hot gimmick

vol.12
MIKI
AIHARA

HOT GIMMICK
CONTENTS

Chapter 52

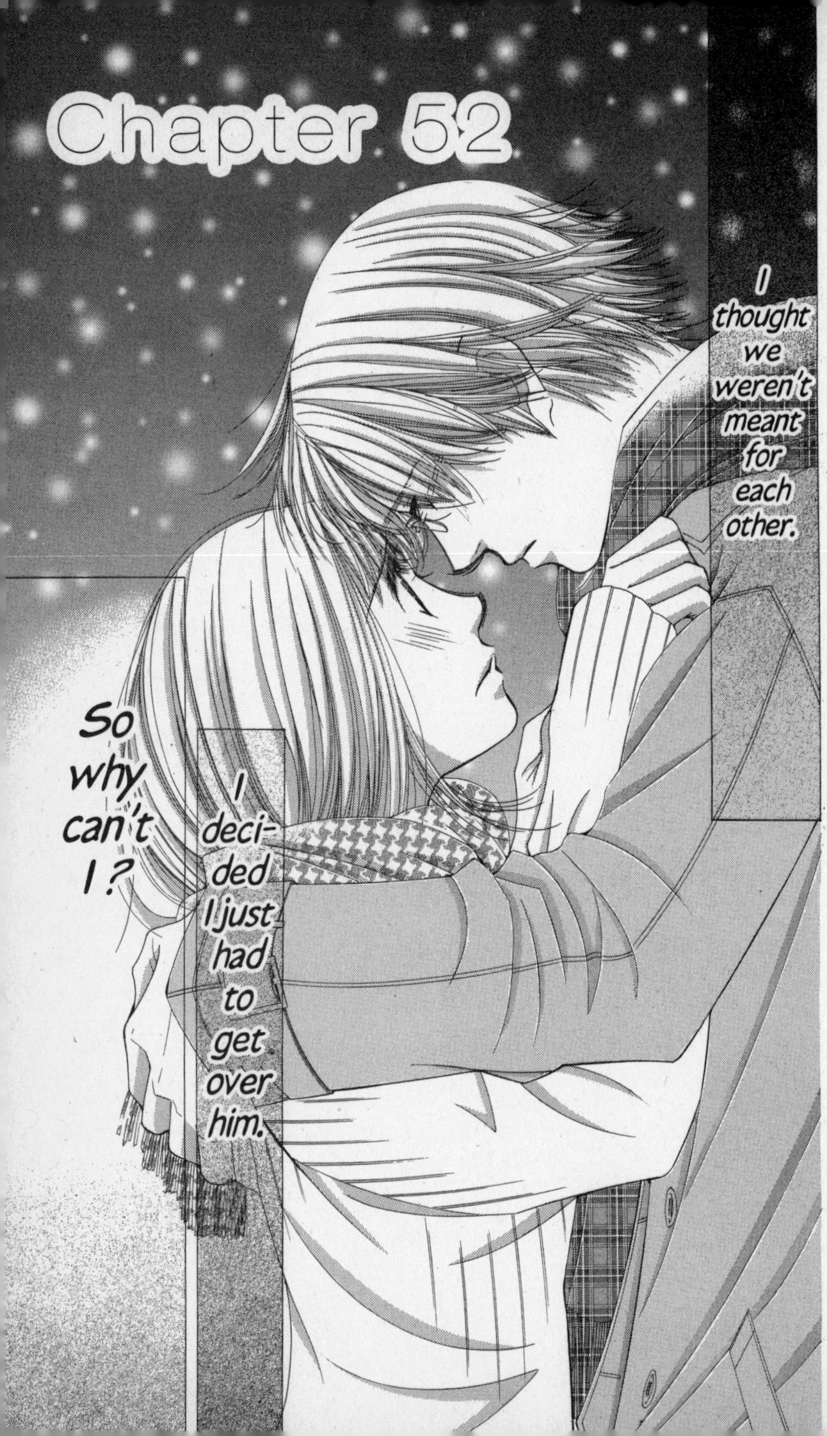
I thought we weren't meant for each other.
I decided I just had to get over him.
So why can't I?

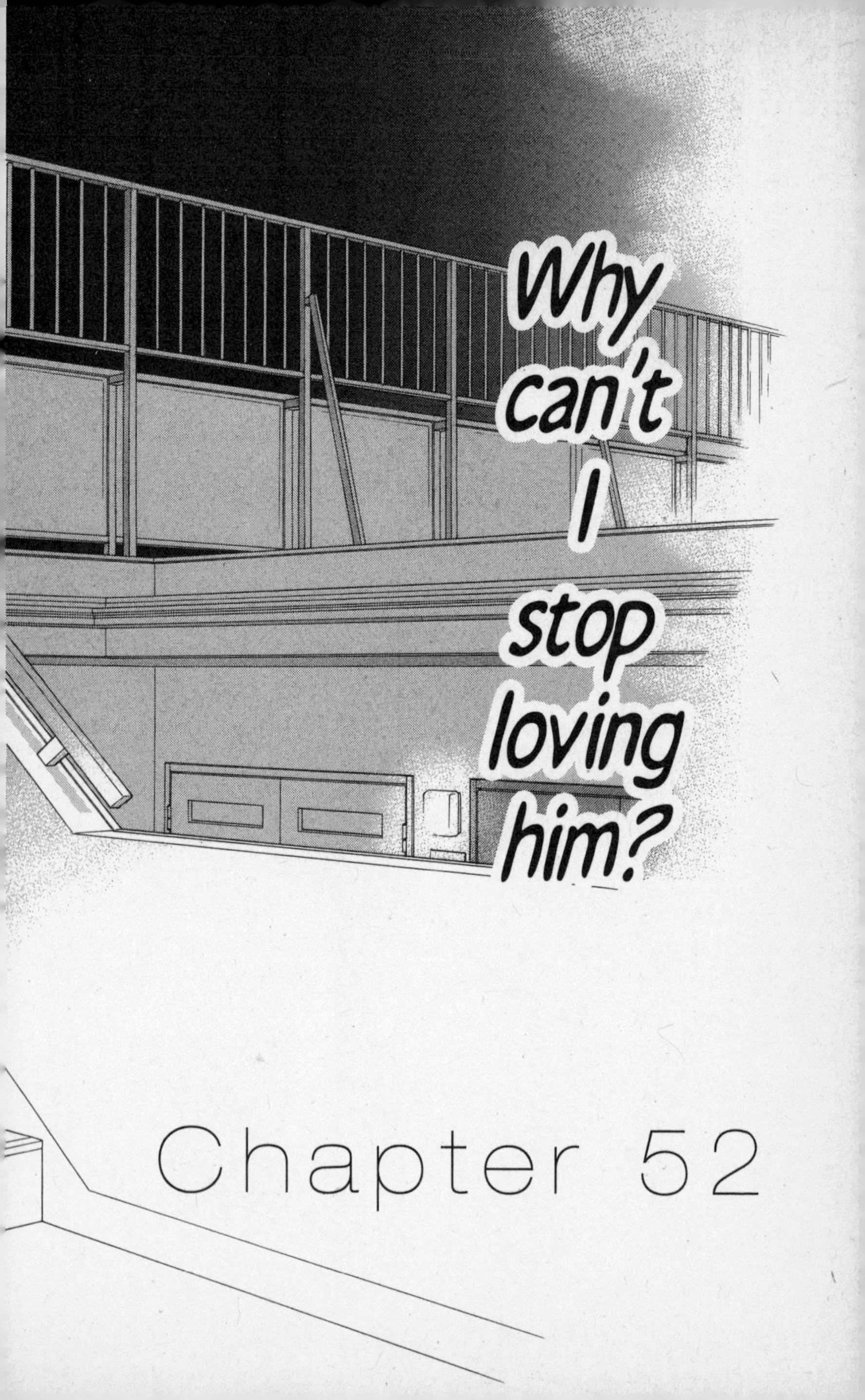
Why can't I stop loving him?

Chapter 52

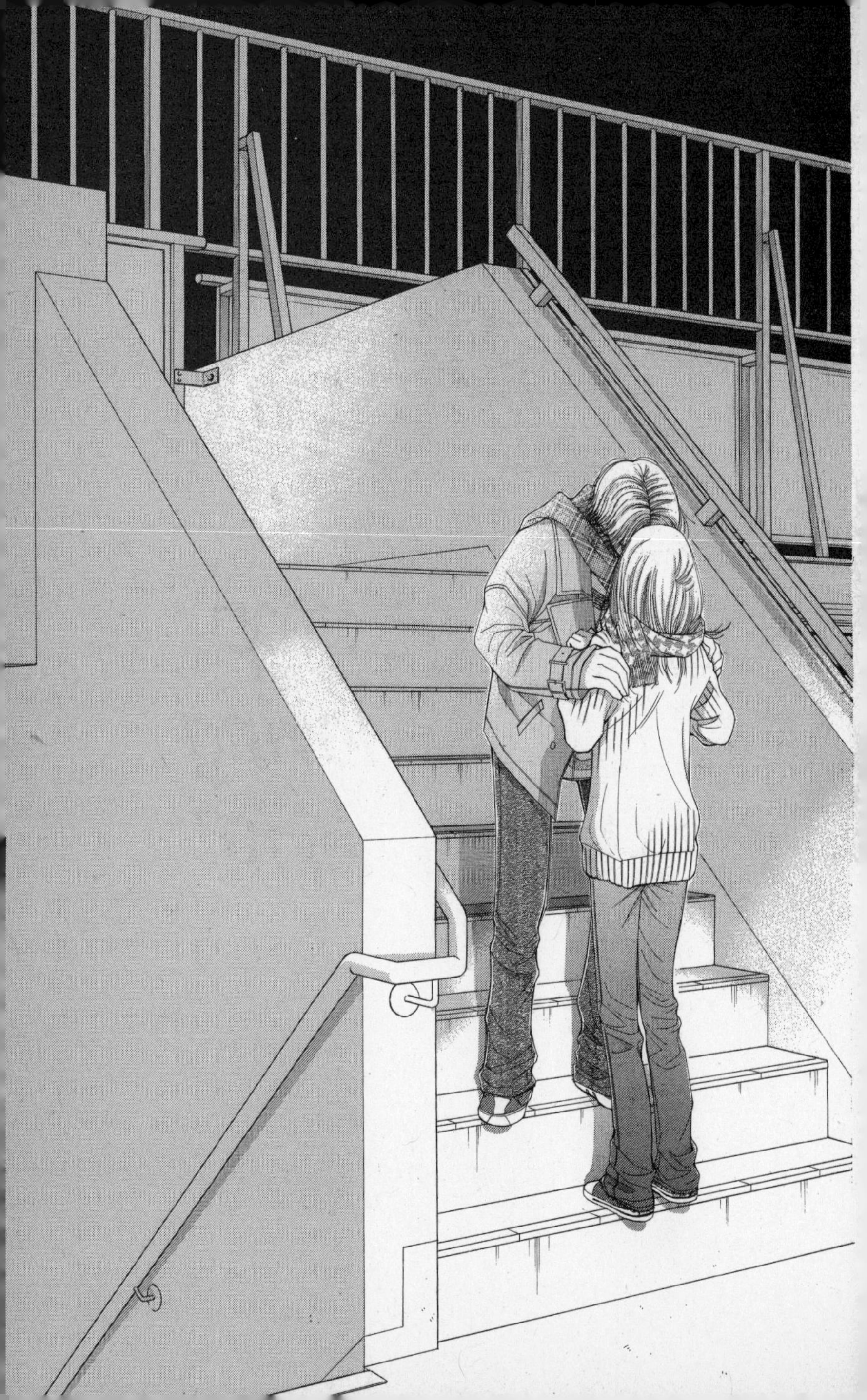

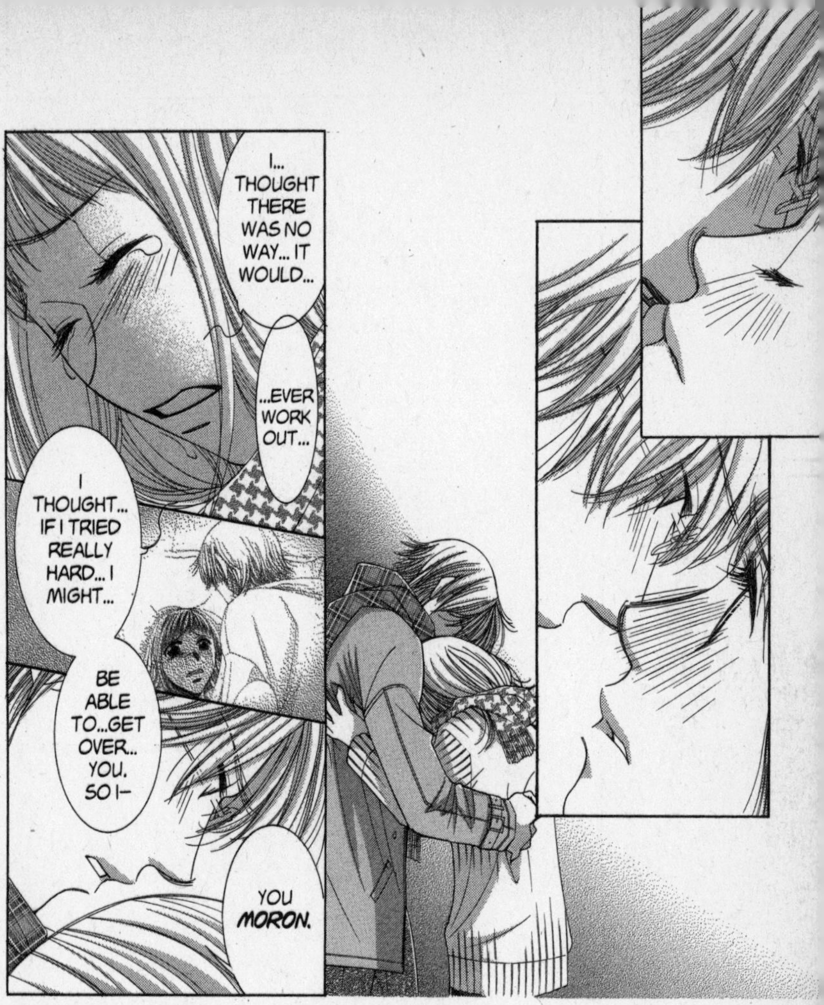
I... THOUGHT THERE WAS NO WAY... IT WOULD...
...EVER WORK OUT...
I THOUGHT... IF I TRIED REALLY HARD... I MIGHT...
BE ABLE TO...GET OVER.. YOU. SO I–
YOU MORON.

hot gimmick

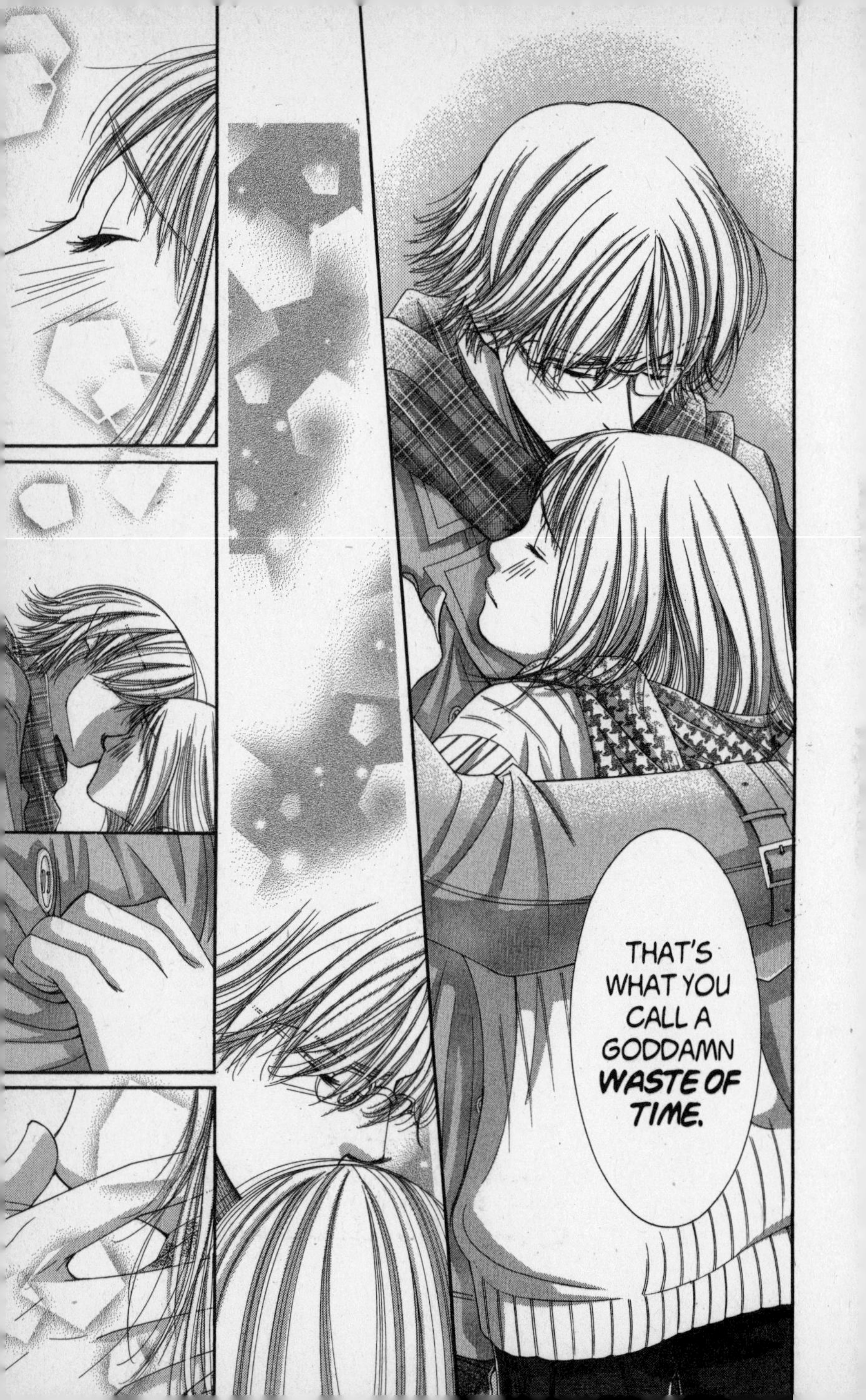
THAT'S WHAT YOU CALL A GODDAMN WASTE OF TIME.

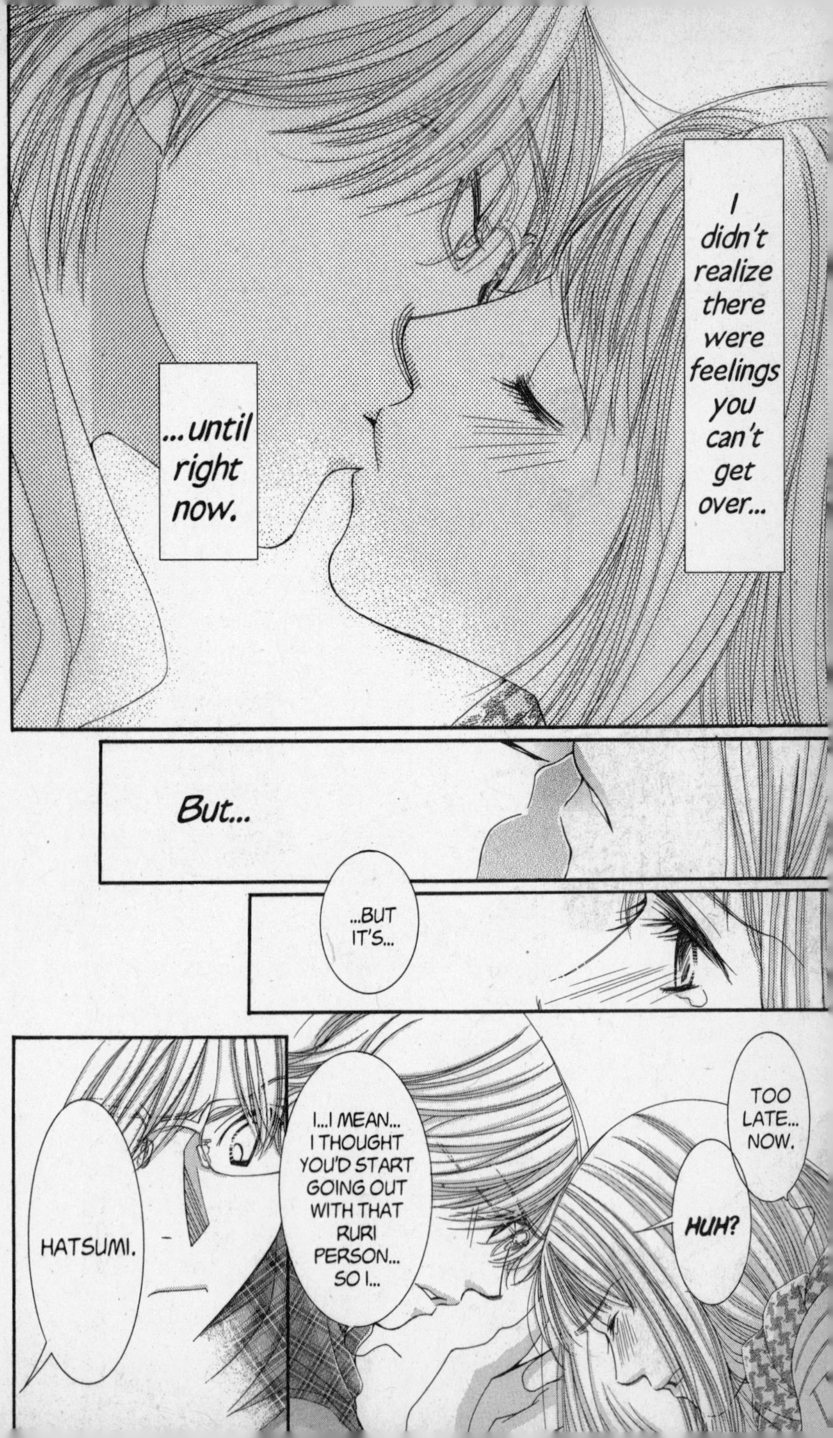

I didn't realize there were feelings you can't get over...
...until right now.
But...
...BUT IT'S...
TOO LATE... NOW.
HUH?
I...I MEAN... I THOUGHT YOU'D START GOING OUT WITH THAT RURI PERSON... SO I...
HATSUMI.

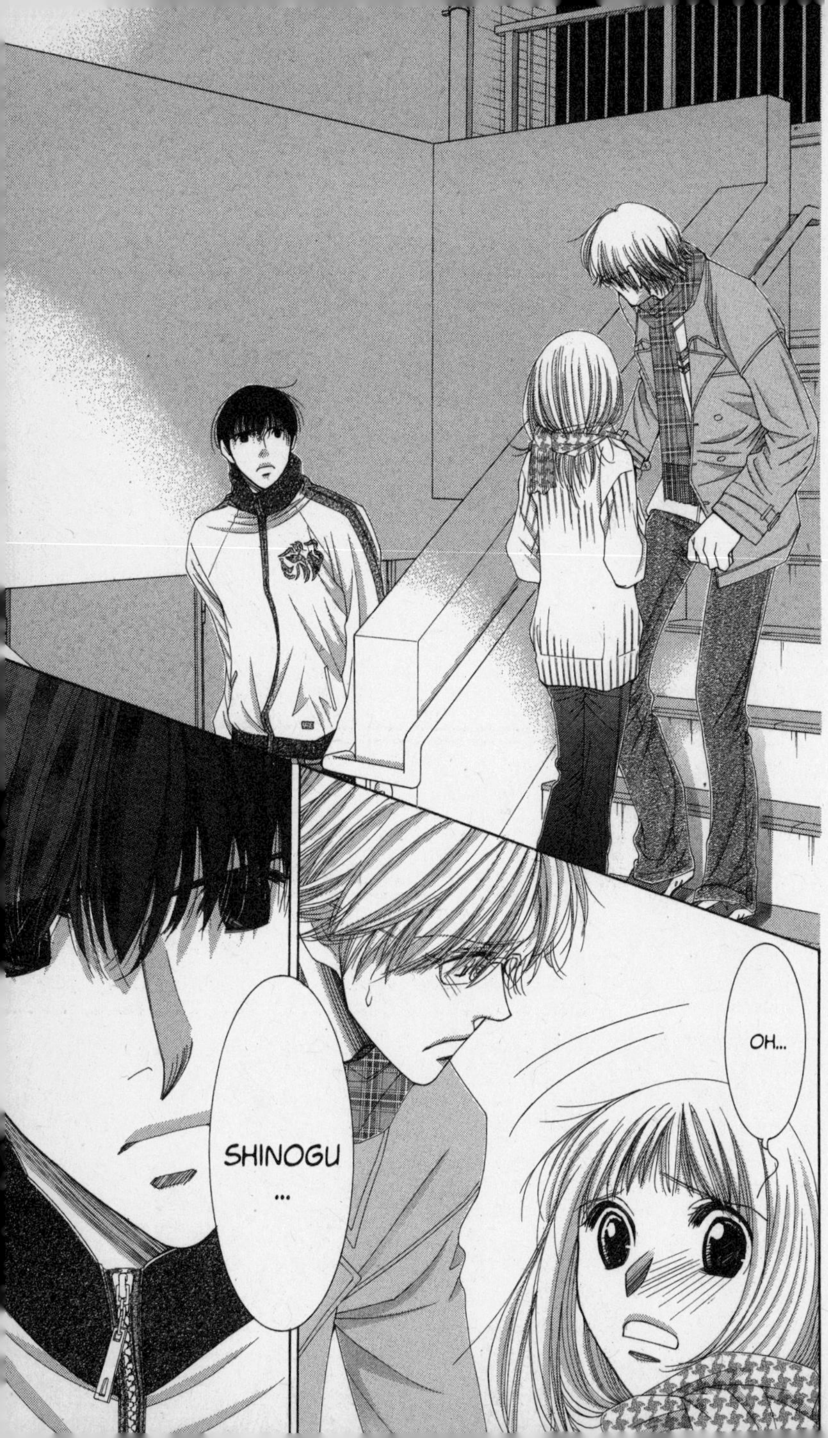
OH...
SHINOGU ...

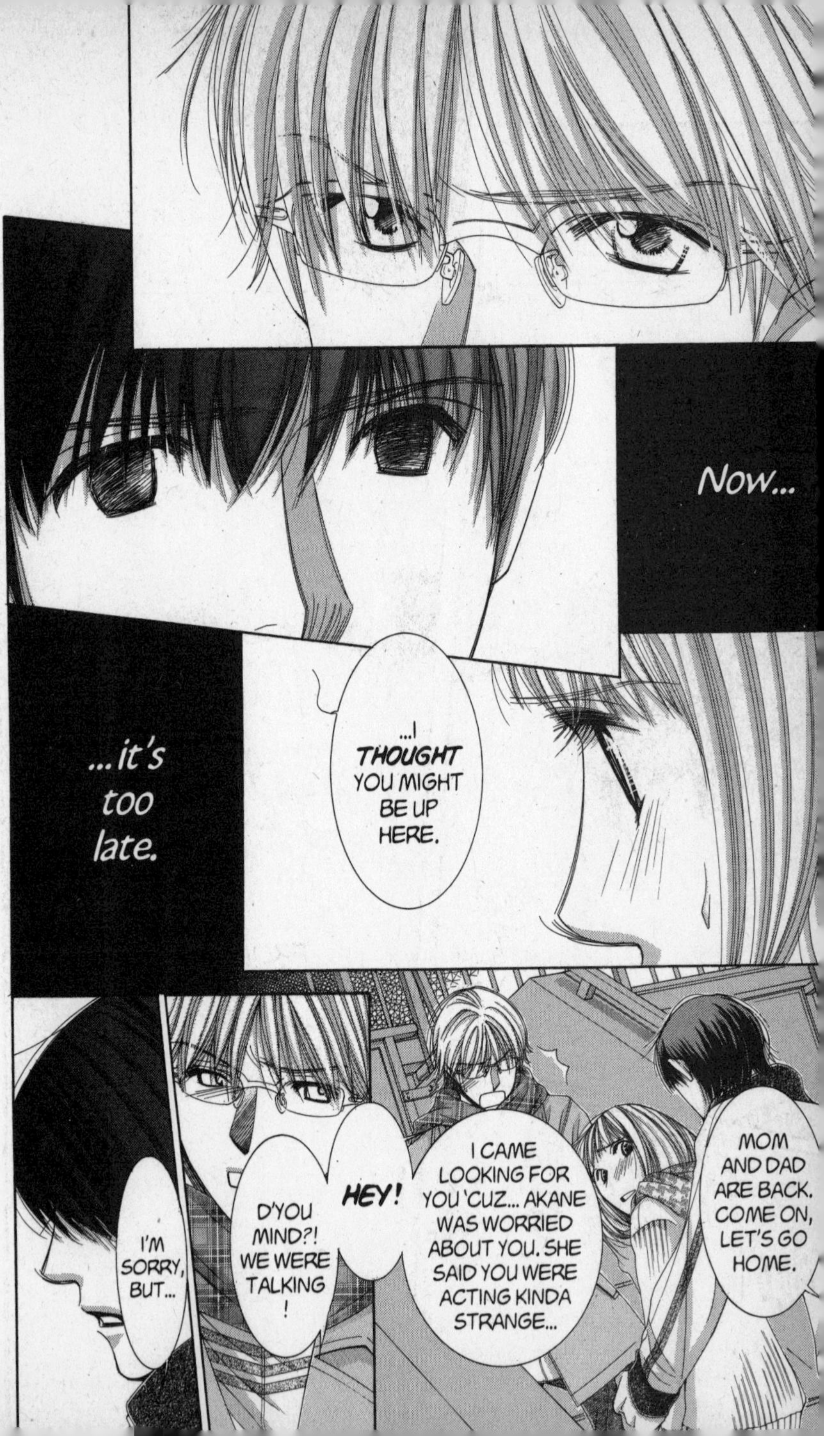
Now...
...it's too late.
...I THOUGHT YOU MIGHT BE UP HERE.
MOM AND DAD ARE BACK. COME ON, LET'S GO HOME.
I CAME LOOKING FOR YOU 'CUZ... AKANE WAS WORRIED ABOUT YOU. SHE SAID YOU WERE ACTING KINDA STRANGE...
HEY!
D'YOU MIND?! WE WERE TALKING!
I'M SORRY, BUT...

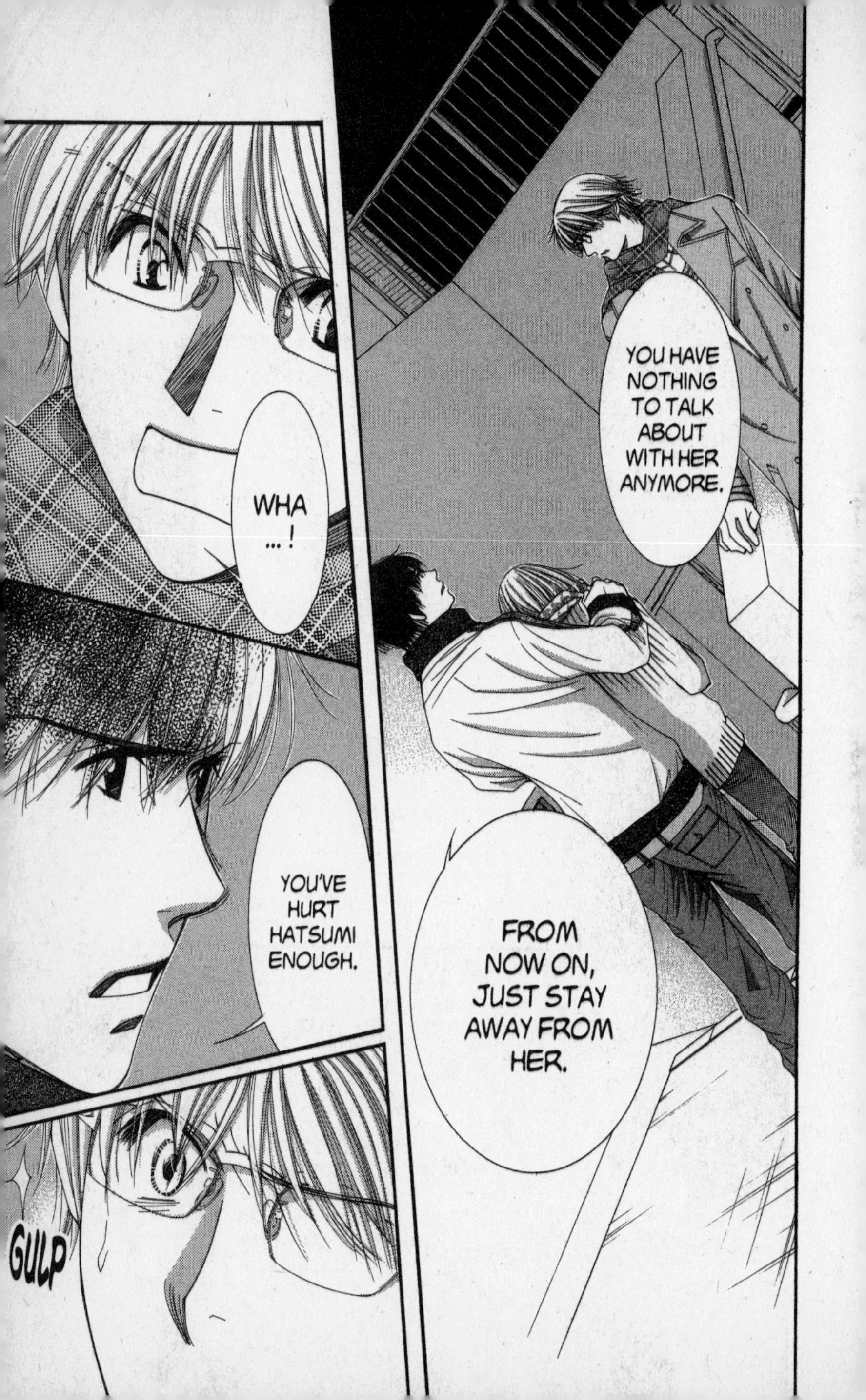

YOU HAVE NOTHING TO TALK ABOUT WITH HER ANYMORE.
FROM NOW ON, JUST STAY AWAY FROM HER.
WHA ...!
YOU'VE HURT HATSUMI ENOUGH.
GULP

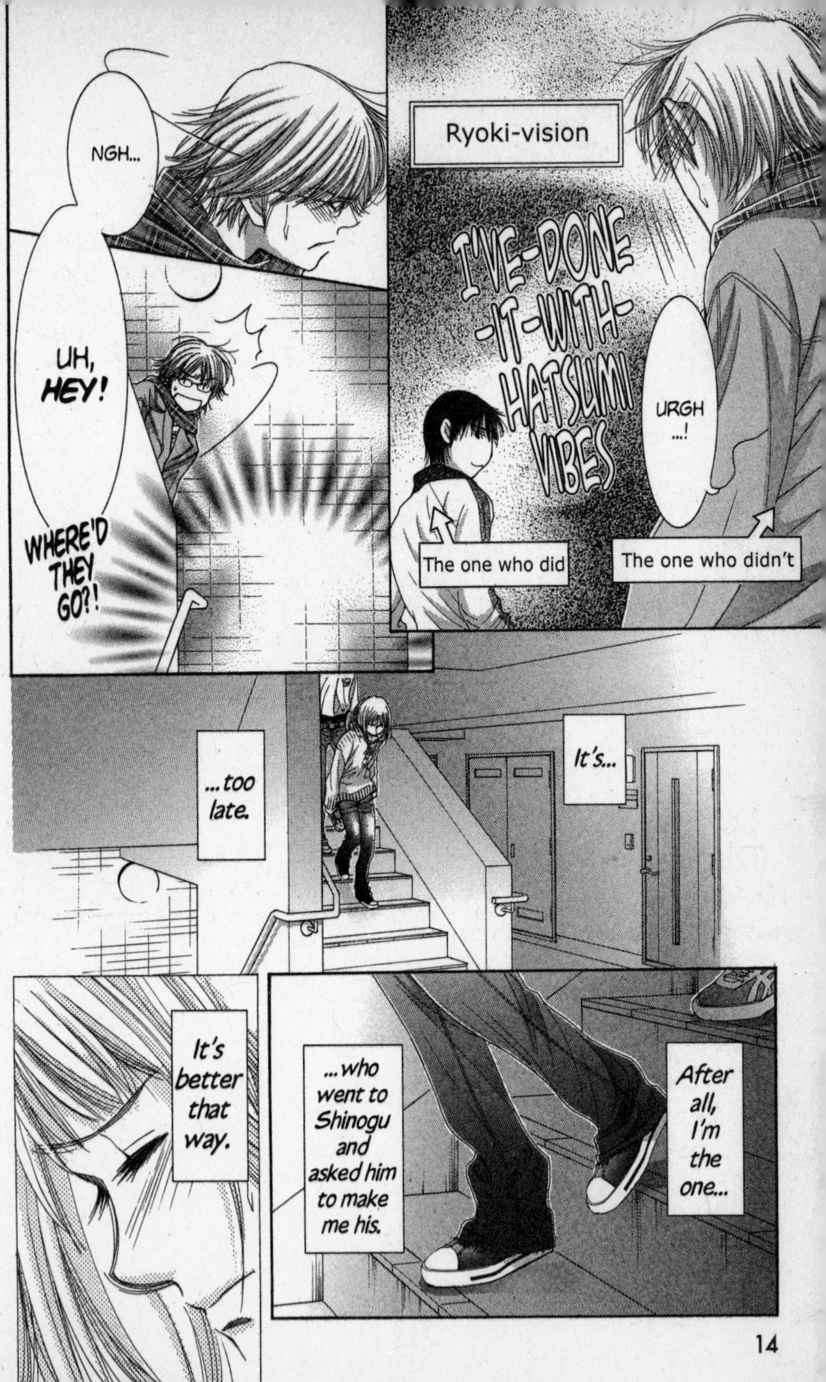
Ryoki-vision
I'VE-DONE-IT-WITH-HATSUMI VIBES
URGH ...!
The one who didn't
The one who did
NGH...
UH, HEY!
WHERE'D THEY GO?!
It's...
...too late.
After all, I'm the one...
...who went to Shinogu and asked him to make me his.
It's better that way.

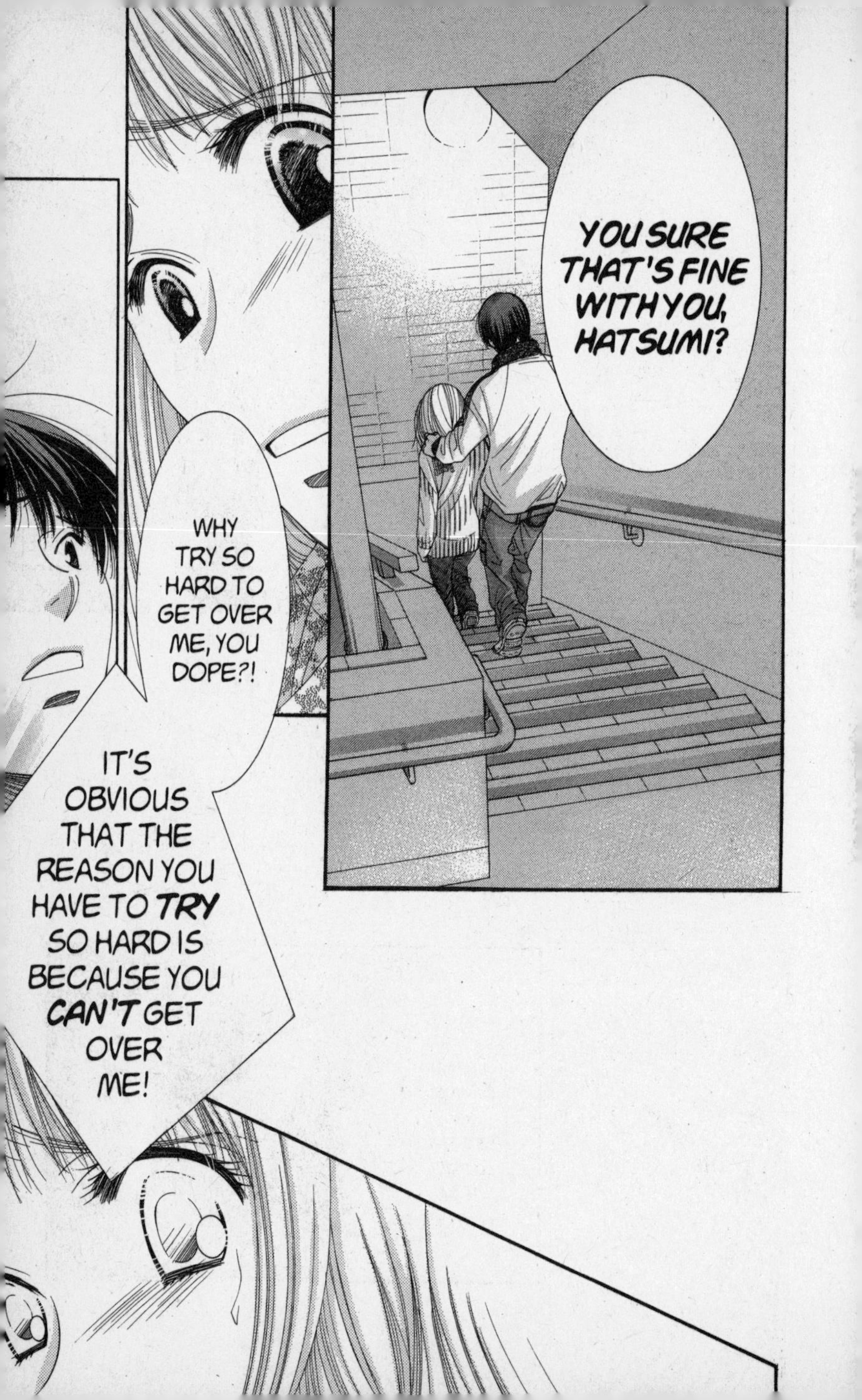
YOU SURE THAT'S FINE WITH YOU, HATSUMI?
WHY TRY SO HARD TO GET OVER ME, YOU DOPE?!
IT'S OBVIOUS THAT THE REASON YOU HAVE TO TRY SO HARD IS BECAUSE YOU CAN'T GET OVER ME!

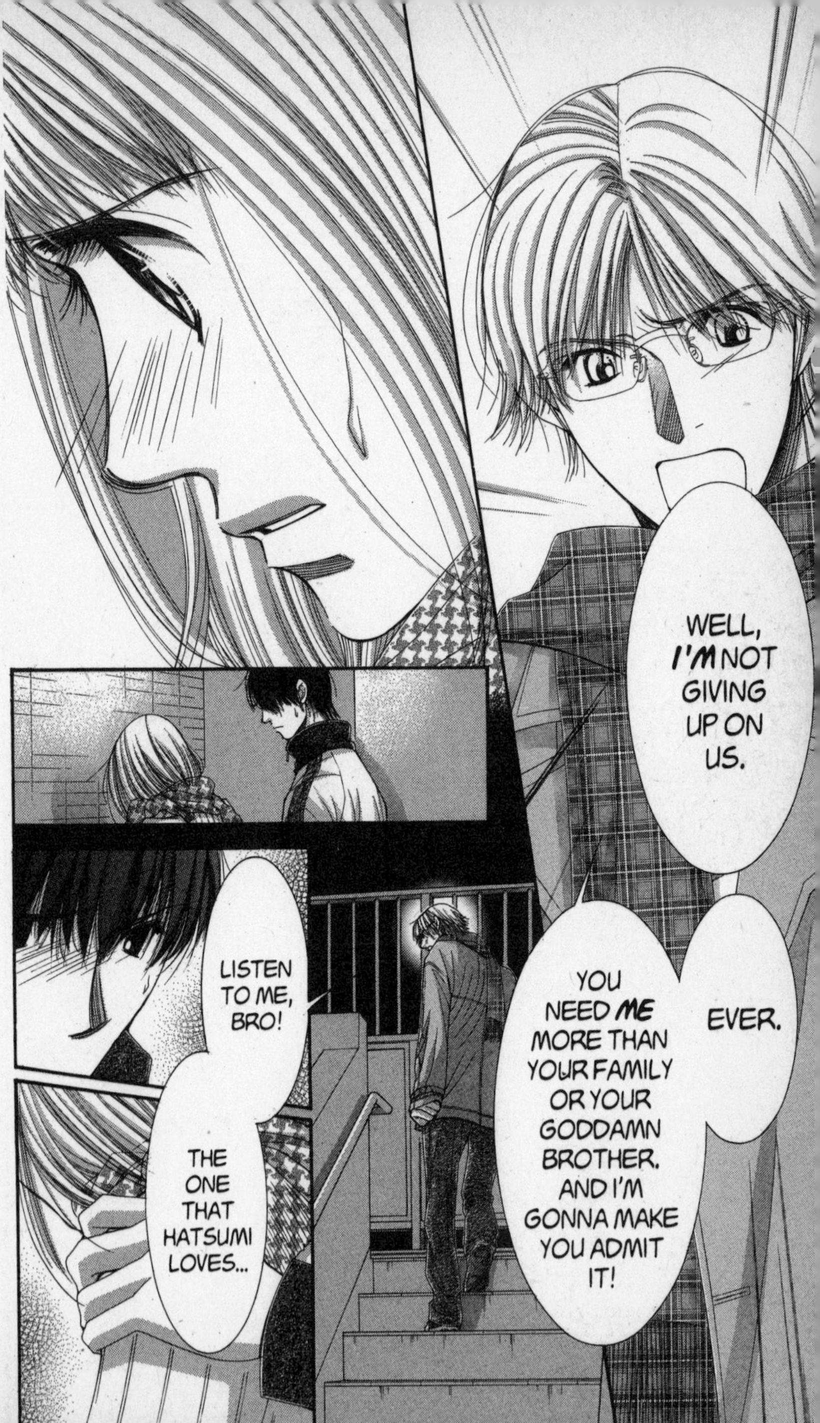
WELL, ***I'M*** NOT GIVING UP ON US.
EVER.
YOU NEED ***ME*** MORE THAN YOUR FAMILY OR YOUR GODDAMN BROTHER. AND I'M GONNA MAKE YOU ADMIT IT!
LISTEN TO ME, BRO!
THE ONE THAT HATSUMI LOVES...

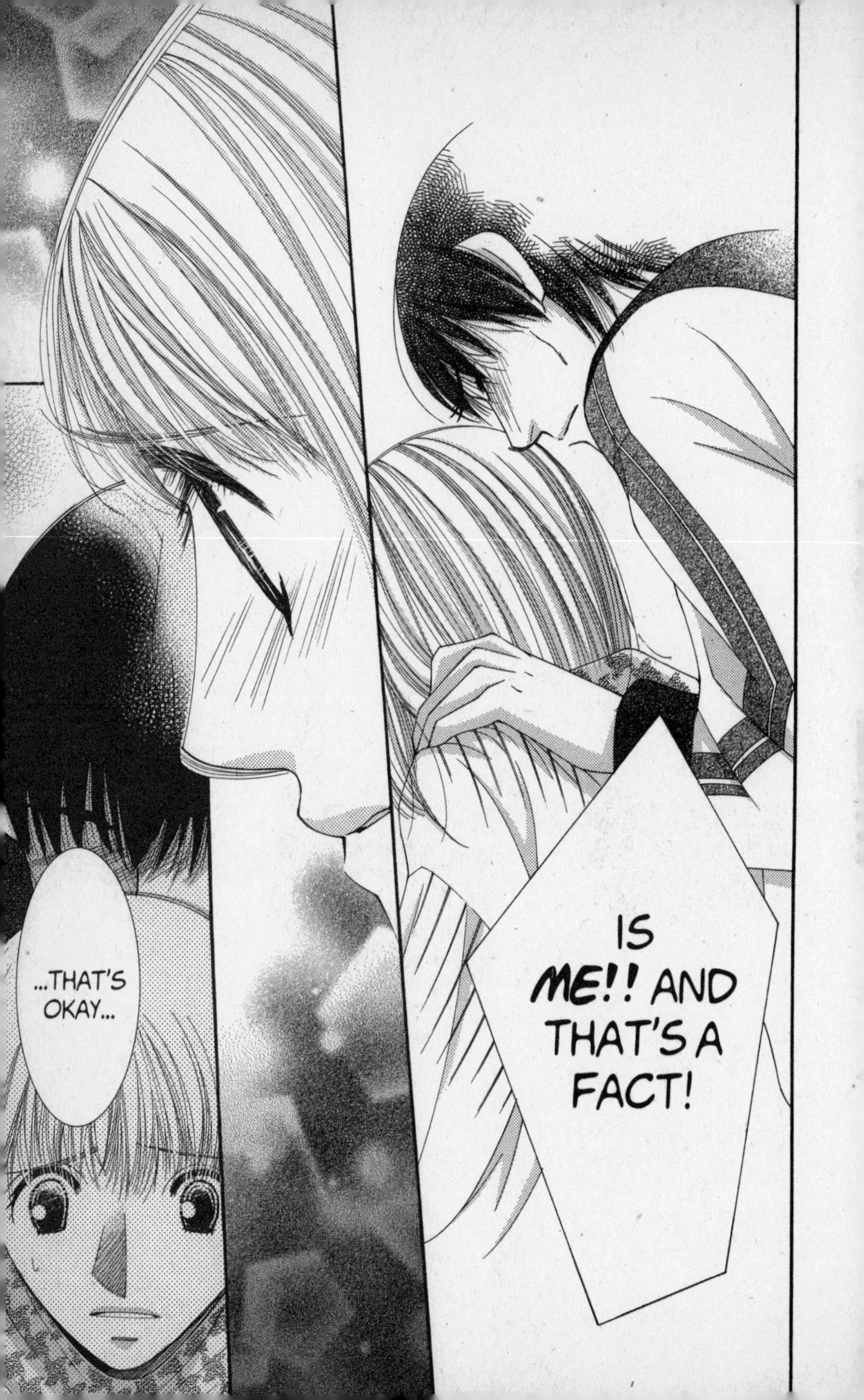
IS *ME!!* AND THAT'S A FACT!
...THAT'S OKAY...

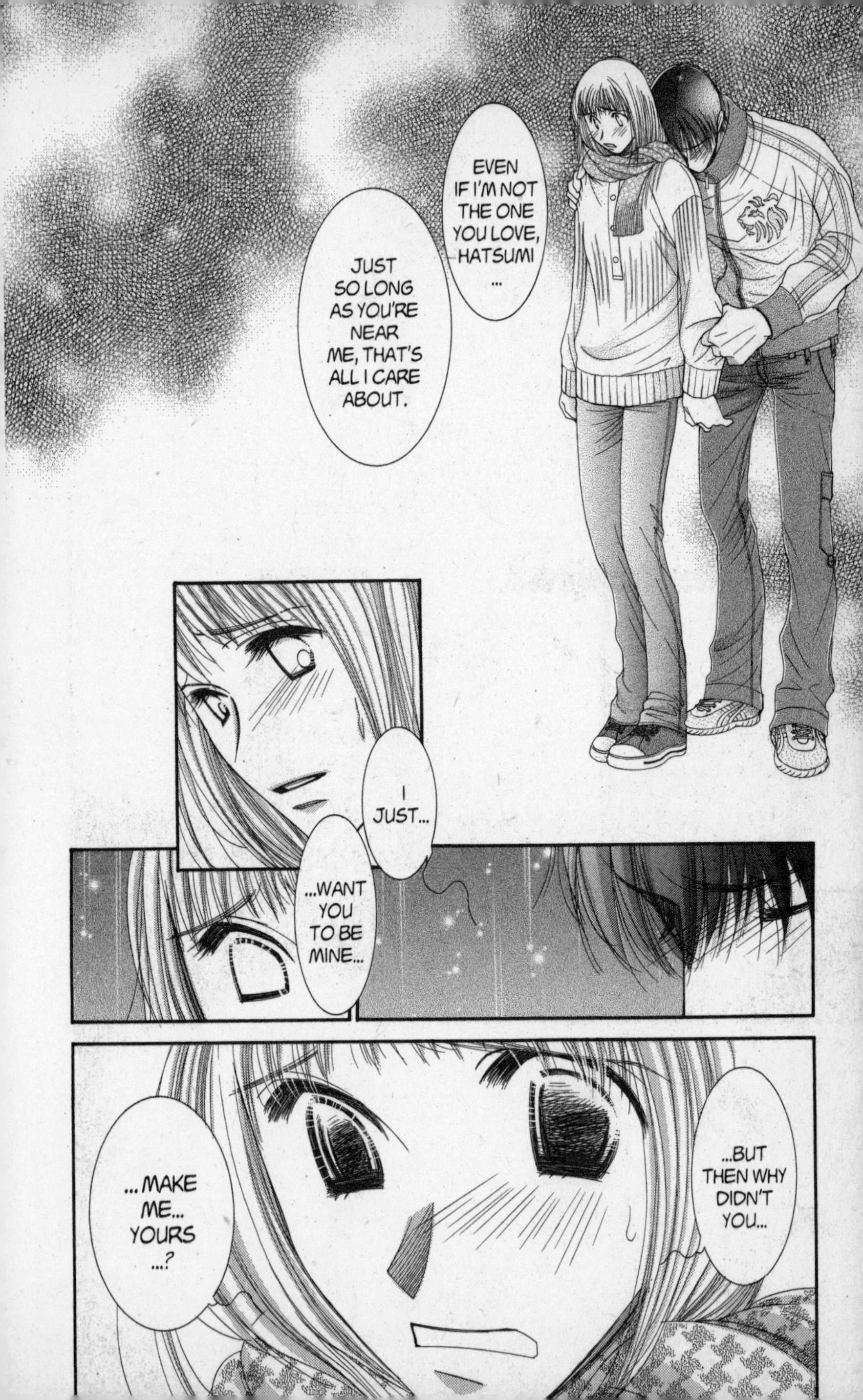
EVEN IF I'M NOT THE ONE YOU LOVE, HATSUMI...
JUST SO LONG AS YOU'RE NEAR ME, THAT'S ALL I CARE ABOUT.
I JUST...
...WANT YOU TO BE MINE...
...BUT THEN WHY DIDN'T YOU...
...MAKE ME... YOURS...?

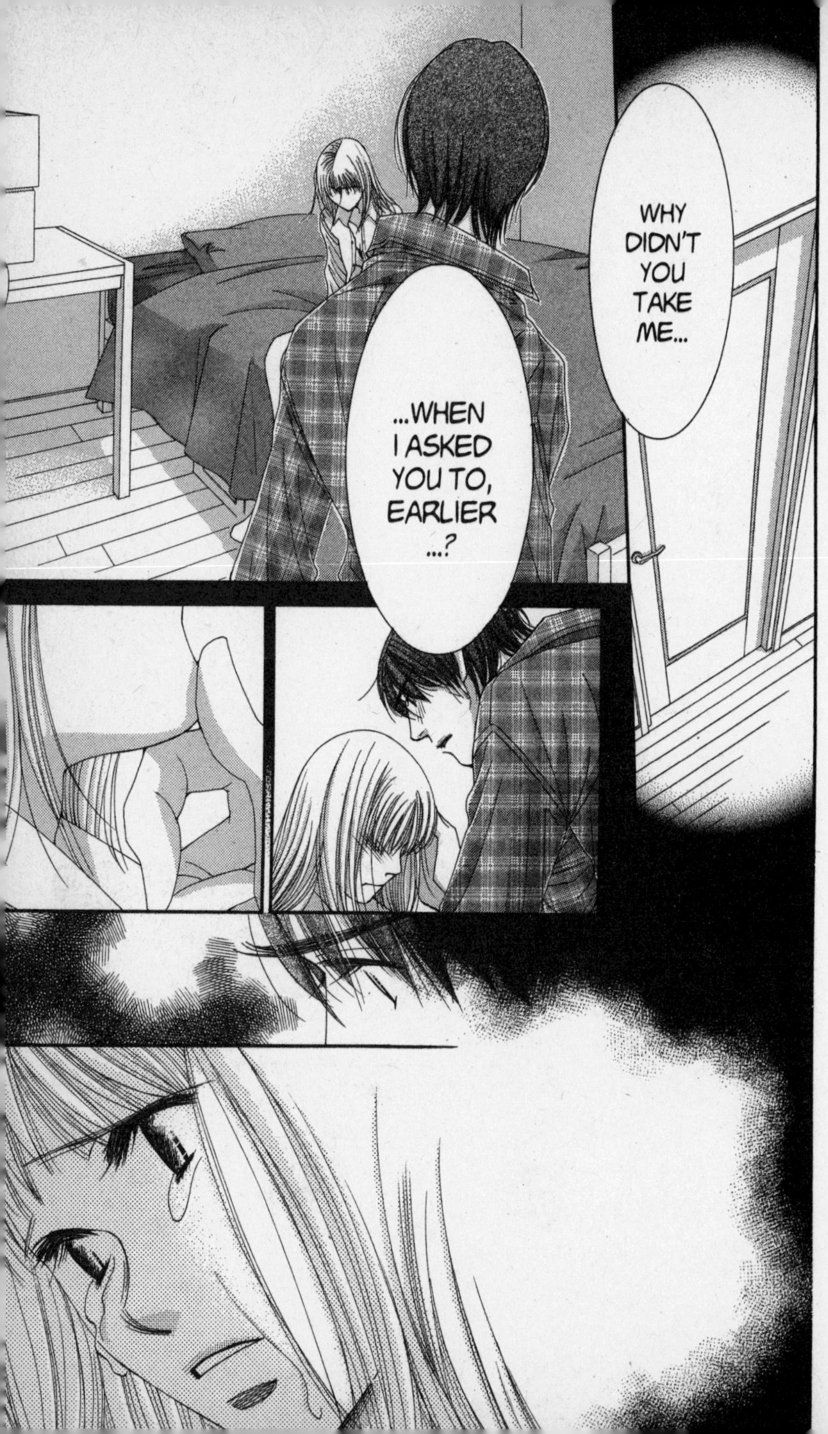
WHY DIDN'T YOU TAKE ME...
...WHEN I ASKED YOU TO, EARLIER ...?

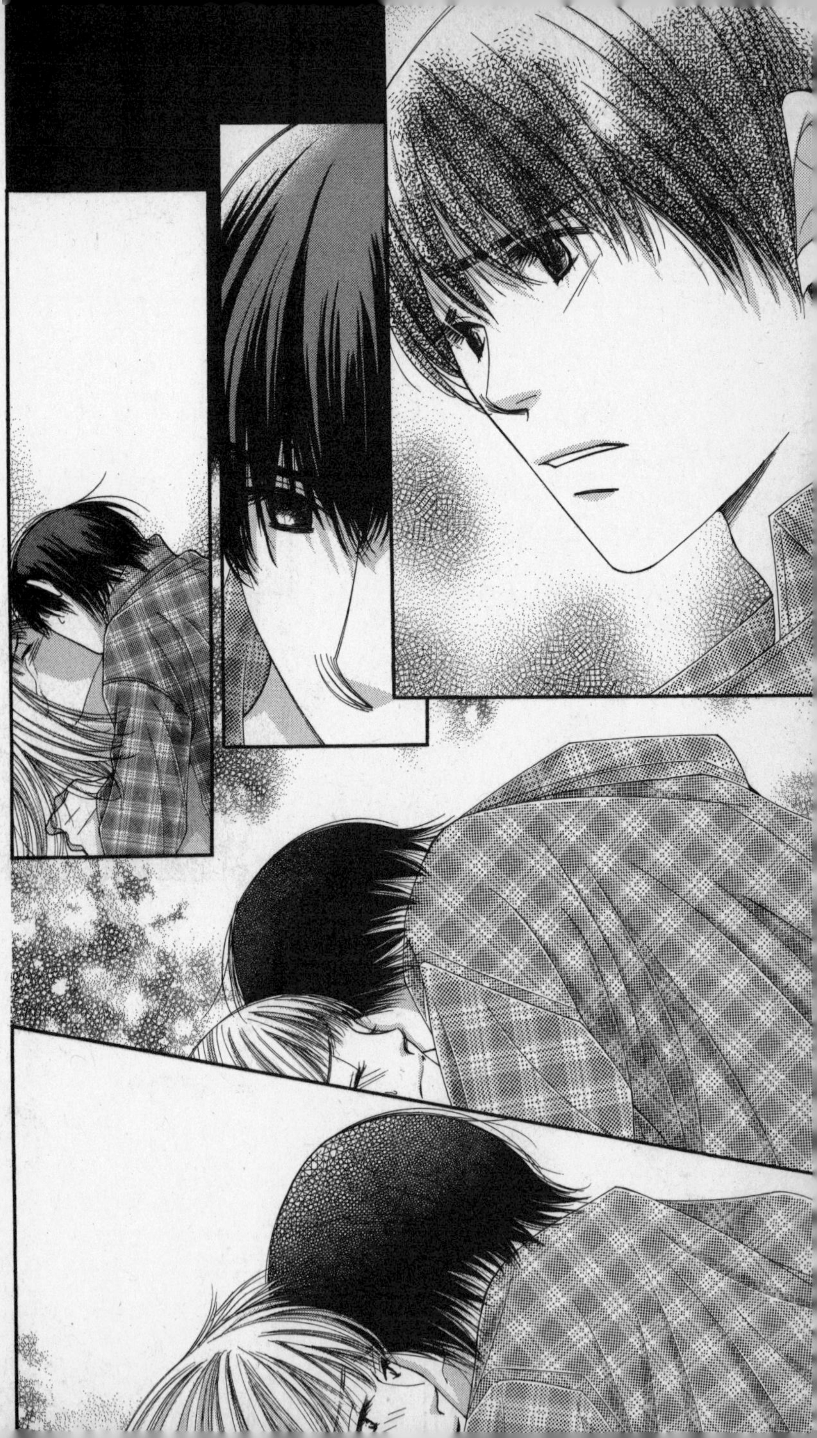

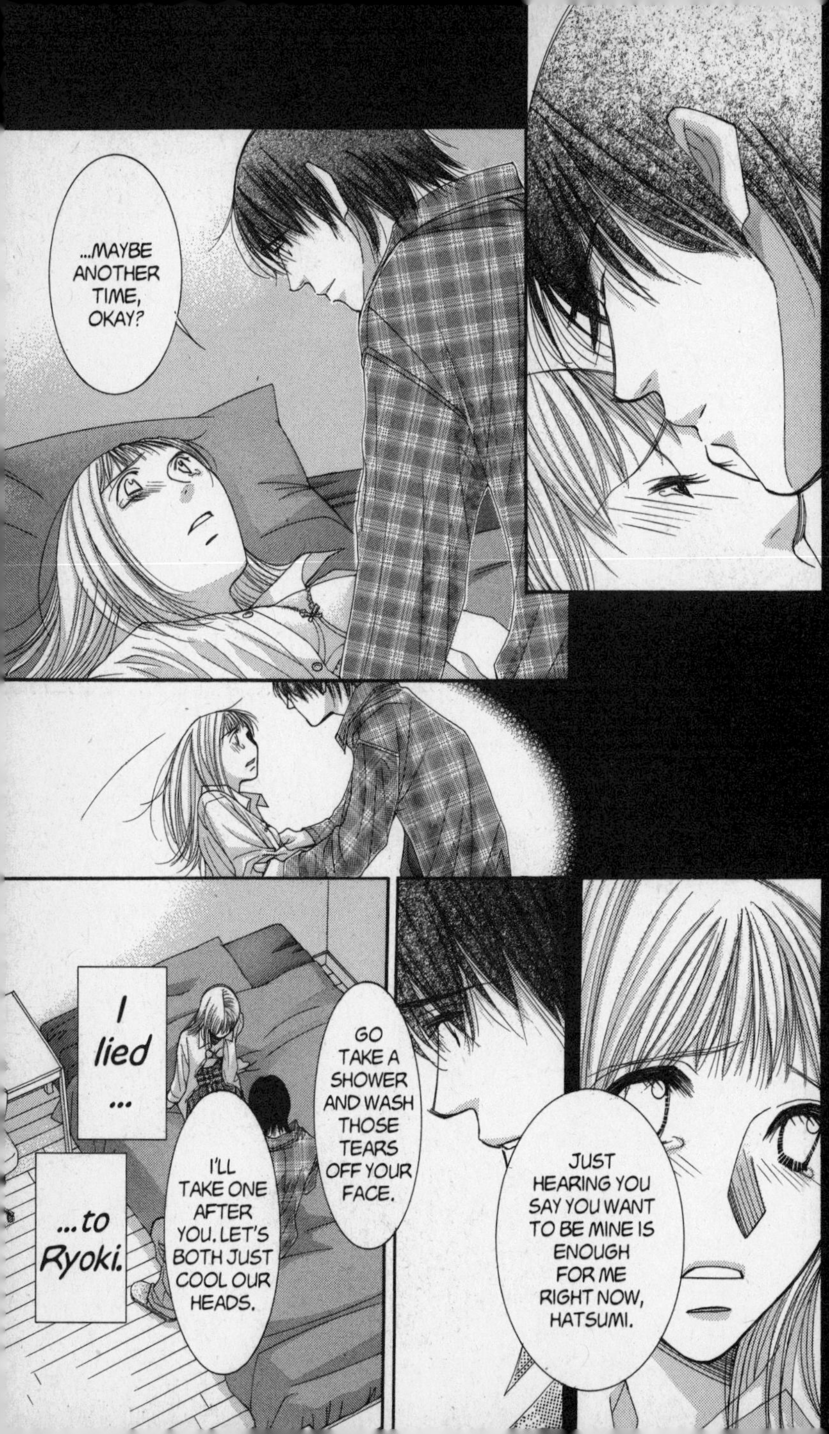
...MAYBE ANOTHER TIME, OKAY?
JUST HEARING YOU SAY YOU WANT TO BE MINE IS ENOUGH FOR ME RIGHT NOW, HATSUMI.
GO TAKE A SHOWER AND WASH THOSE TEARS OFF YOUR FACE.
I'LL TAKE ONE AFTER YOU. LET'S BOTH JUST COOL OUR HEADS.
I lied ...
...to Ryoki.

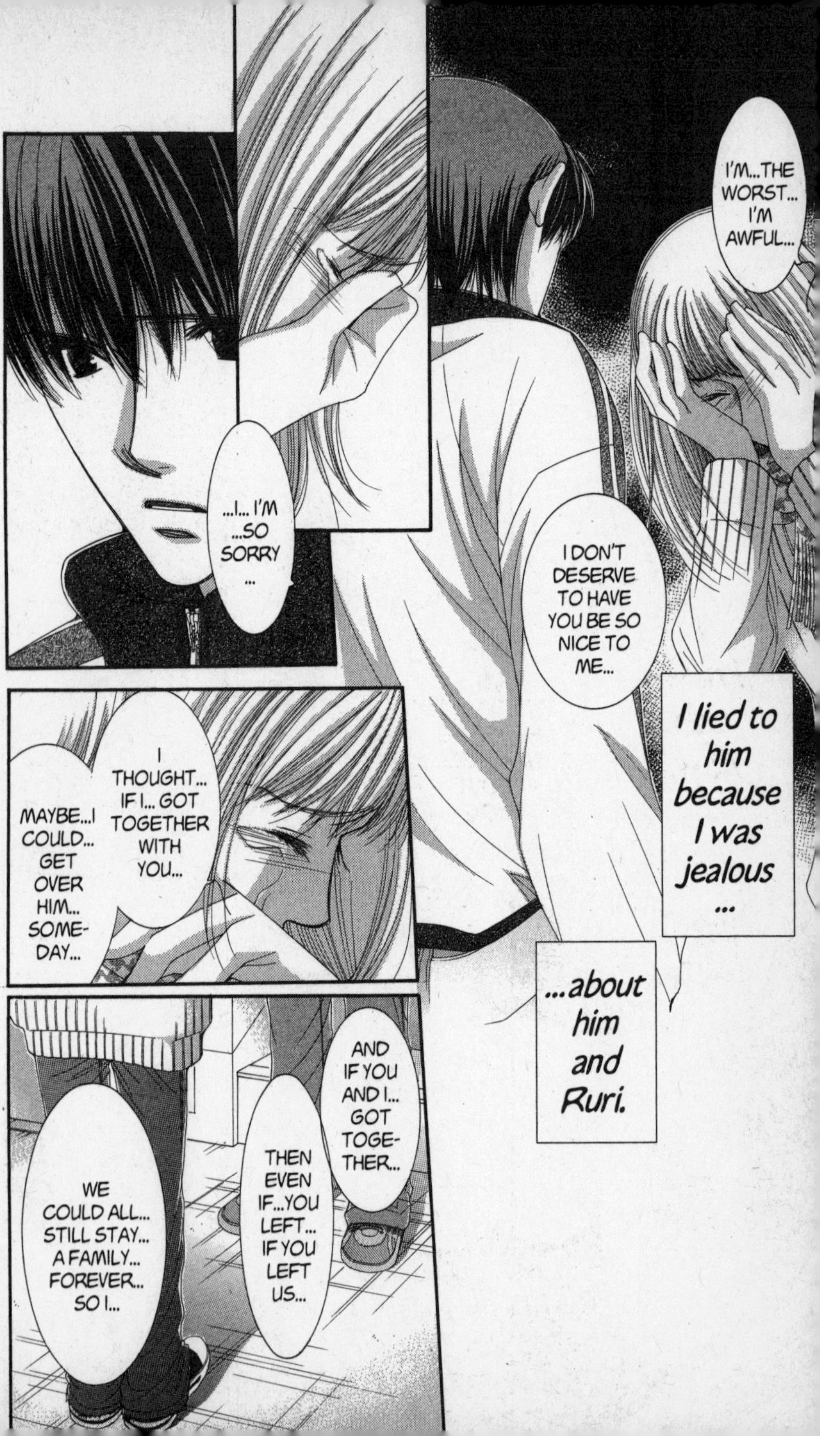
I'M...THE WORST... I'M AWFUL...
I DON'T DESERVE TO HAVE YOU BE SO NICE TO ME...
I lied to him because I was jealous...
...about him and Ruri.
...I... I'M ...SO SORRY ...
I THOUGHT... IF I... GOT TOGETHER WITH YOU...
MAYBE...I COULD... GET OVER HIM... SOME-DAY...
AND IF YOU AND I... GOT TOGE-THER...
THEN EVEN IF...YOU LEFT... IF YOU LEFT US...
WE COULD ALL... STILL STAY... A FAMILY... FOREVER... SO I...

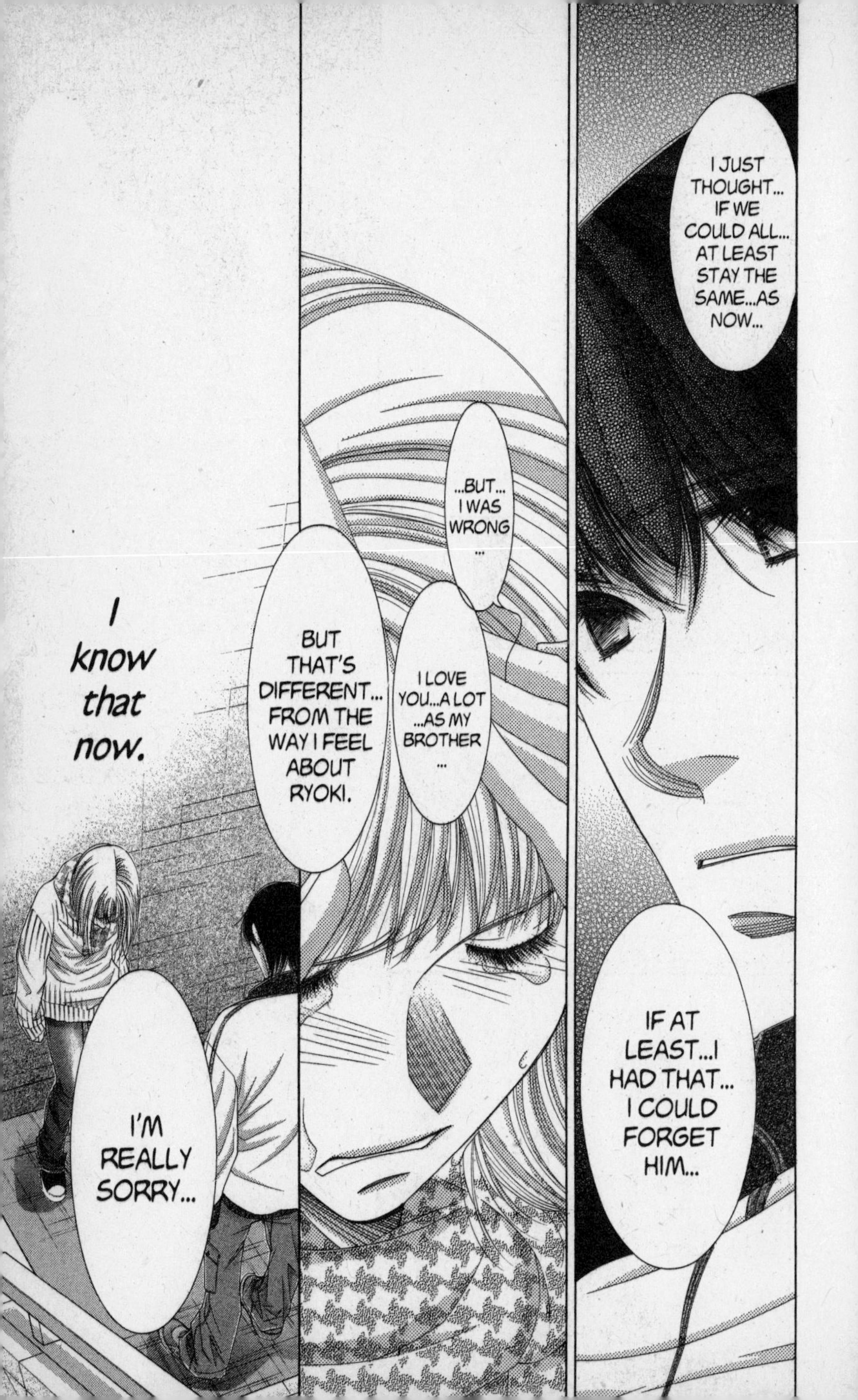
I JUST THOUGHT... IF WE COULD ALL... AT LEAST STAY THE SAME...AS NOW...
IF AT LEAST...I HAD THAT... I COULD FORGET HIM...
...BUT... I WAS WRONG ...
I LOVE YOU...A LOT ...AS MY BROTHER ...
BUT THAT'S DIFFERENT... FROM THE WAY I FEEL ABOUT RYOKI.
I know that now.
I'M REALLY SORRY...

NO MATTER HOW LONG... YOU WAIT FOR ME, SHINOGU...
I'LL NEVER LOVE YOU... IN THAT WAY...

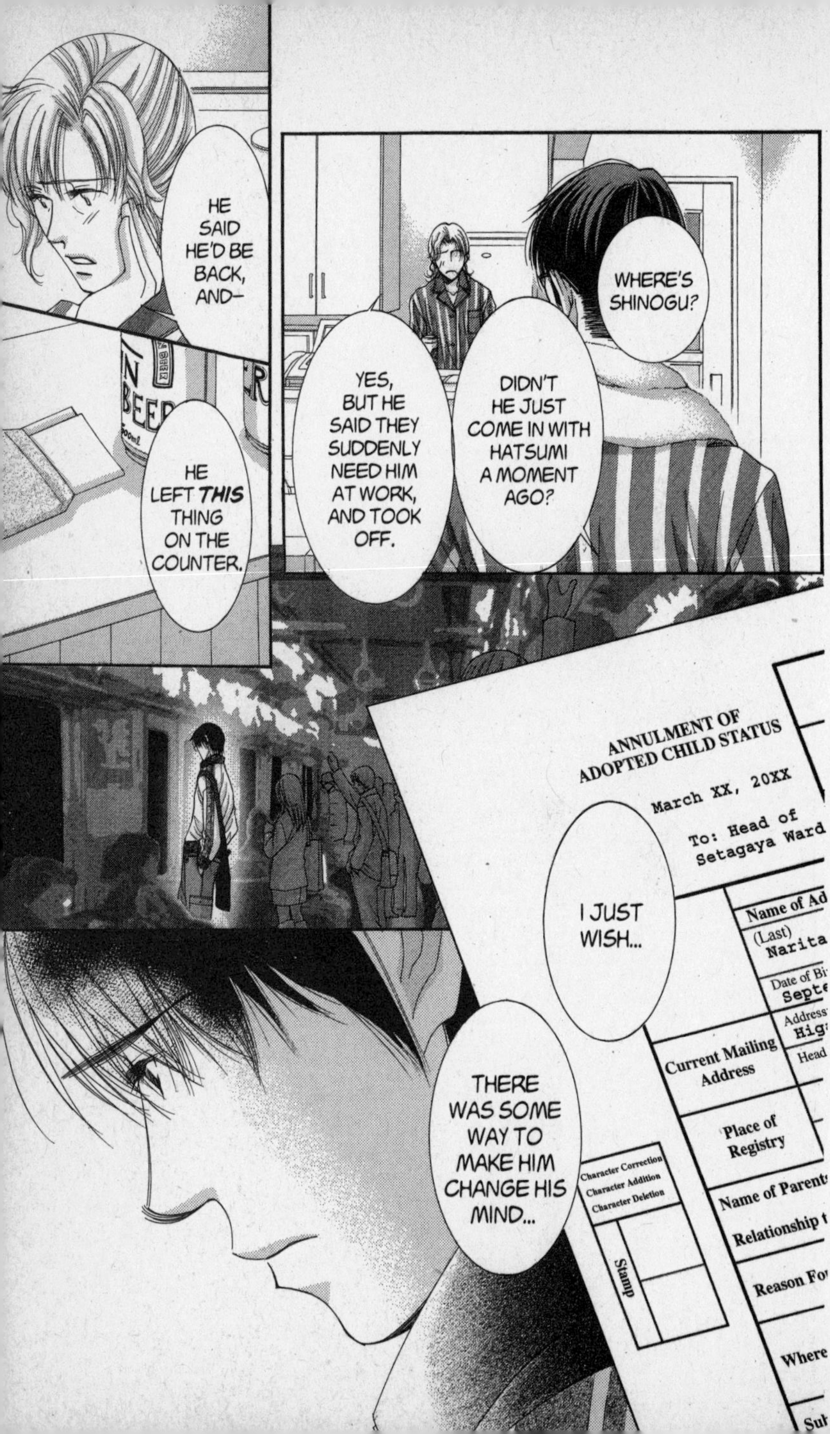
WHERE'S SHINOGU?
DIDN'T HE JUST COME IN WITH HATSUMI A MOMENT AGO?
YES, BUT HE SAID THEY SUDDENLY NEED HIM AT WORK, AND TOOK OFF.
HE SAID HE'D BE BACK, AND—
HE LEFT **THIS** THING ON THE COUNTER.
ANNULMENT OF ADOPTED CHILD STATUS
March XX, 20XX
To: Head of Setagaya Ward
Current Mailing Address
Place of Registry
Character Correction
Character Addition
Character Deletion
Stamp
I JUST WISH...
THERE WAS SOME WAY TO MAKE HIM CHANGE HIS MIND...

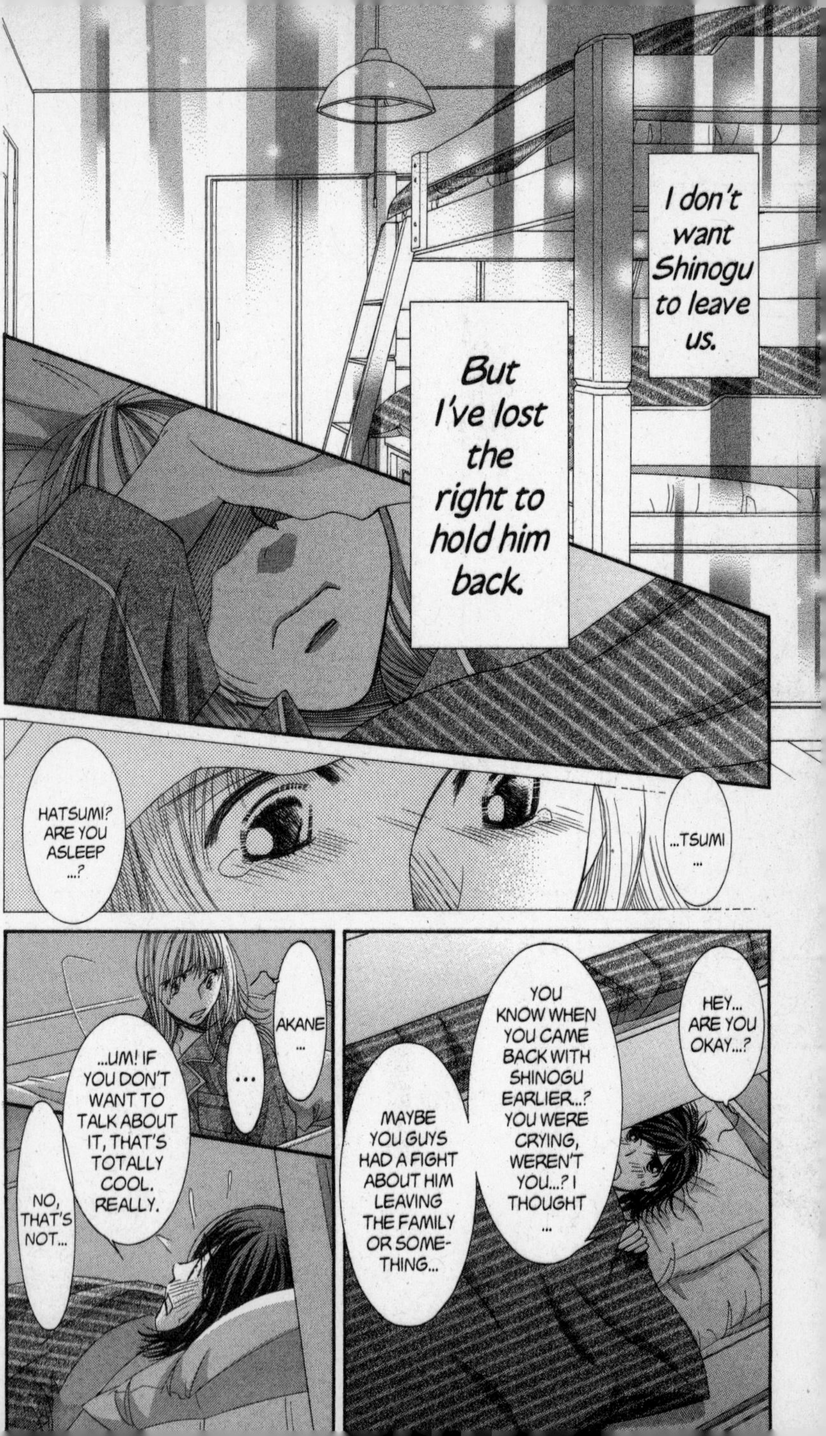
I don't want Shinogu to leave us.
But I've lost the right to hold him back.
...TSUMI ...
HATSUMI? ARE YOU ASLEEP ...?
HEY... ARE YOU OKAY...?
YOU KNOW WHEN YOU CAME BACK WITH SHINOGU EARLIER...? YOU WERE CRYING, WEREN'T YOU...? I THOUGHT ...
MAYBE YOU GUYS HAD A FIGHT ABOUT HIM LEAVING THE FAMILY OR SOME-THING...
AKANE ...
...
...UM! IF YOU DON'T WANT TO TALK ABOUT IT, THAT'S TOTALLY COOL. REALLY.
NO, THAT'S NOT...

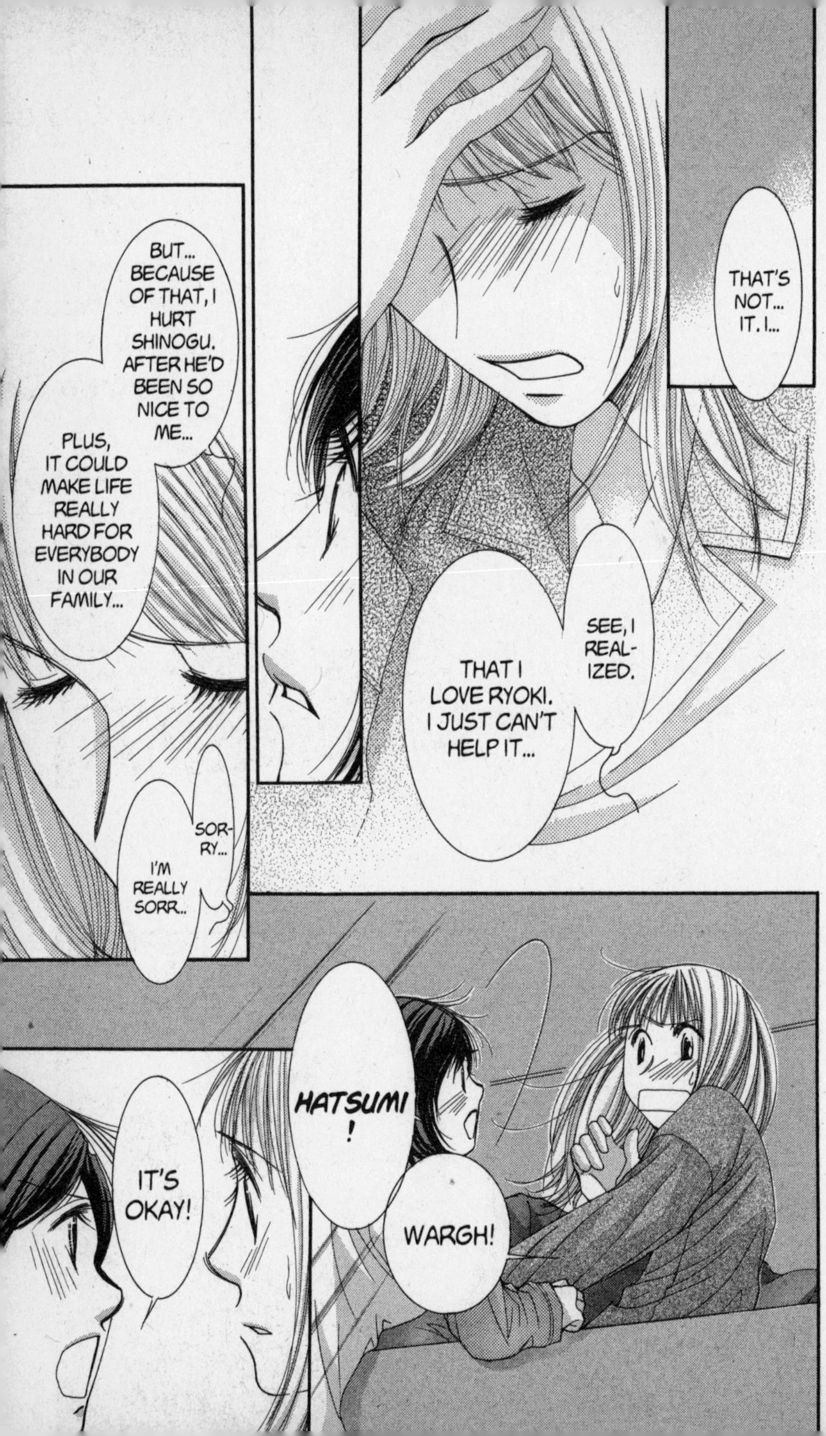
THAT'S NOT... IT. I...
SEE, I REALIZED.
THAT I LOVE RYOKI. I JUST CAN'T HELP IT...
BUT... BECAUSE OF THAT, I HURT SHINOGU. AFTER HE'D BEEN SO NICE TO ME...
PLUS, IT COULD MAKE LIFE REALLY HARD FOR EVERYBODY IN OUR FAMILY...
SORRY...
I'M REALLY SORR...
HATSUMI!
WARGH!
IT'S OKAY!

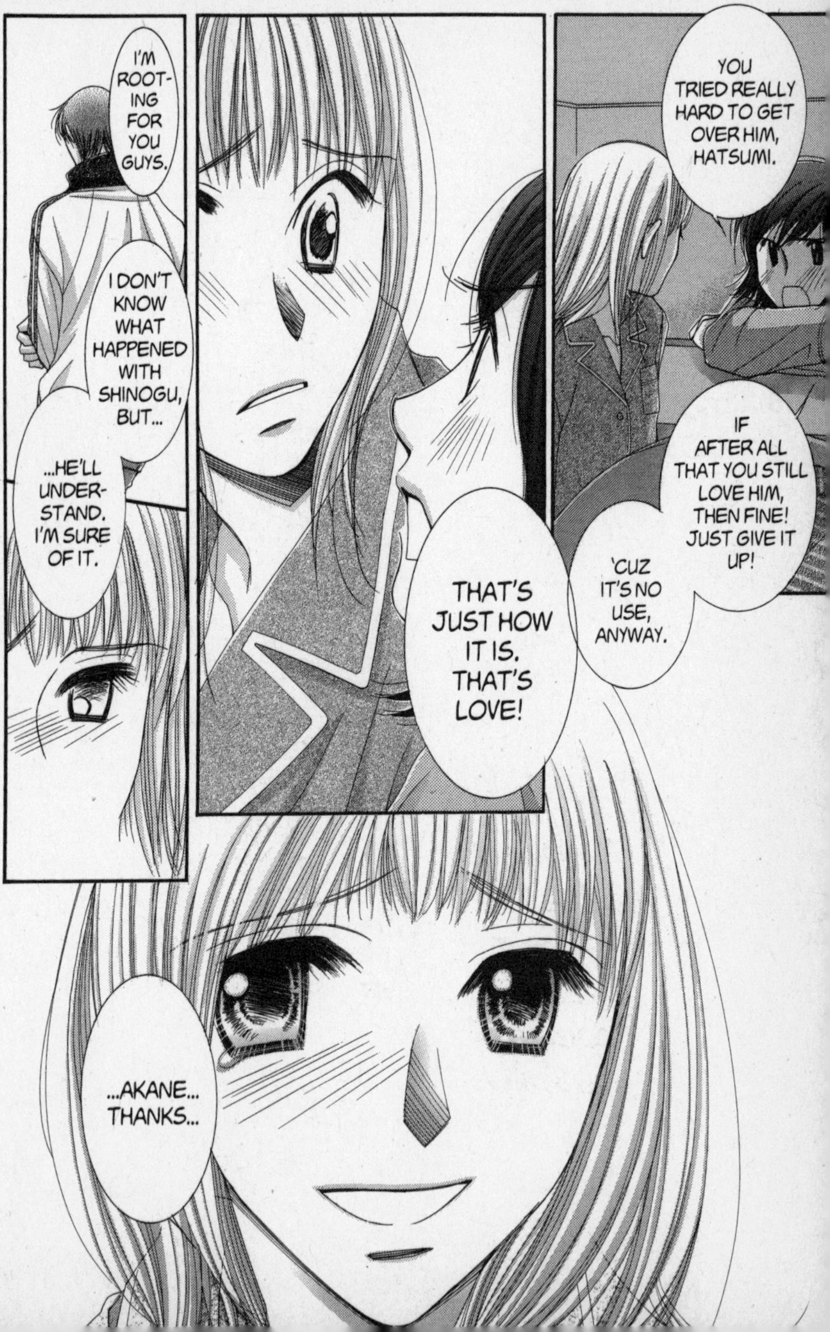
YOU TRIED REALLY HARD TO GET OVER HIM, HATSUMI.
IF AFTER ALL THAT YOU STILL LOVE HIM, THEN FINE! JUST GIVE IT UP!
'CUZ IT'S NO USE, ANYWAY.
THAT'S JUST HOW IT IS. THAT'S LOVE!
I'M ROOTING FOR YOU GUYS.
I DON'T KNOW WHAT HAPPENED WITH SHINOGU, BUT...
...HE'LL UNDERSTAND. I'M SURE OF IT.
...AKANE... THANKS...

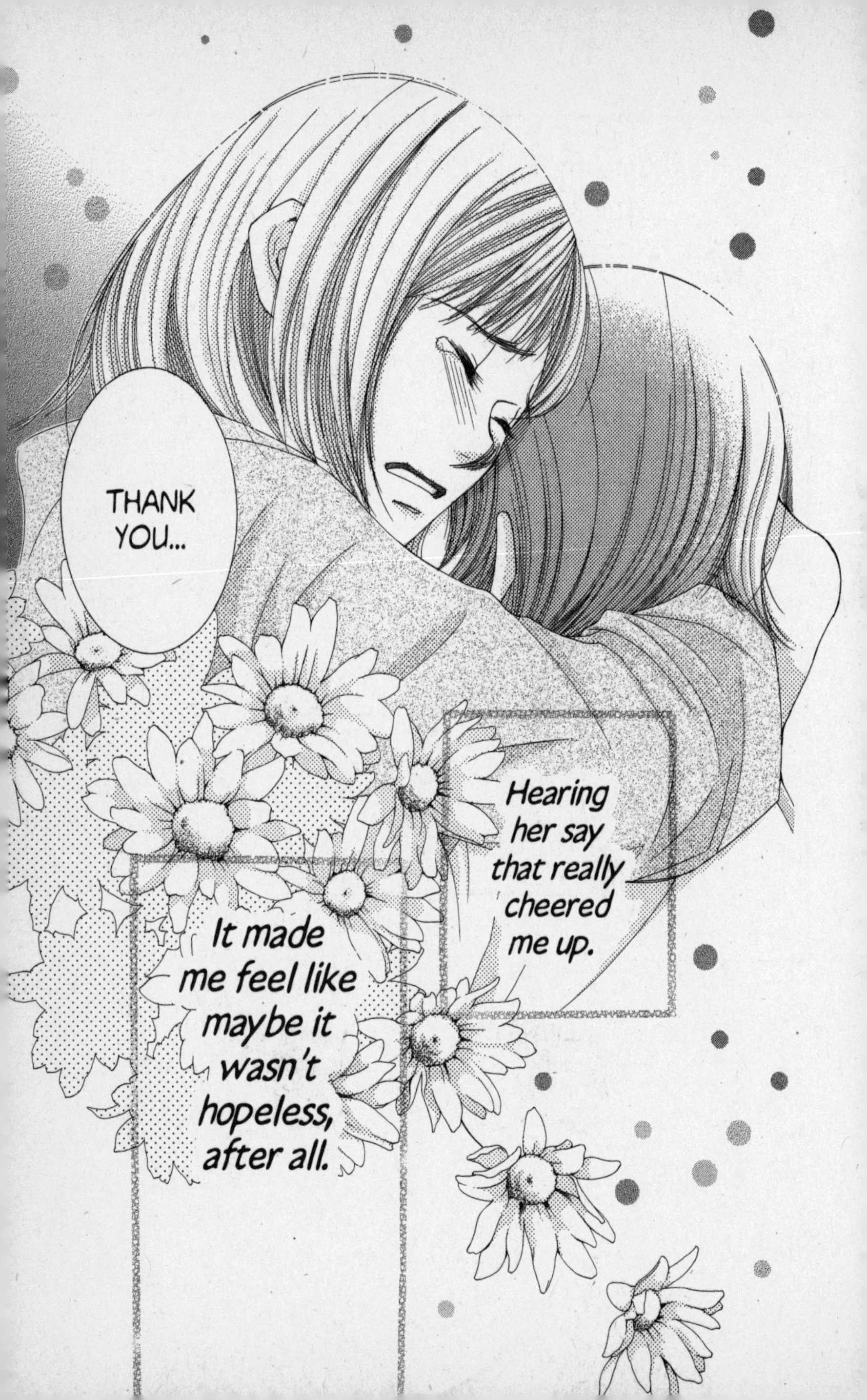
THANK YOU...
Hearing her say that really cheered me up.
It made me feel like maybe it wasn't hopeless, after all.

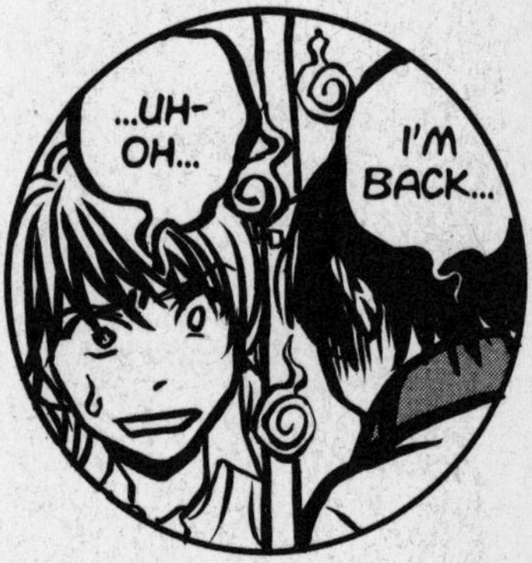
I'M BACK...
...UH-OH...

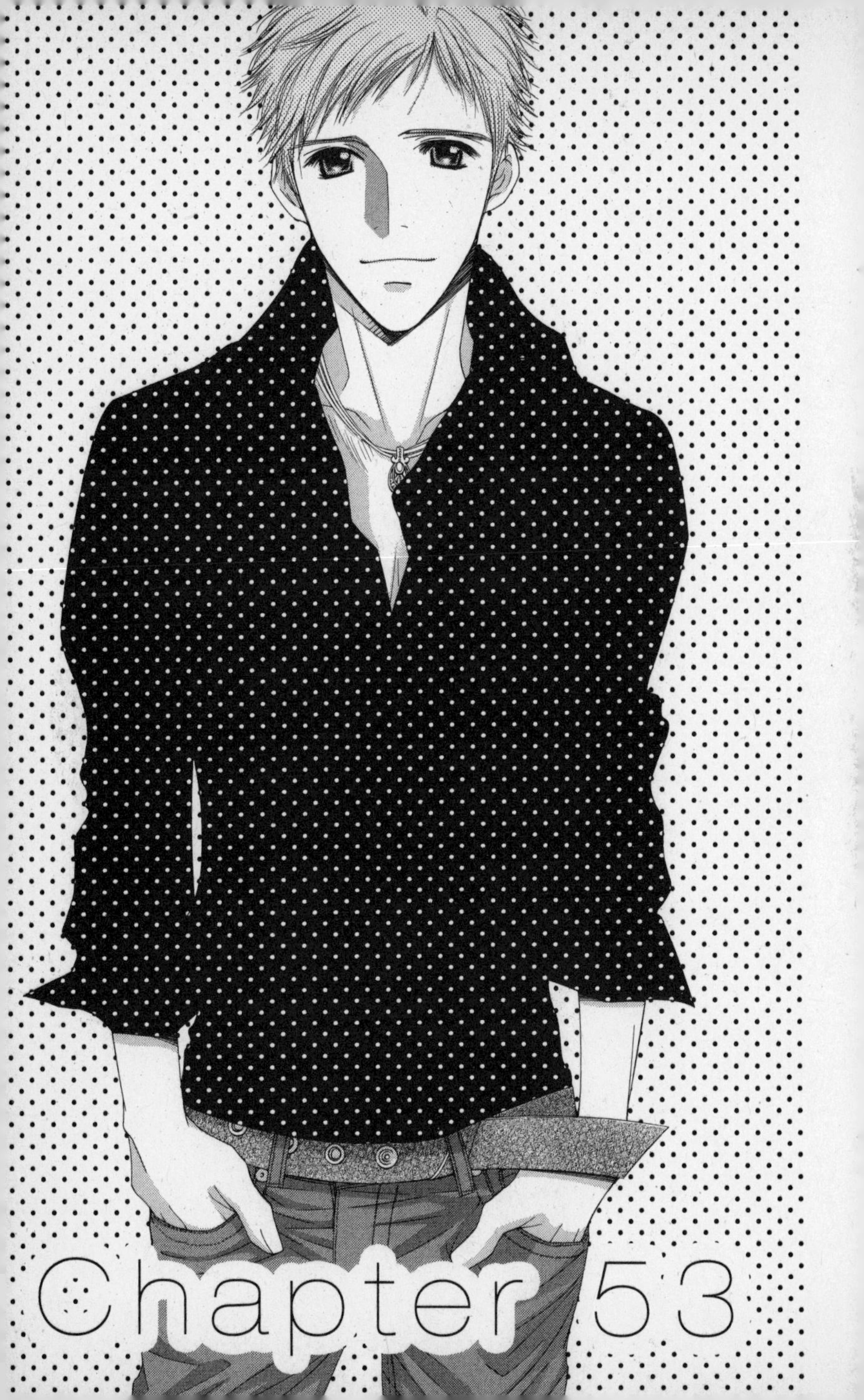
Chapter 53

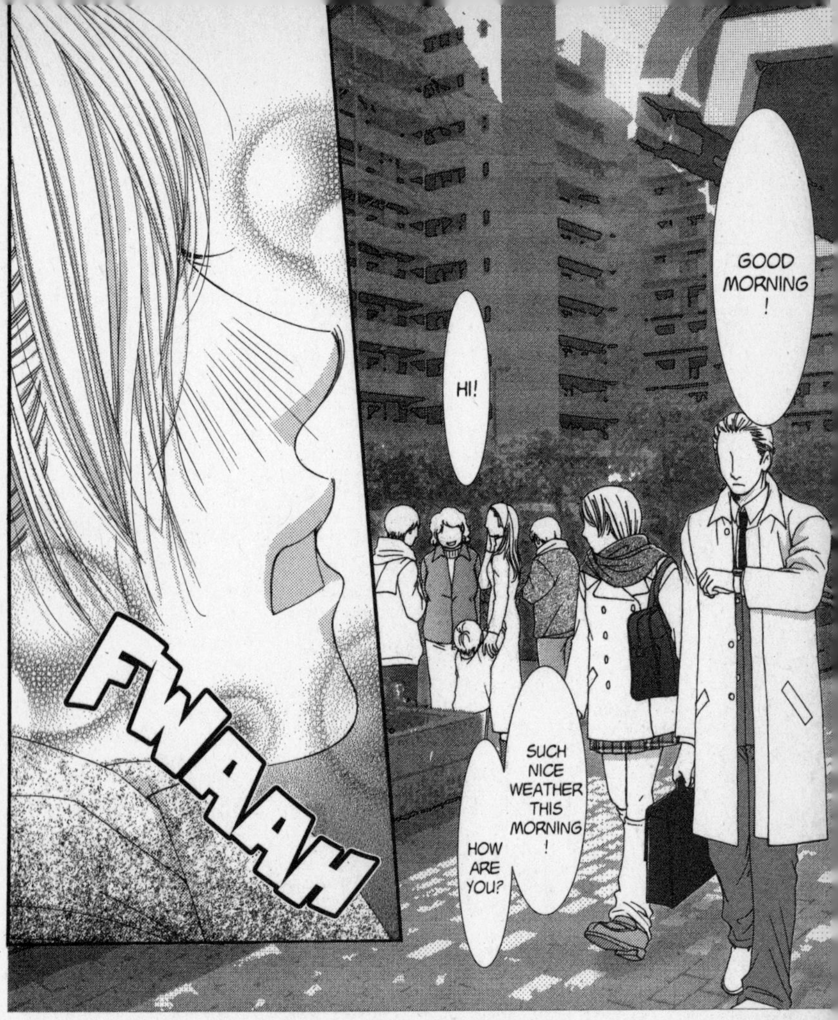
GOOD MORNING!
HI!
SUCH NICE WEATHER THIS MORNING!
HOW ARE YOU?
FWAAAH

hot gimmick

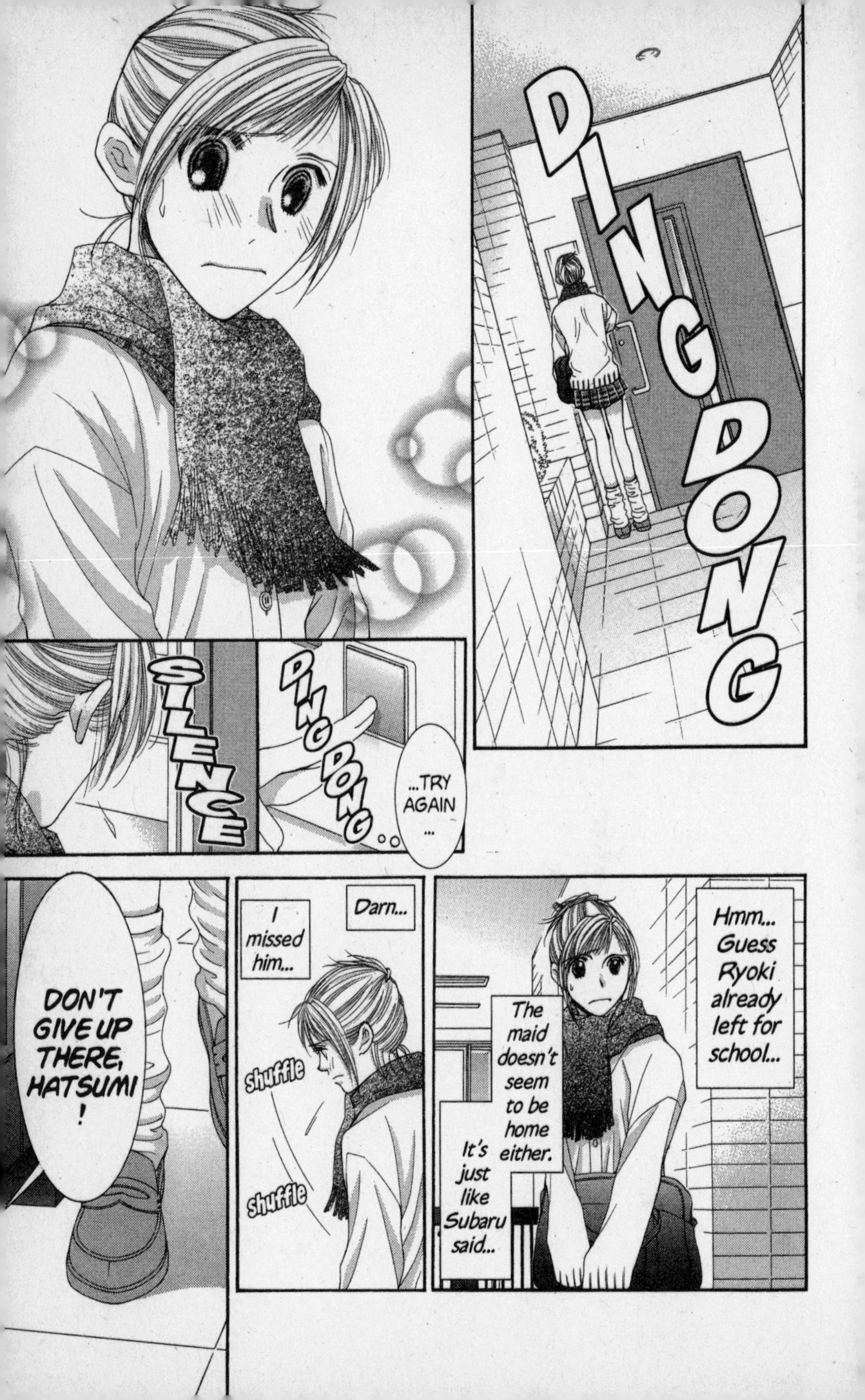
DING DONG
DING DONG
...TRY AGAIN...
SILENCE
Hmm... Guess Ryoki already left for school...
The maid doesn't seem to be home either.
It's just like Subaru said...
Darn...
I missed him...
shuffle
shuffle
DON'T GIVE UP THERE, HATSUMI!

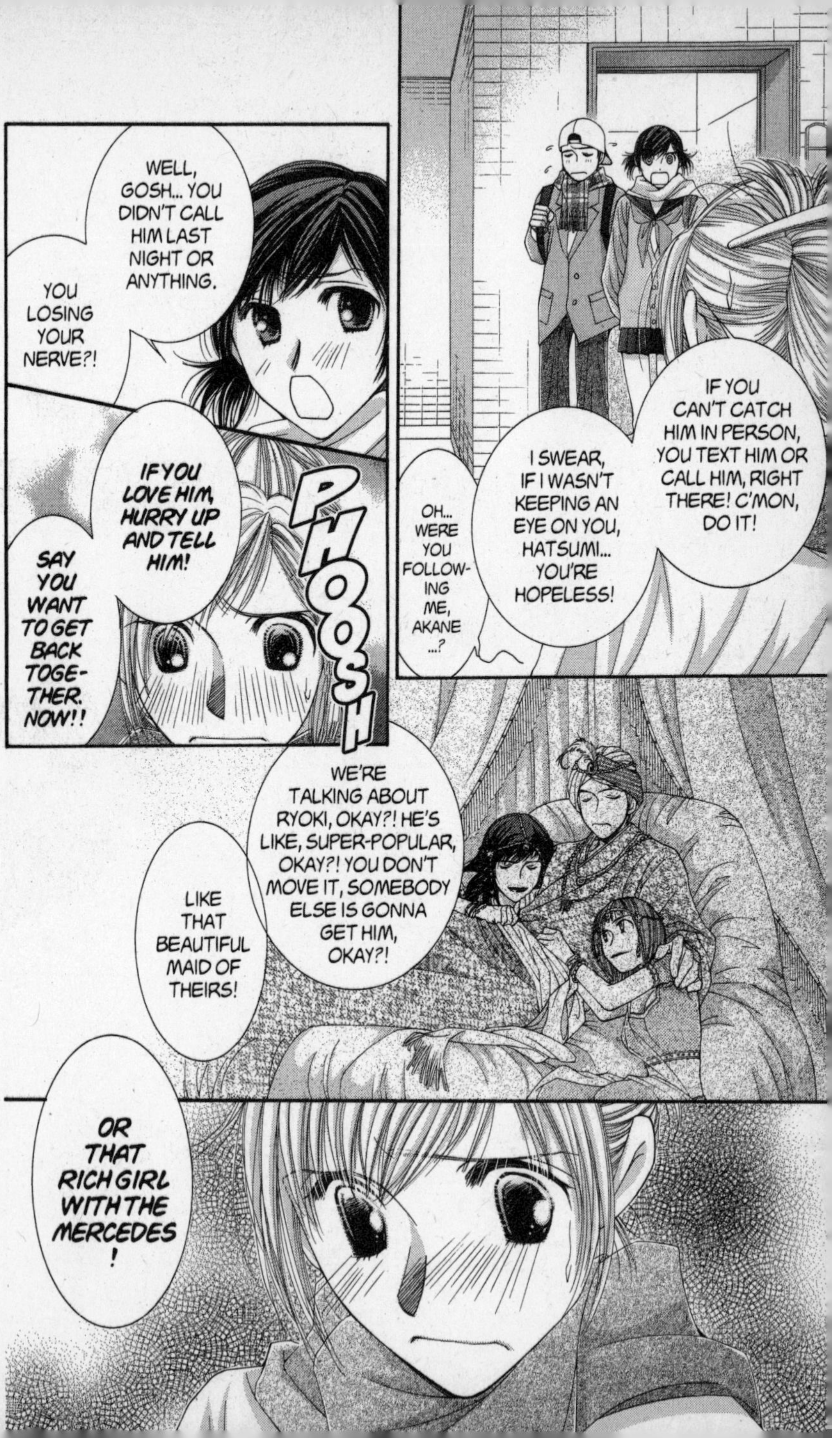
IF YOU CAN'T CATCH HIM IN PERSON, YOU TEXT HIM OR CALL HIM, RIGHT THERE! C'MON, DO IT!
I SWEAR, IF I WASN'T KEEPING AN EYE ON YOU, HATSUMI... YOU'RE HOPELESS!
OH... WERE YOU FOLLOWING ME, AKANE ...?
WELL, GOSH... YOU DIDN'T CALL HIM LAST NIGHT OR ANYTHING.
YOU LOSING YOUR NERVE?!
IF YOU LOVE HIM, HURRY UP AND TELL HIM!
SAY YOU WANT TO GET BACK TOGE-THER. NOW!!
PHOOSH
WE'RE TALKING ABOUT RYOKI, OKAY?! HE'S LIKE, SUPER-POPULAR, OKAY?! YOU DON'T MOVE IT, SOMEBODY ELSE IS GONNA GET HIM, OKAY?!
LIKE THAT BEAUTIFUL MAID OF THEIRS!
OR THAT RICH GIRL WITH THE MERCEDES!

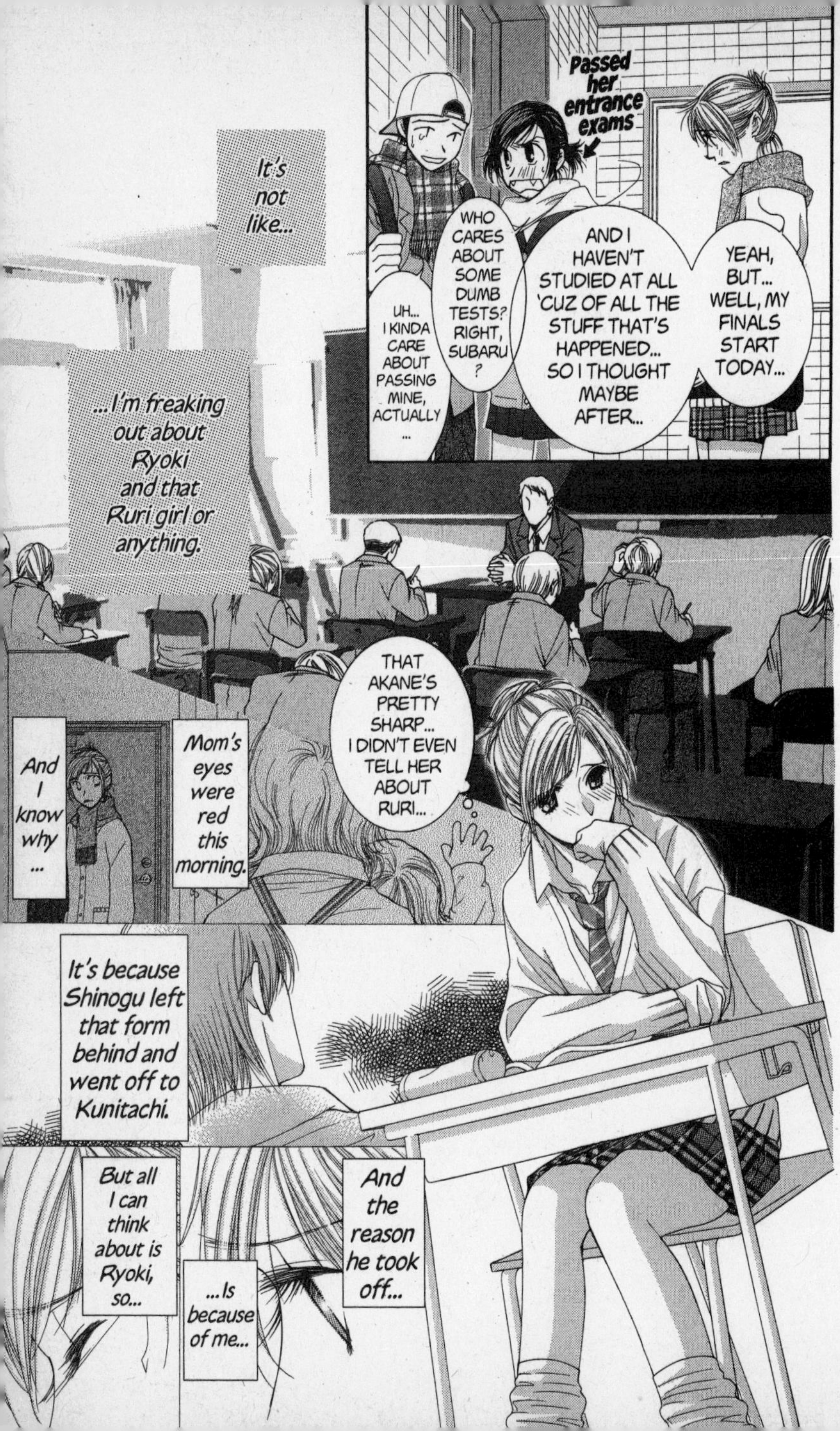
Passed her entrance exams
YEAH, BUT... WELL, MY FINALS START TODAY...
AND I HAVEN'T STUDIED AT ALL 'CUZ OF ALL THE STUFF THAT'S HAPPENED... SO I THOUGHT MAYBE AFTER...
WHO CARES ABOUT SOME DUMB TESTS? RIGHT, SUBARU?
UH... I KINDA CARE ABOUT PASSING MINE, ACTUALLY...
It's not like...
...I'm freaking out about Ryoki and that Ruri girl or anything.
THAT AKANE'S PRETTY SHARP... I DIDN'T EVEN TELL HER ABOUT RURI...
Mom's eyes were red this morning.
And I know why...
It's because Shinogu left that form behind and went off to Kunitachi.
And the reason he took off...
...Is because of me...
But all I can think about is Ryoki, so...

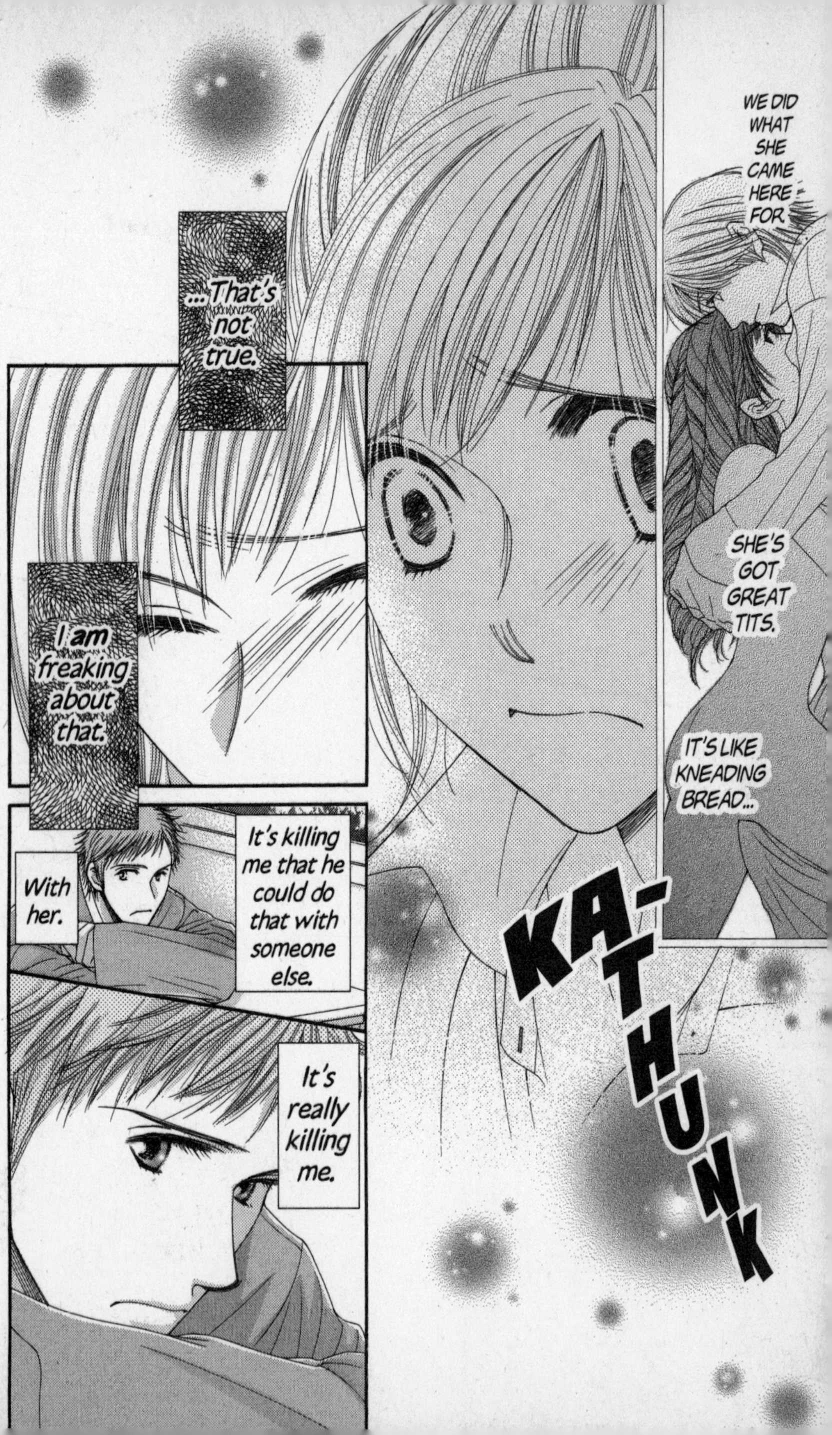
WE DID WHAT SHE CAME HERE FOR.
SHE'S GOT GREAT TITS.
IT'S LIKE KNEADING BREAD...
KA-THUNK
...That's not true.
I am freaking about that.
It's killing me that he could do that with someone else.
With her.
It's really killing me.

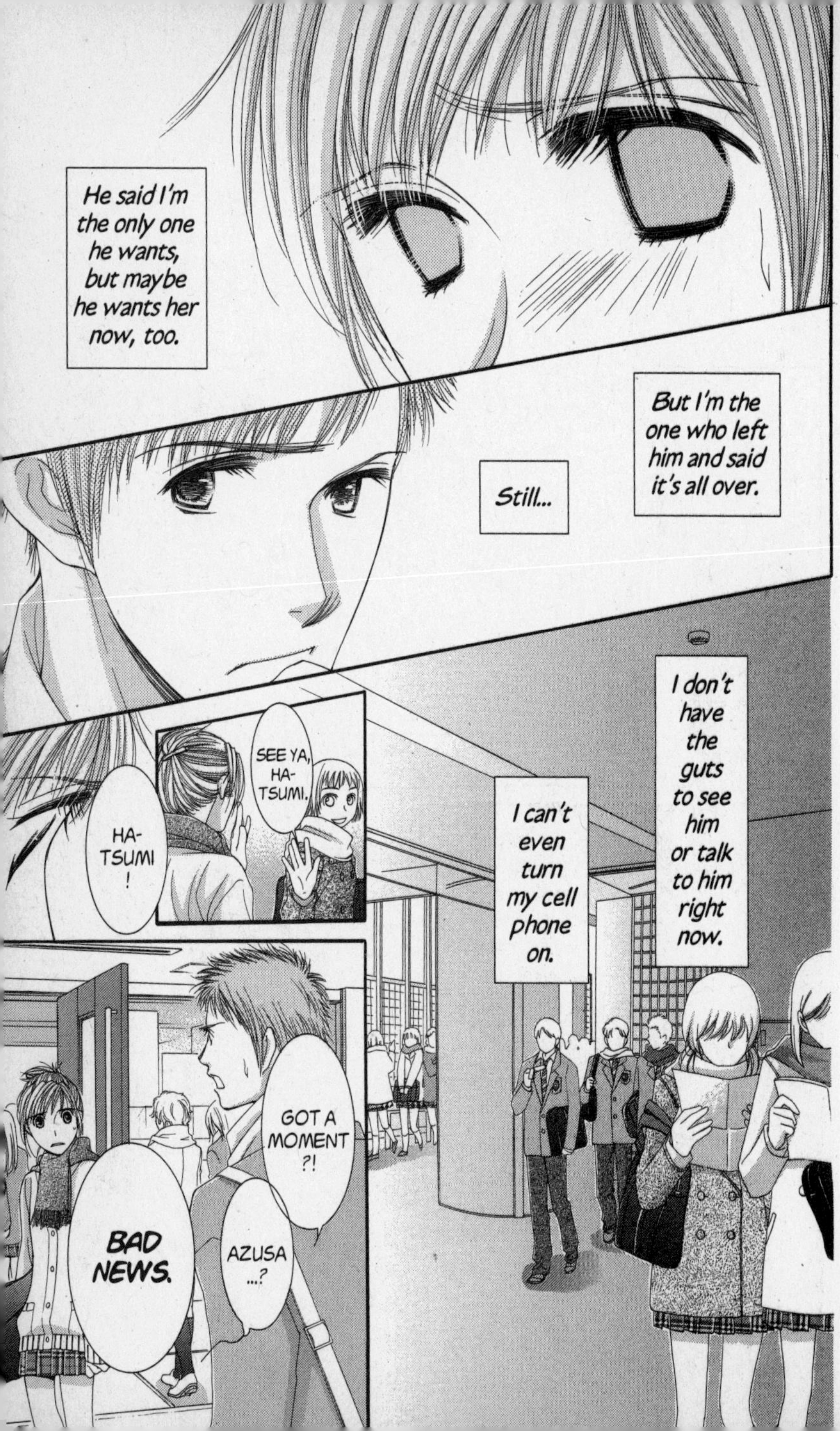
He said I'm the only one he wants, but maybe he wants her now, too.
But I'm the one who left him and said it's all over.
Still...
I don't have the guts to see him or talk to him right now.
I can't even turn my cell phone on.
SEE YA, HA-TSUMI.
HA-TSUMI!
GOT A MOMENT?!
AZUSA ...?
BAD NEWS.

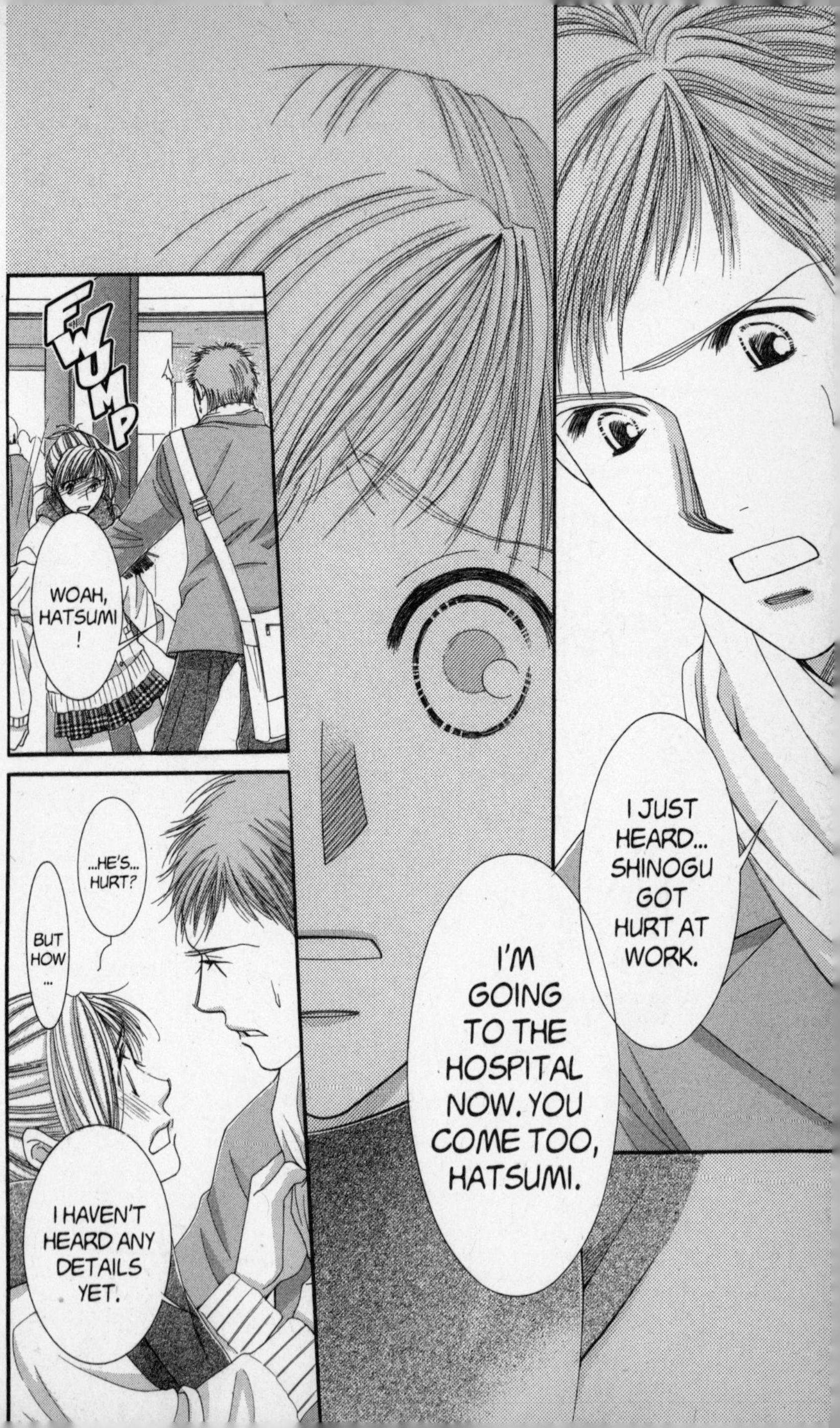
I JUST HEARD... SHINOGU GOT HURT AT WORK.
I'M GOING TO THE HOSPITAL NOW. YOU COME TOO, HATSUMI.
FWUMP
WOAH, HATSUMI!
...HE'S... HURT?
BUT HOW...
I HAVEN'T HEARD ANY DETAILS YET.

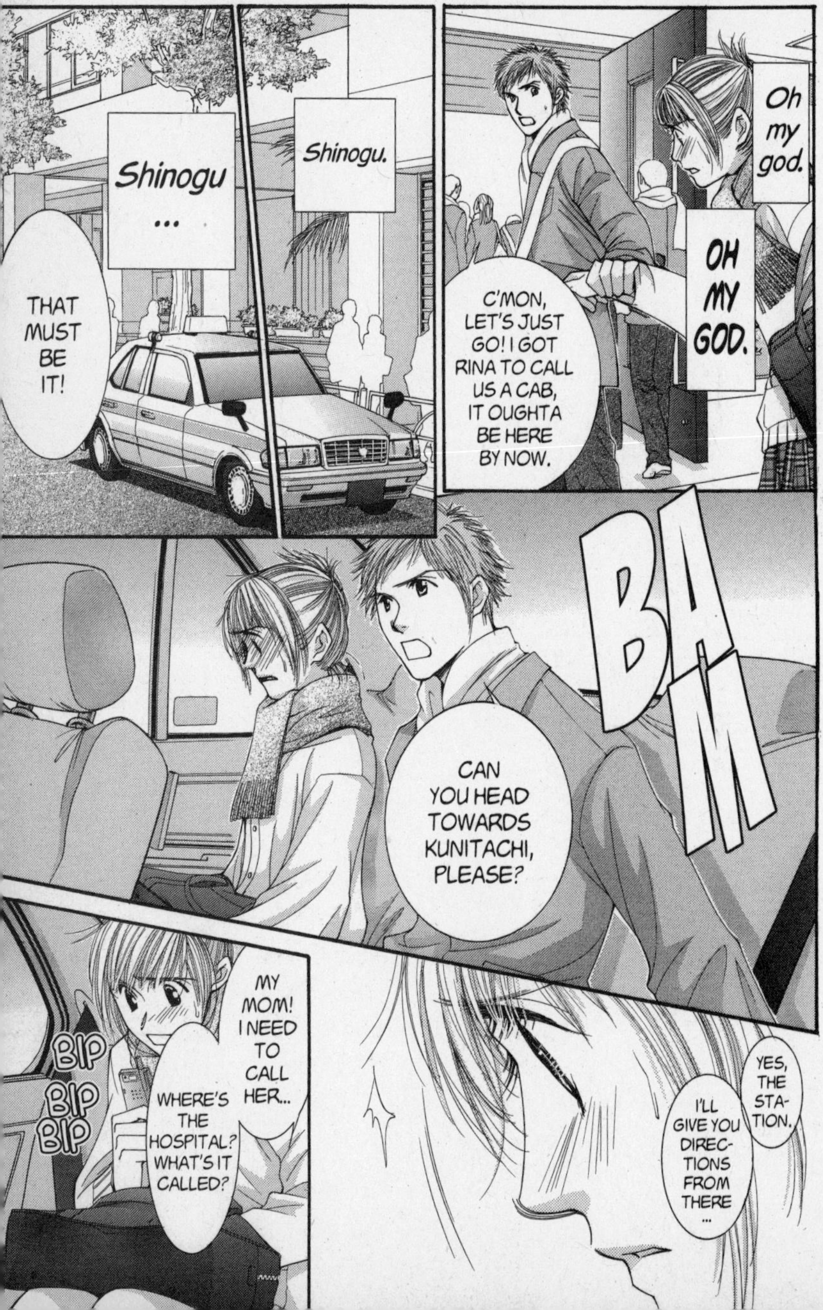
Oh my god.
OH MY GOD.
C'MON, LET'S JUST GO! I GOT RINA TO CALL US A CAB, IT OUGHTA BE HERE BY NOW.
Shinogu.
Shinogu ...
THAT MUST BE IT!
BAM
CAN YOU HEAD TOWARDS KUNITACHI, PLEASE?
YES, THE STA-TION.
I'LL GIVE YOU DIREC-TIONS FROM THERE ...
MY MOM! I NEED TO CALL HER...
WHERE'S THE HOSPITAL? WHAT'S IT CALLED?
BIP BIP BIP

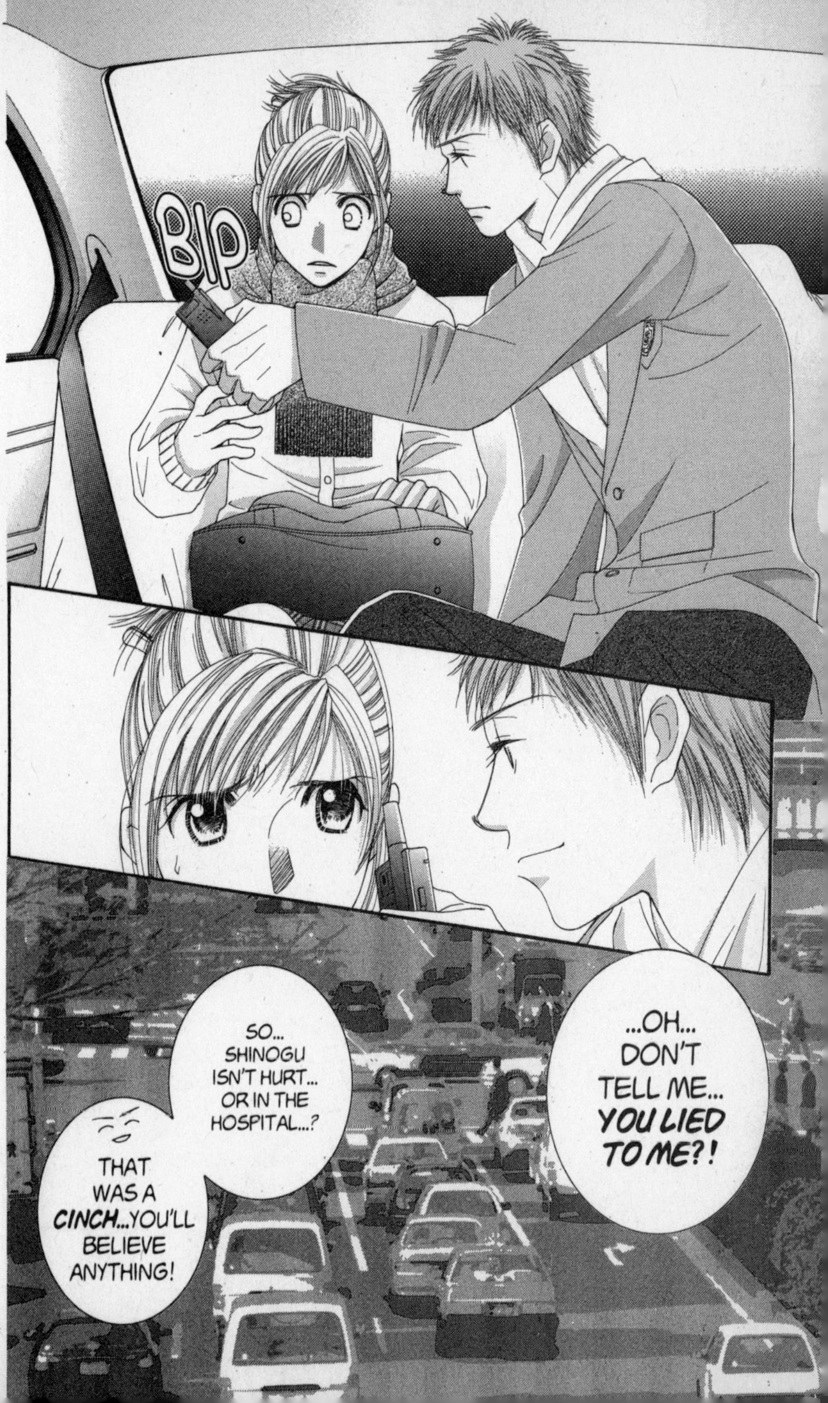
BIP
...OH... DON'T TELL ME... YOU LIED TO ME?!
SO... SHINOGU ISN'T HURT... OR IN THE HOSPITAL...?
THAT WAS A CINCH...YOU'LL BELIEVE ANYTHING!

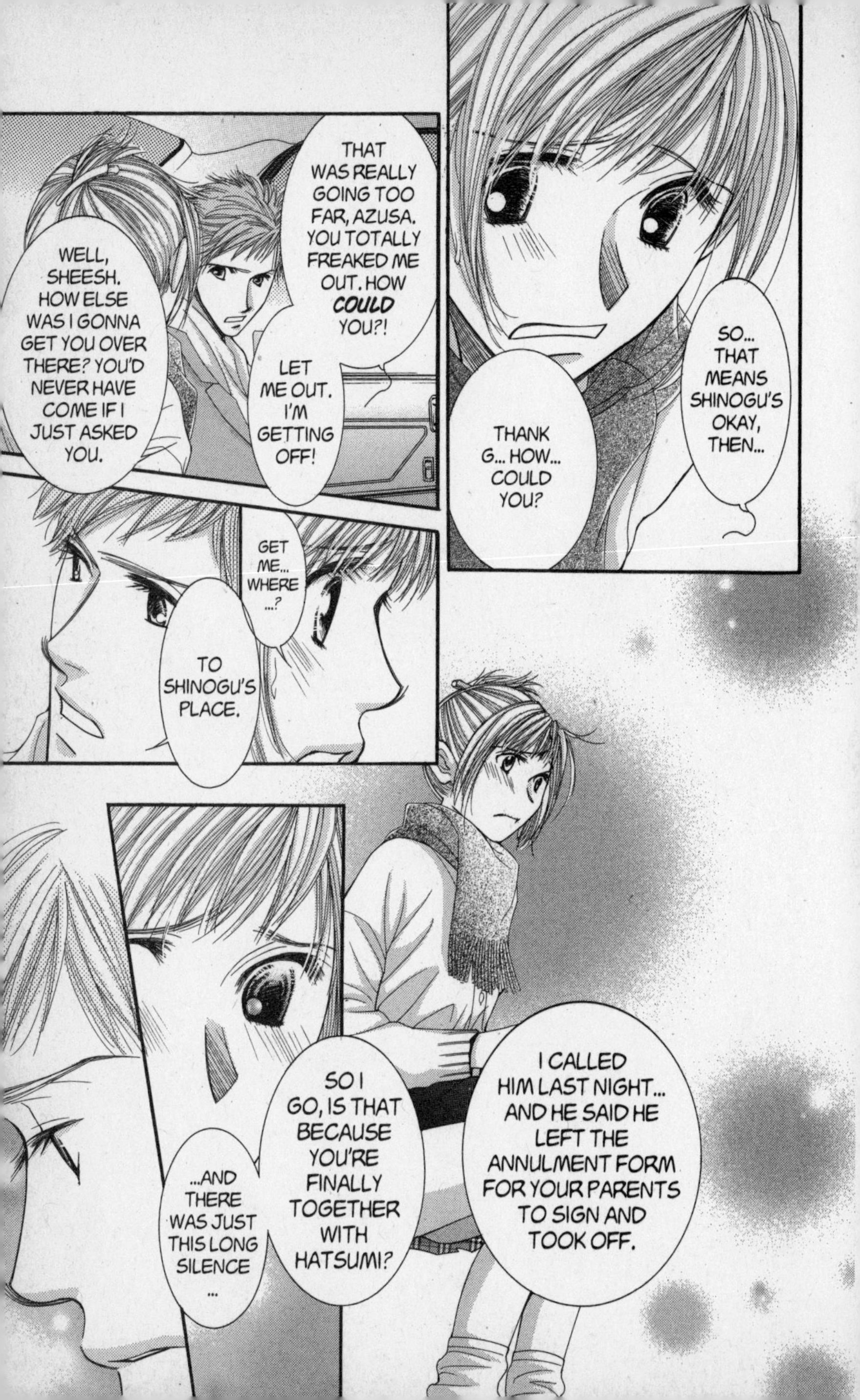
SO... THAT MEANS SHINOGU'S OKAY, THEN...
THANK G... HOW... COULD YOU?
THAT WAS REALLY GOING TOO FAR, AZUSA. YOU TOTALLY FREAKED ME OUT. HOW **COULD** YOU?!
LET ME OUT. I'M GETTING OFF!
WELL, SHEESH. HOW ELSE WAS I GONNA GET YOU OVER THERE? YOU'D NEVER HAVE COME IF I JUST ASKED YOU.
GET ME... WHERE ...?
TO SHINOGU'S PLACE.
I CALLED HIM LAST NIGHT... AND HE SAID HE LEFT THE ANNULMENT FORM FOR YOUR PARENTS TO SIGN AND TOOK OFF.
SO I GO, IS THAT BECAUSE YOU'RE FINALLY TOGETHER WITH HATSUMI?
...AND THERE WAS JUST THIS LONG SILENCE ...

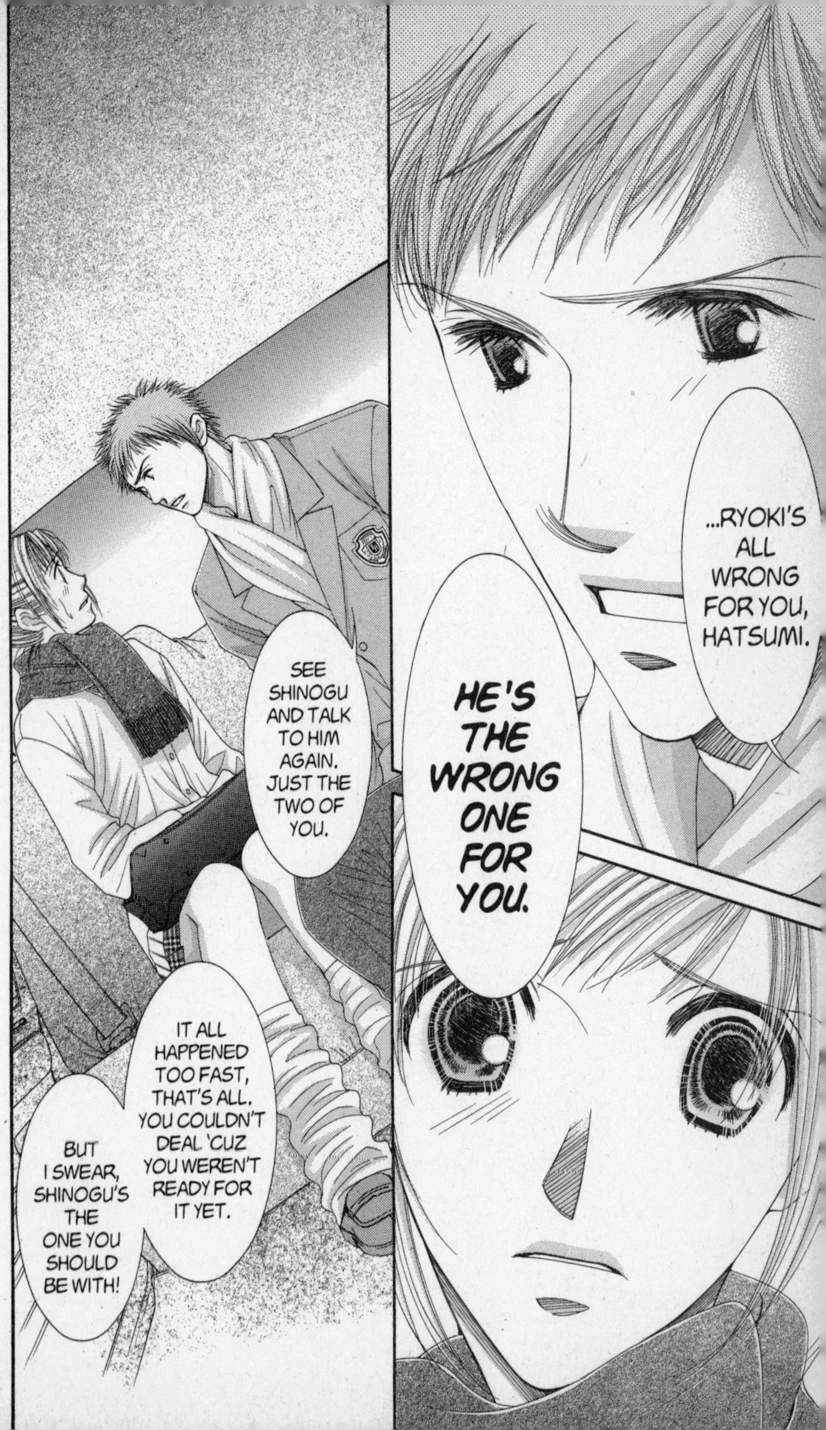
...RYOKI'S ALL WRONG FOR YOU, HATSUMI.
HE'S THE WRONG ONE FOR YOU.
SEE SHINOGU AND TALK TO HIM AGAIN. JUST THE TWO OF YOU.
IT ALL HAPPENED TOO FAST, THAT'S ALL. YOU COULDN'T DEAL 'CUZ YOU WEREN'T READY FOR IT YET.
BUT I SWEAR, SHINOGU'S THE ONE YOU SHOULD BE WITH!

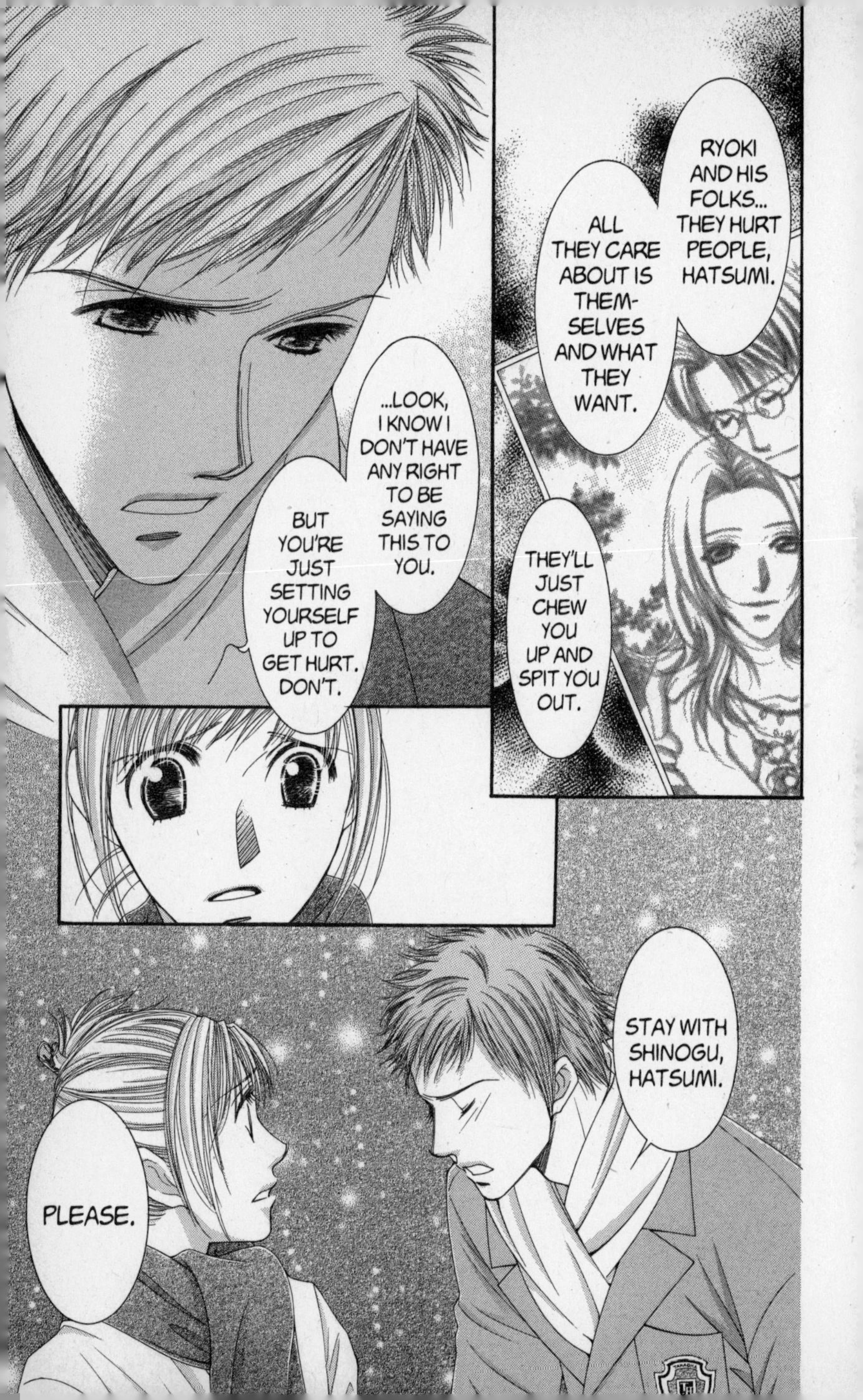
RYOKI AND HIS FOLKS... THEY HURT PEOPLE, HATSUMI.
ALL THEY CARE ABOUT IS THEM-SELVES AND WHAT THEY WANT.
THEY'LL JUST CHEW YOU UP AND SPIT YOU OUT.
...LOOK, I KNOW I DON'T HAVE ANY RIGHT TO BE SAYING THIS TO YOU.
BUT YOU'RE JUST SETTING YOURSELF UP TO GET HURT. DON'T.
STAY WITH SHINOGU, HATSUMI.
PLEASE.

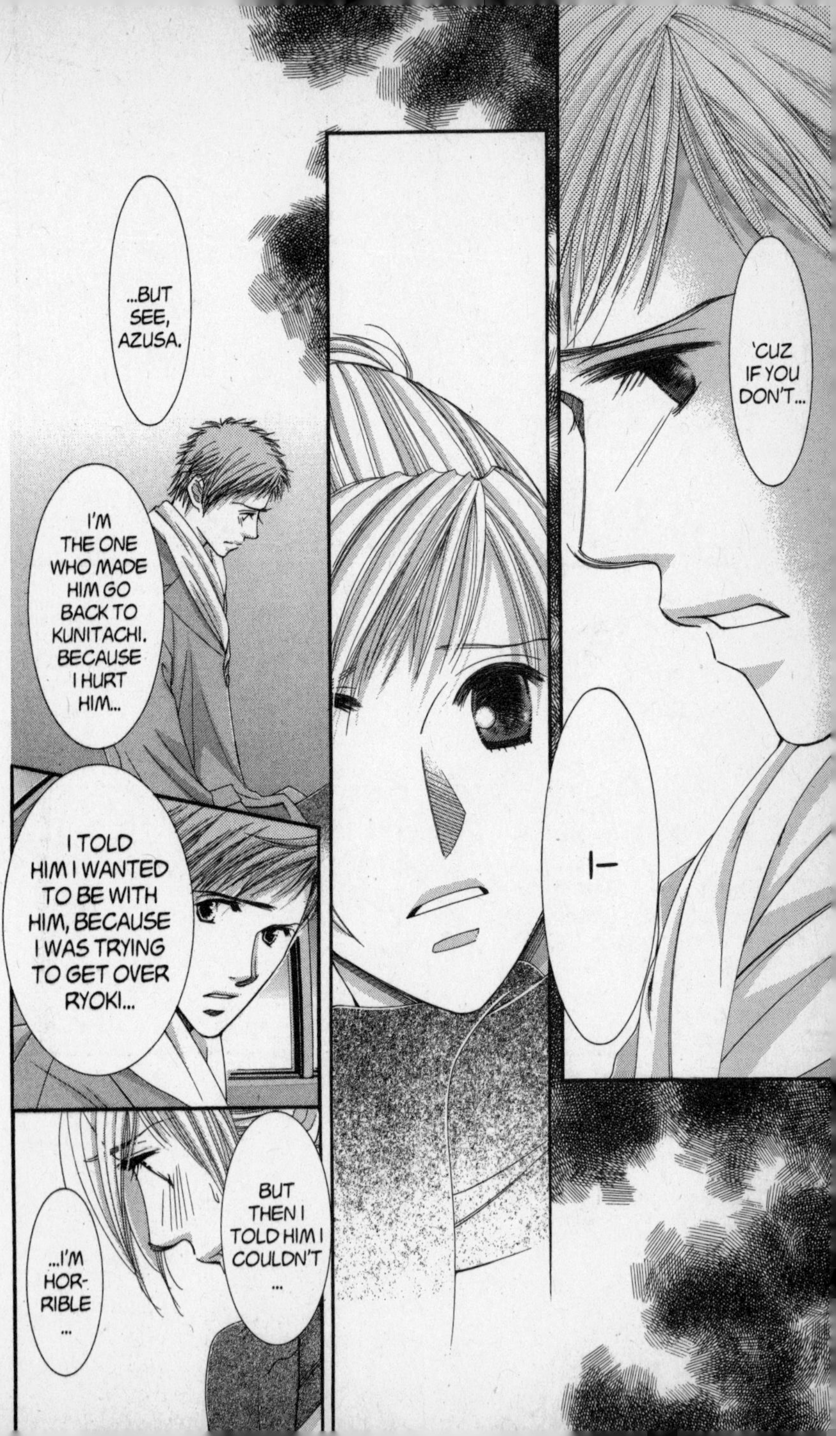
'CUZ IF YOU DON'T...
I-
...BUT SEE, AZUSA.
I'M THE ONE WHO MADE HIM GO BACK TO KUNITACHI. BECAUSE I HURT HIM...
I TOLD HIM I WANTED TO BE WITH HIM, BECAUSE I WAS TRYING TO GET OVER RYOKI...
BUT THEN I TOLD HIM I COULDN'T ...
...I'M HOR-RIBLE ...

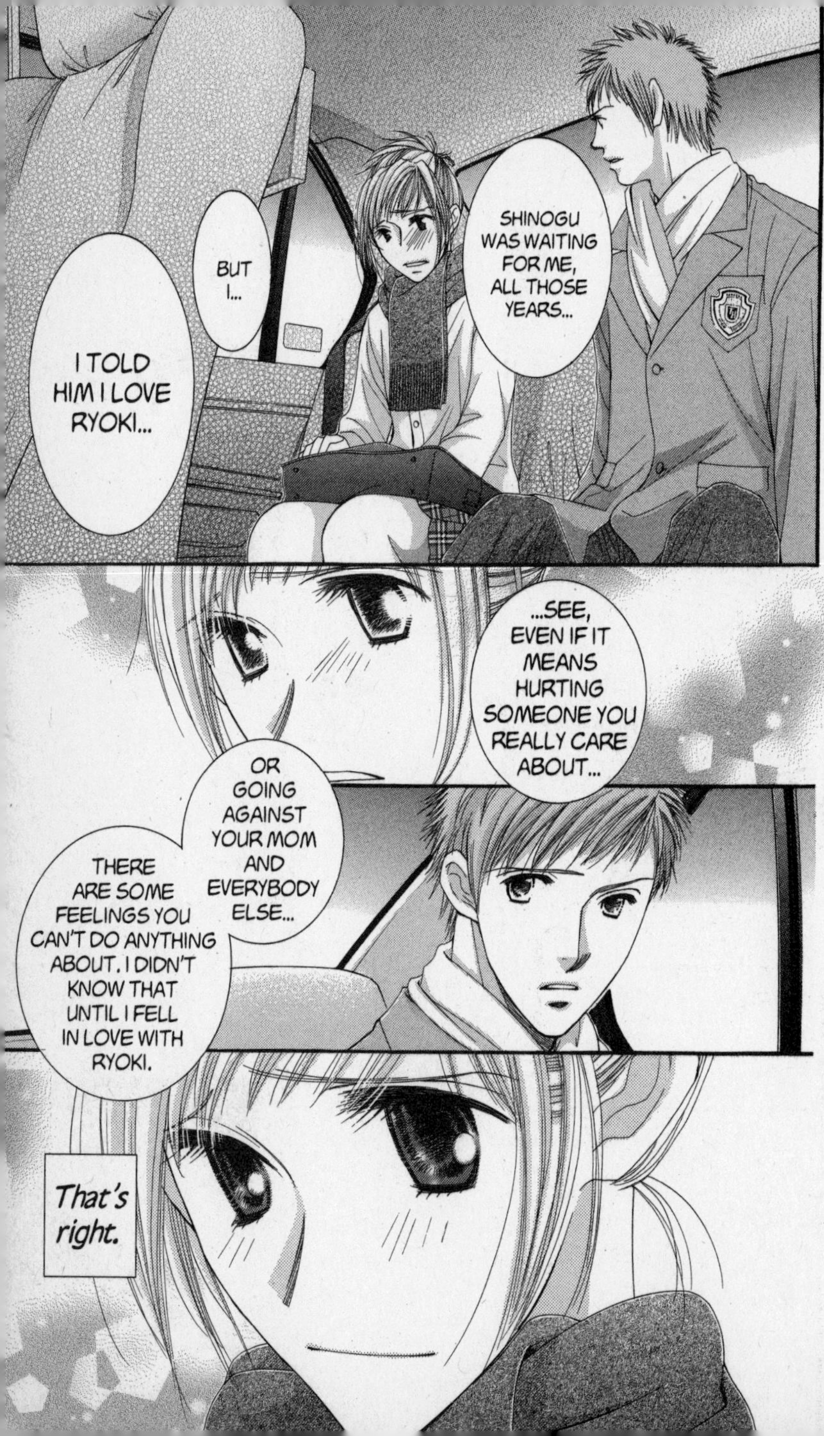
SHINOGU WAS WAITING FOR ME, ALL THOSE YEARS...
BUT I...
I TOLD HIM I LOVE RYOKI...
...SEE, EVEN IF IT MEANS HURTING SOMEONE YOU REALLY CARE ABOUT...
OR GOING AGAINST YOUR MOM AND EVERYBODY ELSE...
THERE ARE SOME FEELINGS YOU CAN'T DO ANYTHING ABOUT. I DIDN'T KNOW THAT UNTIL I FELL IN LOVE WITH RYOKI.
That's right.

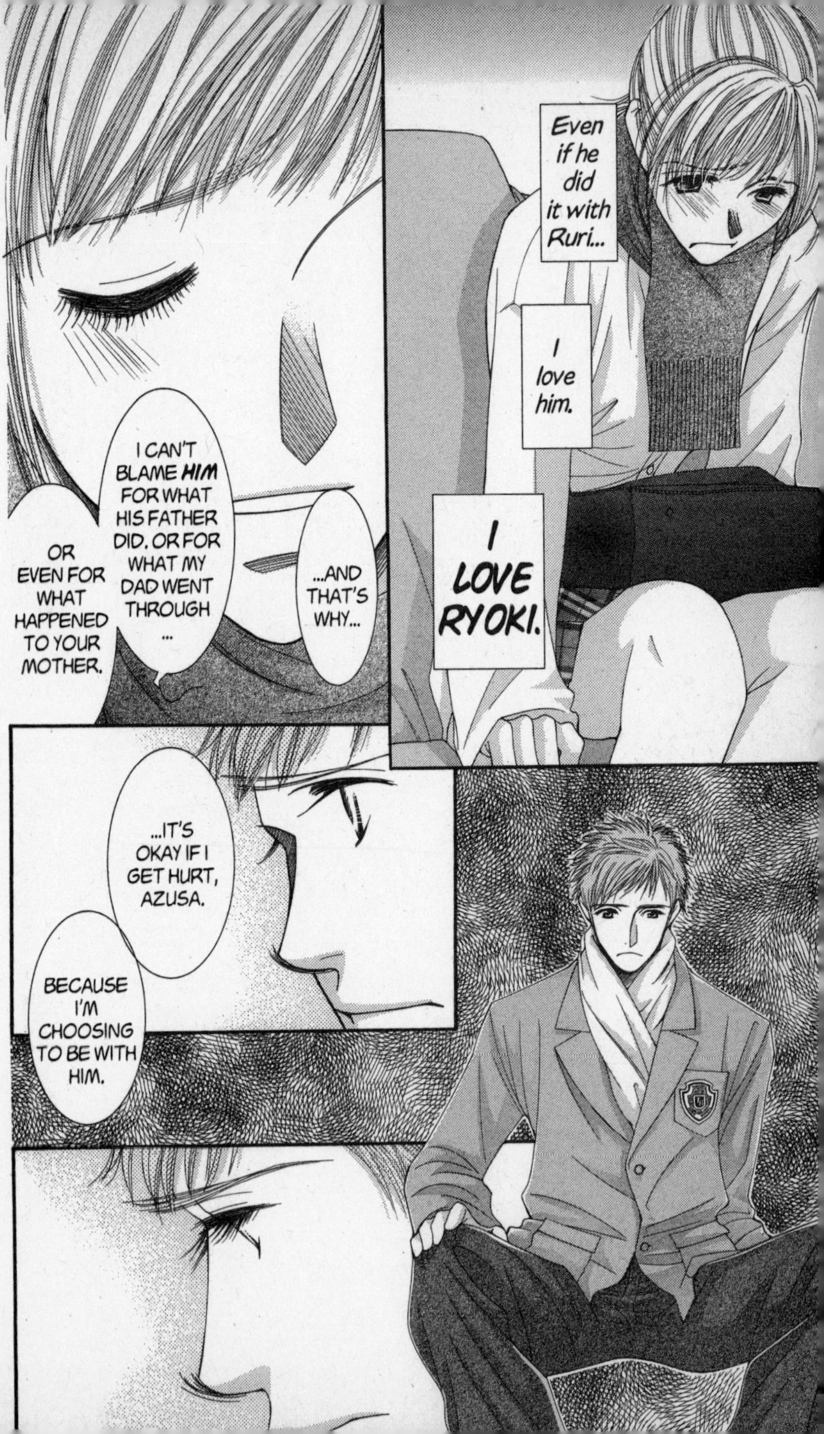
Even if he did it with Ruri...
I love him.
I LOVE RYOKI.
I CAN'T BLAME **HIM** FOR WHAT HIS FATHER DID. OR FOR WHAT MY DAD WENT THROUGH ...
OR EVEN FOR WHAT HAPPENED TO YOUR MOTHER.
...AND THAT'S WHY...
...IT'S OKAY IF I GET HURT, AZUSA.
BECAUSE I'M CHOOSING TO BE WITH HIM.

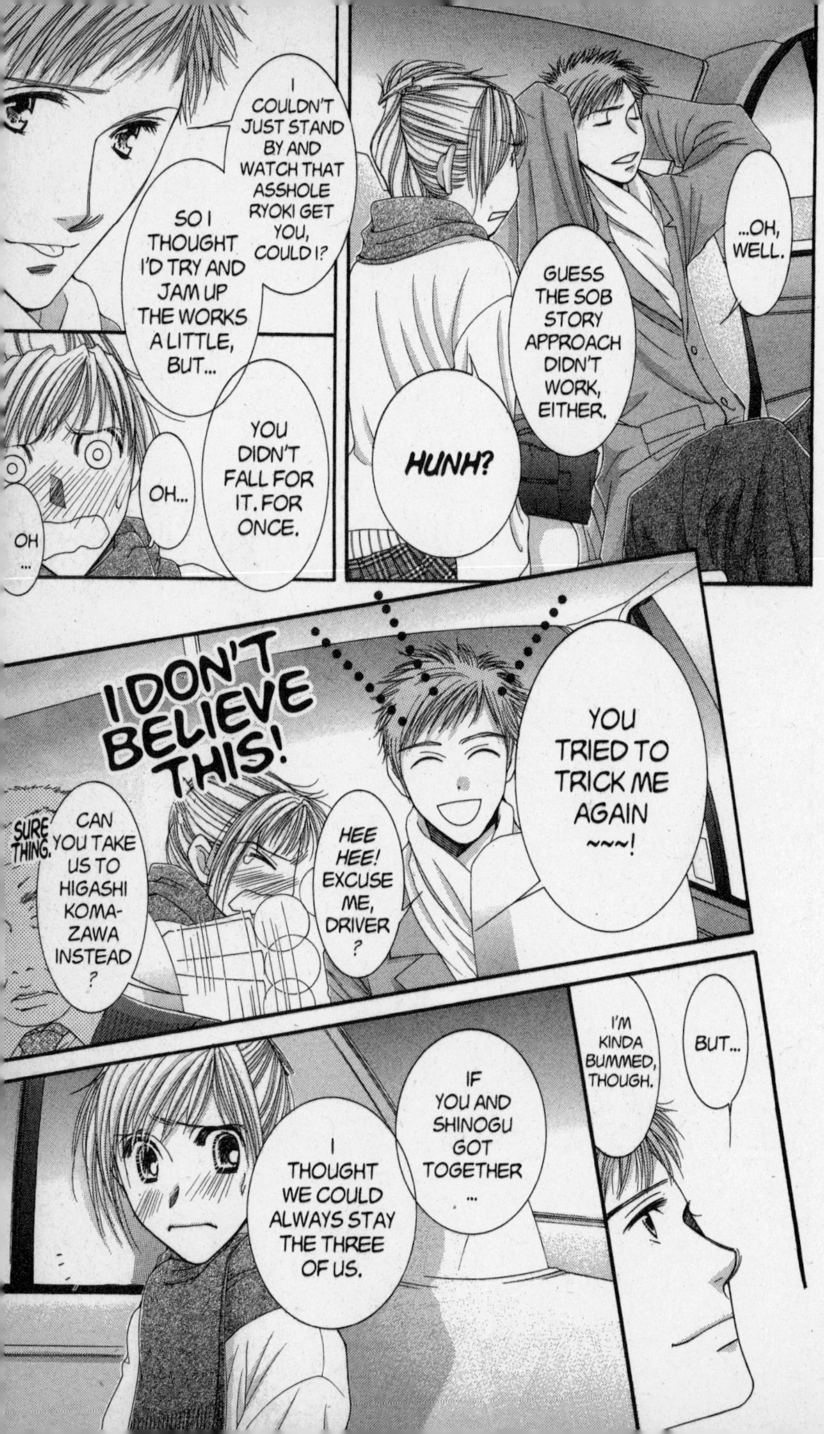
...OH, WELL.
GUESS THE SOB STORY APPROACH DIDN'T WORK, EITHER.
HUNH?
I COULDN'T JUST STAND BY AND WATCH THAT ASSHOLE RYOKI GET YOU, COULD I?
SO I THOUGHT I'D TRY AND JAM UP THE WORKS A LITTLE, BUT...
YOU DIDN'T FALL FOR IT. FOR ONCE.
OH...
OH ...
YOU TRIED TO TRICK ME AGAIN ~~~!
I DON'T BELIEVE THIS!
HEE HEE! EXCUSE ME, DRIVER?
CAN YOU TAKE US TO HIGASHI KOMA-ZAWA INSTEAD?
SURE THING.
BUT...
I'M KINDA BUMMED, THOUGH.
IF YOU AND SHINOGU GOT TOGETHER ...
I THOUGHT WE COULD ALWAYS STAY THE THREE OF US.

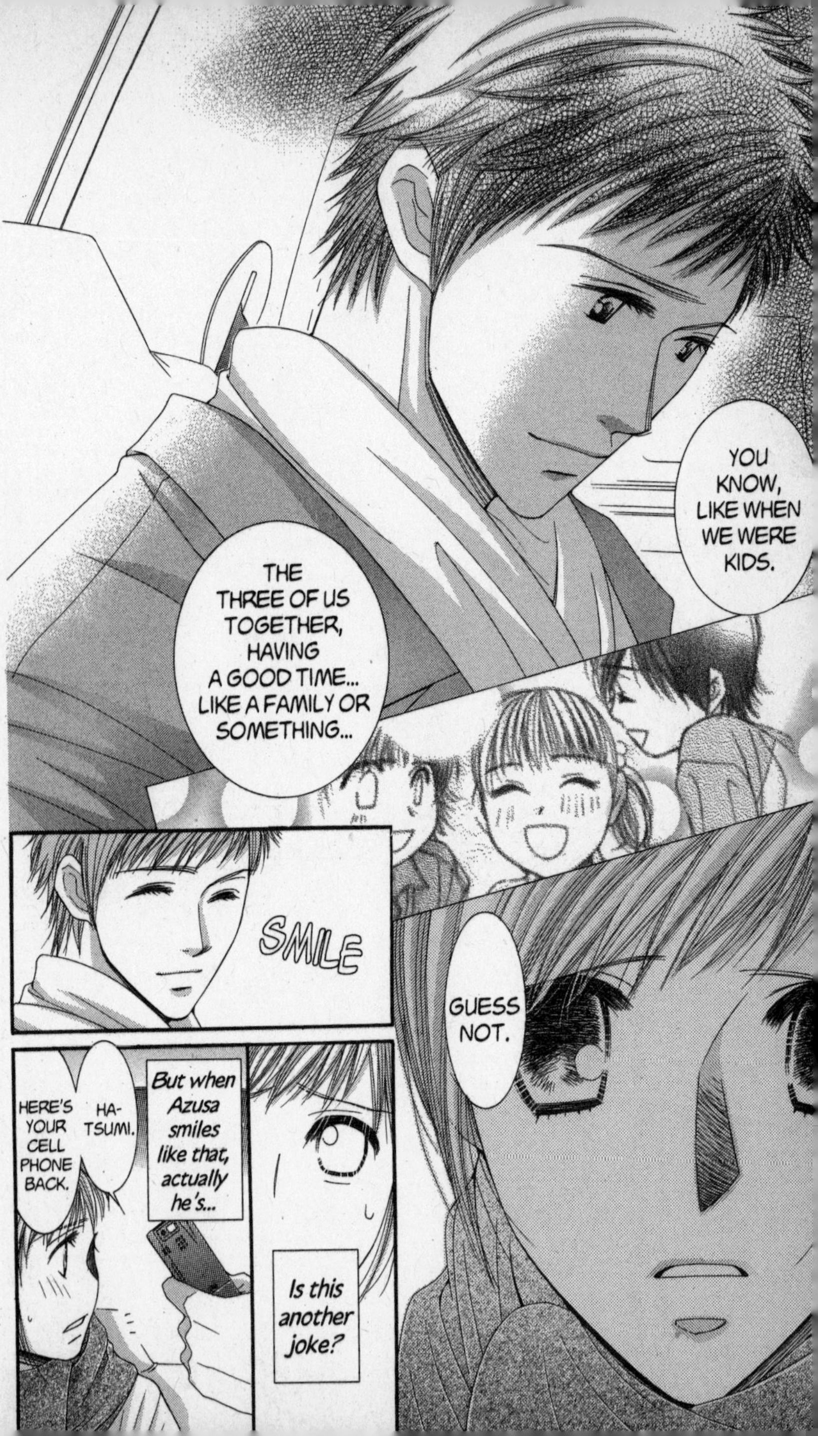
YOU KNOW, LIKE WHEN WE WERE KIDS.
THE THREE OF US TOGETHER, HAVING A GOOD TIME... LIKE A FAMILY OR SOMETHING...
GUESS NOT.
SMILE
But when Azusa smiles like that, actually he's...
HA-TSUMI.
HERE'S YOUR CELL PHONE BACK.
Is this another joke?

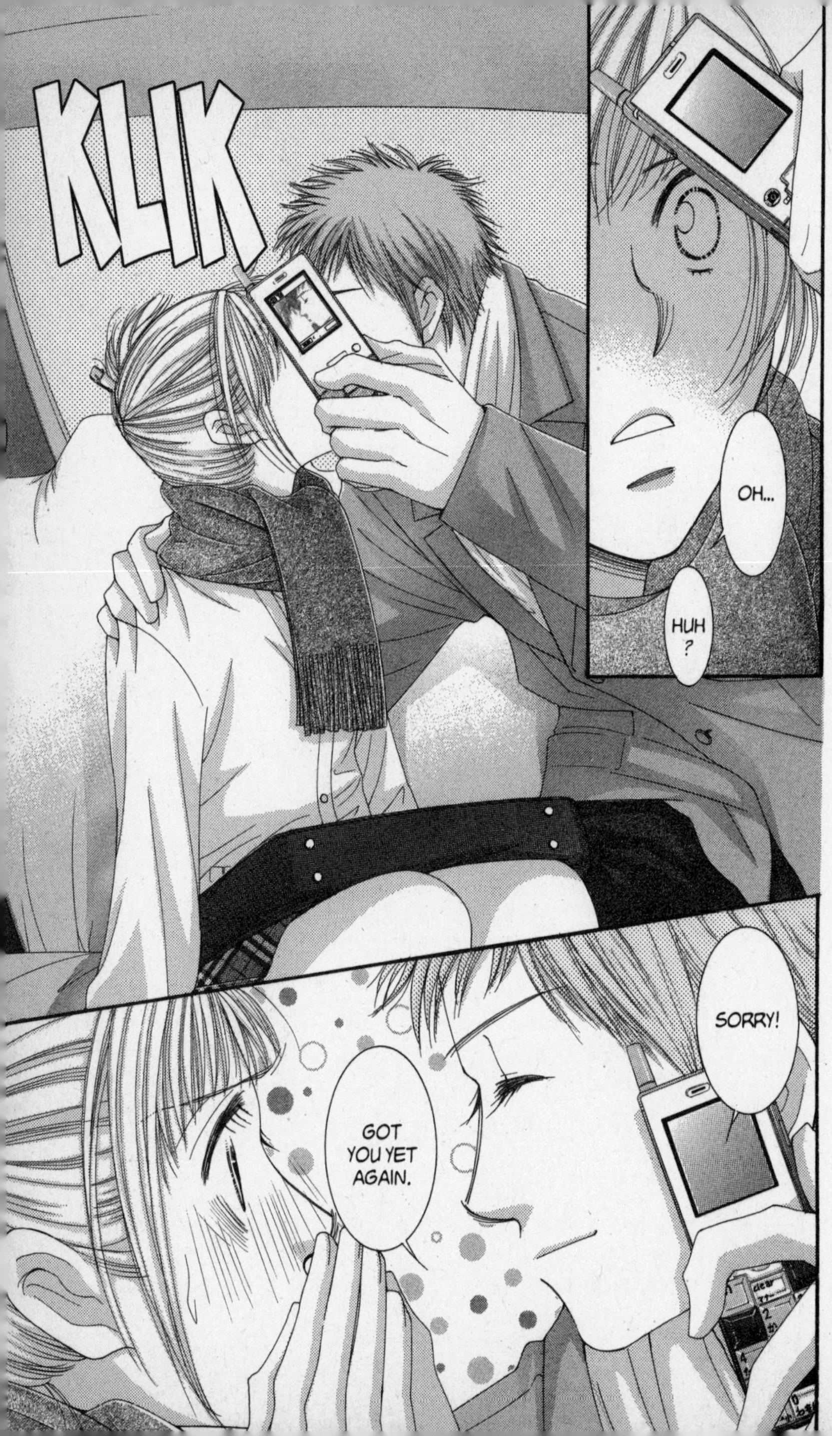
OH...
HUH ?
KLIK
SORRY!
GOT YOU YET AGAIN.

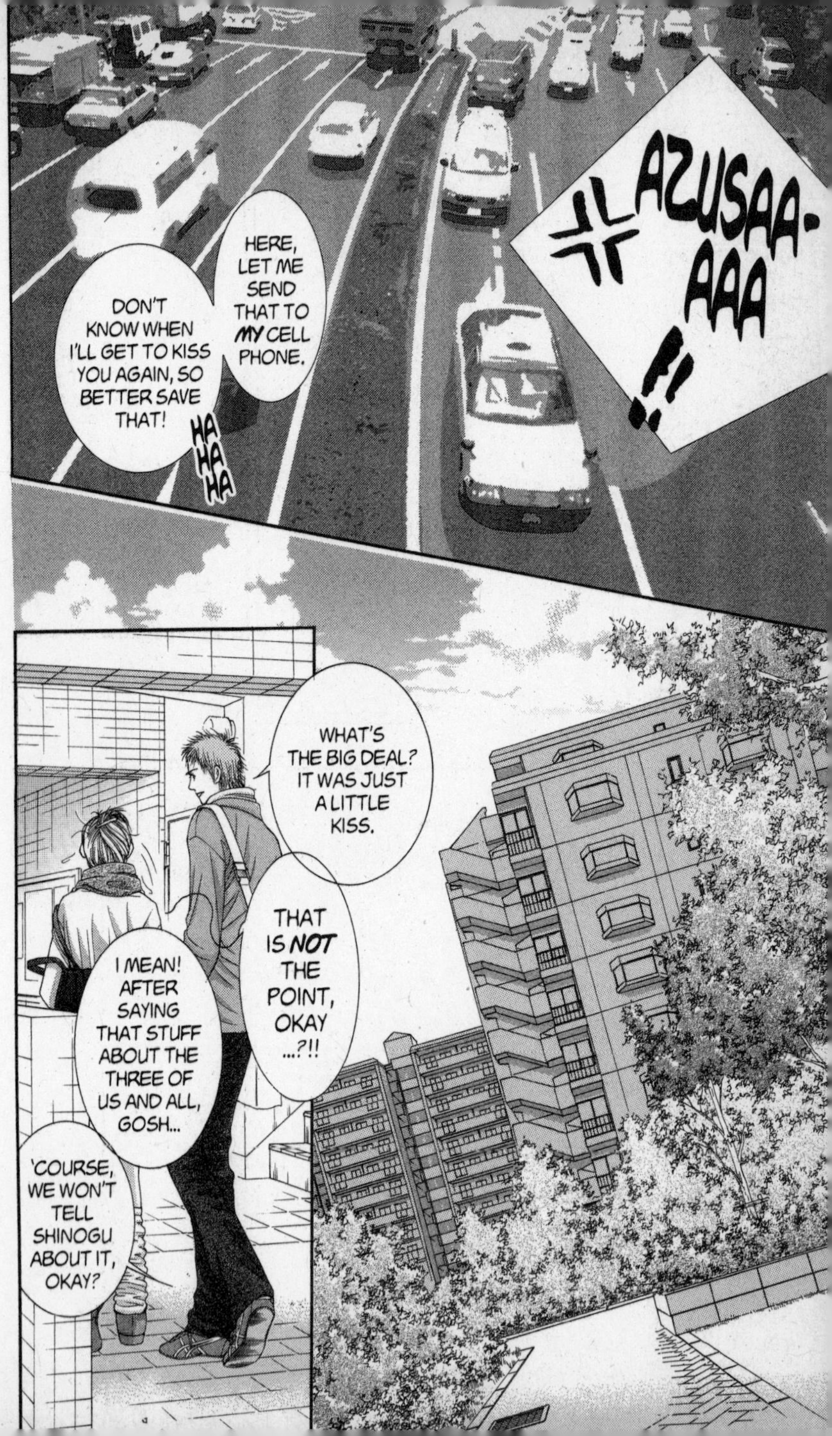
AZUSAA-AAA!!
HERE, LET ME SEND THAT TO *MY* CELL PHONE.
DON'T KNOW WHEN I'LL GET TO KISS YOU AGAIN, SO BETTER SAVE THAT!
HA HA HA
WHAT'S THE BIG DEAL? IT WAS JUST A LITTLE KISS.
THAT IS *NOT* THE POINT, OKAY ...?!!
I MEAN! AFTER SAYING THAT STUFF ABOUT THE THREE OF US AND ALL, GOSH...
'COURSE, WE WON'T TELL SHINOGU ABOUT IT, OKAY?

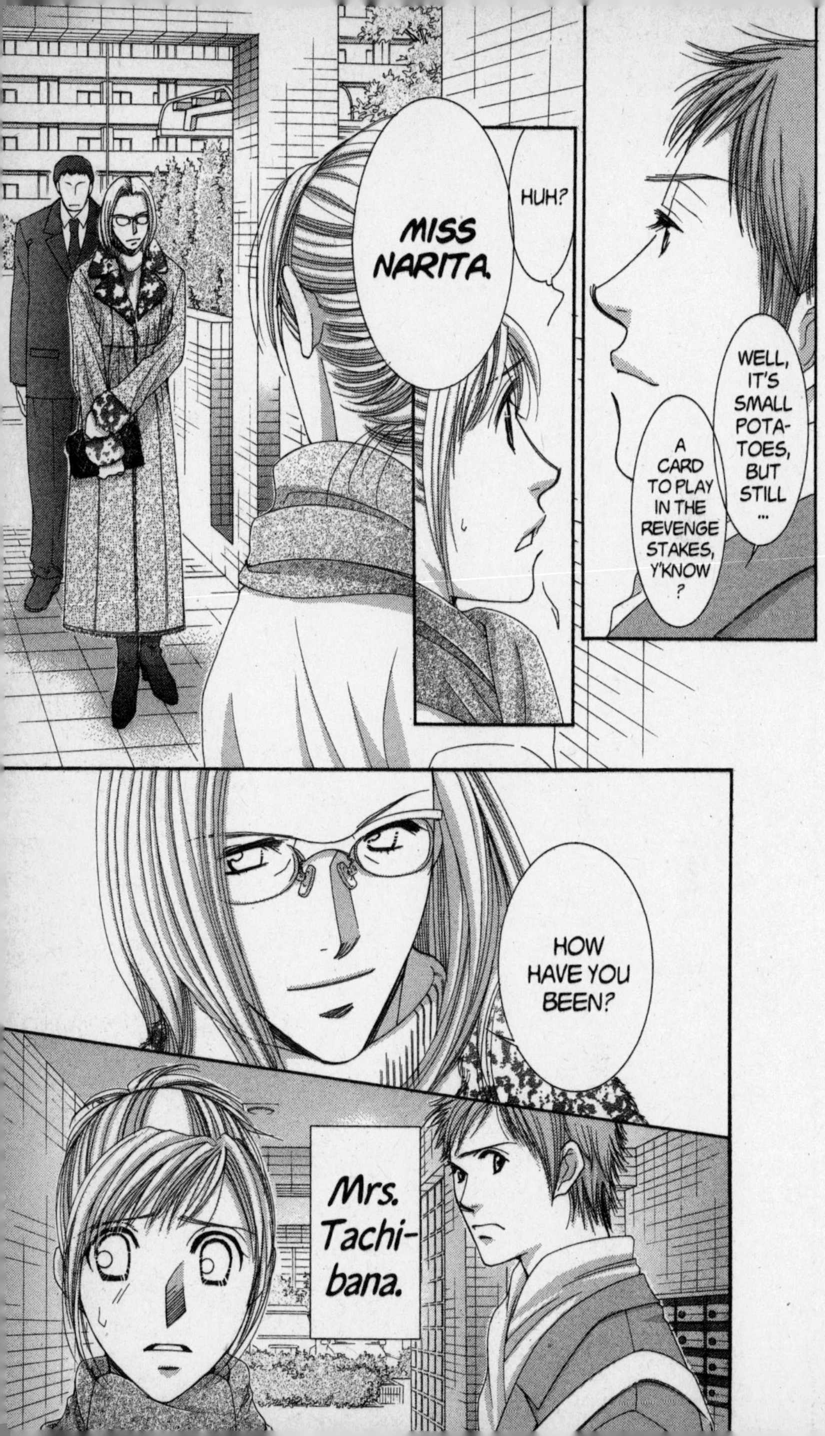
WELL, IT'S SMALL POTATOES, BUT STILL ...
A CARD TO PLAY IN THE REVENGE STAKES, Y'KNOW?
HUH?
MISS NARITA.
HOW HAVE YOU BEEN?
Mrs. Tachibana.

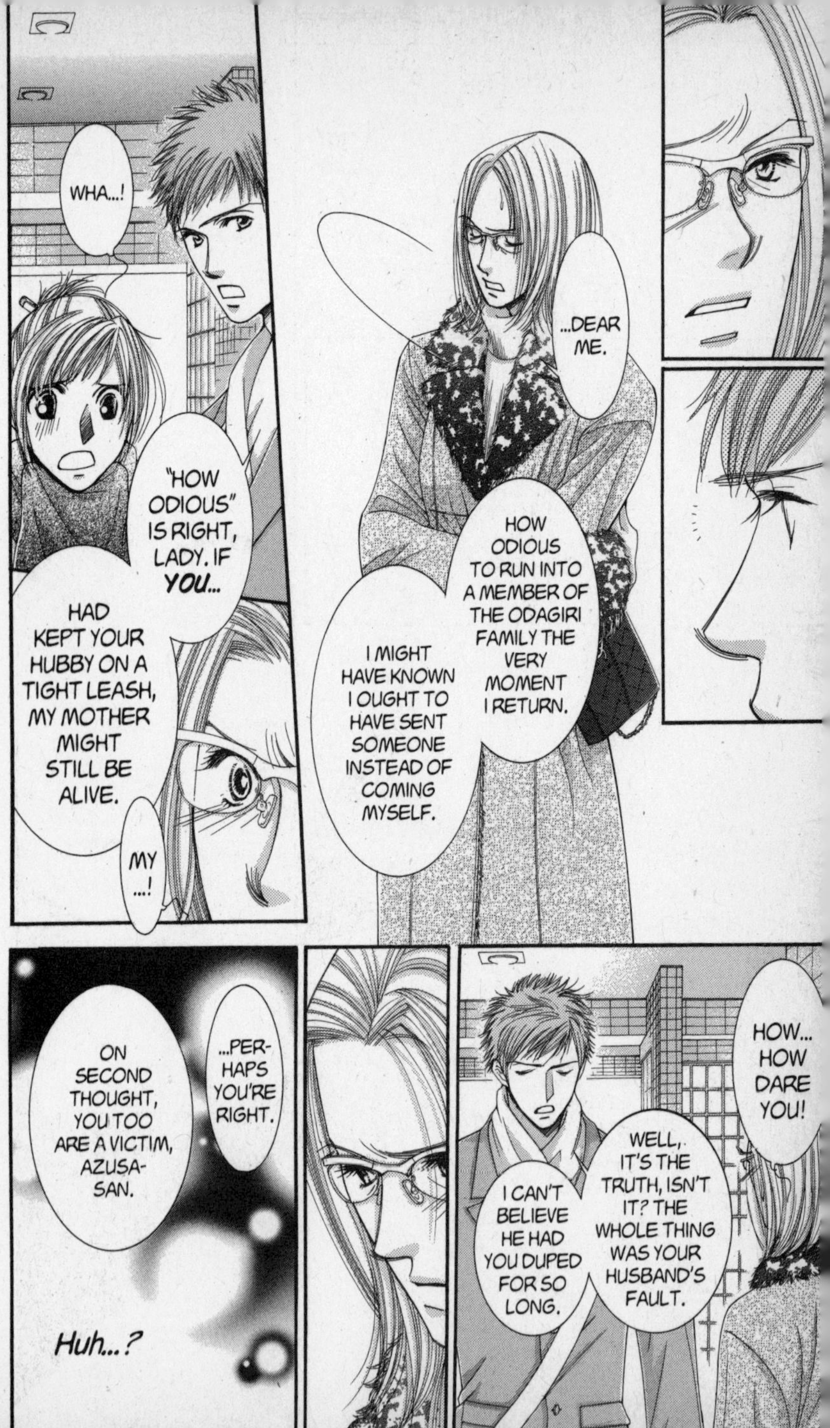
...DEAR ME.
HOW ODIOUS TO RUN INTO A MEMBER OF THE ODAGIRI FAMILY THE VERY MOMENT I RETURN.
I MIGHT HAVE KNOWN I OUGHT TO HAVE SENT SOMEONE INSTEAD OF COMING MYSELF.
WHA...!
"HOW ODIOUS" IS RIGHT, LADY. IF **YOU...**
HAD KEPT YOUR HUBBY ON A TIGHT LEASH, MY MOTHER MIGHT STILL BE ALIVE.
MY ...!
HOW... HOW DARE YOU!
WELL, IT'S THE TRUTH, ISN'T IT? THE WHOLE THING WAS YOUR HUSBAND'S FAULT.
I CAN'T BELIEVE HE HAD YOU DUPED FOR SO LONG.
...PER-HAPS YOU'RE RIGHT.
ON SECOND THOUGHT, YOU TOO ARE A VICTIM, AZUSA-SAN.
Huh...?

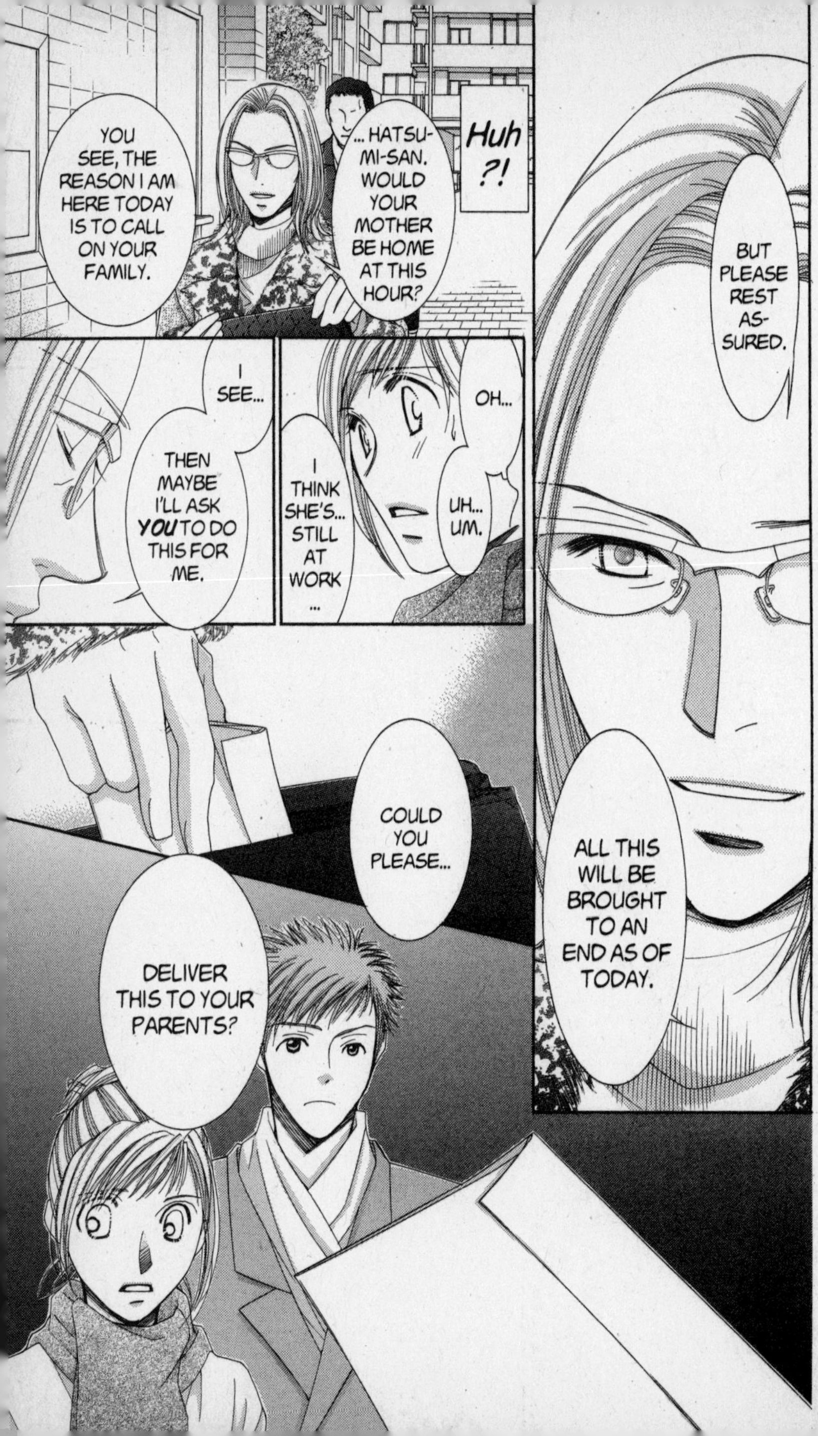
BUT PLEASE REST AS-SURED.
ALL THIS WILL BE BROUGHT TO AN END AS OF TODAY.
Huh ?!
... HATSU-MI-SAN. WOULD YOUR MOTHER BE HOME AT THIS HOUR?
YOU SEE, THE REASON I AM HERE TODAY IS TO CALL ON YOUR FAMILY.
OH...
UH... UM.
I THINK SHE'S... STILL AT WORK ...
I SEE...
THEN MAYBE I'LL ASK **YOU** TO DO THIS FOR ME.
COULD YOU PLEASE...
DELIVER THIS TO YOUR PARENTS?

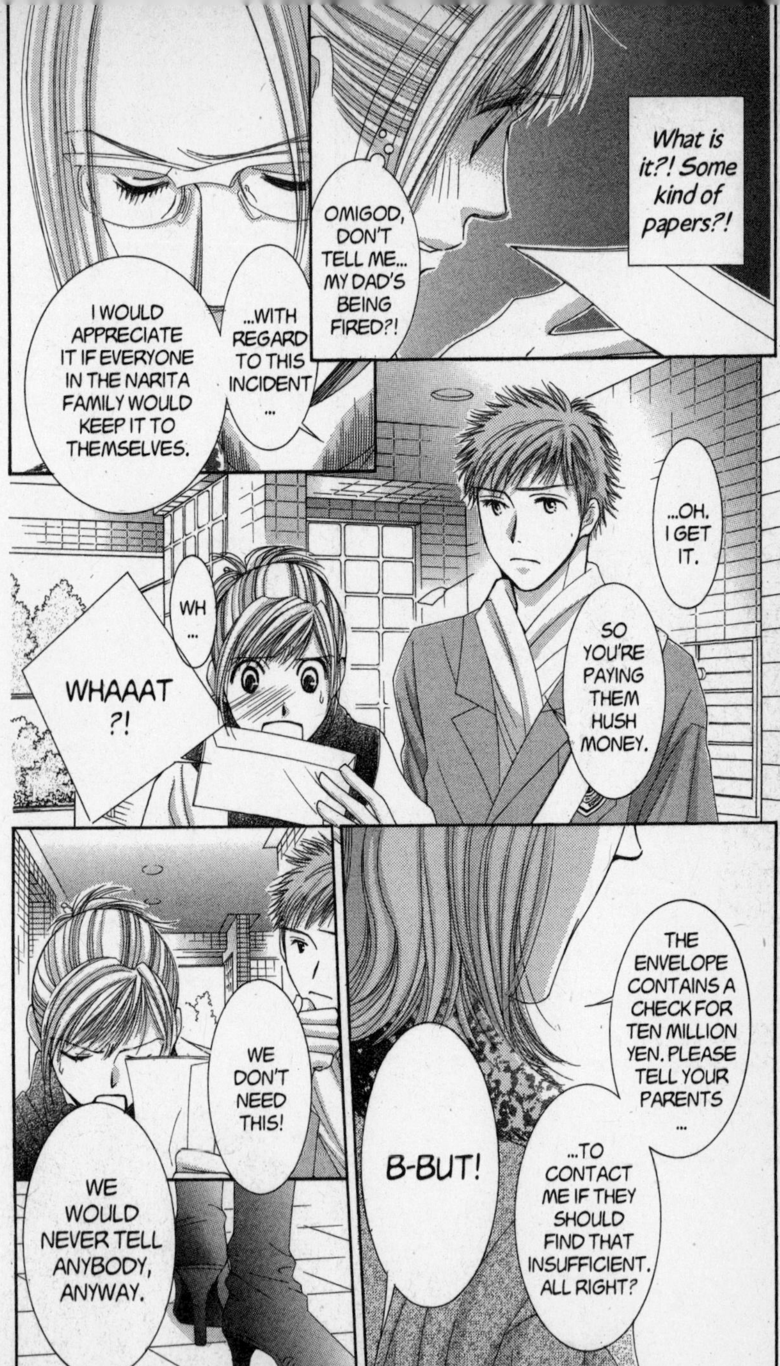
What is it?! Some kind of papers?!
OMIGOD, DON'T TELL ME... MY DAD'S BEING FIRED?!
...WITH REGARD TO THIS INCIDENT...
I WOULD APPRECIATE IT IF EVERYONE IN THE NARITA FAMILY WOULD KEEP IT TO THEMSELVES.
...OH. I GET IT.
SO YOU'RE PAYING THEM HUSH MONEY.
WH...
WHAAAT?!
THE ENVELOPE CONTAINS A CHECK FOR TEN MILLION YEN. PLEASE TELL YOUR PARENTS...
...TO CONTACT ME IF THEY SHOULD FIND THAT INSUFFICIENT. ALL RIGHT?
B-BUT!
WE DON'T NEED THIS!
WE WOULD NEVER TELL ANYBODY, ANYWAY.

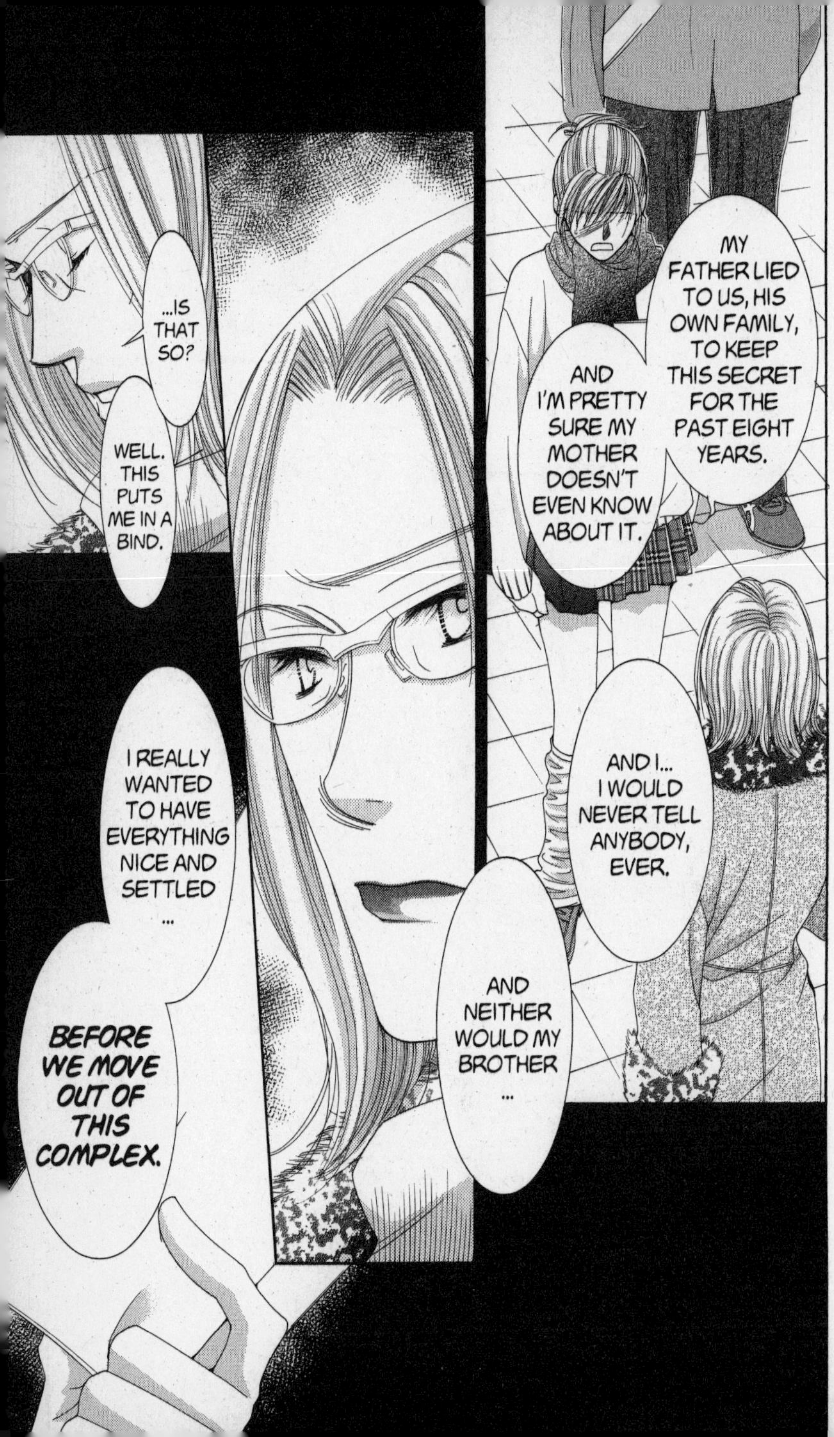
MY FATHER LIED TO US, HIS OWN FAMILY, TO KEEP THIS SECRET FOR THE PAST EIGHT YEARS.
AND I'M PRETTY SURE MY MOTHER DOESN'T EVEN KNOW ABOUT IT.
AND I... I WOULD NEVER TELL ANYBODY, EVER.
AND NEITHER WOULD MY BROTHER ...
...IS THAT SO?
WELL. THIS PUTS ME IN A BIND.
I REALLY WANTED TO HAVE EVERYTHING NICE AND SETTLED ...
BEFORE WE MOVE OUT OF THIS COMPLEX.

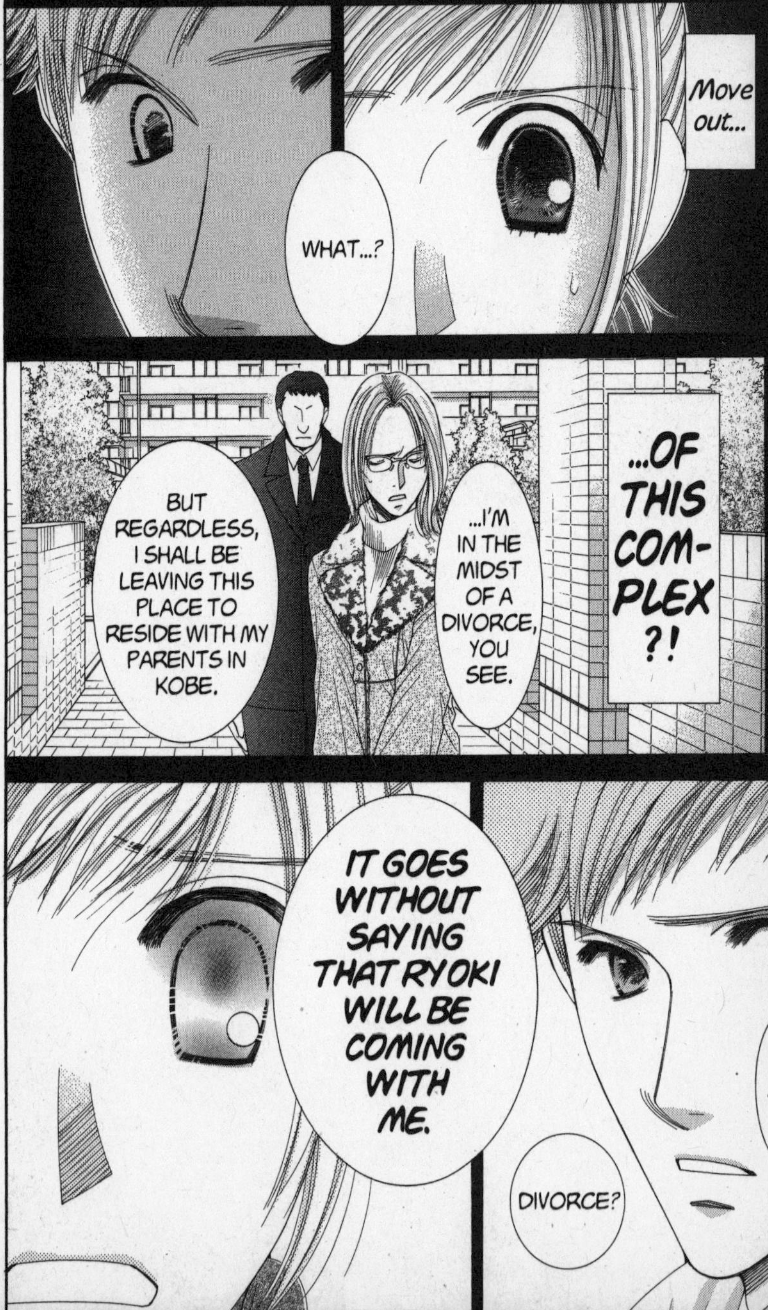
Move out...
WHAT...?
...OF THIS COMPLEX?!
...I'M IN THE MIDST OF A DIVORCE, YOU SEE.
BUT REGARDLESS, I SHALL BE LEAVING THIS PLACE TO RESIDE WITH MY PARENTS IN KOBE.
...A...
DIVORCE?
IT GOES WITHOUT SAYING THAT RYOKI WILL BE COMING WITH ME.

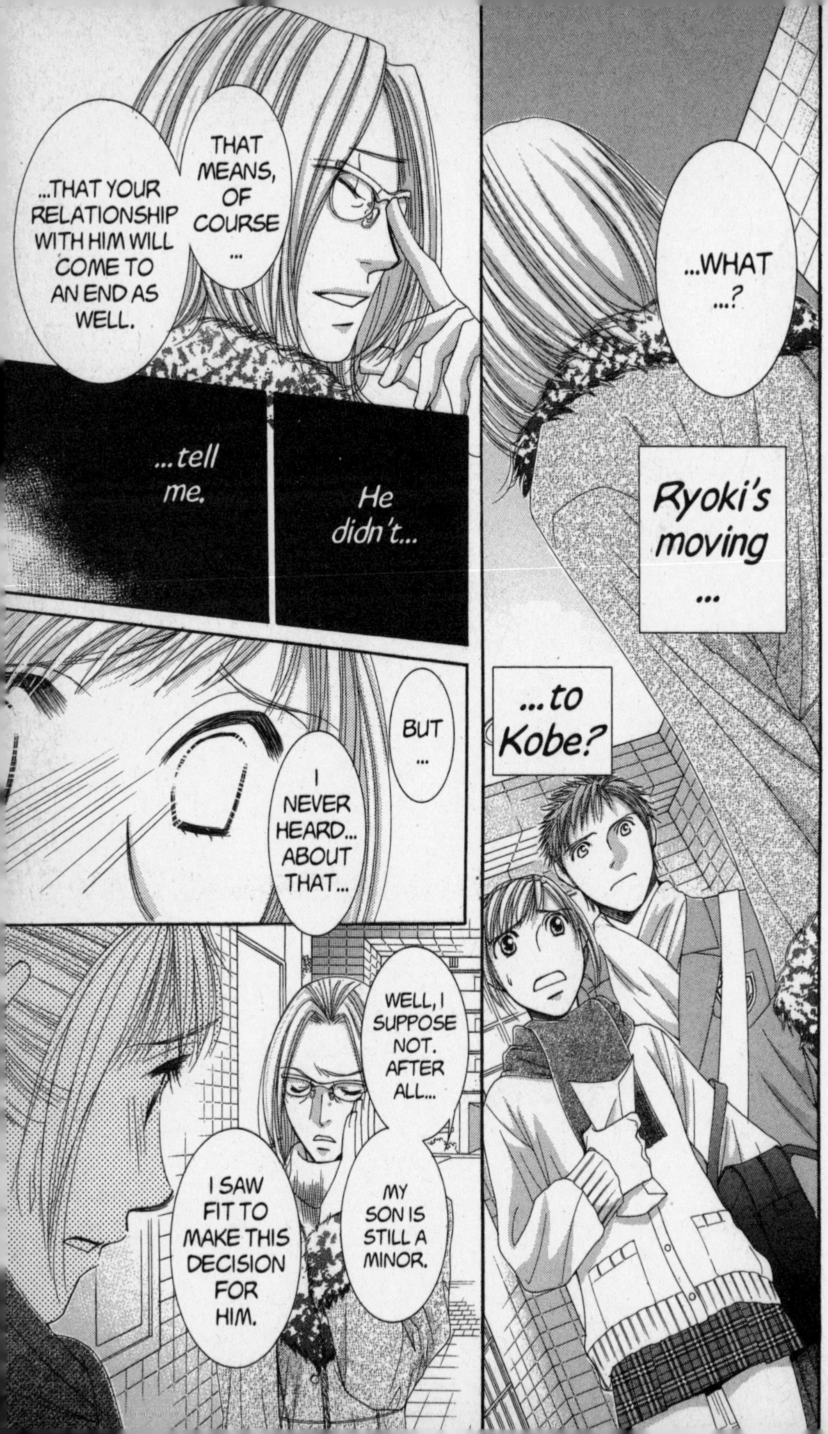
...WHAT ...?
Ryoki's moving ...
...to Kobe?
THAT MEANS, OF COURSE ...
...THAT YOUR RELATIONSHIP WITH HIM WILL COME TO AN END AS WELL.
He didn't...
...tell me.
BUT ...
I NEVER HEARD... ABOUT THAT...
WELL, I SUPPOSE NOT. AFTER ALL...
MY SON IS STILL A MINOR.
I SAW FIT TO MAKE THIS DECISION FOR HIM.

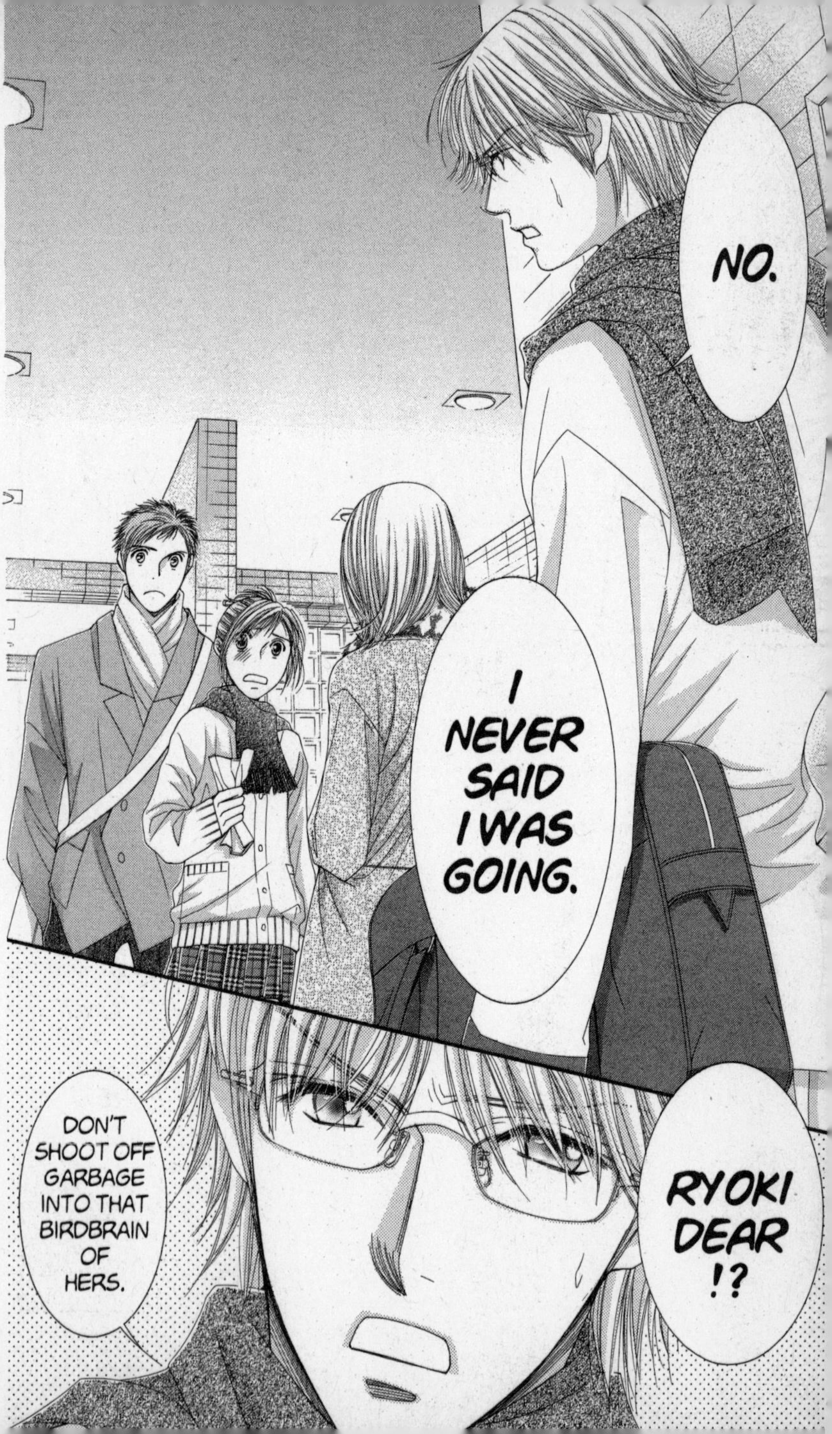
NO.
I NEVER SAID I WAS GOING.
RYOKI DEAR !?
DON'T SHOOT OFF GARBAGE INTO THAT BIRDBRAIN OF HERS.

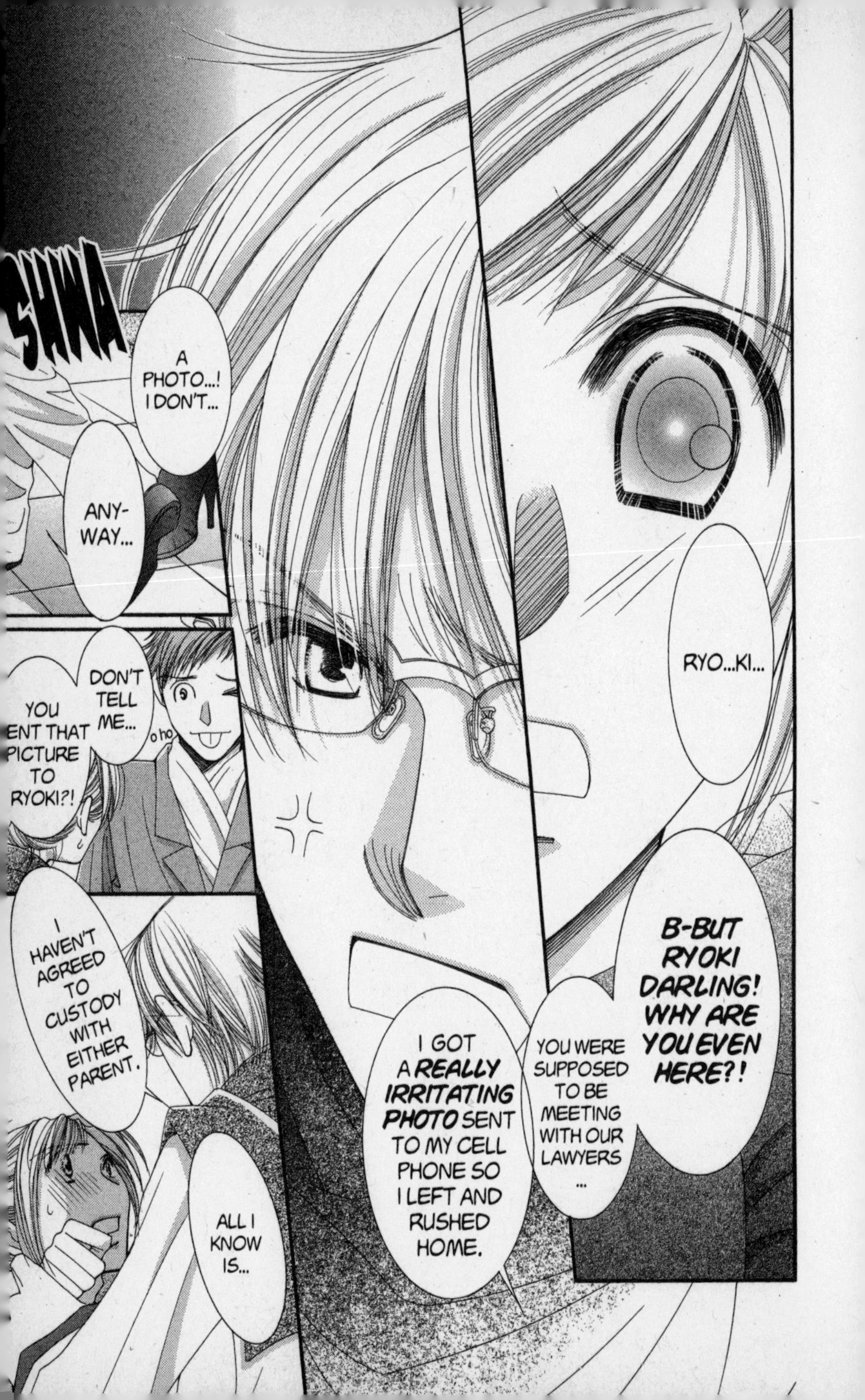

RYO...KI...
B-BUT RYOKI DARLING! WHY ARE YOU EVEN HERE?!
YOU WERE SUPPOSED TO BE MEETING WITH OUR LAWYERS...
I GOT A **REALLY IRRITATING PHOTO** SENT TO MY CELL PHONE SO I LEFT AND RUSHED HOME.
SHWA
A PHOTO...! I DON'T...
ANY-WAY...
DON'T TELL ME...
oho
YOU ENT THAT PICTURE TO RYOKI?!
I HAVEN'T AGREED TO CUSTODY WITH EITHER PARENT.
ALL I KNOW IS...

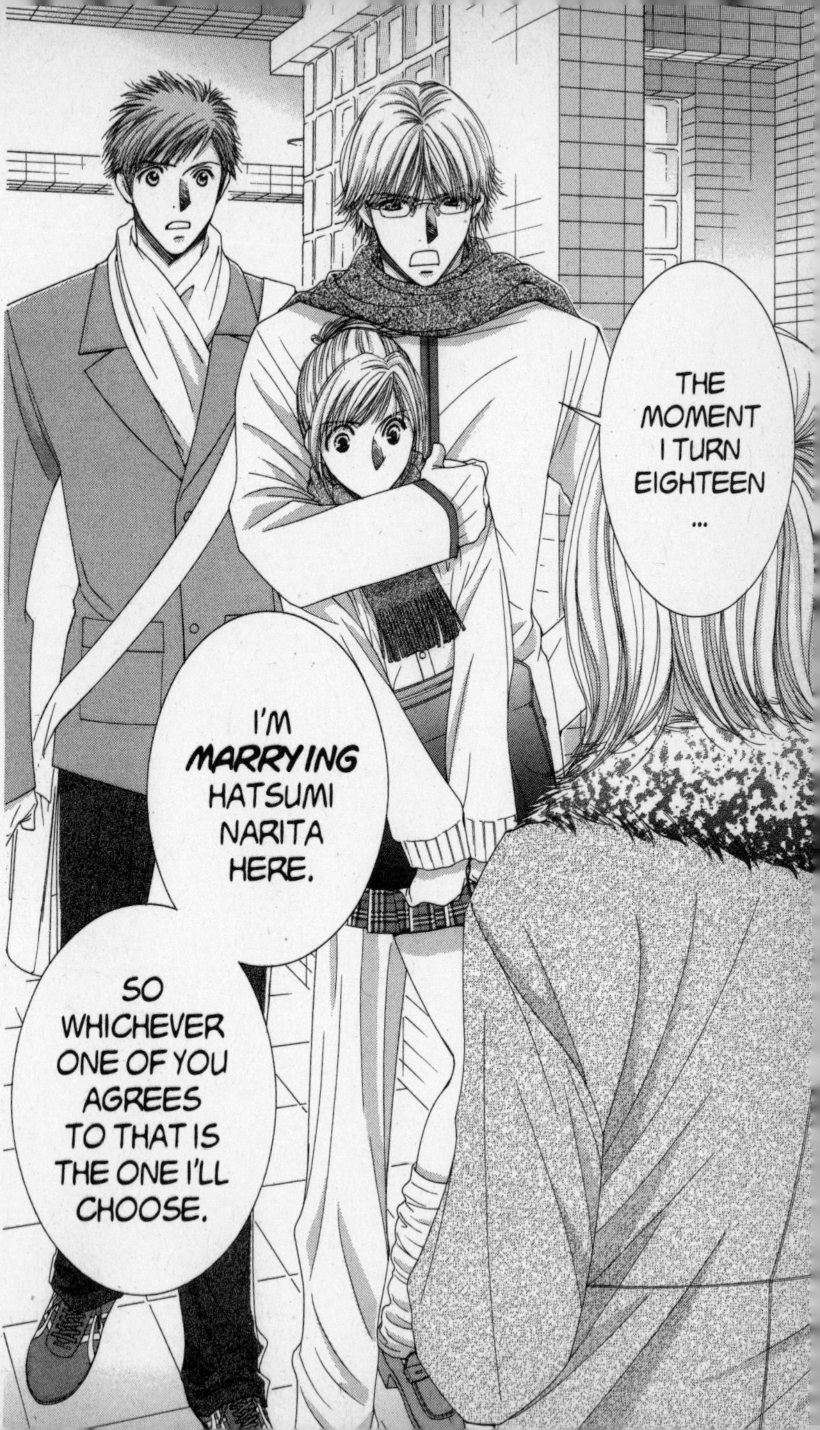
THE MOMENT I TURN EIGHTEEN ...
I'M **MARRYING** HATSUMI NARITA HERE.
SO WHICHEVER ONE OF YOU AGREES TO THAT IS THE ONE I'LL CHOOSE.

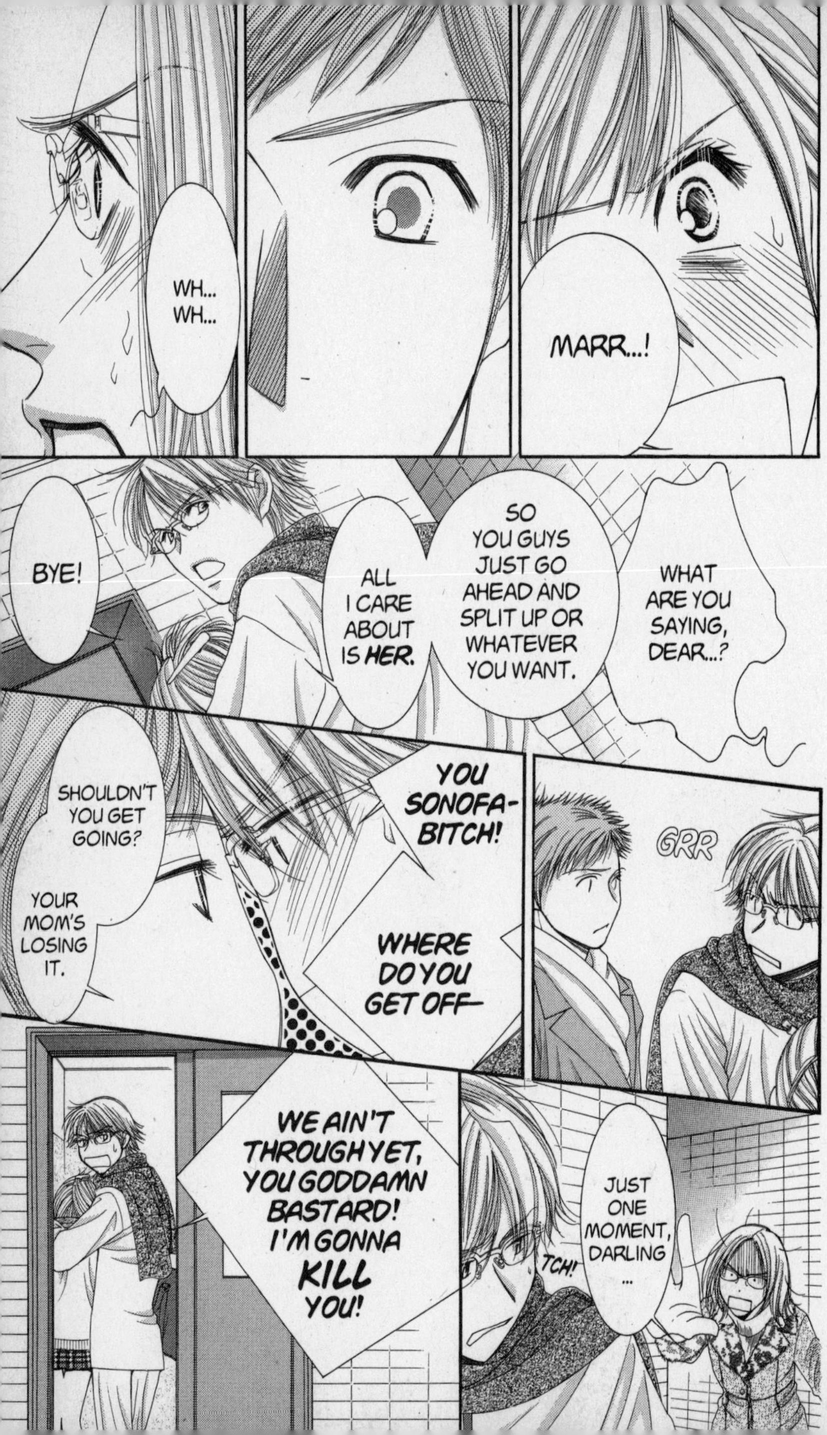
MARR...!
WH... WH...
WHAT ARE YOU SAYING, DEAR...?
SO YOU GUYS JUST GO AHEAD AND SPLIT UP OR WHATEVER YOU WANT.
ALL I CARE ABOUT IS **HER.**
BYE!
GRR
YOU SONOFA-BITCH!
WHERE DO YOU GET OFF—
SHOULDN'T YOU GET GOING?
YOUR MOM'S LOSING IT.
JUST ONE MOMENT, DARLING ...
TCH!
WE AIN'T THROUGH YET, YOU GODDAMN BASTARD! I'M GONNA KILL YOU!

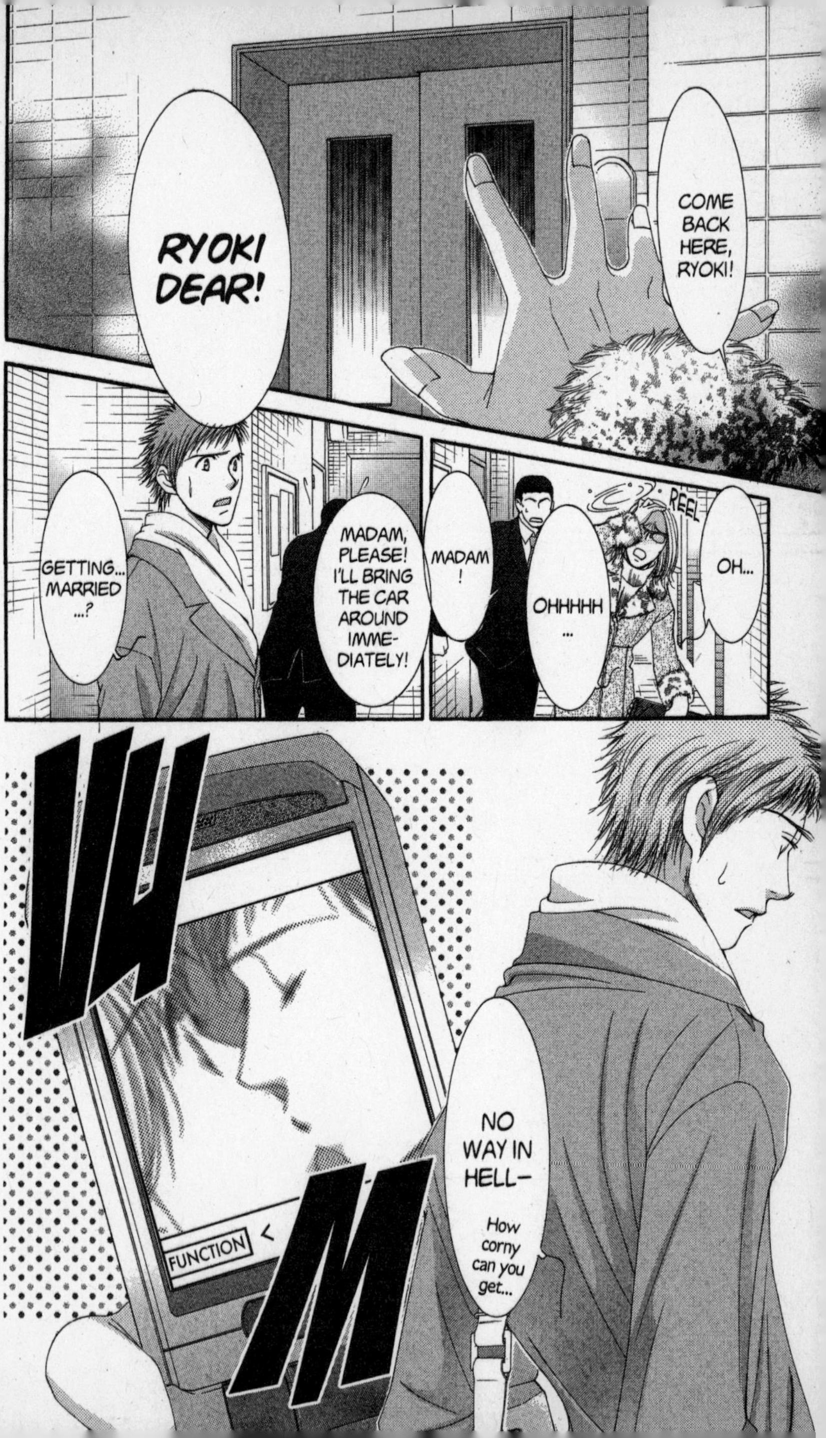
COME BACK HERE, RYOKI!
RYOKI DEAR!
REEL
OH...
OHHHHH...
MADAM!
MADAM, PLEASE! I'LL BRING THE CAR AROUND IMMEDIATELY!
GETTING... MARRIED...?
NO WAY IN HELL—
How corny can you get...
FUNCTION

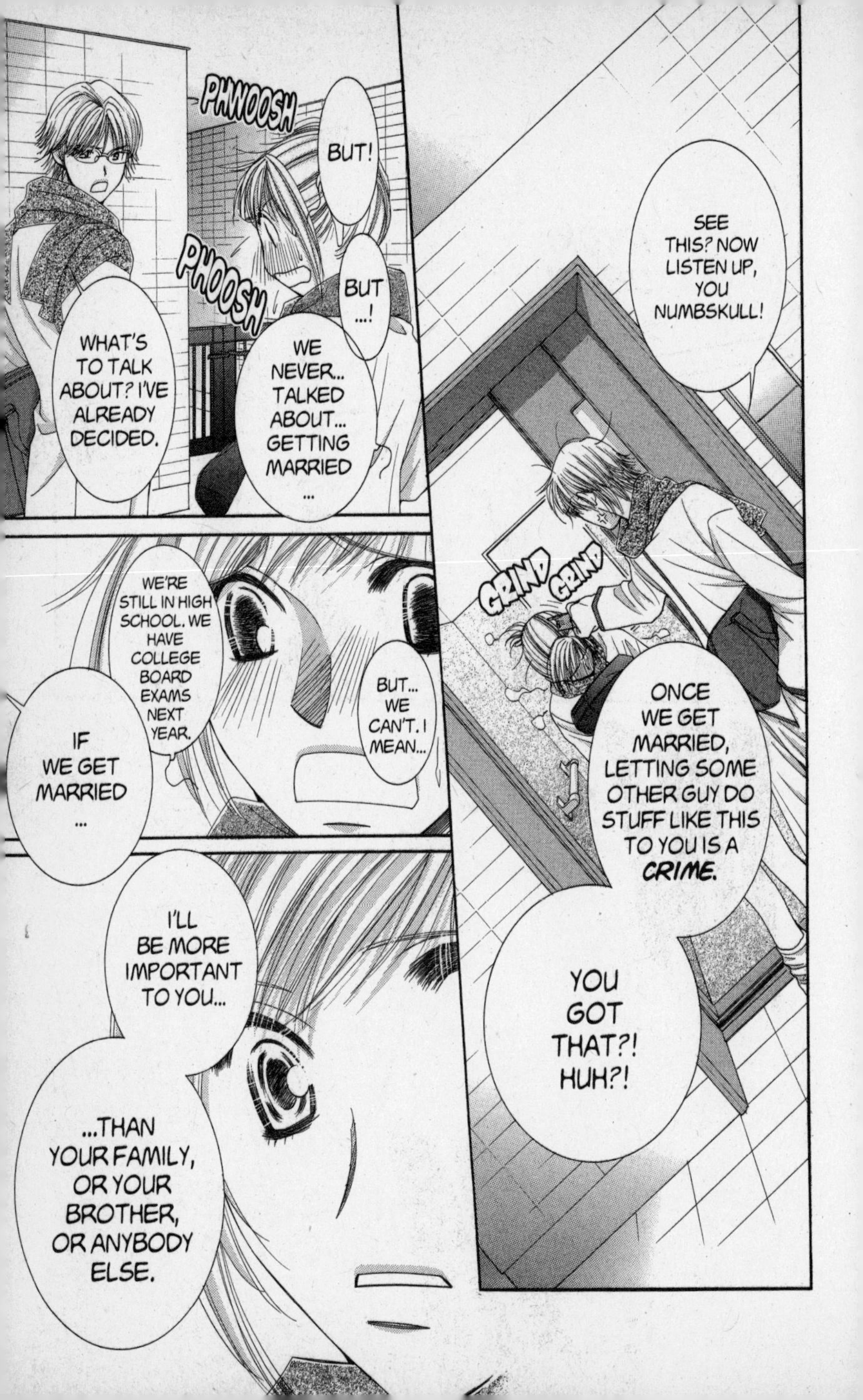
SEE THIS? NOW LISTEN UP, YOU NUMBSKULL!
GRIND GRIND
ONCE WE GET MARRIED, LETTING SOME OTHER GUY DO STUFF LIKE THIS TO YOU IS A **CRIME.**
YOU GOT THAT?! HUH?!
PHWOOSH
BUT!
PHOOSH
BUT ...!
WE NEVER... TALKED ABOUT... GETTING MARRIED ...
WHAT'S TO TALK ABOUT? I'VE ALREADY DECIDED.
BUT... WE CAN'T. I MEAN...
WE'RE STILL IN HIGH SCHOOL. WE HAVE COLLEGE BOARD EXAMS NEXT YEAR.
IF WE GET MARRIED ...
I'LL BE MORE IMPORTANT TO YOU...
...THAN YOUR FAMILY, OR YOUR BROTHER, OR ANYBODY ELSE.

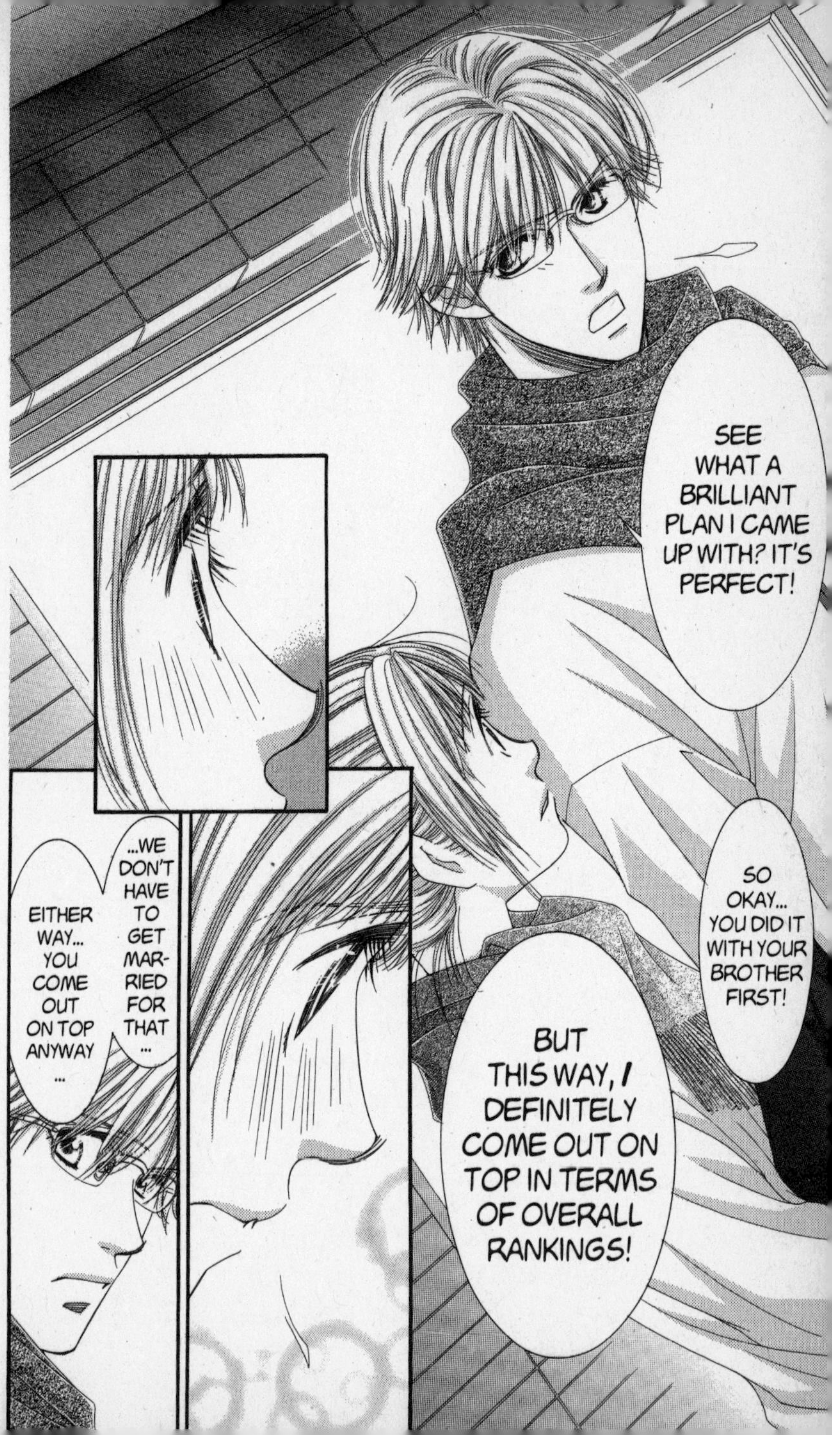
SEE WHAT A BRILLIANT PLAN I CAME UP WITH? IT'S PERFECT!
SO OKAY... YOU DID IT WITH YOUR BROTHER FIRST!
BUT THIS WAY, I DEFINITELY COME OUT ON TOP IN TERMS OF OVERALL RANKINGS!
...WE DON'T HAVE TO GET MAR-RIED FOR THAT...
EITHER WAY... YOU COME OUT ON TOP ANYWAY...

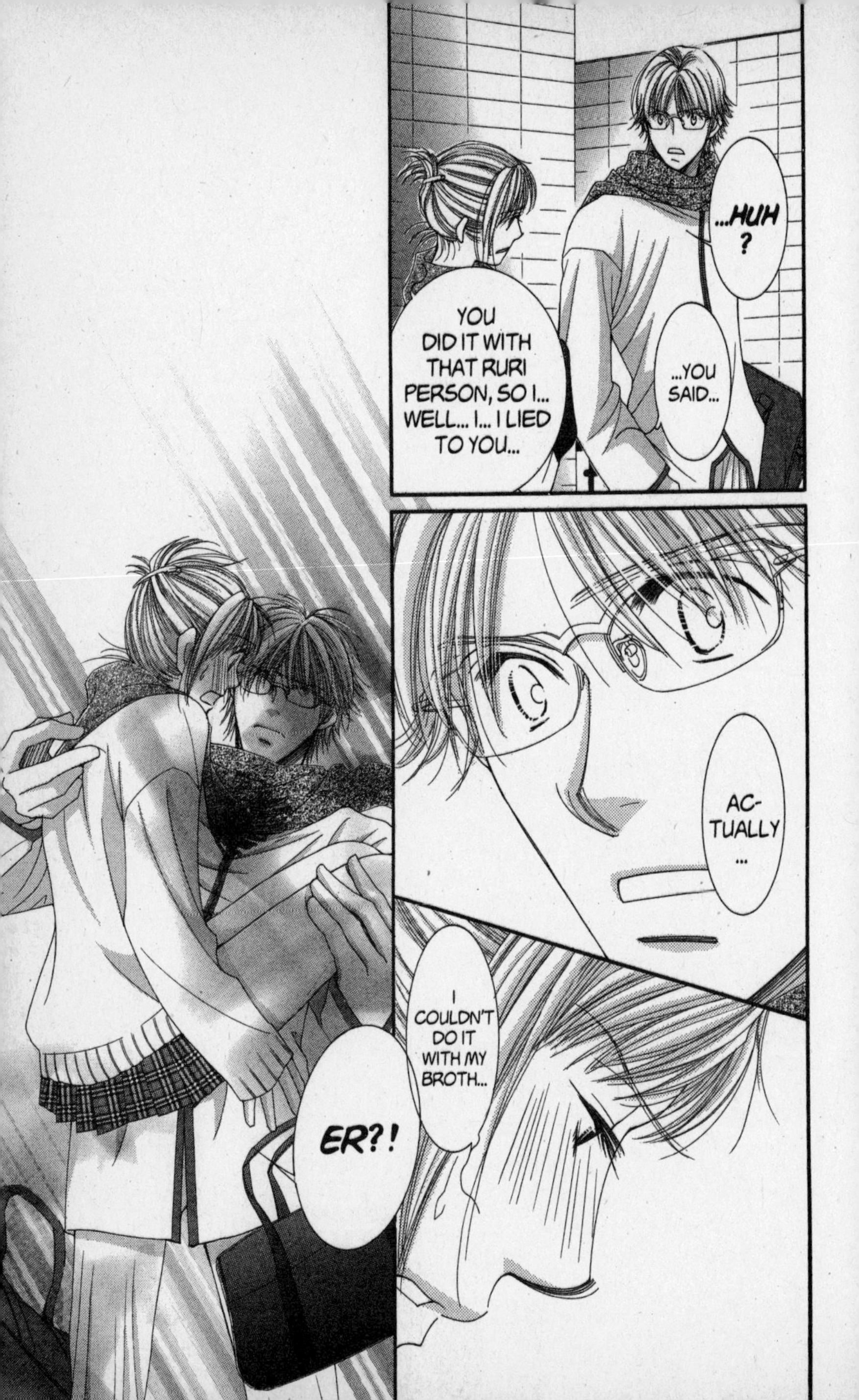
...HUH?
...YOU SAID...
YOU DID IT WITH THAT RURI PERSON, SO I... WELL... I... I LIED TO YOU...
ACTUALLY...
I COULDN'T DO IT WITH MY BROTH...
ER?!

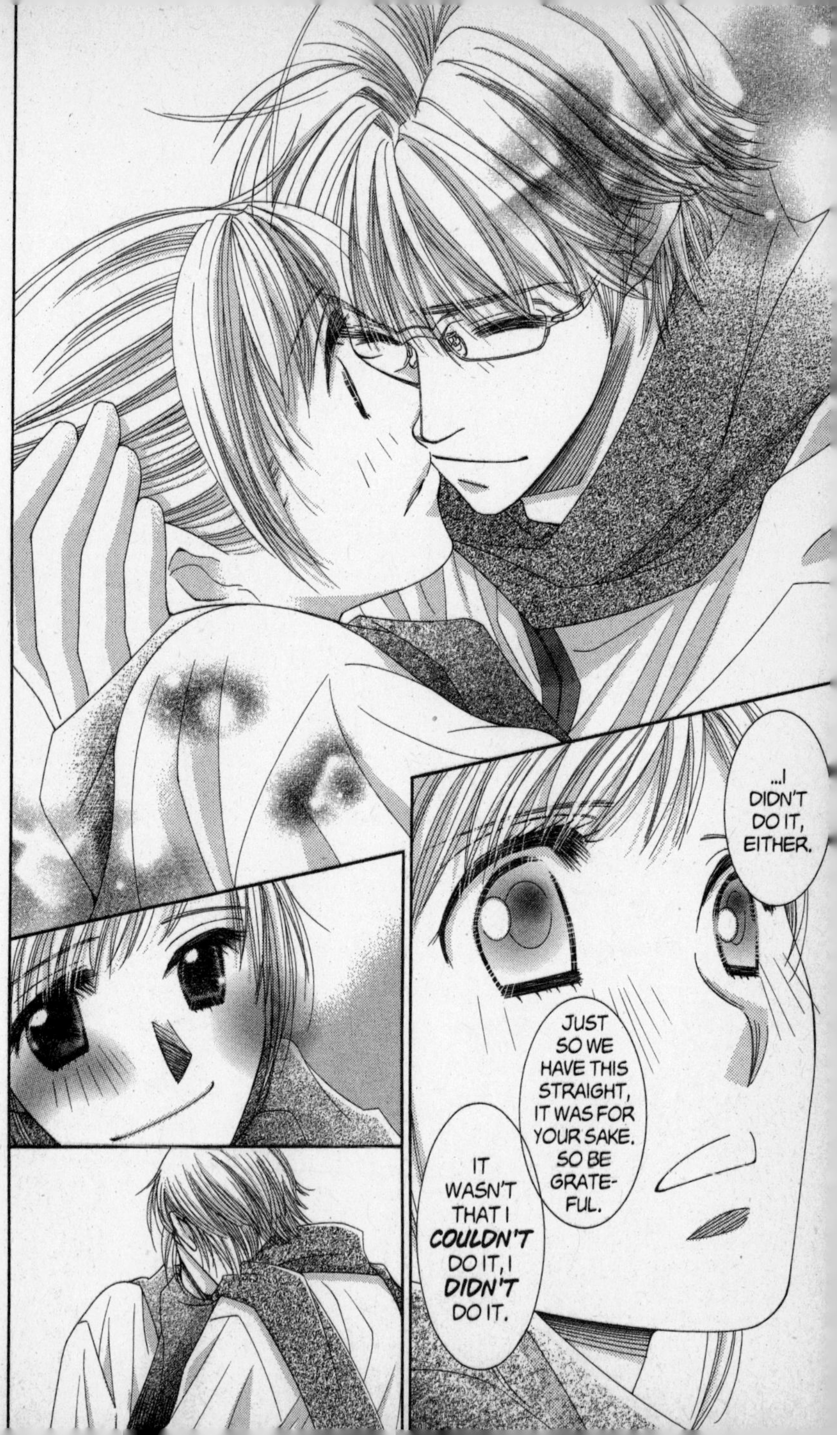
...I DIDN'T DO IT, EITHER.
JUST SO WE HAVE THIS STRAIGHT, IT WAS FOR YOUR SAKE. SO BE GRATE-FUL.
IT WASN'T THAT I **COULDN'T** DO IT, I **DIDN'T** DO IT.

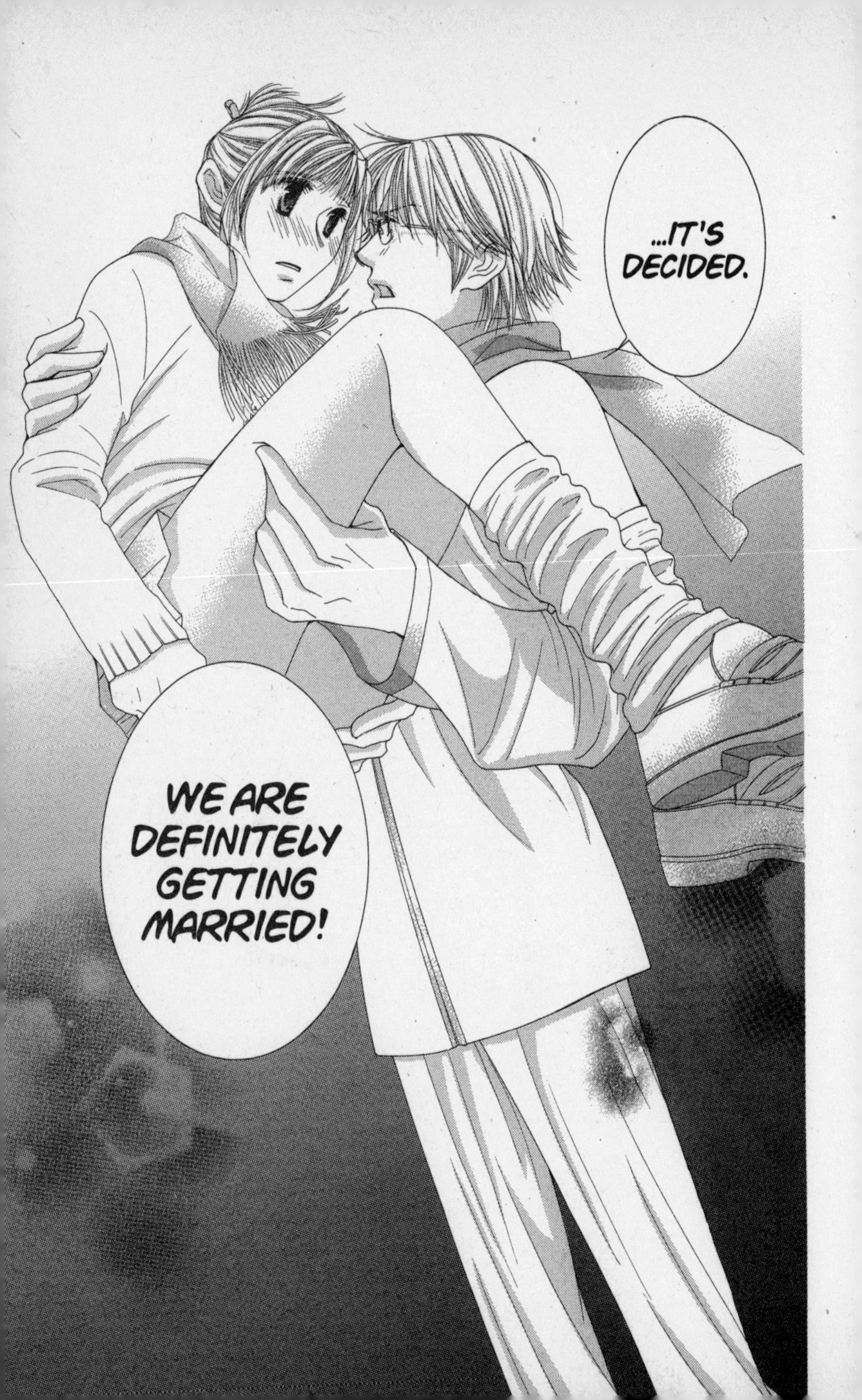
...IT'S DECIDED.
WE ARE DEFINITELY GETTING MARRIED!

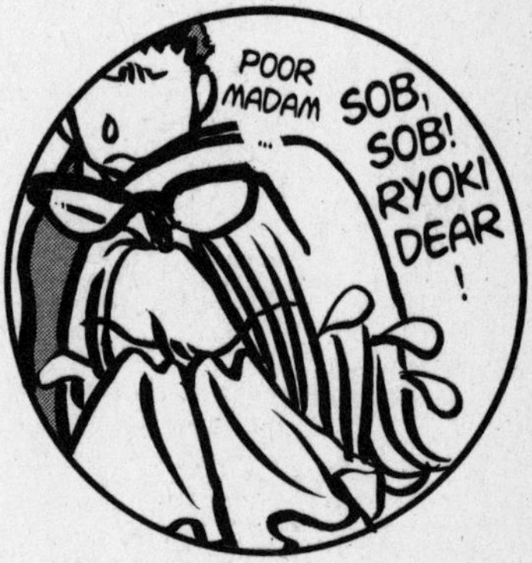
POOR MADAM ...
SOB, SOB! RYOKI DEAR!

Final Chapter

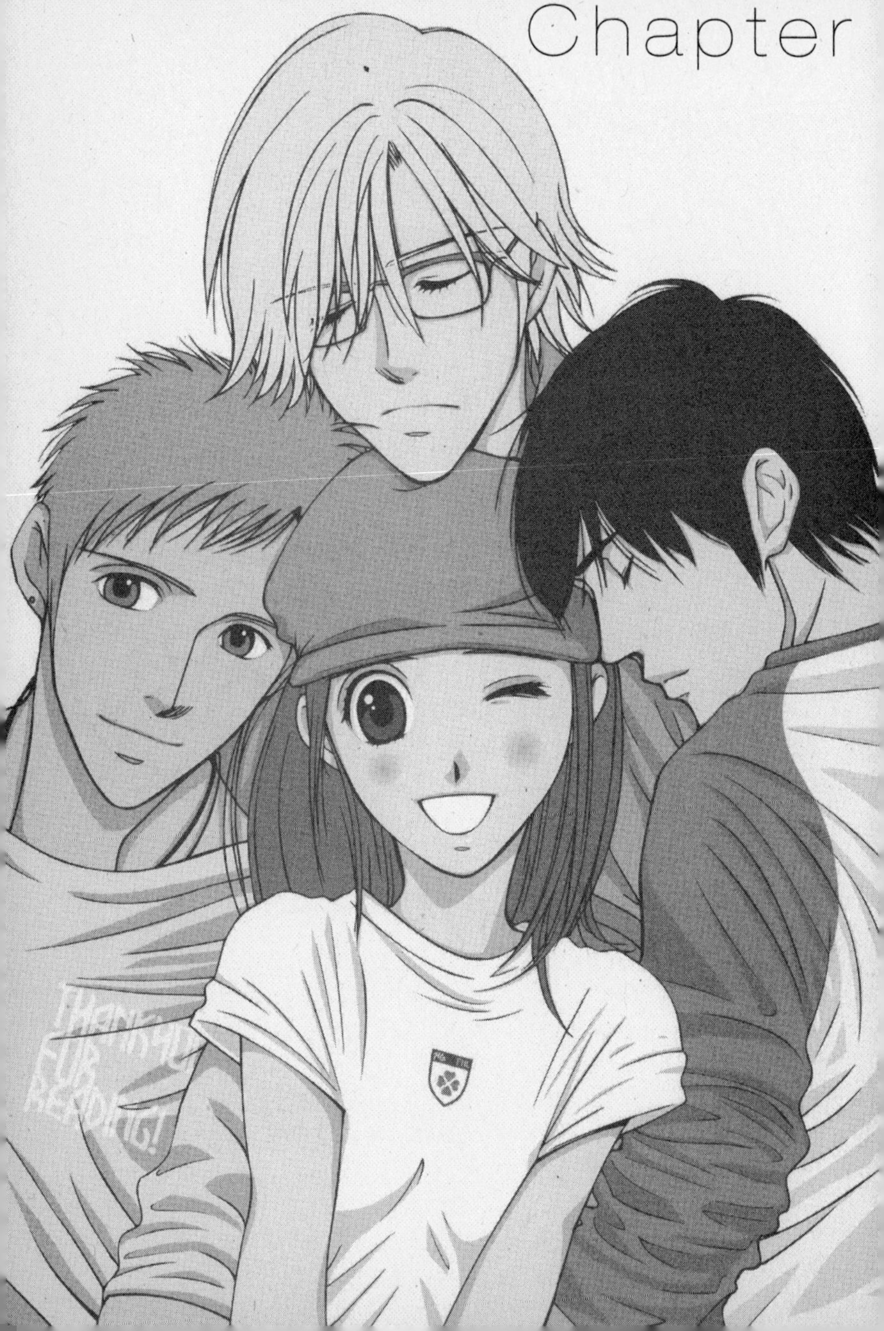
THANK YOU FOR READING!

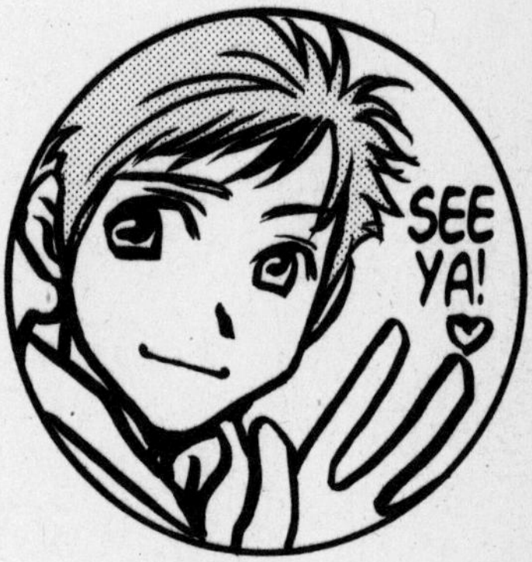
SEE YA!

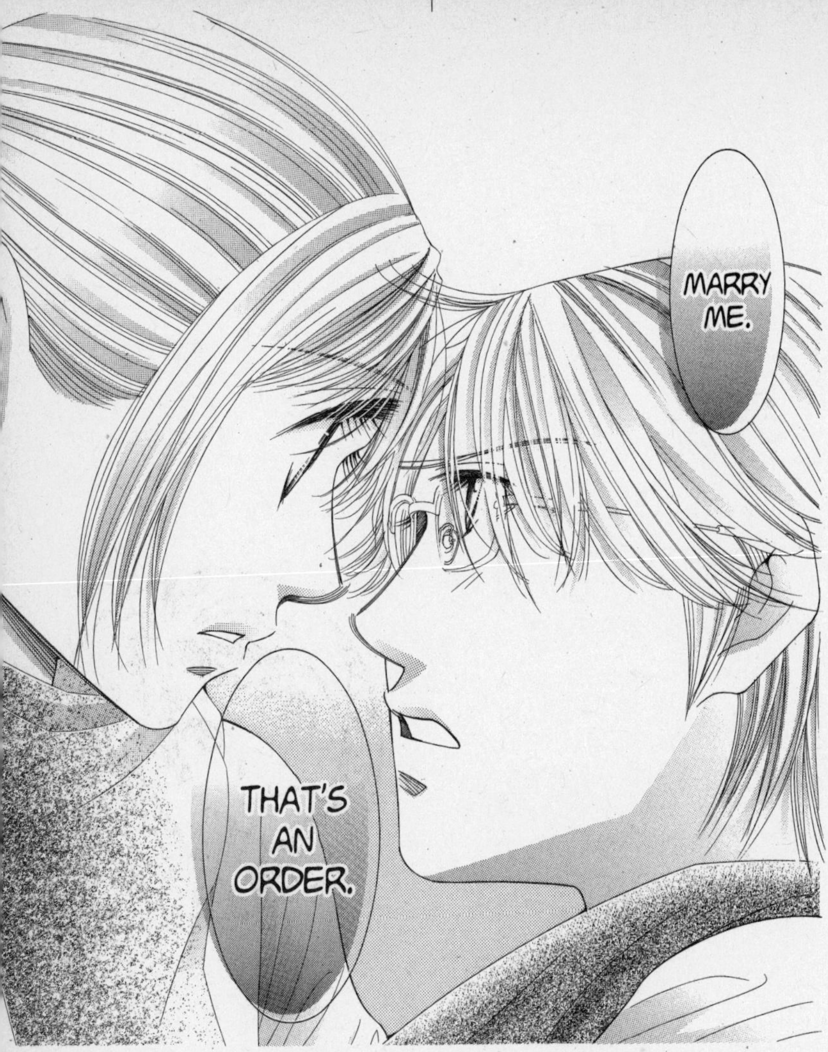
MARRY ME.
THAT'S AN ORDER.

hot gimmick

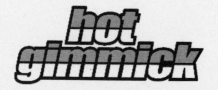

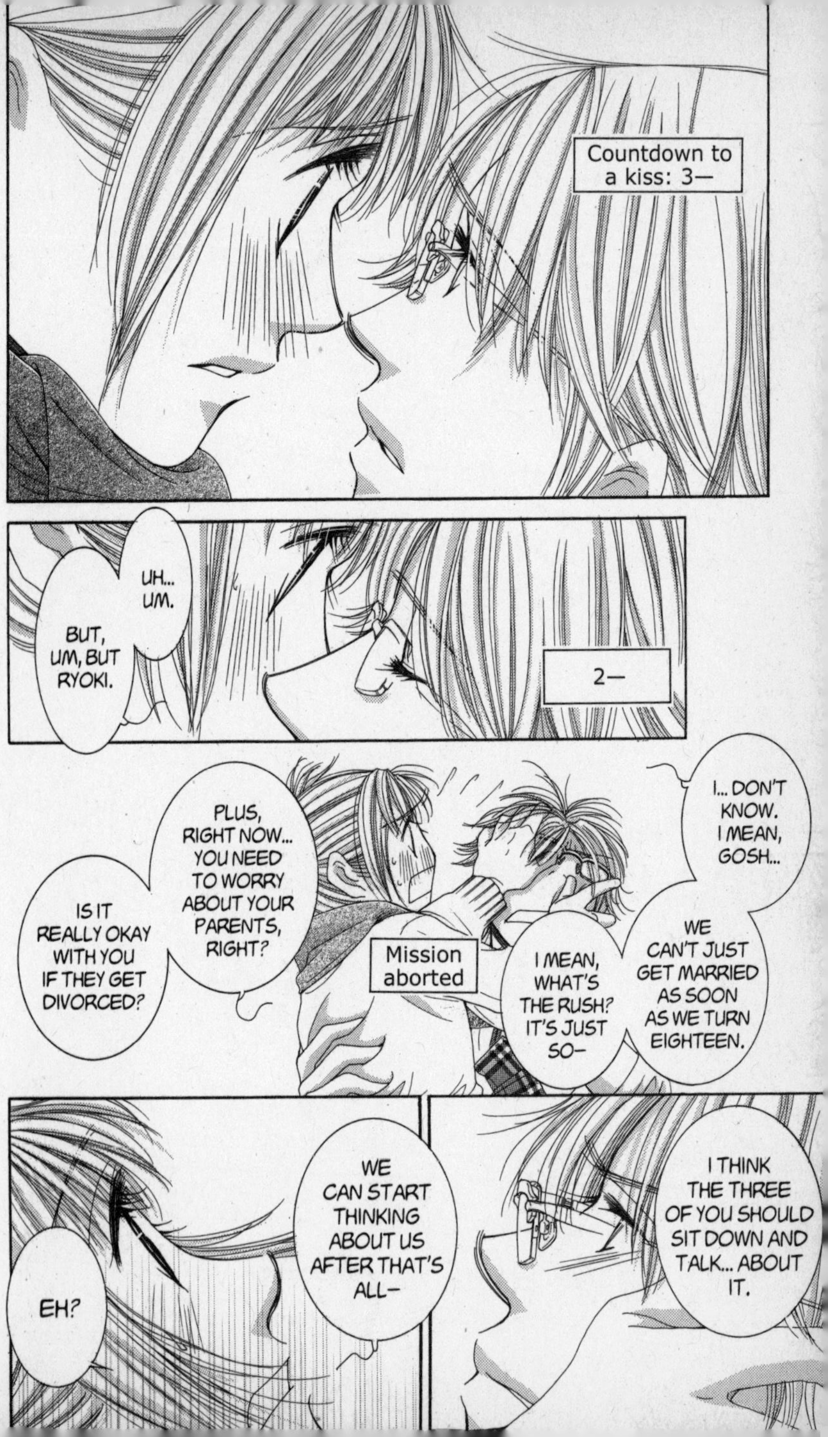
Countdown to a kiss: 3—
2—
UH... UM.
BUT, UM, BUT RYOKI.
I... DON'T KNOW. I MEAN, GOSH...
WE CAN'T JUST GET MARRIED AS SOON AS WE TURN EIGHTEEN.
I MEAN, WHAT'S THE RUSH? IT'S JUST SO—
Mission aborted
PLUS, RIGHT NOW... YOU NEED TO WORRY ABOUT YOUR PARENTS, RIGHT?
IS IT REALLY OKAY WITH YOU IF THEY GET DIVORCED?
I THINK THE THREE OF YOU SHOULD SIT DOWN AND TALK... ABOUT IT.
WE CAN START THINKING ABOUT US AFTER THAT'S ALL—
EH?

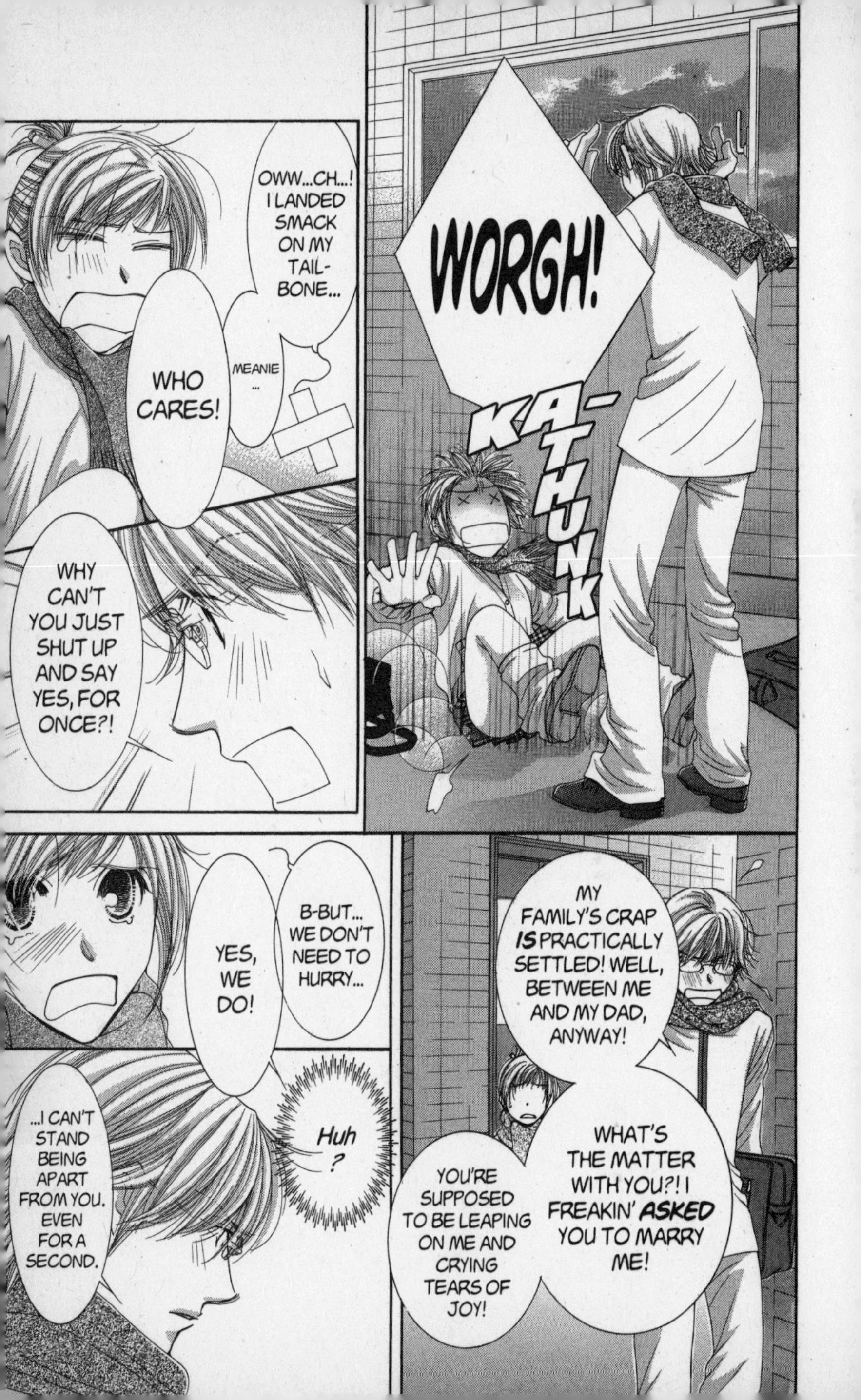
WORGH!
KA-THUNK
OWW...CH...! I LANDED SMACK ON MY TAIL-BONE...
MEANIE...
WHO CARES!
WHY CAN'T YOU JUST SHUT UP AND SAY YES, FOR ONCE?!
MY FAMILY'S CRAP **IS** PRACTICALLY SETTLED! WELL, BETWEEN ME AND MY DAD, ANYWAY!
WHAT'S THE MATTER WITH YOU?! I FREAKIN' **ASKED** YOU TO MARRY ME!
YOU'RE SUPPOSED TO BE LEAPING ON ME AND CRYING TEARS OF JOY!
B-BUT... WE DON'T NEED TO HURRY...
YES, WE DO!
Huh?
...I CAN'T STAND BEING APART FROM YOU. EVEN FOR A SECOND.

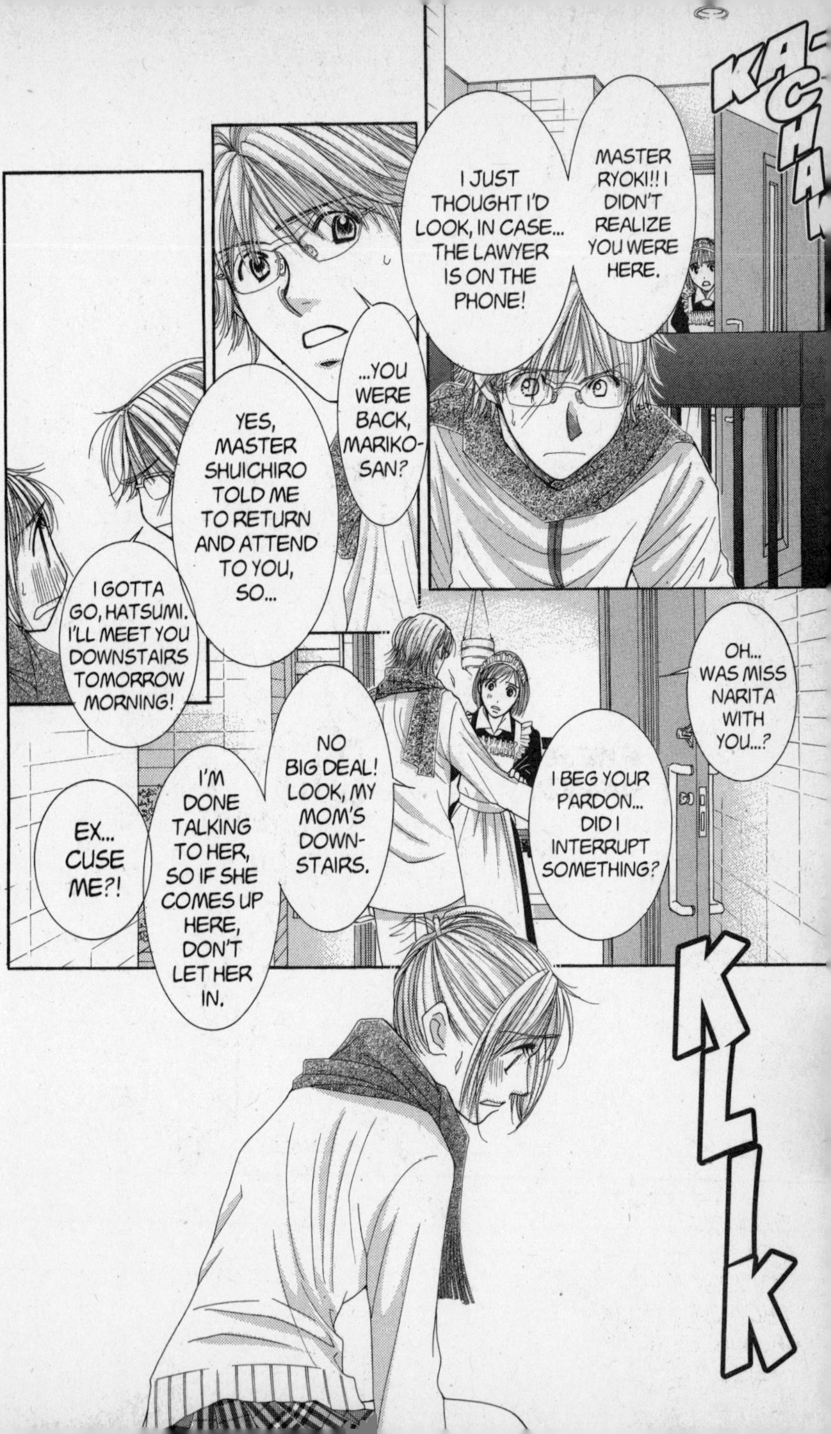
KA-CHAK
MASTER RYOKI!!! I DIDN'T REALIZE YOU WERE HERE.
I JUST THOUGHT I'D LOOK, IN CASE... THE LAWYER IS ON THE PHONE!
...YOU WERE BACK, MARIKO-SAN?
YES, MASTER SHUICHIRO TOLD ME TO RETURN AND ATTEND TO YOU, SO...
I GOTTA GO, HATSUMI. I'LL MEET YOU DOWNSTAIRS TOMORROW MORNING!
OH... WAS MISS NARITA WITH YOU...?
I BEG YOUR PARDON... DID I INTERRUPT SOMETHING?
NO BIG DEAL! LOOK, MY MOM'S DOWN-STAIRS.
I'M DONE TALKING TO HER, SO IF SHE COMES UP HERE, DON'T LET HER IN.
EX... CUSE ME?!
KLIK

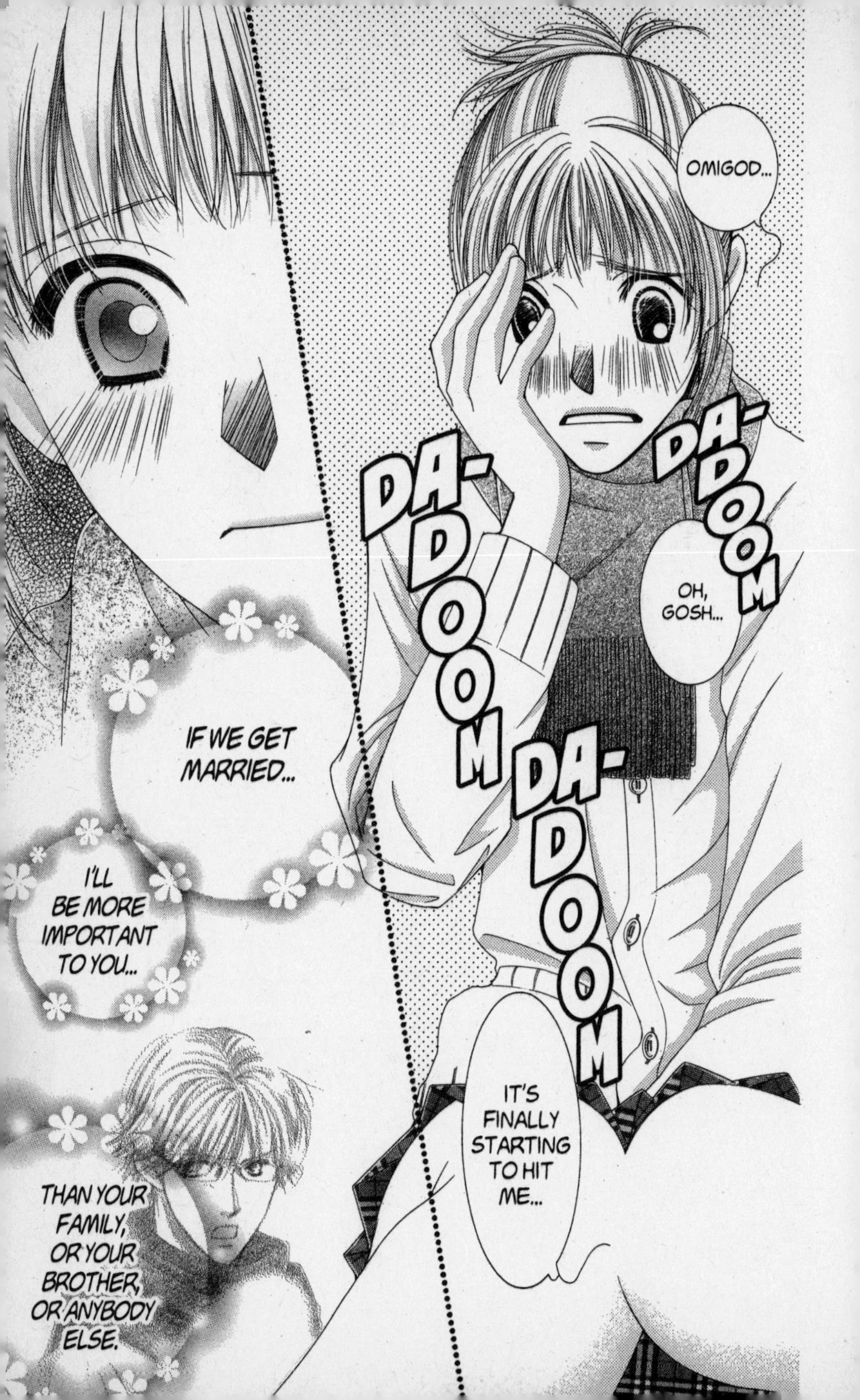
OMIGOD...
DA-DOOM
OH, GOSH...
DA-DOOM
DA-DOOM
IT'S FINALLY STARTING TO HIT ME...
IF WE GET MARRIED...
I'LL BE MORE IMPORTANT TO YOU...
THAN YOUR FAMILY, OR YOUR BROTHER, OR ANYBODY ELSE.

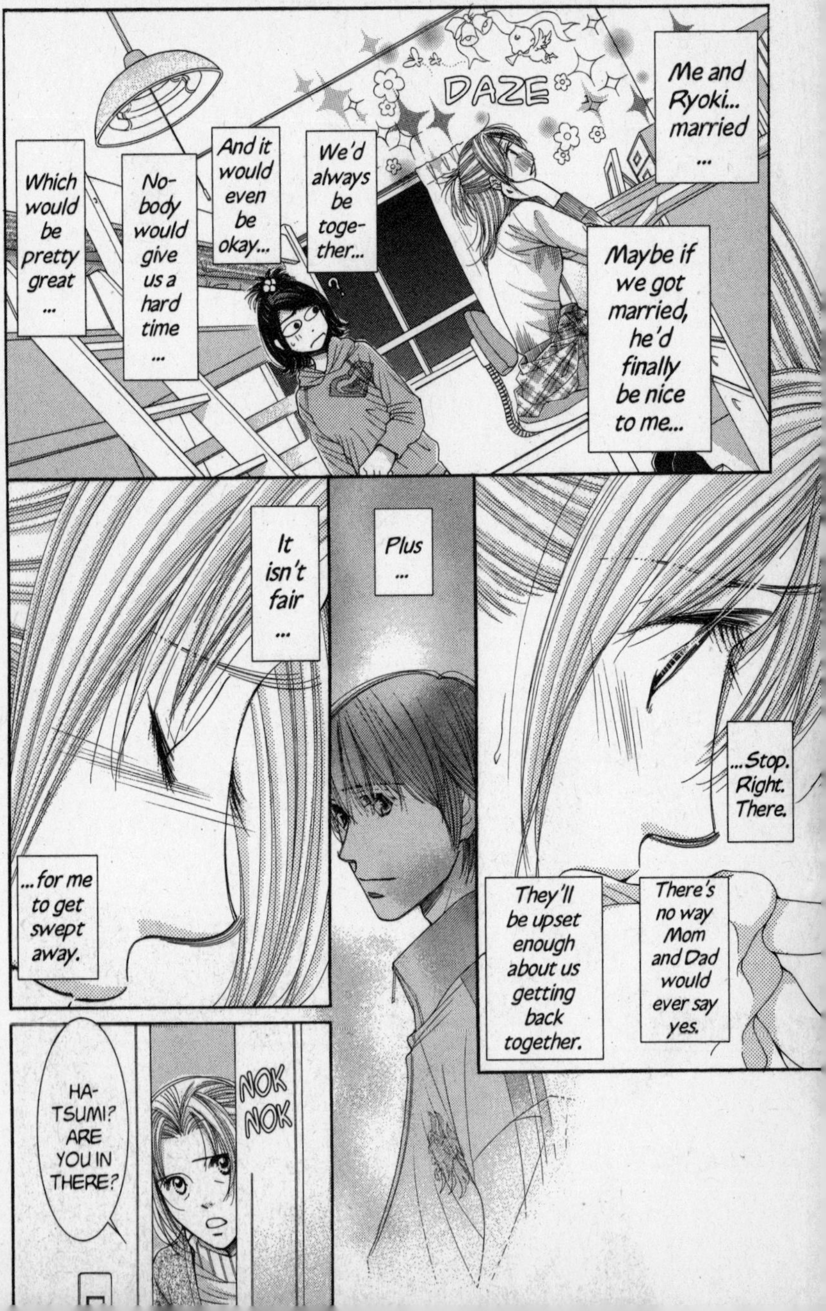
Me and Ryoki... married...
DAZE
Maybe if we got married, he'd finally be nice to me...
We'd always be toge-ther...
And it would even be okay...
No-body would give us a hard time...
Which would be pretty great...
...Stop. Right. There.
There's no way Mom and Dad would ever say yes.
They'll be upset enough about us getting back together.
Plus...
It isn't fair...
...for me to get swept away.
NOK NOK
HA-TSUMI? ARE YOU IN THERE?

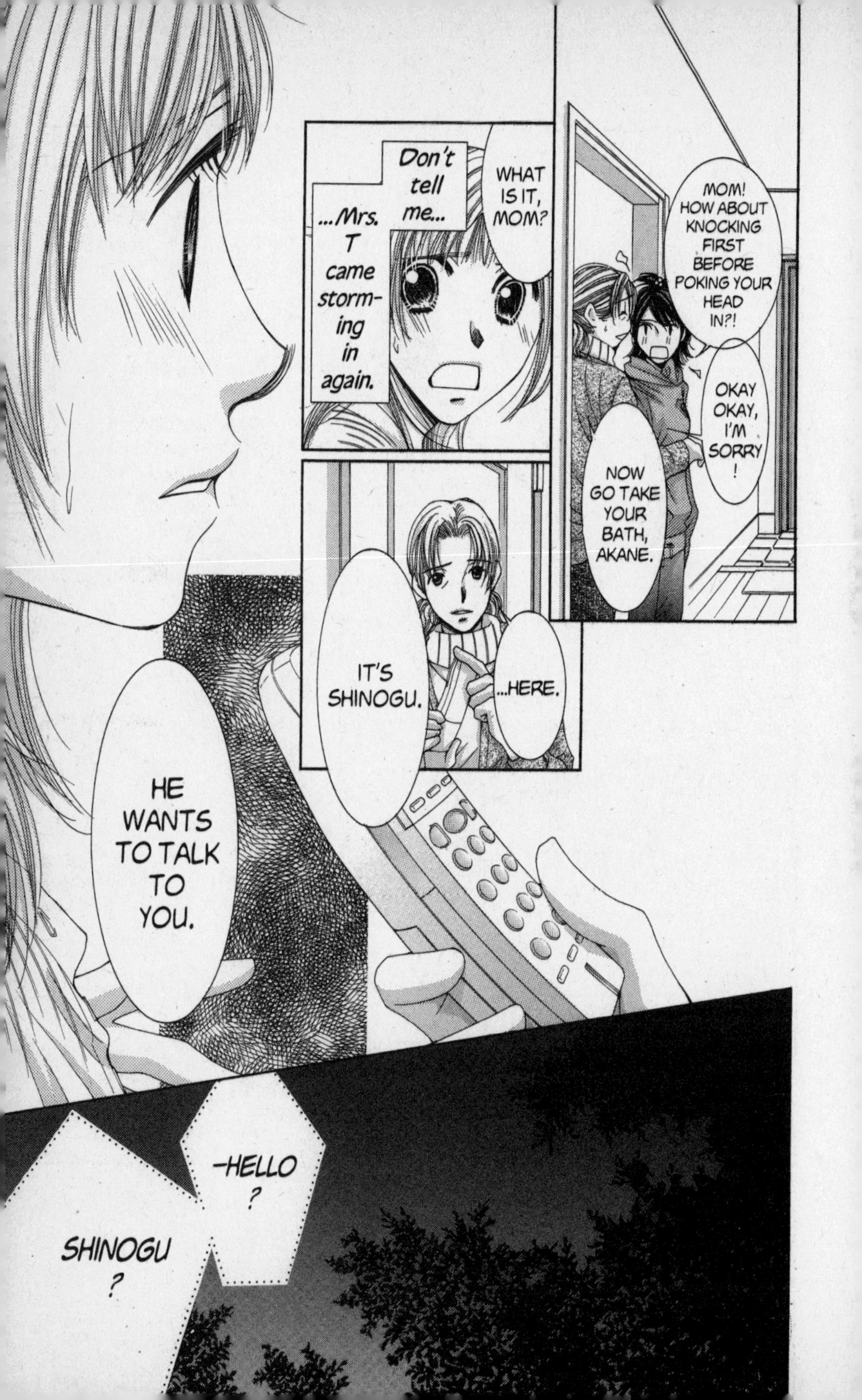
MOM! HOW ABOUT KNOCKING FIRST BEFORE POKING YOUR HEAD IN?!
OKAY OKAY, I'M SORRY!
NOW GO TAKE YOUR BATH, AKANE.
WHAT IS IT, MOM?
Don't tell me...
...Mrs. T came storming in again.
...HERE.
IT'S SHINOGU.
HE WANTS TO TALK TO YOU.
-HELLO?
SHINOGU?

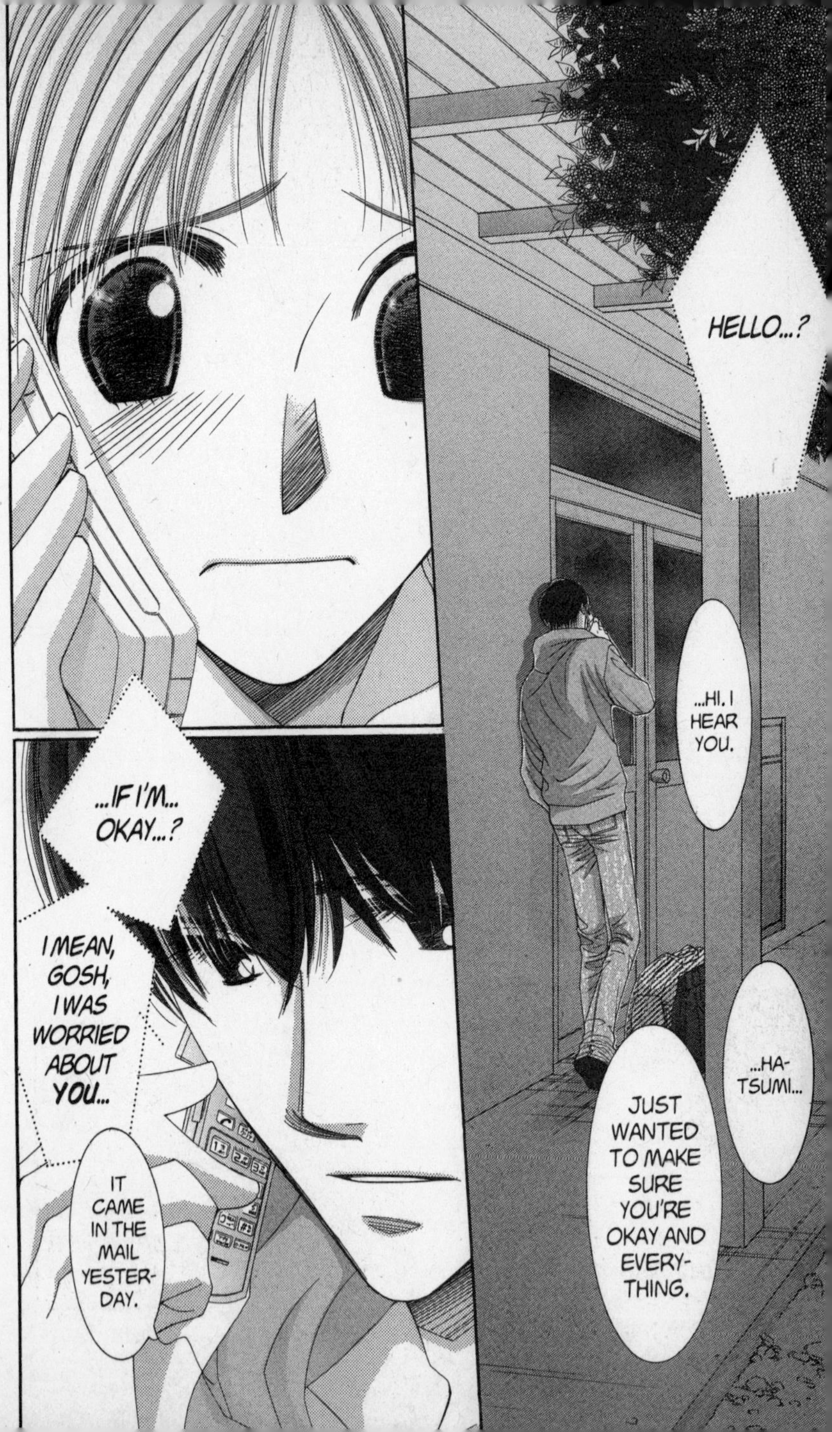
HELLO...?
...HI. I HEAR YOU.
...HA-TSUMI...
JUST WANTED TO MAKE SURE YOU'RE OKAY AND EVERY-THING.
...IF I'M... OKAY...?
I MEAN, GOSH, I WAS WORRIED ABOUT YOU...
IT CAME IN THE MAIL YESTER-DAY.

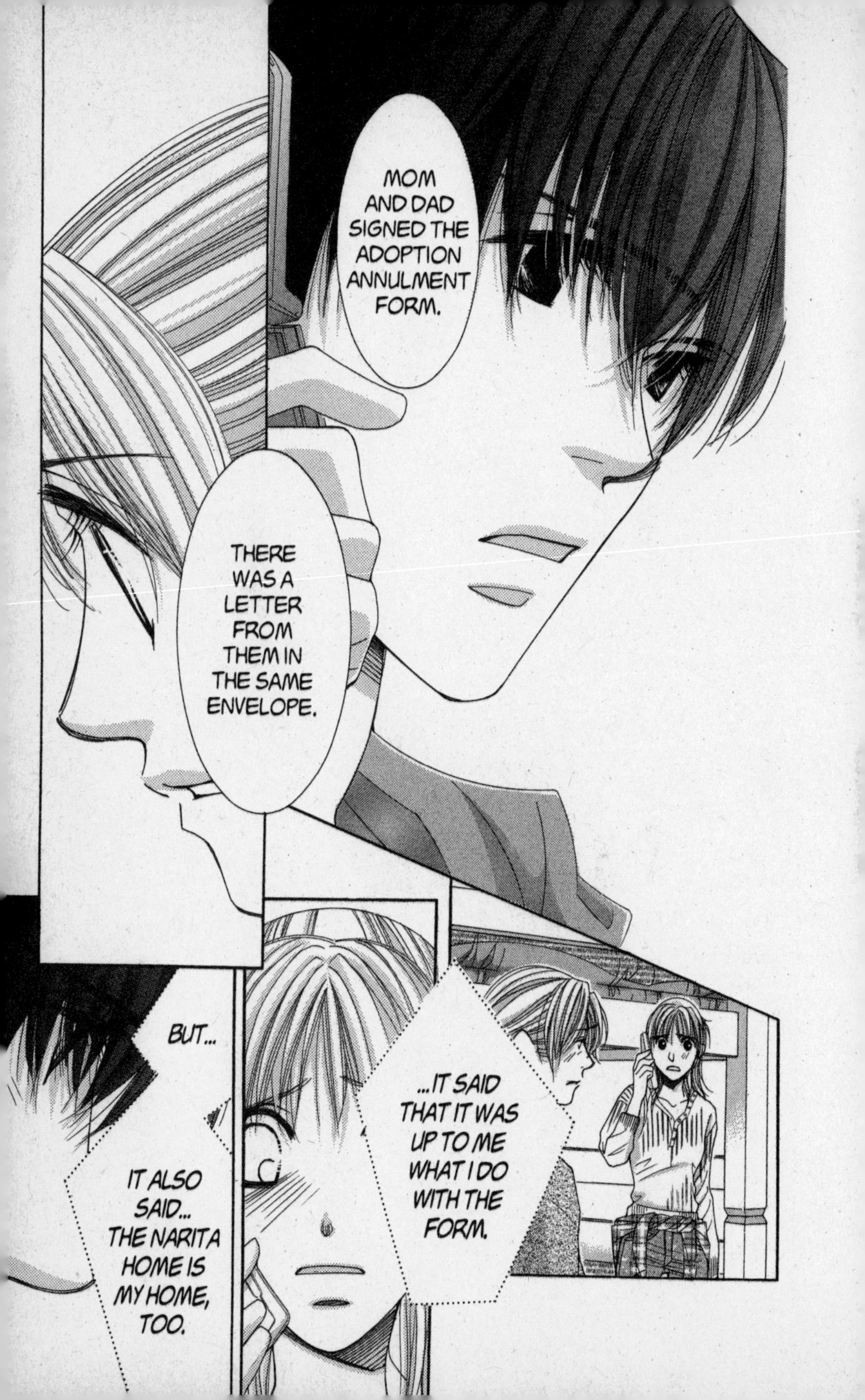
MOM AND DAD SIGNED THE ADOPTION ANNULMENT FORM.
THERE WAS A LETTER FROM THEM IN THE SAME ENVELOPE.
BUT...
...IT SAID THAT IT WAS UP TO ME WHAT I DO WITH THE FORM.
IT ALSO SAID... THE NARITA HOME IS MY HOME, TOO.

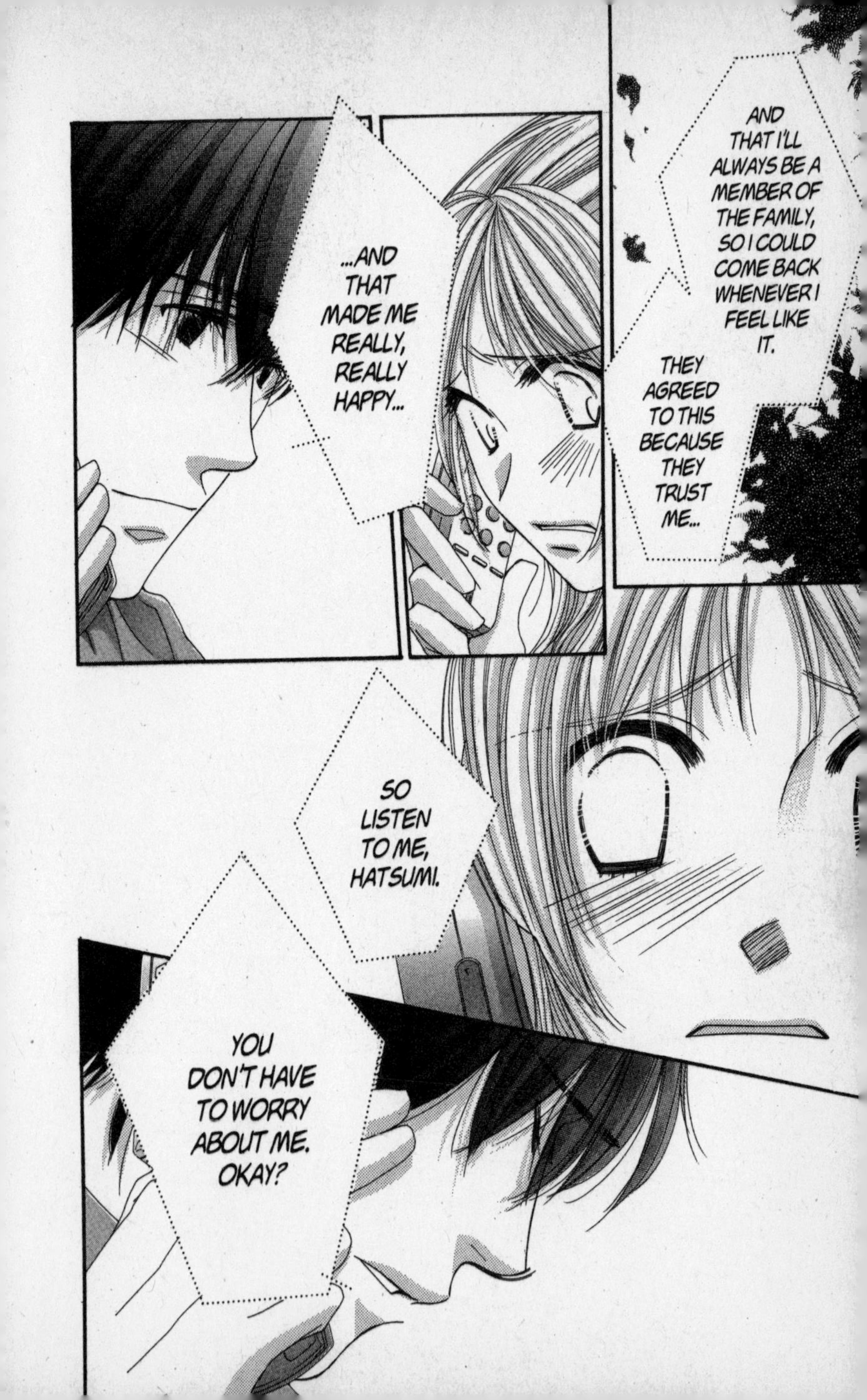
AND THAT I'LL ALWAYS BE A MEMBER OF THE FAMILY, SO I COULD COME BACK WHENEVER I FEEL LIKE IT.
THEY AGREED TO THIS BECAUSE THEY TRUST ME...
...AND THAT MADE ME REALLY, REALLY HAPPY...
SO LISTEN TO ME, HATSUMI.
YOU DON'T HAVE TO WORRY ABOUT ME. OKAY?

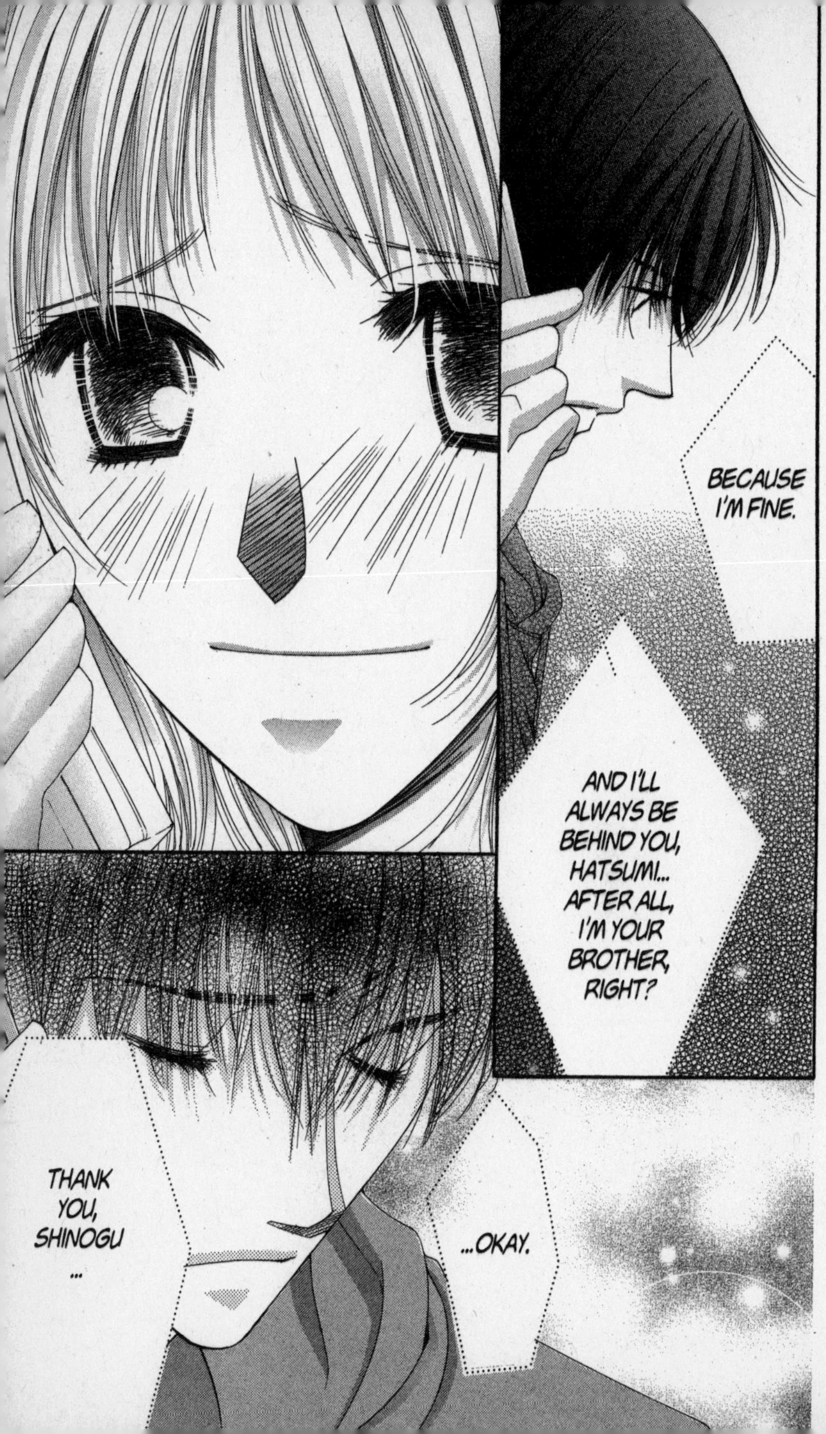
BECAUSE I'M FINE.
AND I'LL ALWAYS BE BEHIND YOU, HATSUMI... AFTER ALL, I'M YOUR BROTHER, RIGHT?
...OKAY.
THANK YOU, SHINOGU ...

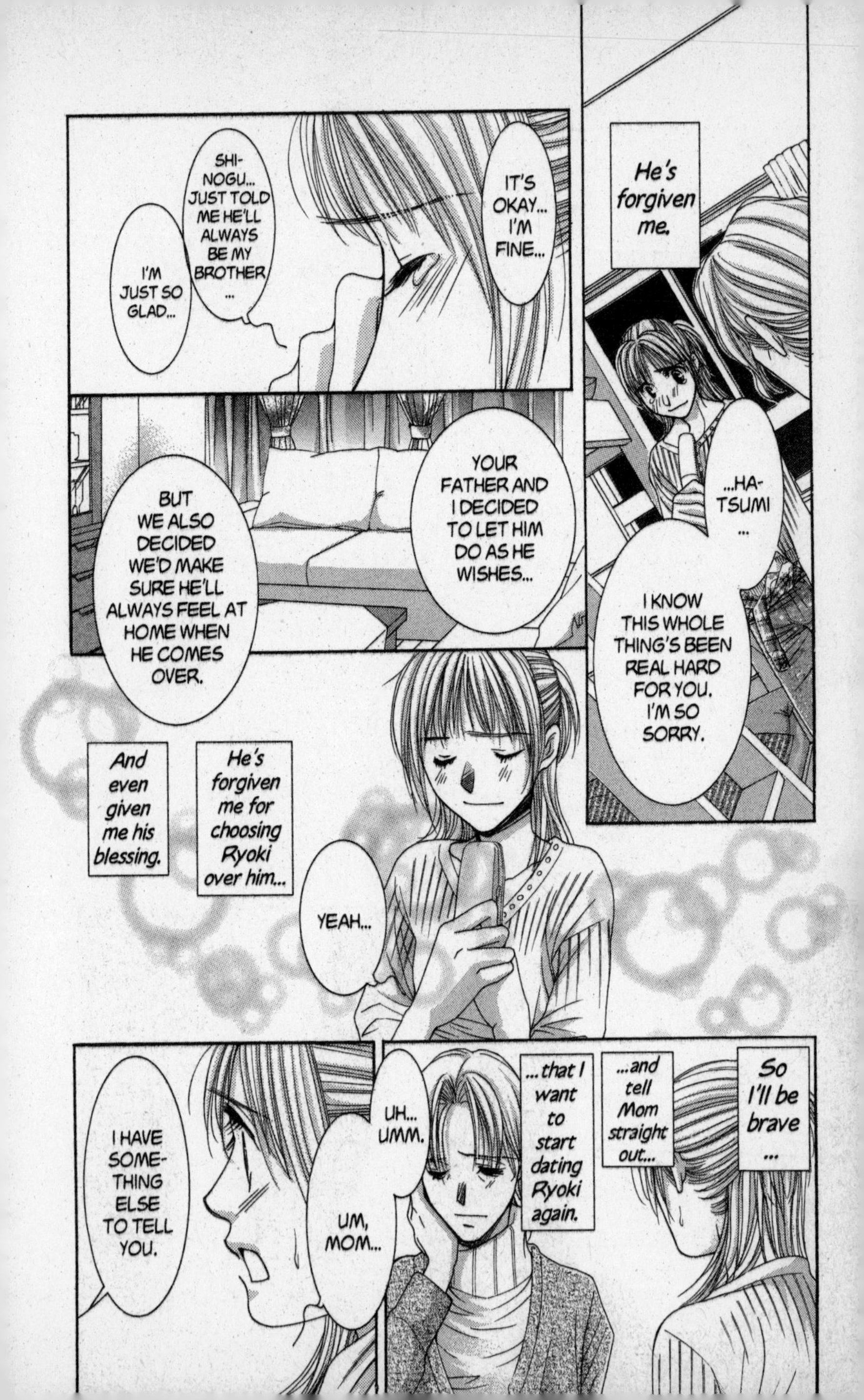
He's forgiven me.
...HA-TSUMI...
I KNOW THIS WHOLE THING'S BEEN REAL HARD FOR YOU. I'M SO SORRY.
IT'S OKAY... I'M FINE...
SHI-NOGU... JUST TOLD ME HE'LL ALWAYS BE MY BROTHER...
I'M JUST SO GLAD...
YOUR FATHER AND I DECIDED TO LET HIM DO AS HE WISHES...
BUT WE ALSO DECIDED WE'D MAKE SURE HE'LL ALWAYS FEEL AT HOME WHEN HE COMES OVER.
He's forgiven me for choosing Ryoki over him...
And even given me his blessing.
YEAH...
So I'll be brave...
...and tell Mom straight out...
...that I want to start dating Ryoki again.
UH... UMM.
UM, MOM...
I HAVE SOMETHING ELSE TO TELL YOU.

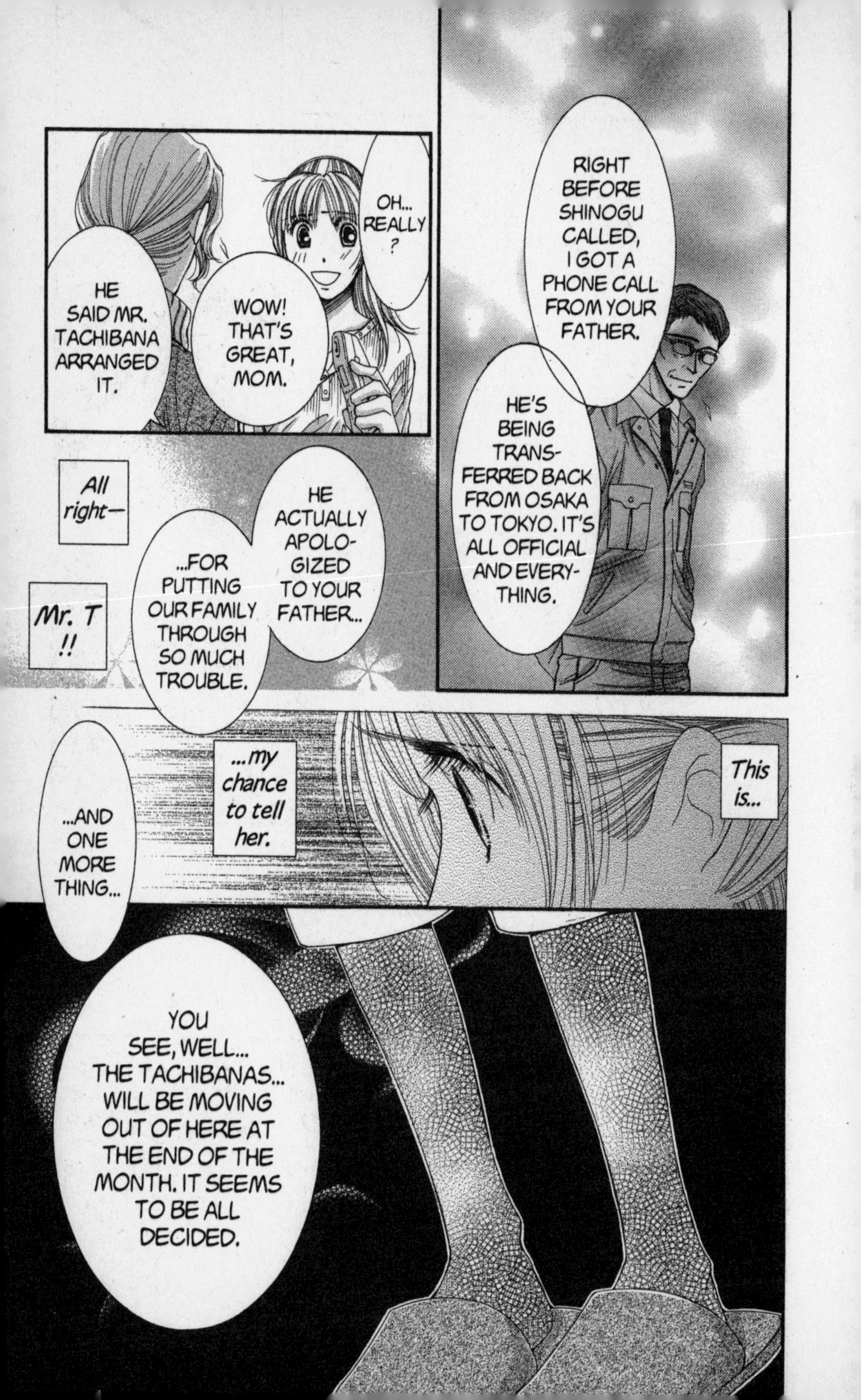
RIGHT BEFORE SHINOGU CALLED, I GOT A PHONE CALL FROM YOUR FATHER.
HE'S BEING TRANS-FERRED BACK FROM OSAKA TO TOKYO. IT'S ALL OFFICIAL AND EVERY-THING.
OH... REALLY?
WOW! THAT'S GREAT, MOM.
HE SAID MR. TACHIBANA ARRANGED IT.
HE ACTUALLY APOLO-GIZED TO YOUR FATHER...
...FOR PUTTING OUR FAMILY THROUGH SO MUCH TROUBLE.
All right—
Mr. T !!
This is...
...my chance to tell her.
...AND ONE MORE THING...
YOU SEE, WELL... THE TACHIBANAS... WILL BE MOVING OUT OF HERE AT THE END OF THE MONTH. IT SEEMS TO BE ALL DECIDED.

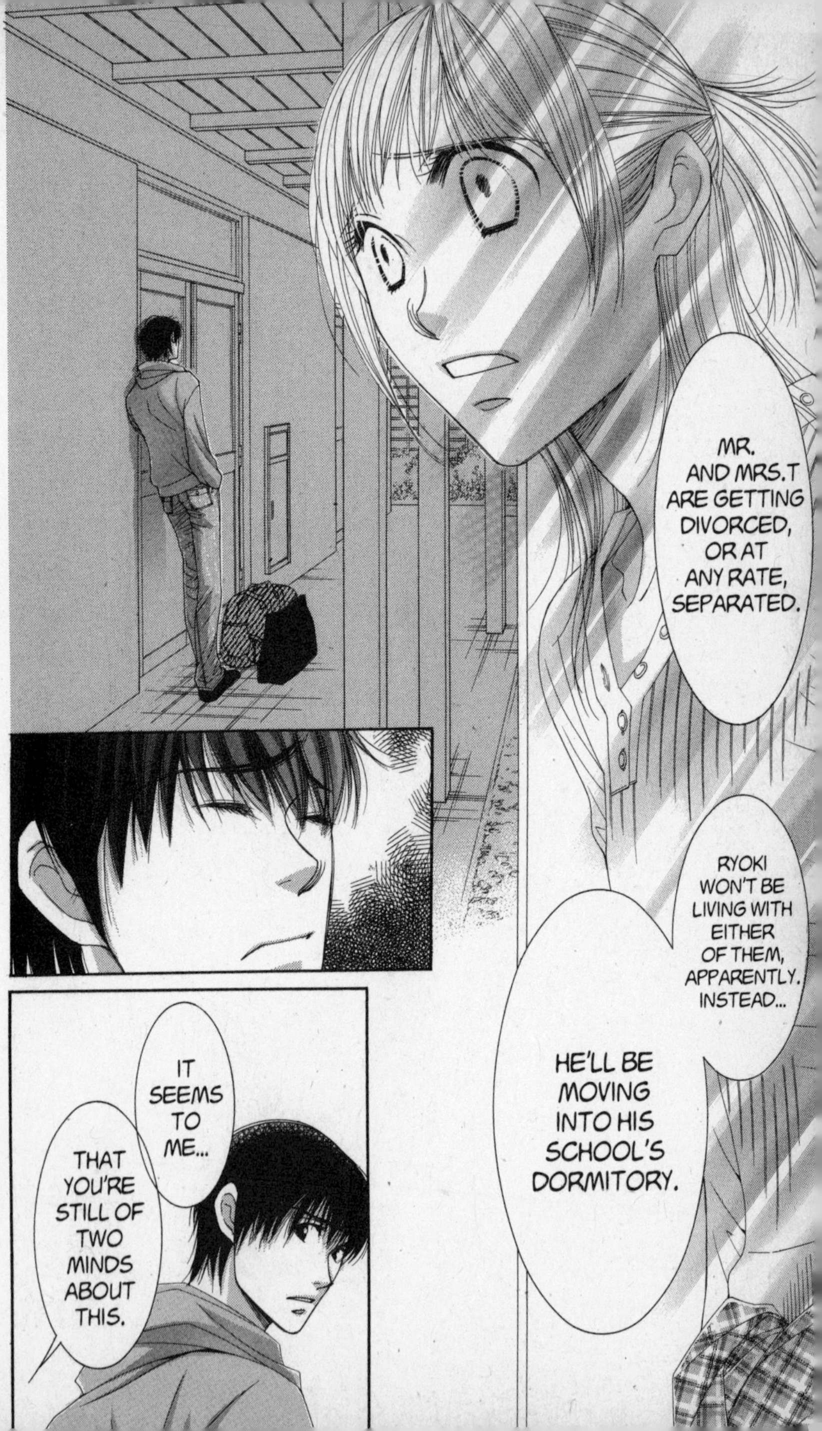
MR. AND MRS.T ARE GETTING DIVORCED, OR AT ANY RATE, SEPARATED.
RYOKI WON'T BE LIVING WITH EITHER OF THEM, APPARENTLY. INSTEAD...
HE'LL BE MOVING INTO HIS SCHOOL'S DORMITORY.
IT SEEMS TO ME...
THAT YOU'RE STILL OF TWO MINDS ABOUT THIS.

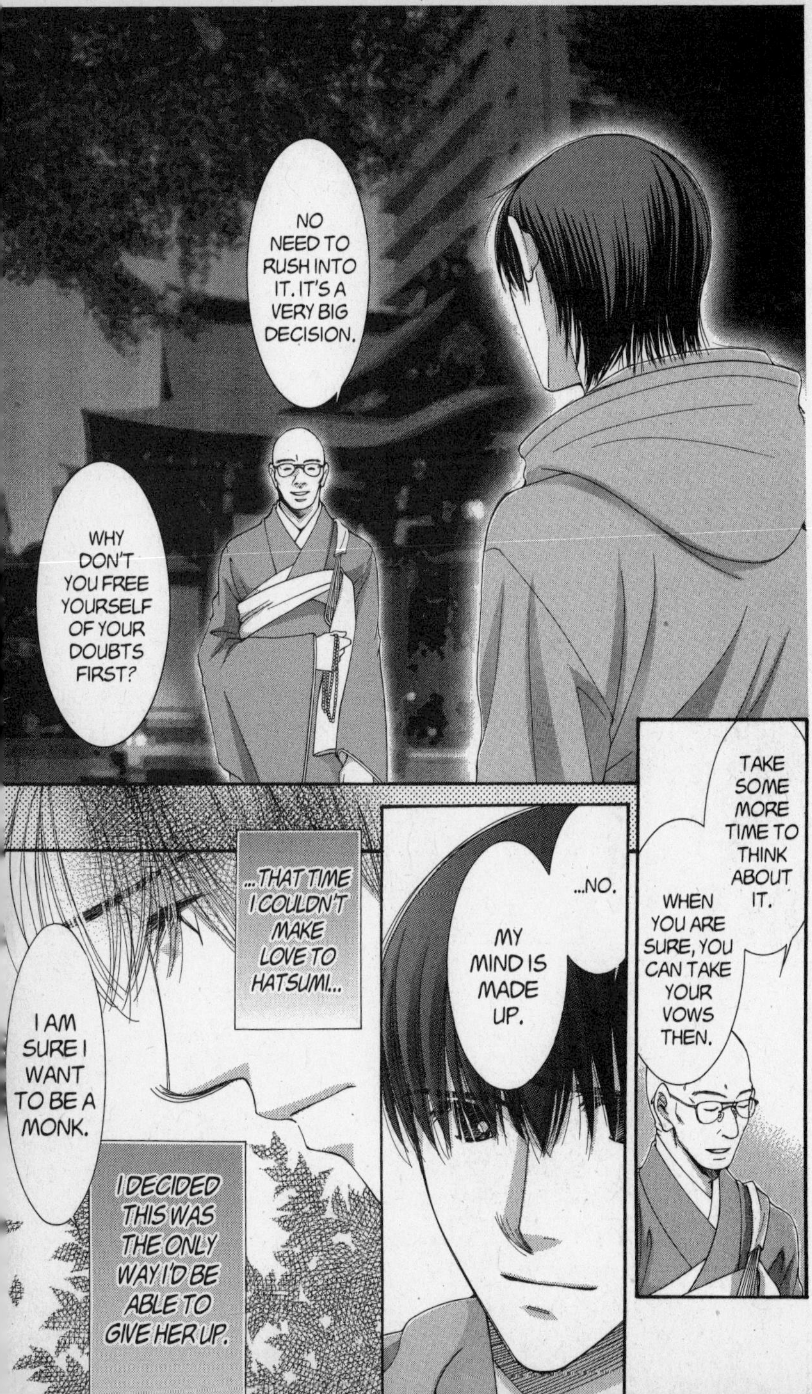
NO NEED TO RUSH INTO IT. IT'S A VERY BIG DECISION.
WHY DON'T YOU FREE YOURSELF OF YOUR DOUBTS FIRST?
TAKE SOME MORE TIME TO THINK ABOUT IT.
WHEN YOU ARE SURE, YOU CAN TAKE YOUR VOWS THEN.
...NO.
MY MIND IS MADE UP.
...THAT TIME I COULDN'T MAKE LOVE TO HATSUMI...
I AM SURE I WANT TO BE A MONK.
I DECIDED THIS WAS THE ONLY WAY I'D BE ABLE TO GIVE HER UP.

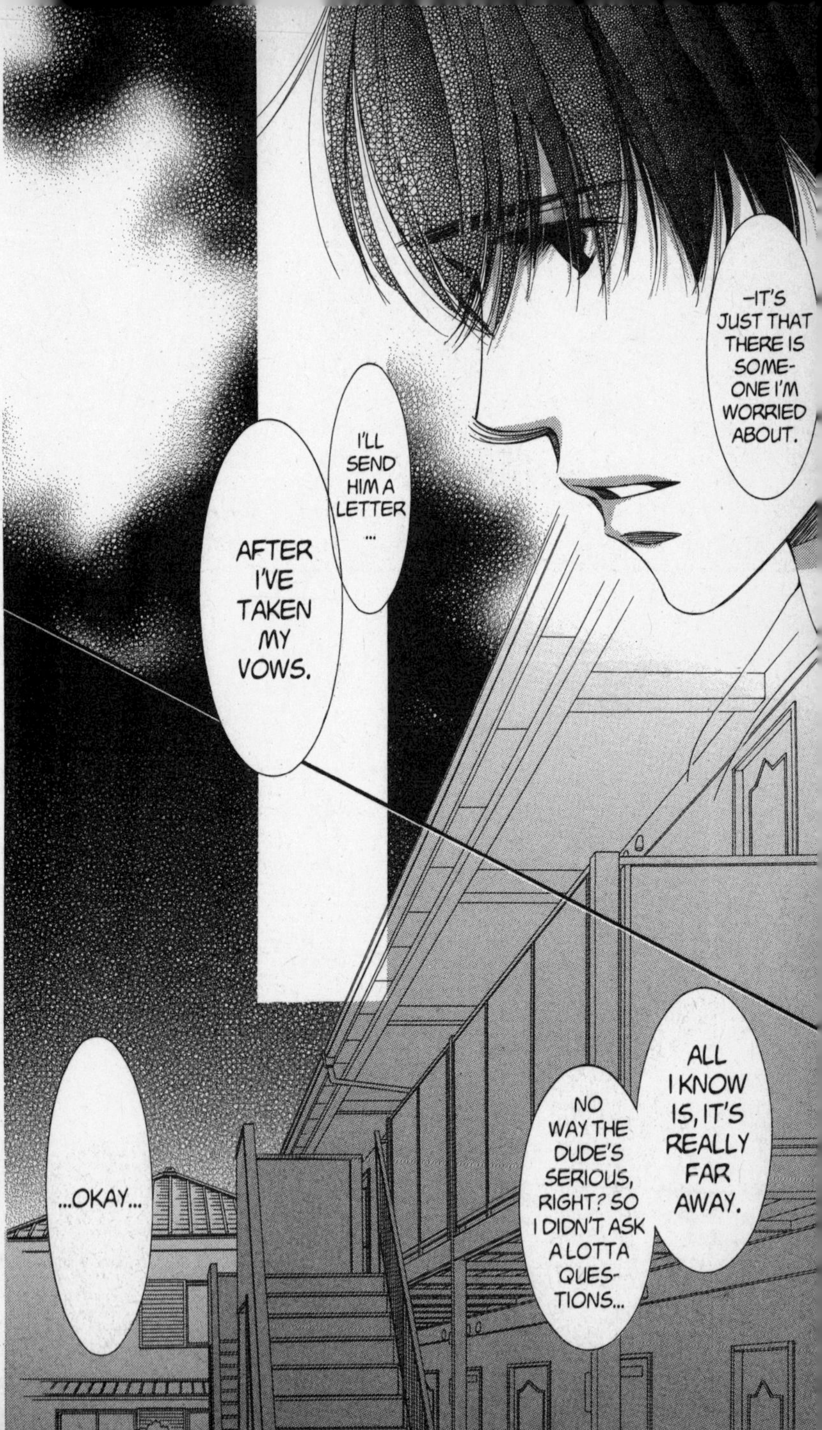
–IT'S JUST THAT THERE IS SOMEONE I'M WORRIED ABOUT.
I'LL SEND HIM A LETTER...
AFTER I'VE TAKEN MY VOWS.
ALL I KNOW IS, IT'S REALLY FAR AWAY.
NO WAY THE DUDE'S SERIOUS, RIGHT? SO I DIDN'T ASK A LOTTA QUESTIONS...
...OKAY...

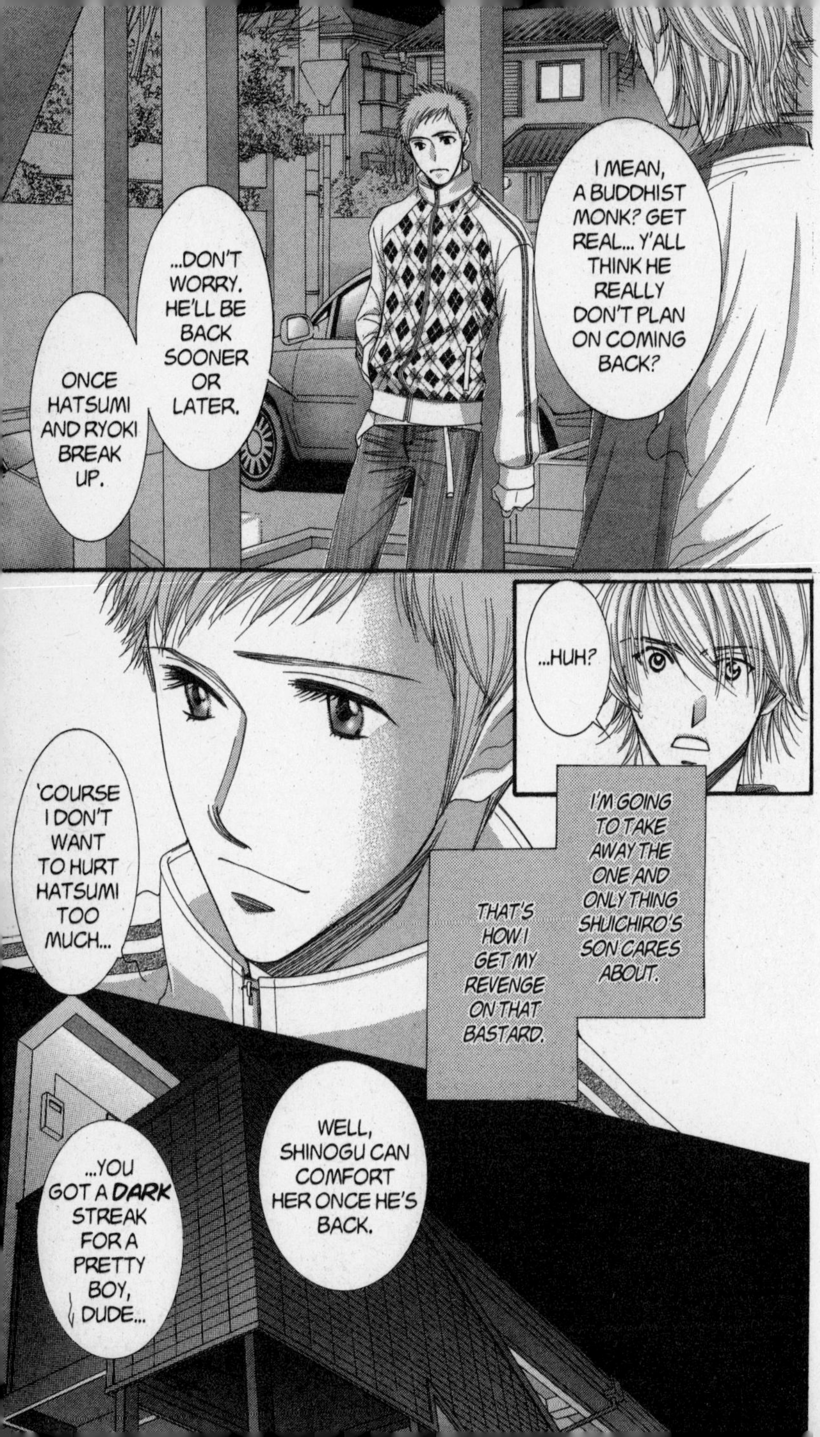
I MEAN, A BUDDHIST MONK? GET REAL... Y'ALL THINK HE REALLY DON'T PLAN ON COMING BACK?
...DON'T WORRY. HE'LL BE BACK SOONER OR LATER.
ONCE HATSUMI AND RYOKI BREAK UP.
...HUH?
I'M GOING TO TAKE AWAY THE ONE AND ONLY THING SHUICHIRO'S SON CARES ABOUT.
THAT'S HOW I GET MY REVENGE ON THAT BASTARD.
'COURSE I DON'T WANT TO HURT HATSUMI TOO MUCH...
WELL, SHINOGU CAN COMFORT HER ONCE HE'S BACK.
...YOU GOT A **DARK** STREAK FOR A PRETTY BOY, DUDE...

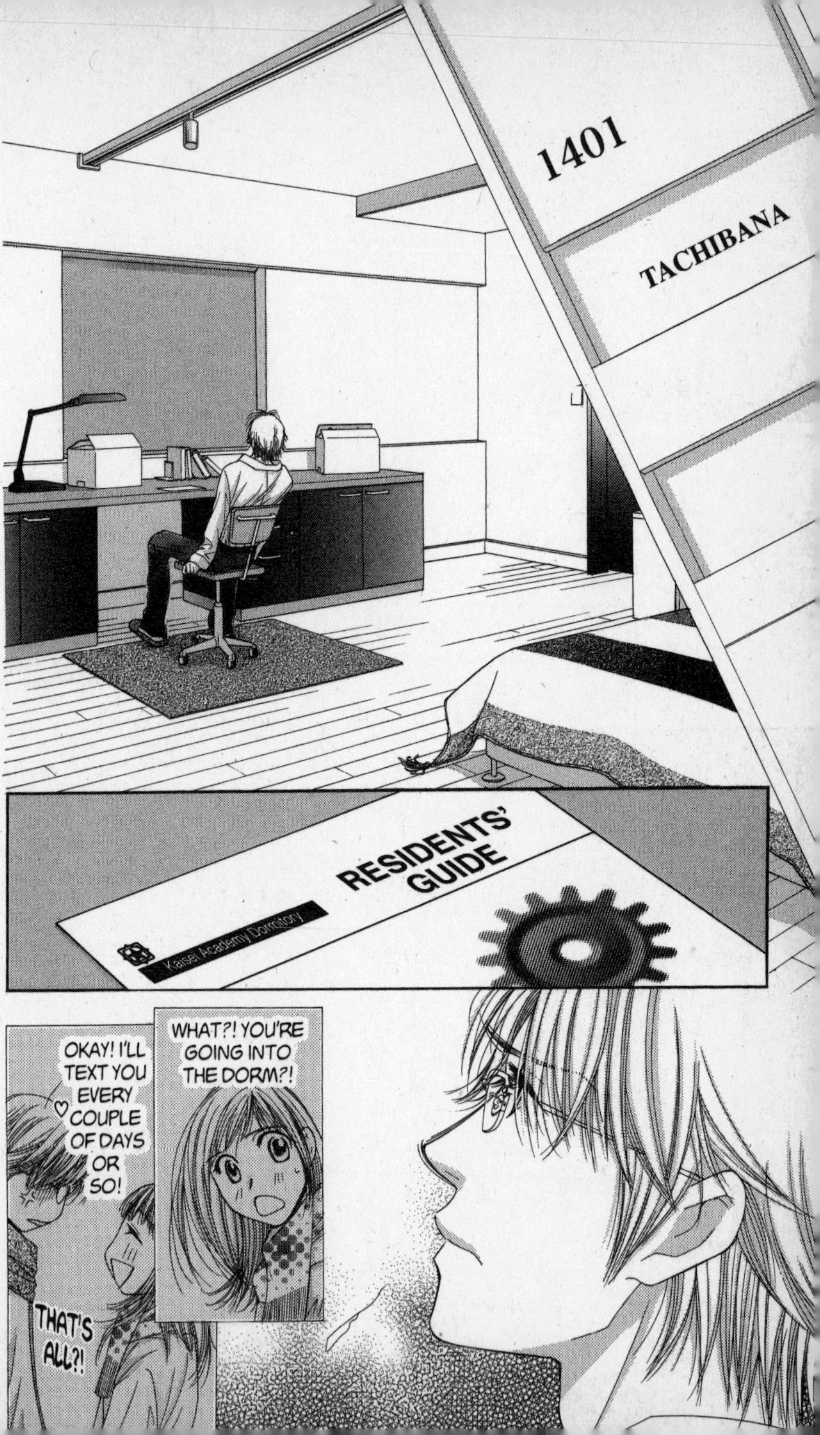
1401
TACHIBANA
RESIDENTS' GUIDE
Kaisei Academy Dormitory
WHAT?! YOU'RE GOING INTO THE DORM?!
OKAY! I'LL TEXT YOU EVERY COUPLE OF DAYS OR SO!
THAT'S ALL?!

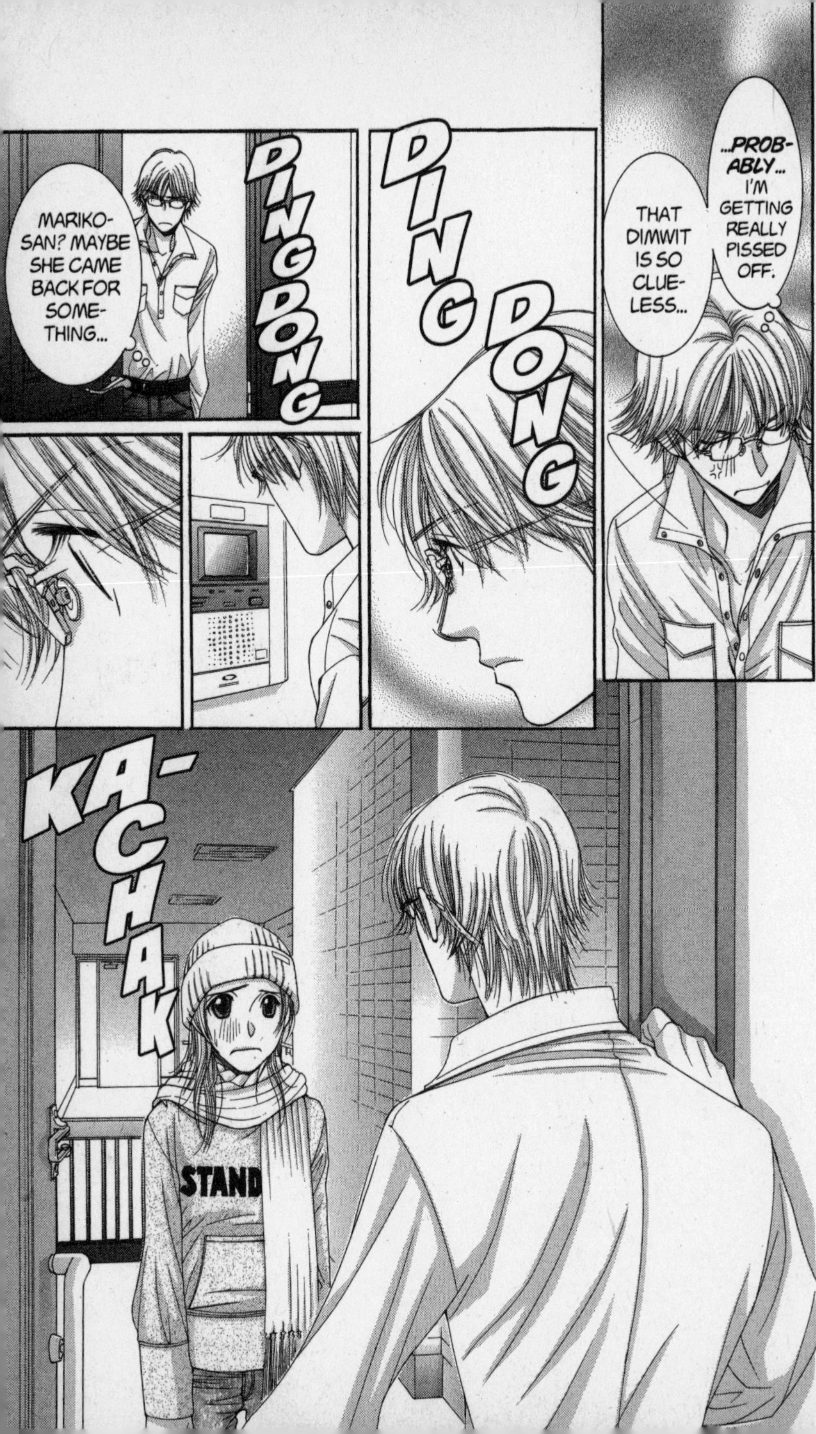
...PROBABLY... I'M GETTING REALLY PISSED OFF.
THAT DIMWIT IS SO CLUELESS...
DING DONG
DING DONG
MARIKO-SAN? MAYBE SHE CAME BACK FOR SOMETHING...
KA-CHAK
STAND

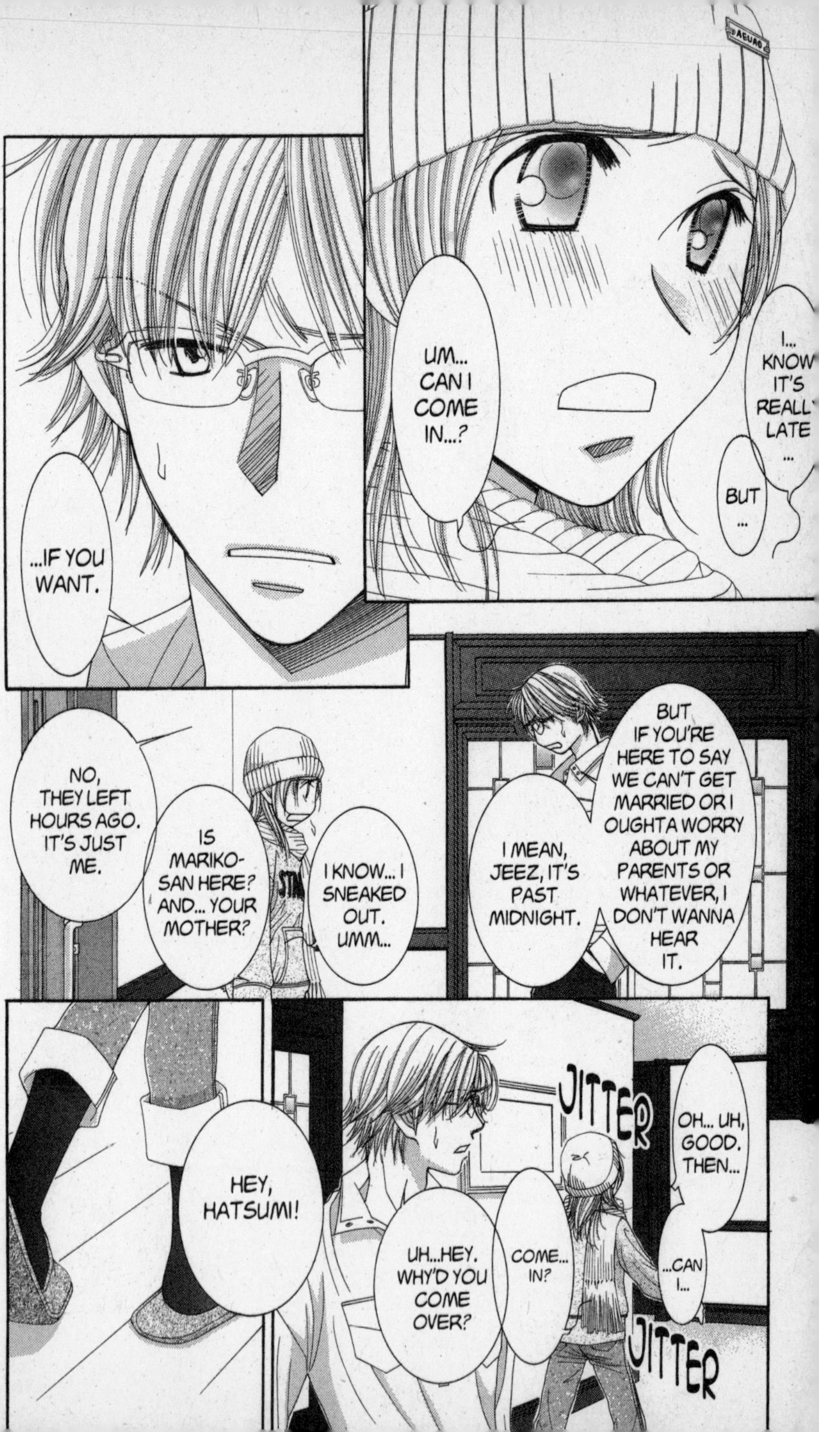
I... KNOW IT'S REALLY LATE ...
BUT ...
UM... CAN I COME IN...?
...IF YOU WANT.
BUT IF YOU'RE HERE TO SAY WE CAN'T GET MARRIED OR I OUGHTA WORRY ABOUT MY PARENTS OR WHATEVER, I DON'T WANNA HEAR IT.
I MEAN, JEEZ, IT'S PAST MIDNIGHT.
I KNOW... I SNEAKED OUT. UMM...
IS MARIKO-SAN HERE? AND... YOUR MOTHER?
NO, THEY LEFT HOURS AGO. IT'S JUST ME.
JITTER
OH... UH, GOOD. THEN...
...CAN I...
JITTER
COME... IN?
UH...HEY. WHY'D YOU COME OVER?
HEY, HATSUMI!

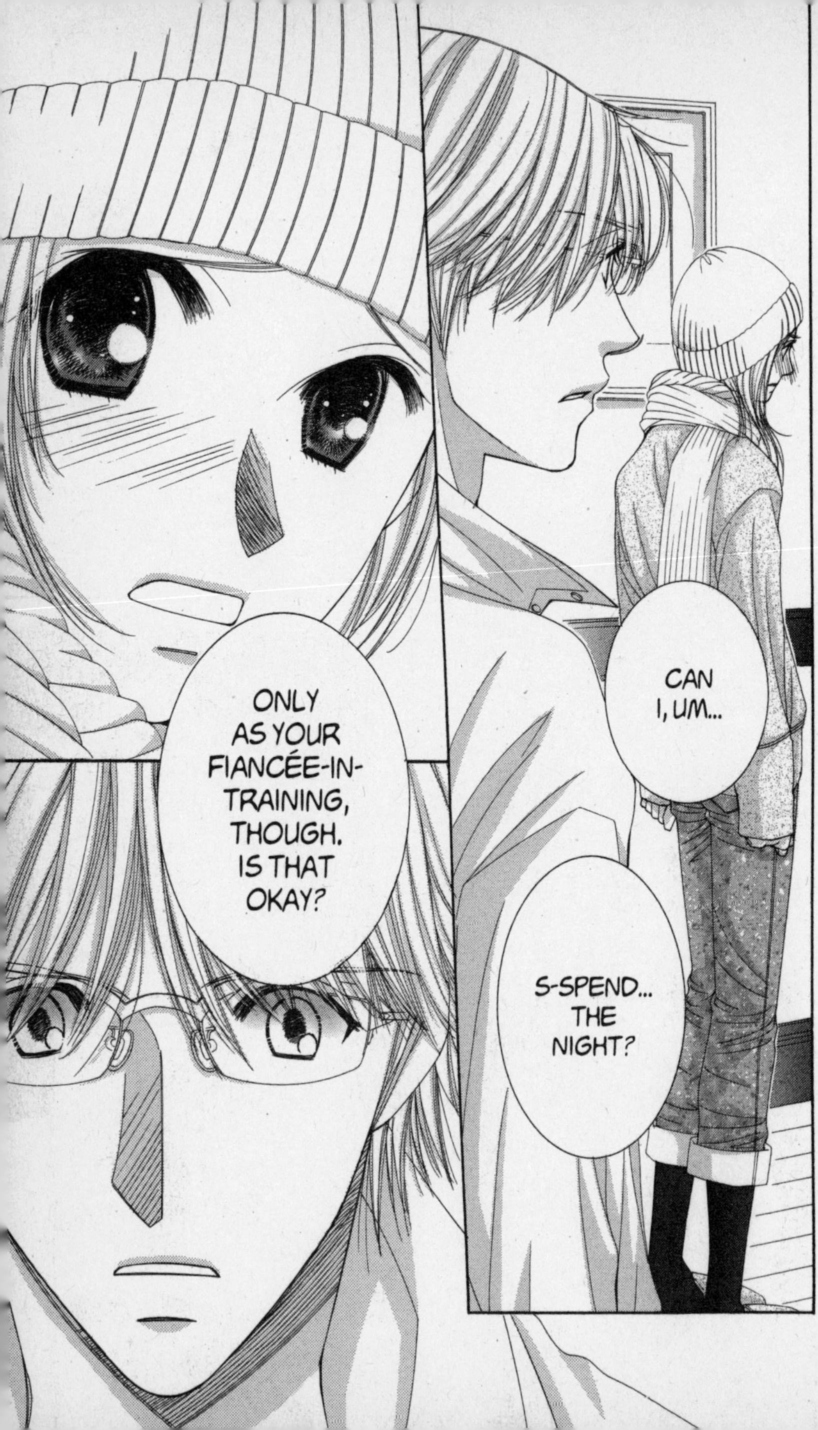
CAN I, UM...
S-SPEND... THE NIGHT?
ONLY AS YOUR FIANCÉE-IN-TRAINING, THOUGH. IS THAT OKAY?

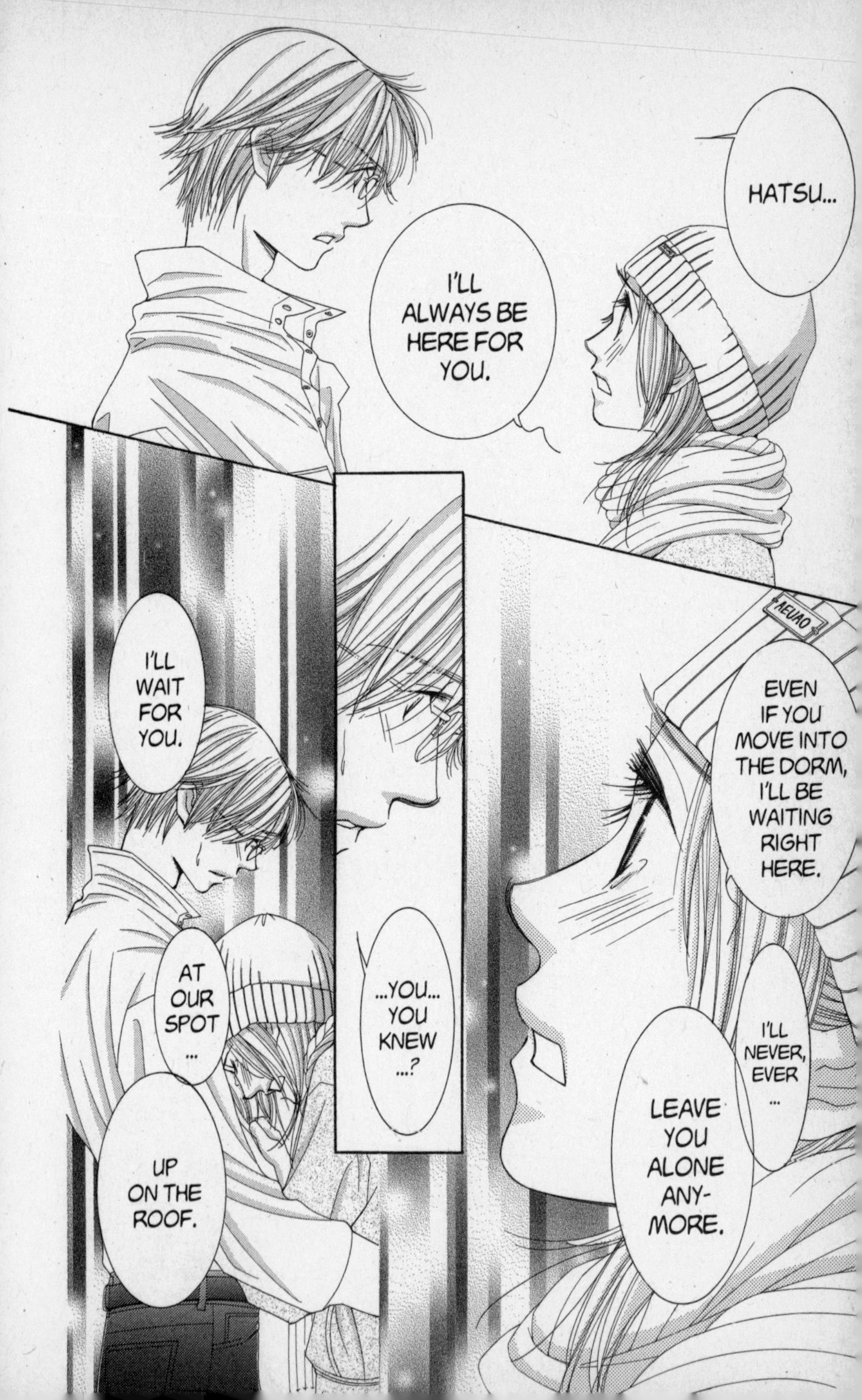
HATSU...
I'LL ALWAYS BE HERE FOR YOU.
EVEN IF YOU MOVE INTO THE DORM, I'LL BE WAITING RIGHT HERE.
I'LL NEVER, EVER ...
LEAVE YOU ALONE ANY-MORE.
...YOU... YOU KNEW ...?
I'LL WAIT FOR YOU.
AT OUR SPOT ...
UP ON THE ROOF.

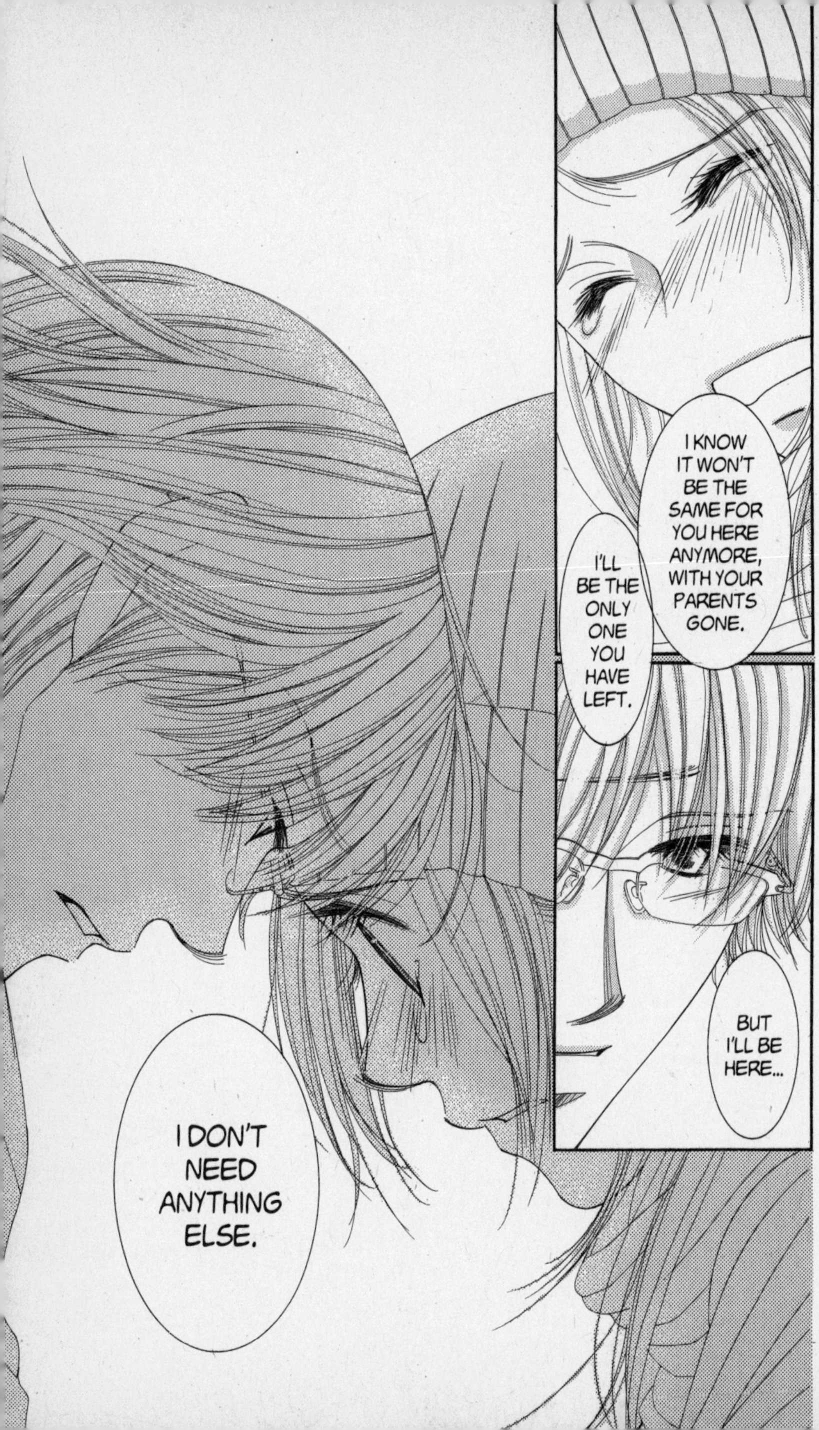
I KNOW IT WON'T BE THE SAME FOR YOU HERE ANYMORE, WITH YOUR PARENTS GONE.
I'LL BE THE ONLY ONE YOU HAVE LEFT.
BUT I'LL BE HERE...
I DON'T NEED ANYTHING ELSE.

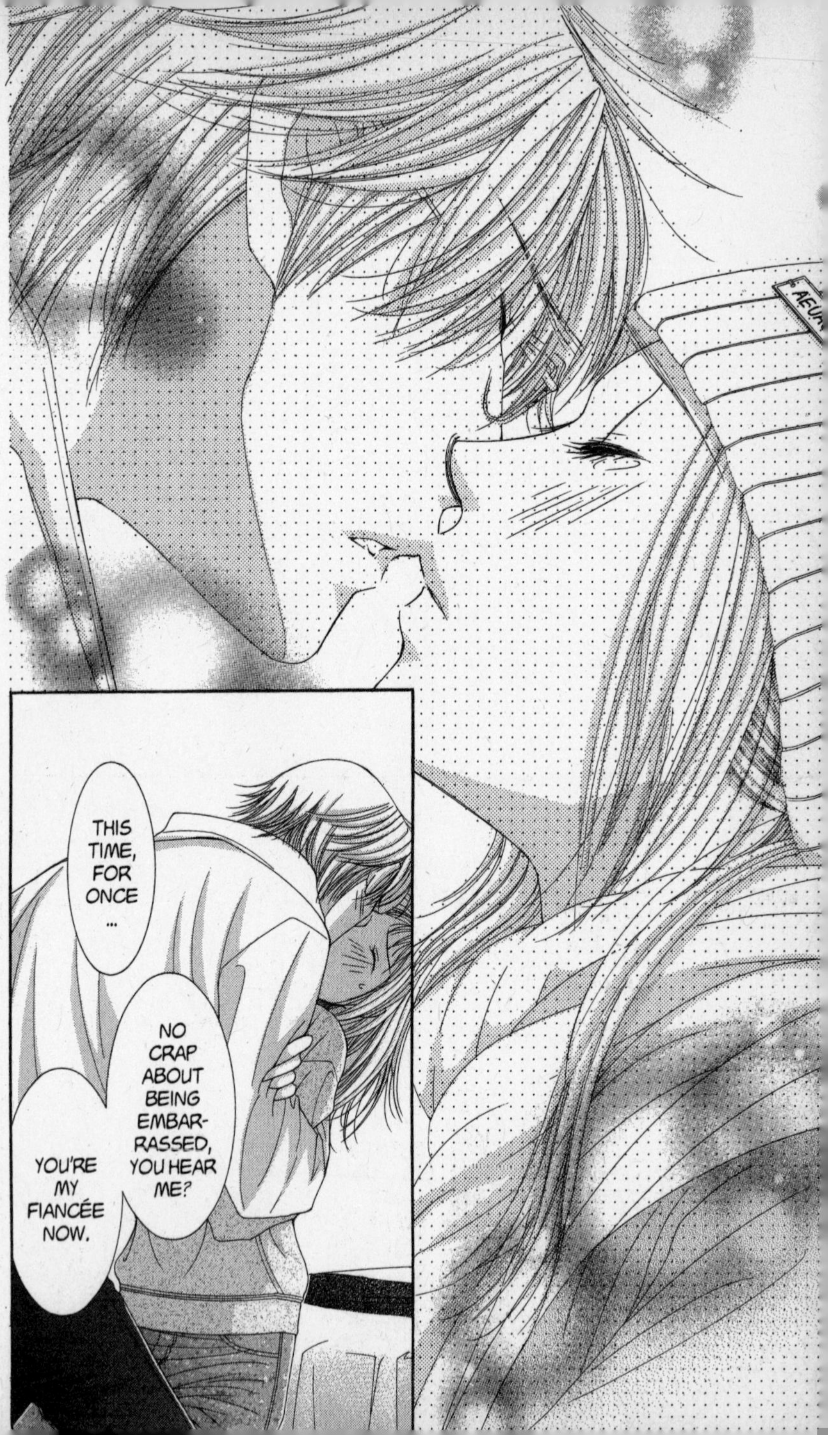
THIS TIME, FOR ONCE ...
NO CRAP ABOUT BEING EMBARRASSED, YOU HEAR ME?
YOU'RE MY FIANCÉE NOW.

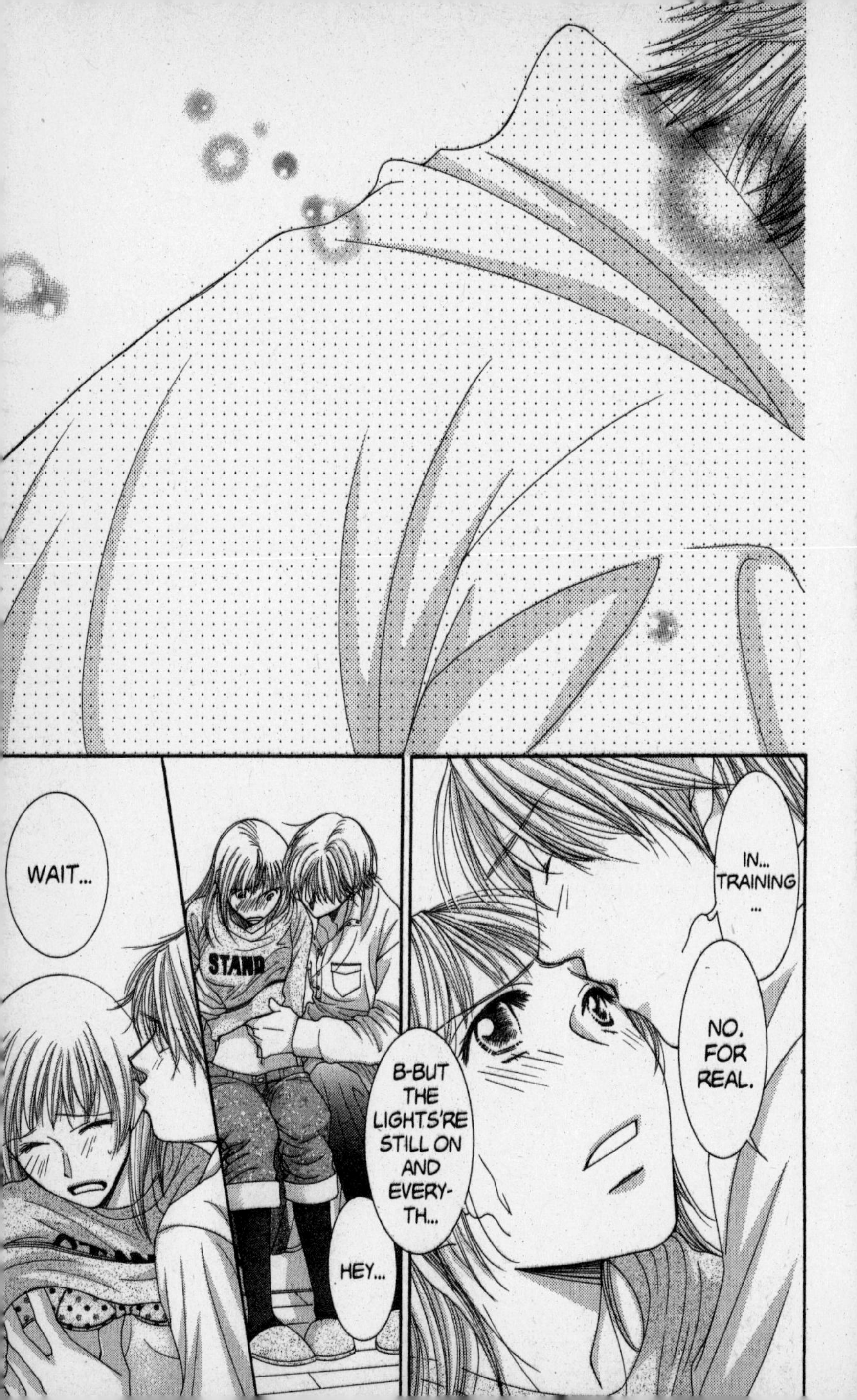
IN... TRAINING ...
NO. FOR REAL.
B-BUT THE LIGHTS'RE STILL ON AND EVERY-TH...
HEY...
STAND
WAIT...

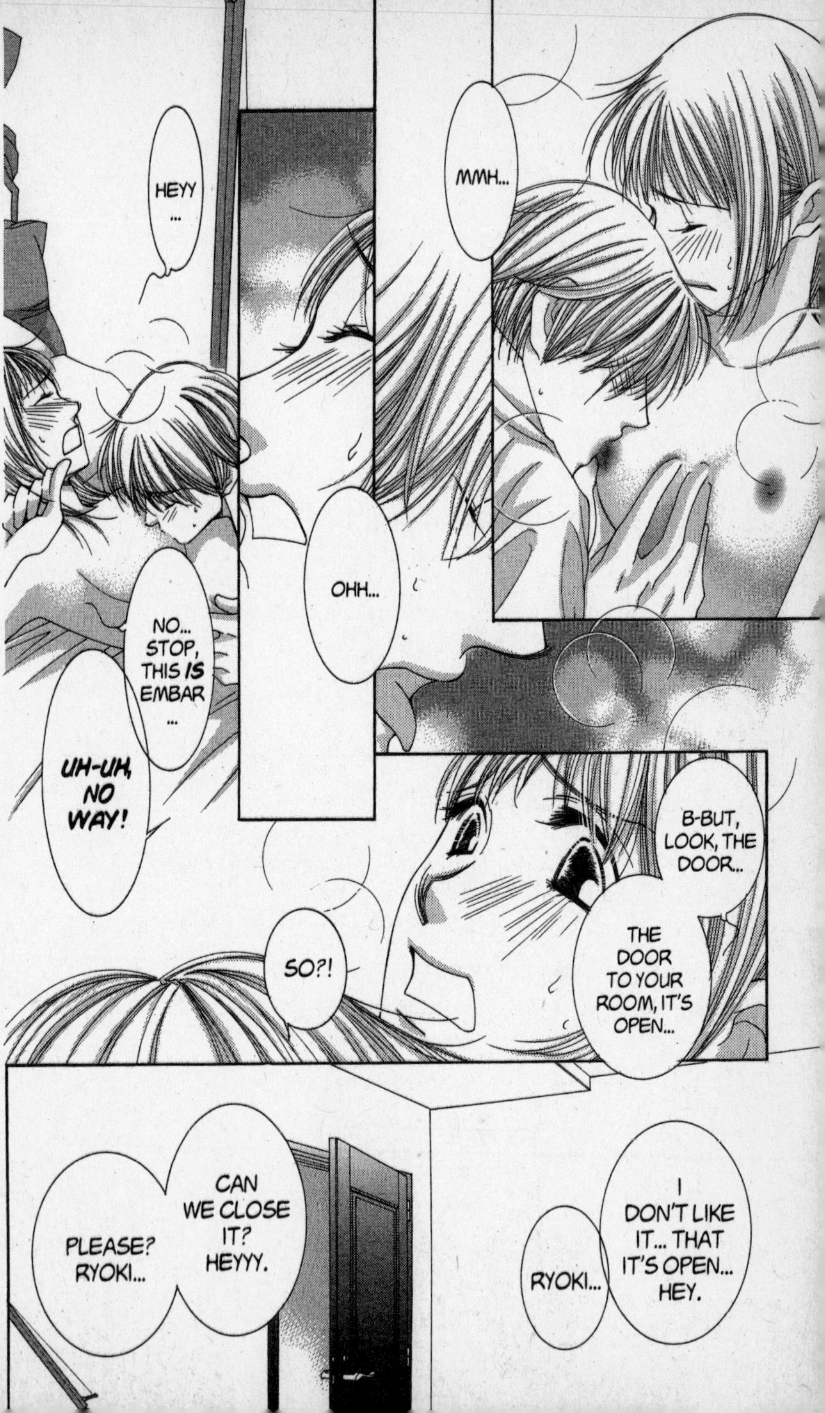
MMH...
OHH...
HEYY ...
NO... STOP, THIS IS EMBAR ...
UH-UH, NO WAY!
B-BUT, LOOK, THE DOOR...
THE DOOR TO YOUR ROOM, IT'S OPEN...
SO?!
I DON'T LIKE IT... THAT IT'S OPEN... HEY.
RYOKI...
CAN WE CLOSE IT? HEYYY.
PLEASE? RYOKI...

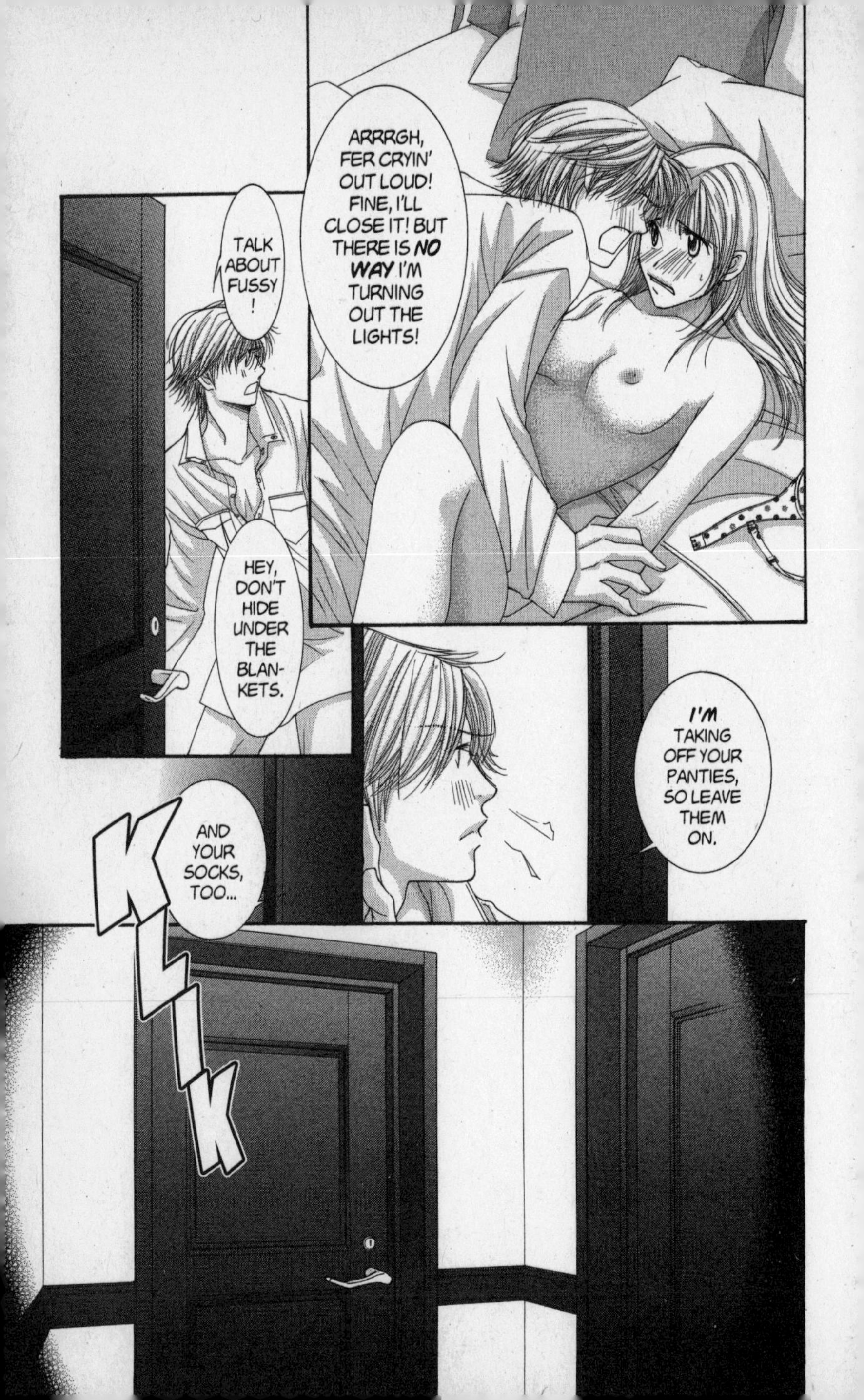
ARRRGH, FER CRYIN' OUT LOUD! FINE, I'LL CLOSE IT! BUT THERE IS **NO WAY** I'M TURNING OUT THE LIGHTS!
TALK ABOUT FUSSY!
HEY, DON'T HIDE UNDER THE BLAN-KETS.
I'M TAKING OFF YOUR PANTIES, SO LEAVE THEM ON.
AND YOUR SOCKS, TOO...
KLIK

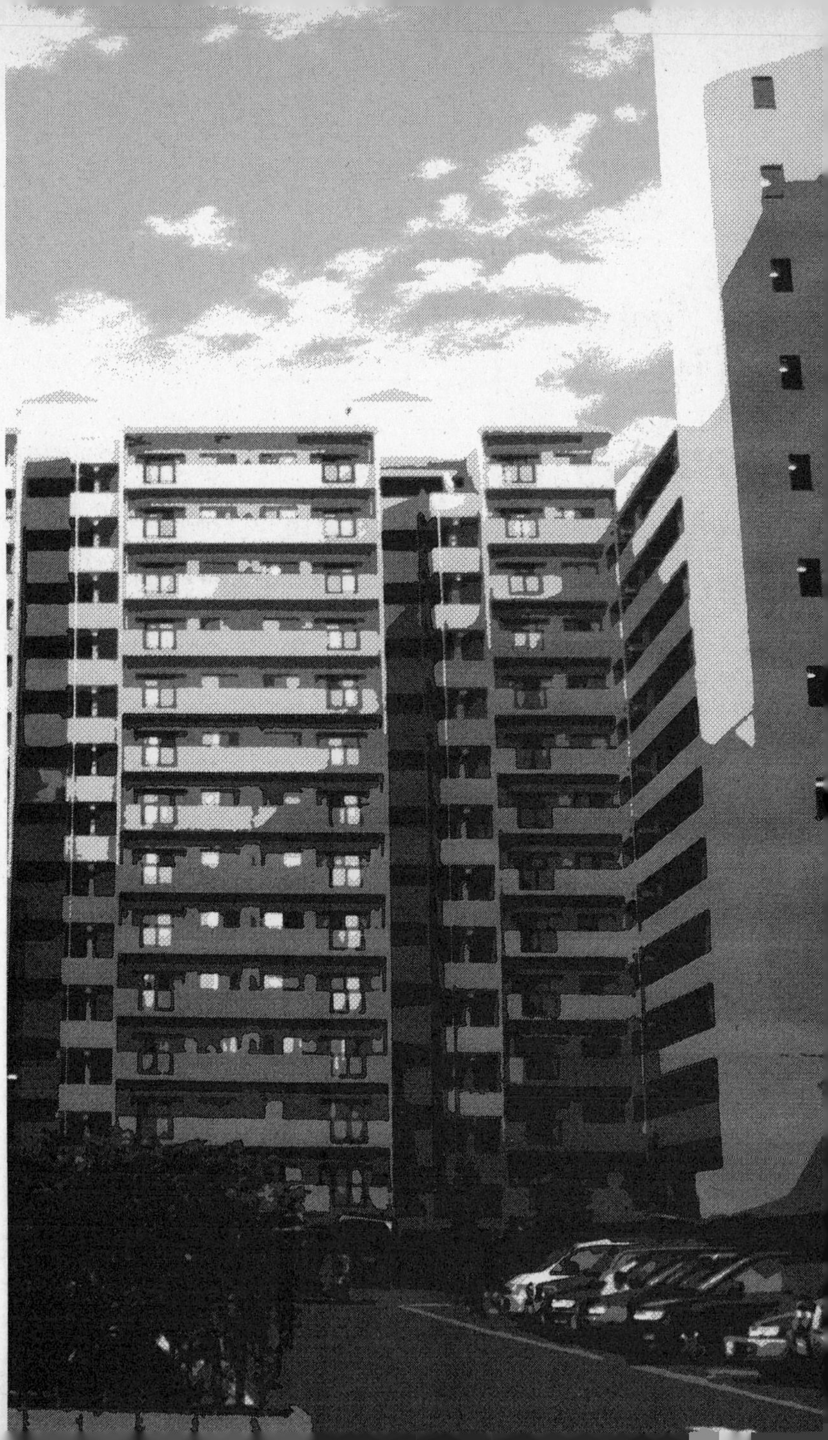

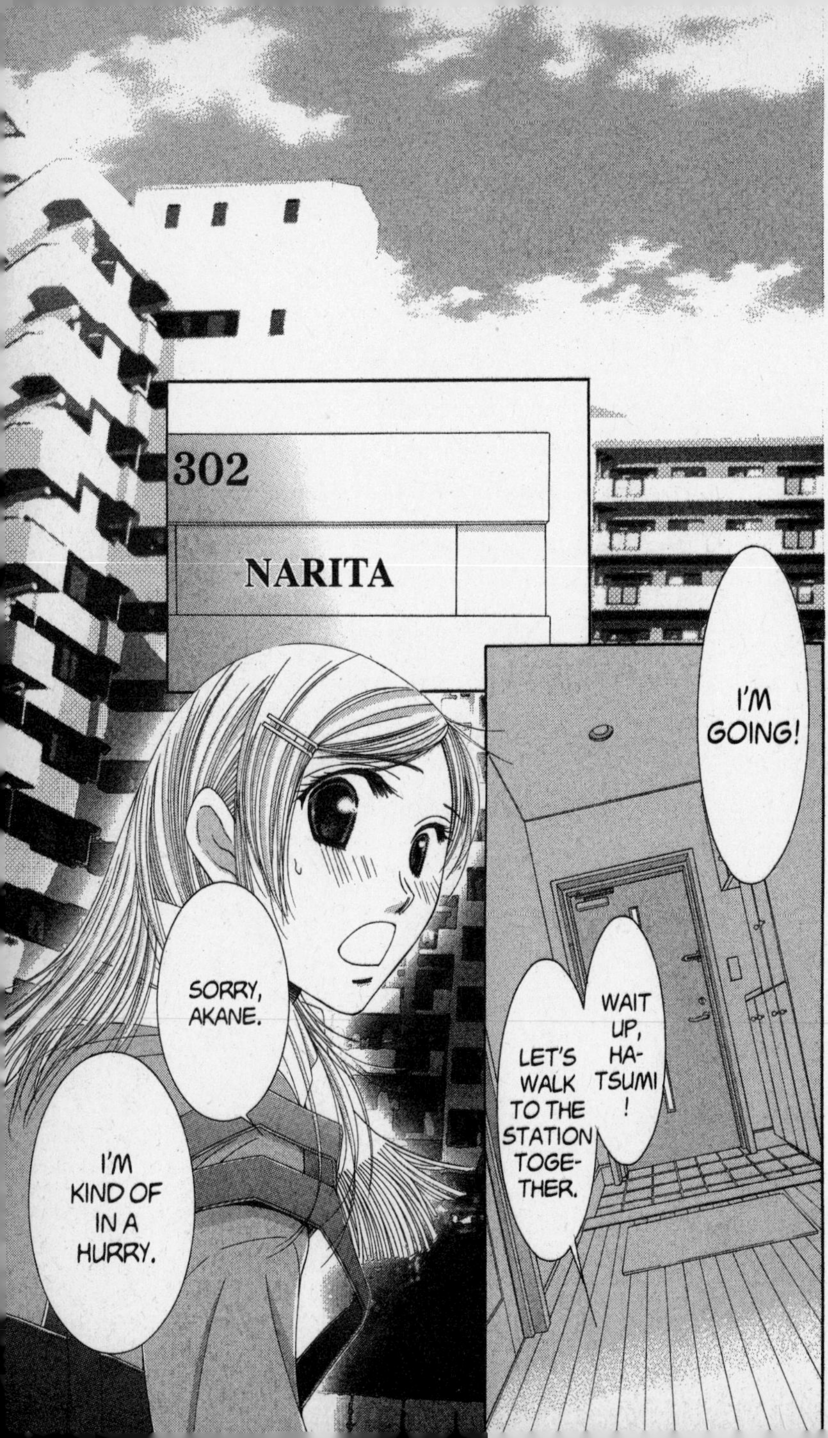
302
NARITA
I'M GOING!
WAIT UP, HATSUMI!
LET'S WALK TO THE STATION TOGETHER.
SORRY, AKANE.
I'M KIND OF IN A HURRY.

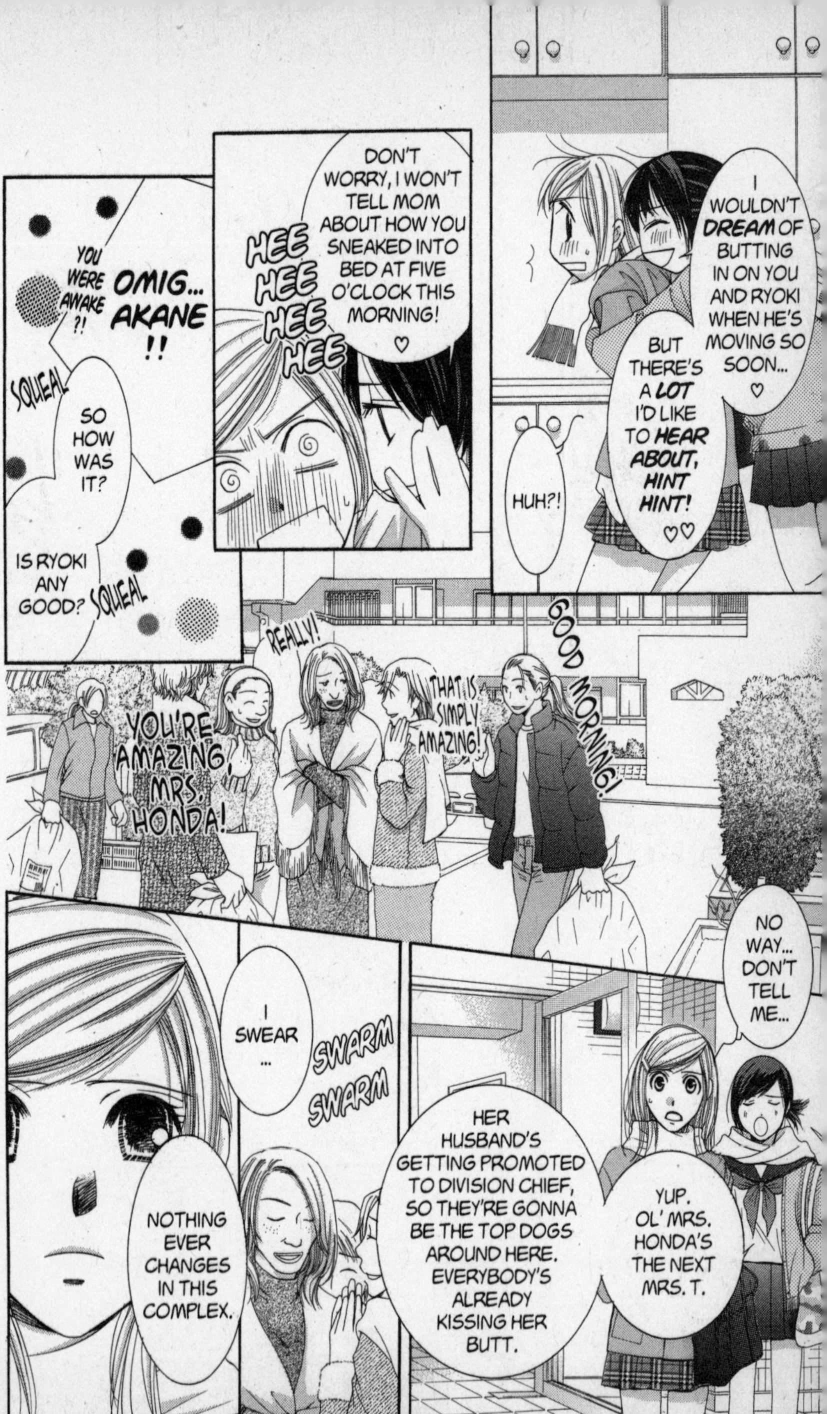
I WOULDN'T DREAM OF BUTTING IN ON YOU AND RYOKI WHEN HE'S MOVING SO SOON... ♡
BUT THERE'S A LOT I'D LIKE TO HEAR ABOUT, HINT HINT! ♡♡
HUH?!
DON'T WORRY, I WON'T TELL MOM ABOUT HOW YOU SNEAKED INTO BED AT FIVE O'CLOCK THIS MORNING! ♡
HEE HEE HEE HEE
OMIG... AKANE!!
YOU WERE AWAKE?!
SQUEAL
SO HOW WAS IT?
IS RYOKI ANY GOOD?
SQUEAL
GOOD MORNING!
THAT IS SIMPLY AMAZING!
REALLY!
YOU'RE AMAZING, MRS. HONDA!
NO WAY... DON'T TELL ME...
YUP. OL' MRS. HONDA'S THE NEXT MRS. T.
HER HUSBAND'S GETTING PROMOTED TO DIVISION CHIEF, SO THEY'RE GONNA BE THE TOP DOGS AROUND HERE. EVERYBODY'S ALREADY KISSING HER BUTT.
SWARM SWARM
I SWEAR...
NOTHING EVER CHANGES IN THIS COMPLEX.

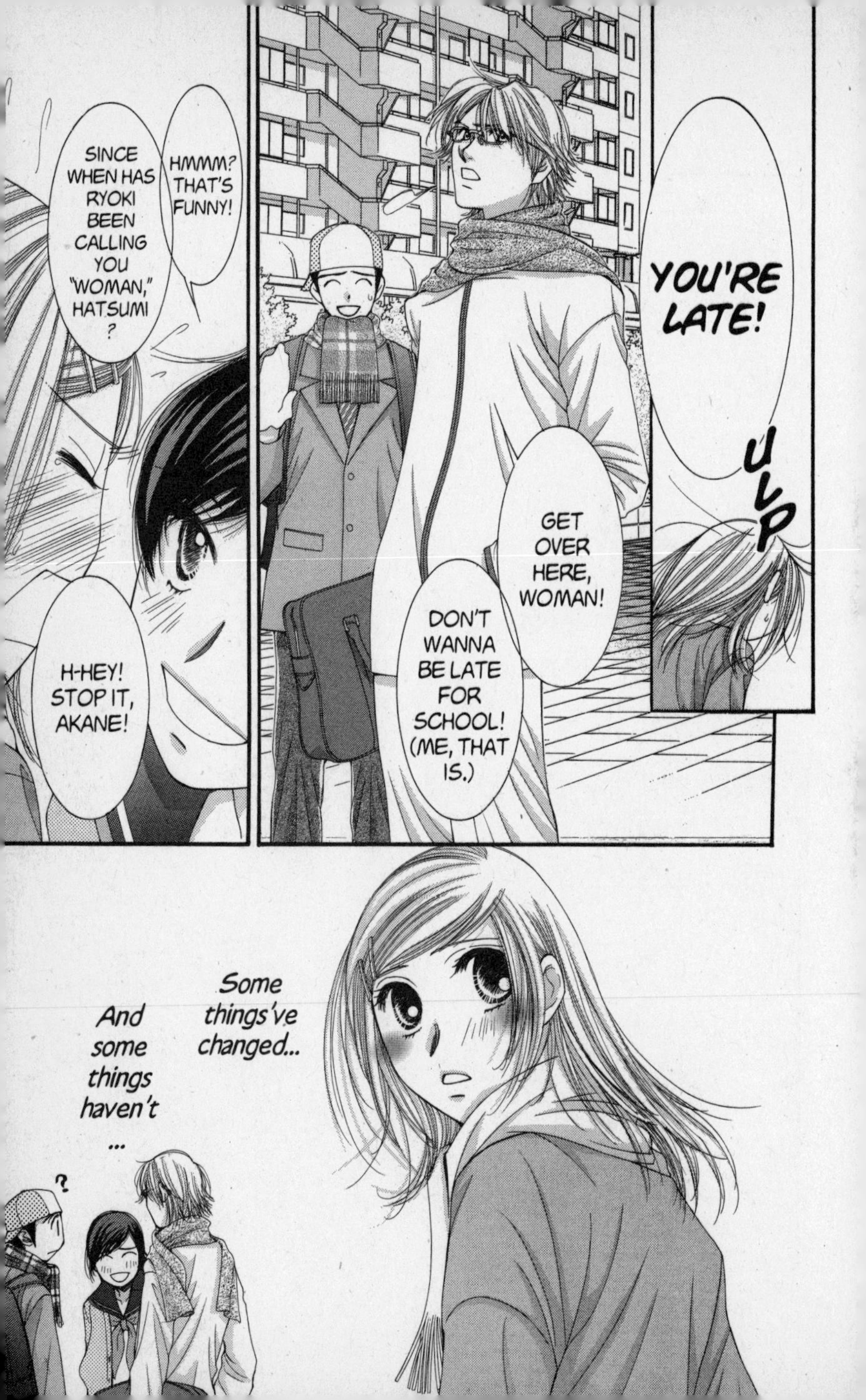
YOU'RE LATE!
ULP
GET OVER HERE, WOMAN!
DON'T WANNA BE LATE FOR SCHOOL! (ME, THAT IS.)
HMMM? THAT'S FUNNY!
SINCE WHEN HAS RYOKI BEEN CALLING YOU "WOMAN," HATSUMI ?
H-HEY! STOP IT, AKANE!
Some things've changed...
And some things haven't ...
?

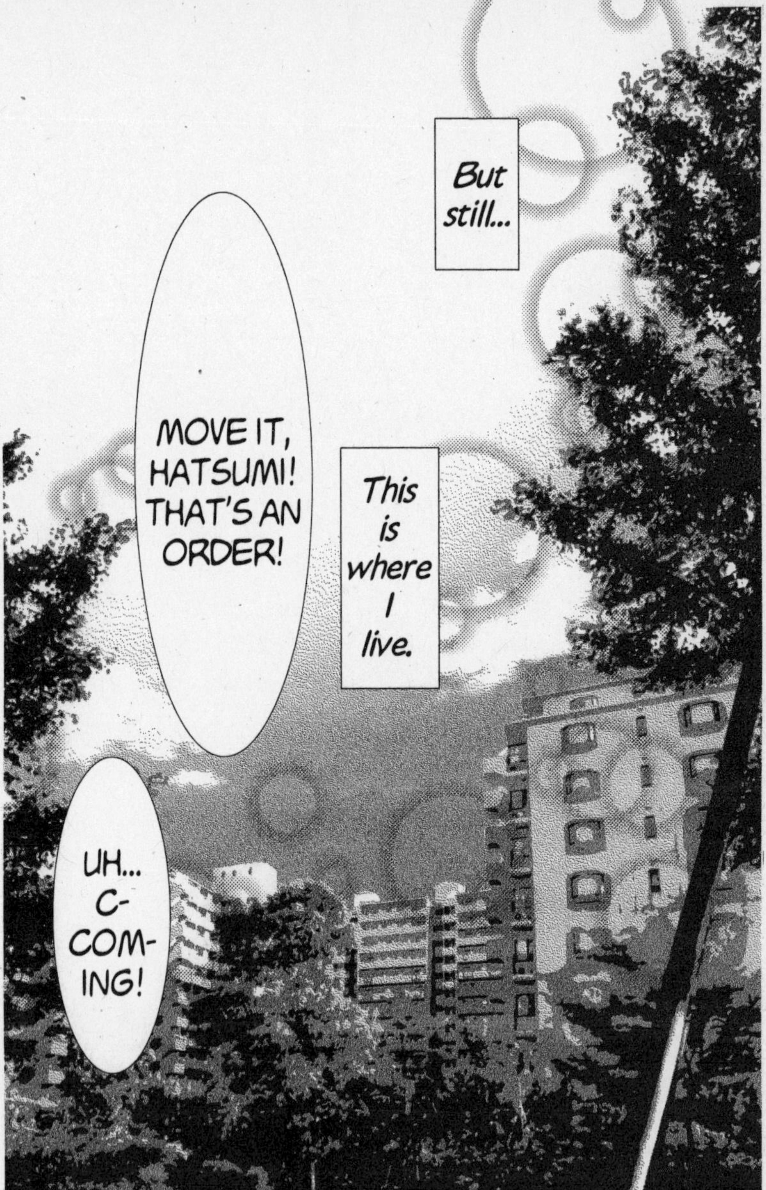
But still...
This is where I live.
MOVE IT, HATSUMI! THAT'S AN ORDER!
UH... C-COMING!

THE END

hot gimmick

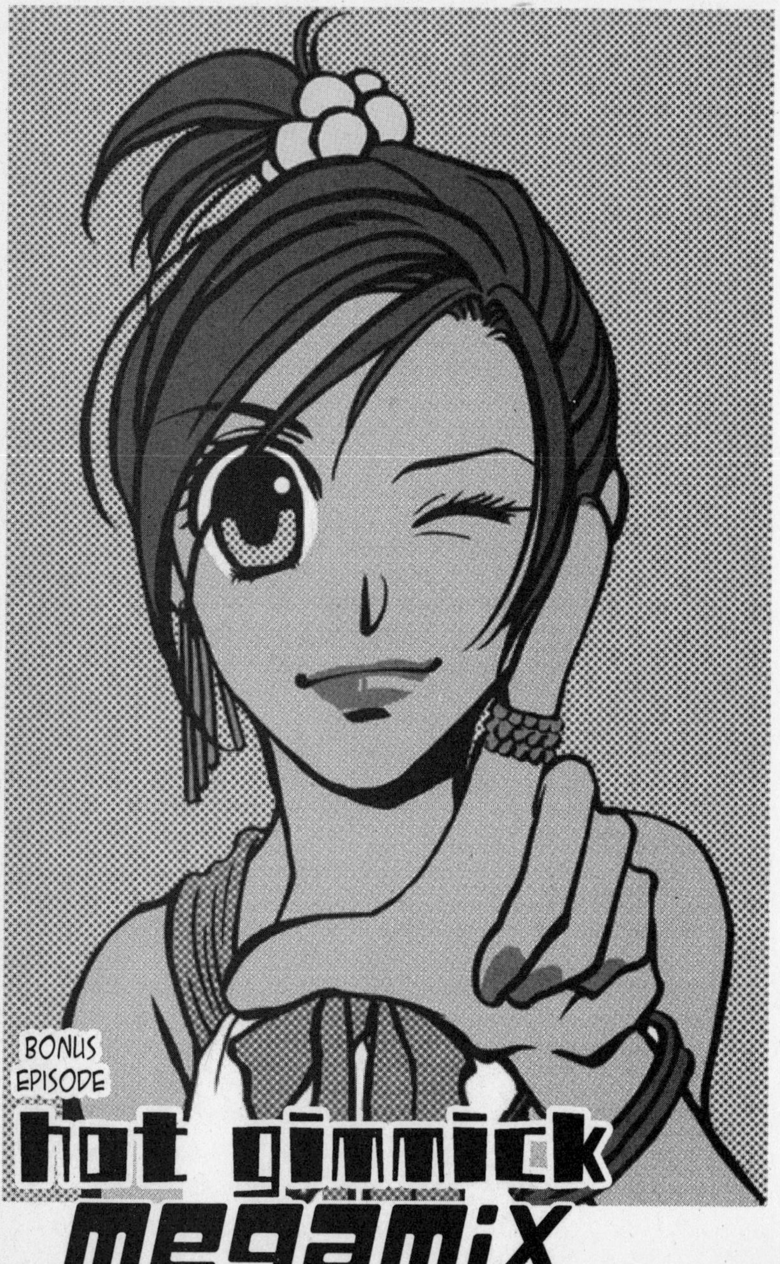
BONUS
EPISODE
hot gimmick
megamiX

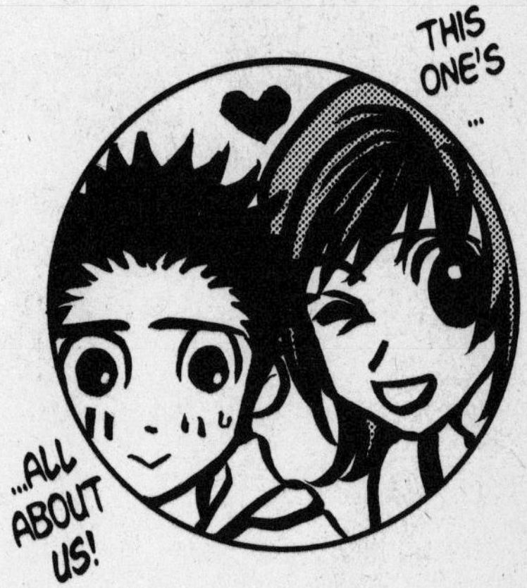
THIS ONE'S ...
...ALL ABOUT US!

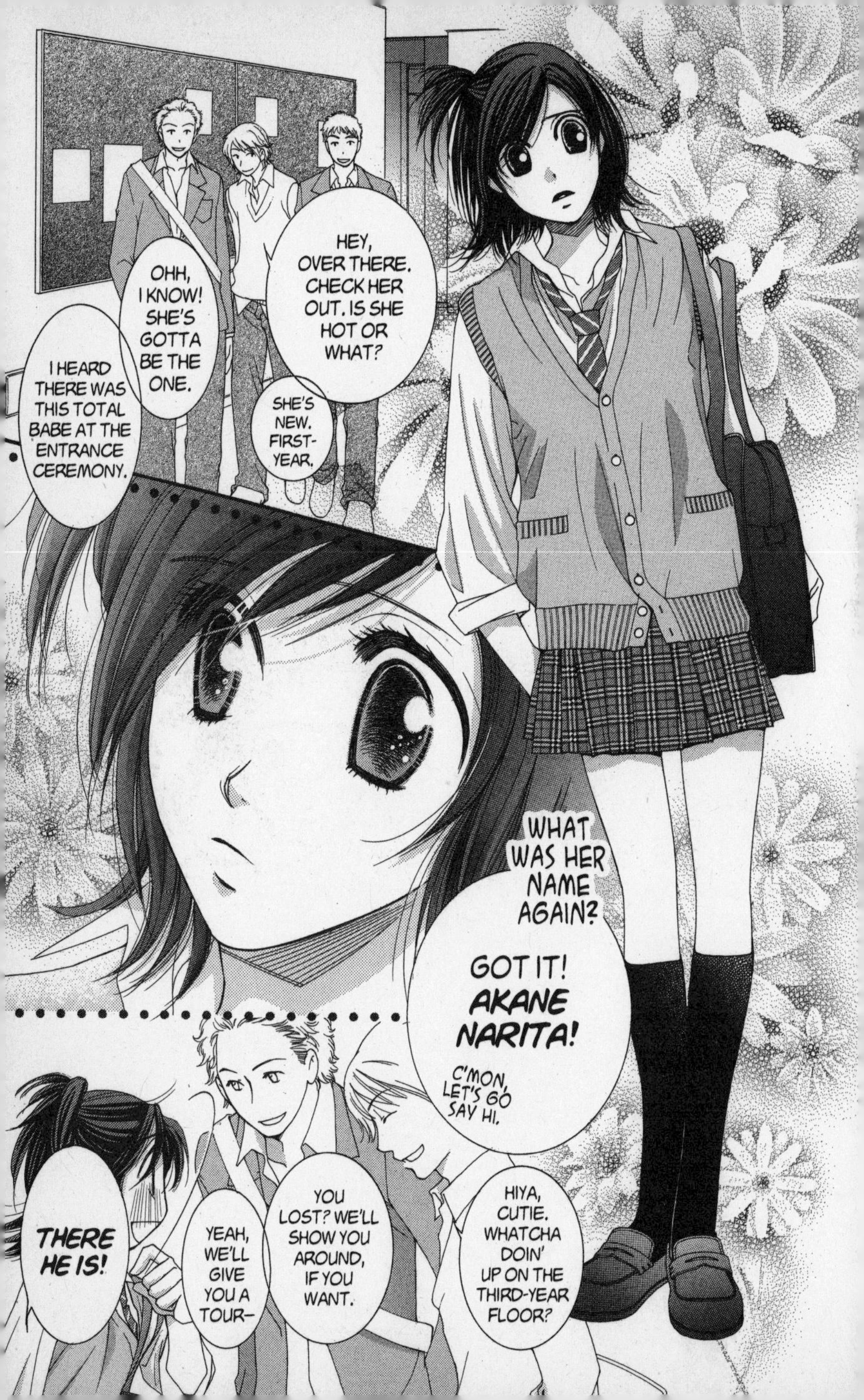
HEY, OVER THERE. CHECK HER OUT. IS SHE HOT OR WHAT?
SHE'S NEW. FIRST-YEAR.
OHH, I KNOW! SHE'S GOTTA BE THE ONE.
I HEARD THERE WAS THIS TOTAL BABE AT THE ENTRANCE CEREMONY.
WHAT WAS HER NAME AGAIN?
GOT IT! AKANE NARITA!
C'MON, LET'S GO SAY HI.
HIYA, CUTIE. WHATCHA DOIN' UP ON THE THIRD-YEAR FLOOR?
YOU LOST? WE'LL SHOW YOU AROUND, IF YOU WANT.
YEAH, WE'LL GIVE YOU A TOUR–
THERE HE IS!

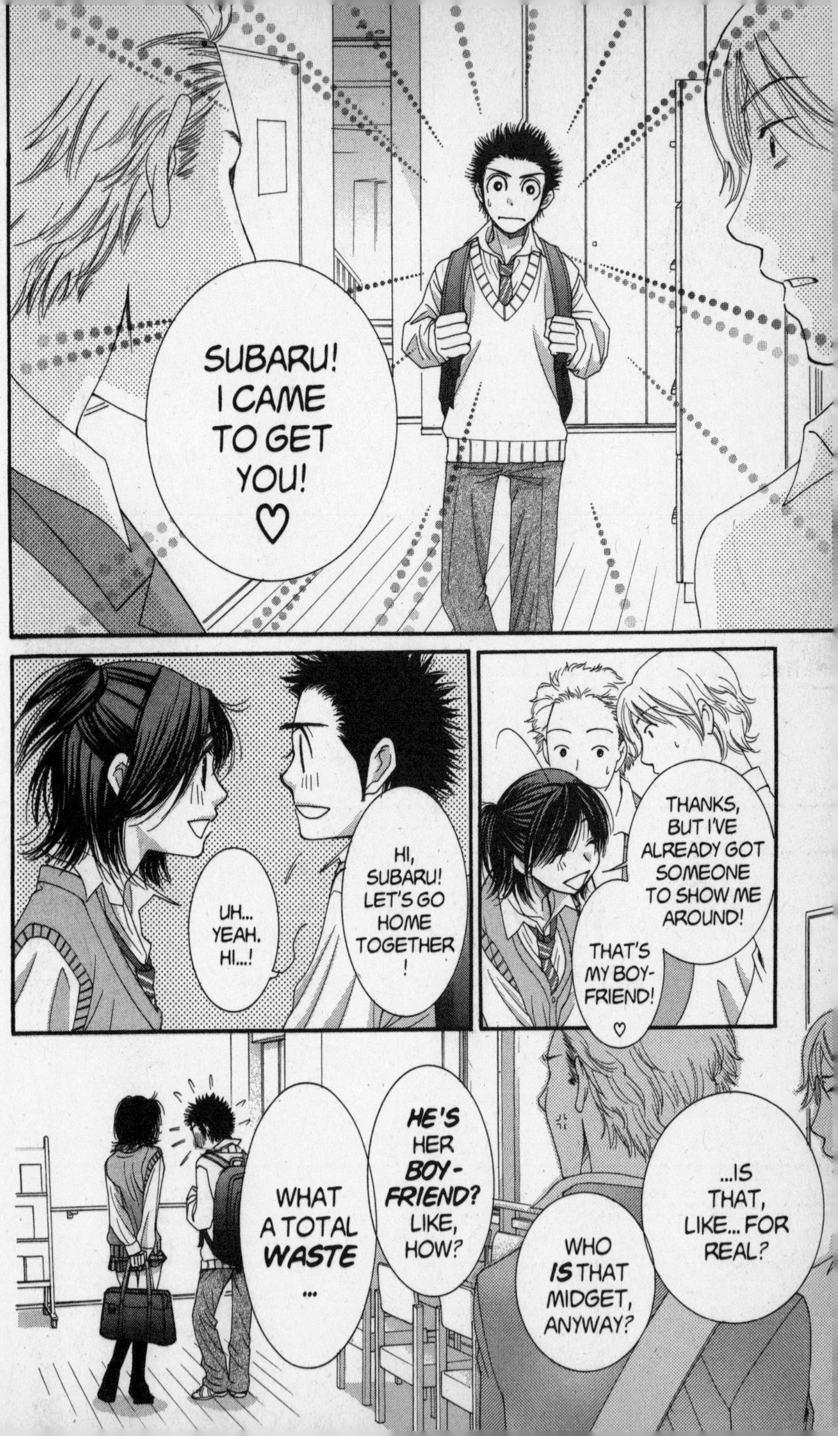
SUBARU! I CAME TO GET YOU! ♡
THANKS, BUT I'VE ALREADY GOT SOMEONE TO SHOW ME AROUND!
THAT'S MY BOY-FRIEND! ♡
HI, SUBARU! LET'S GO HOME TOGETHER!
UH... YEAH. HI...!
...IS THAT, LIKE... FOR REAL?
WHO **IS** THAT MIDGET, ANYWAY?
HE'S HER ***BOY-FRIEND?*** LIKE, HOW?
WHAT A TOTAL ***WASTE***...

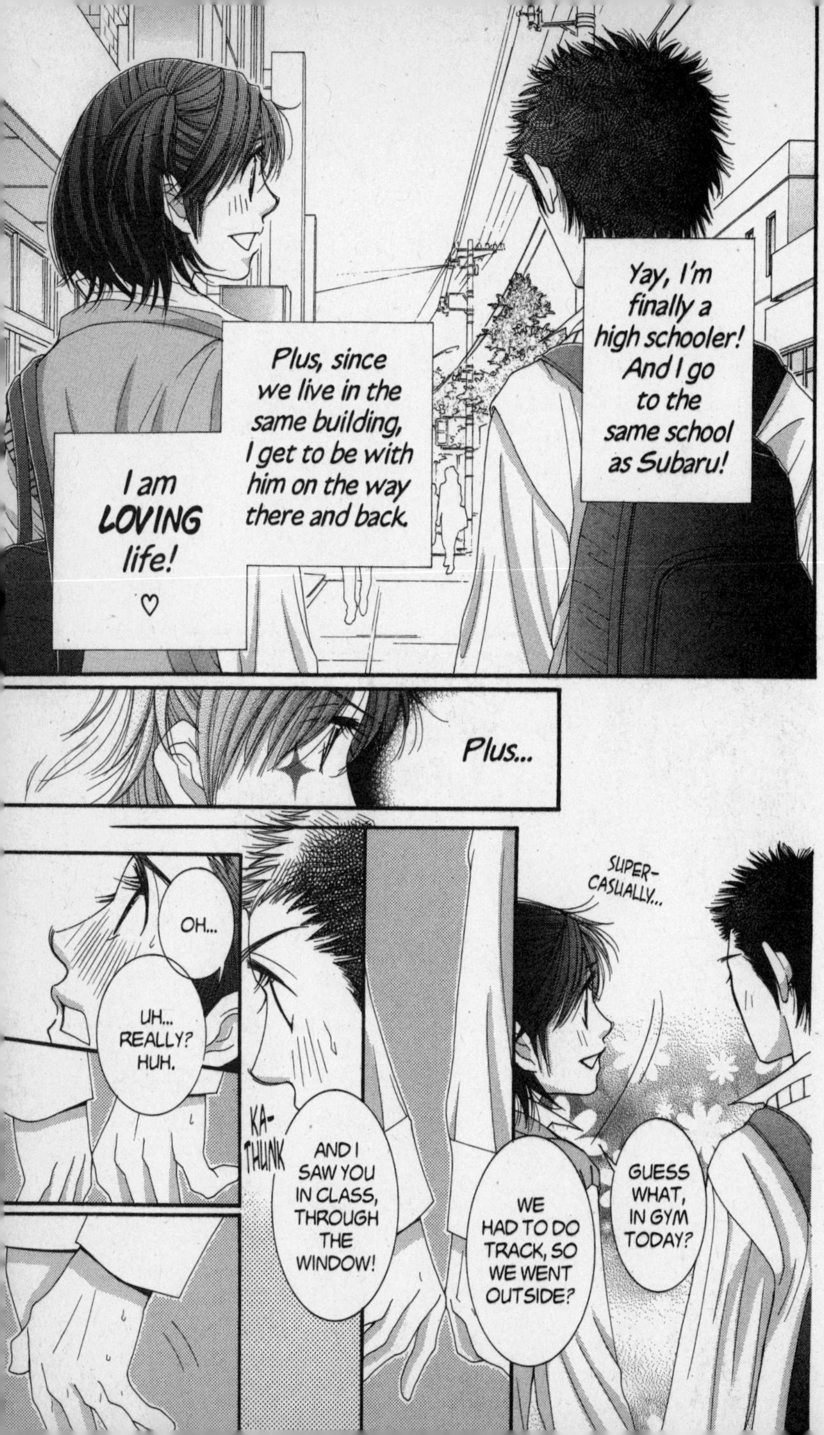
Yay, I'm finally a high schooler! And I go to the same school as Subaru!
Plus, since we live in the same building, I get to be with him on the way there and back.
I am **LOVING** life! ♡
Plus...
SUPER-CASUALLY...
GUESS WHAT, IN GYM TODAY?
WE HAD TO DO TRACK, SO WE WENT OUTSIDE?
AND I SAW YOU IN CLASS, THROUGH THE WINDOW!
KA-THUNK
OH...
UH... REALLY? HUH.

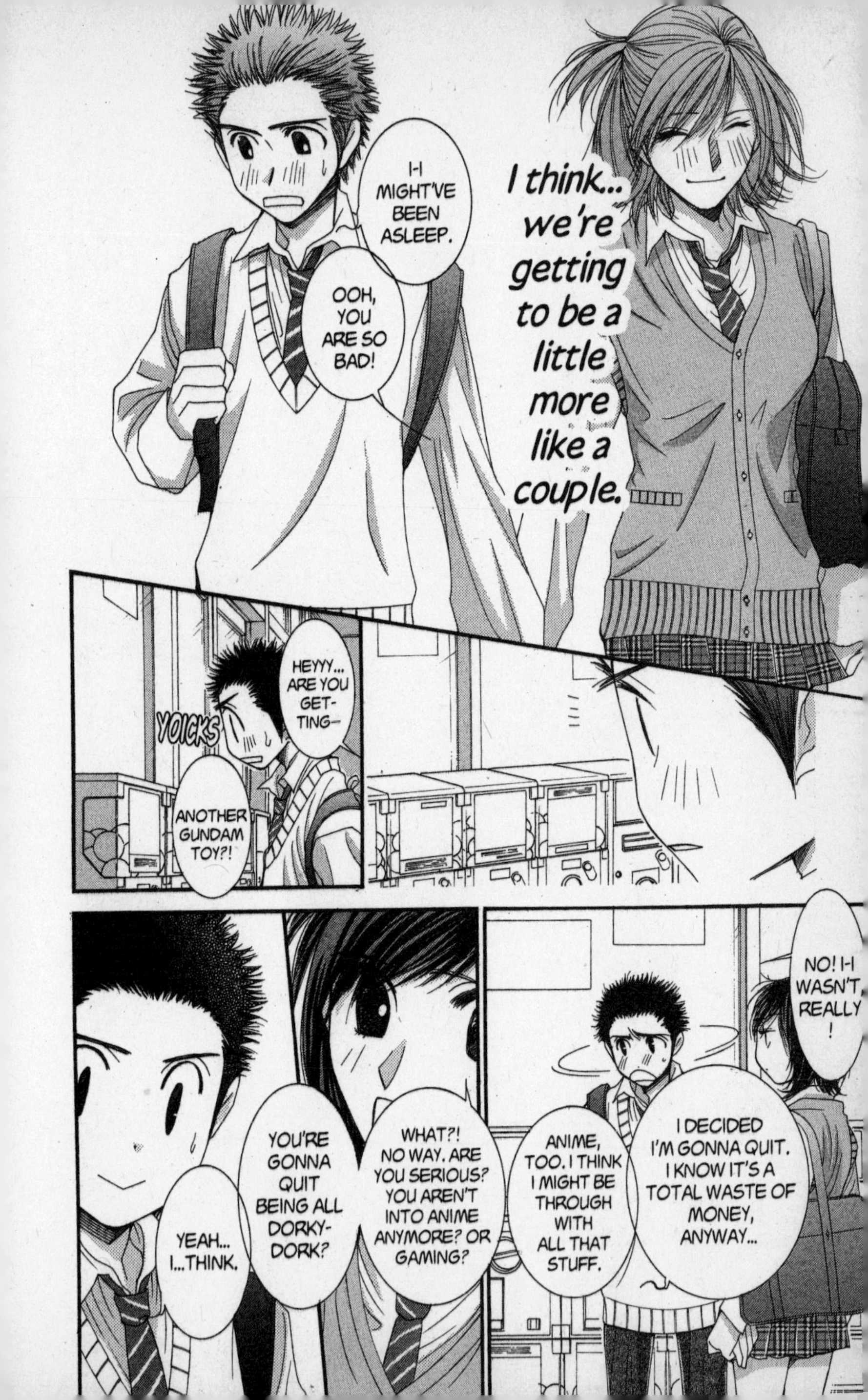
I-I MIGHT'VE BEEN ASLEEP.
OOH, YOU ARE SO BAD!
I think... we're getting to be a little more like a couple.
HEYYY... ARE YOU GET-TING—
YOICKS
ANOTHER GUNDAM TOY?!
NO! I-I WASN'T, REALLY!
I DECIDED I'M GONNA QUIT. I KNOW IT'S A TOTAL WASTE OF MONEY, ANYWAY...
ANIME, TOO. I THINK I MIGHT BE THROUGH WITH ALL THAT STUFF.
WHAT?! NO WAY. ARE YOU SERIOUS? YOU AREN'T INTO ANIME ANYMORE? OR GAMING?
YOU'RE GONNA QUIT BEING ALL DORKY-DORK?
YEAH... I...THINK.

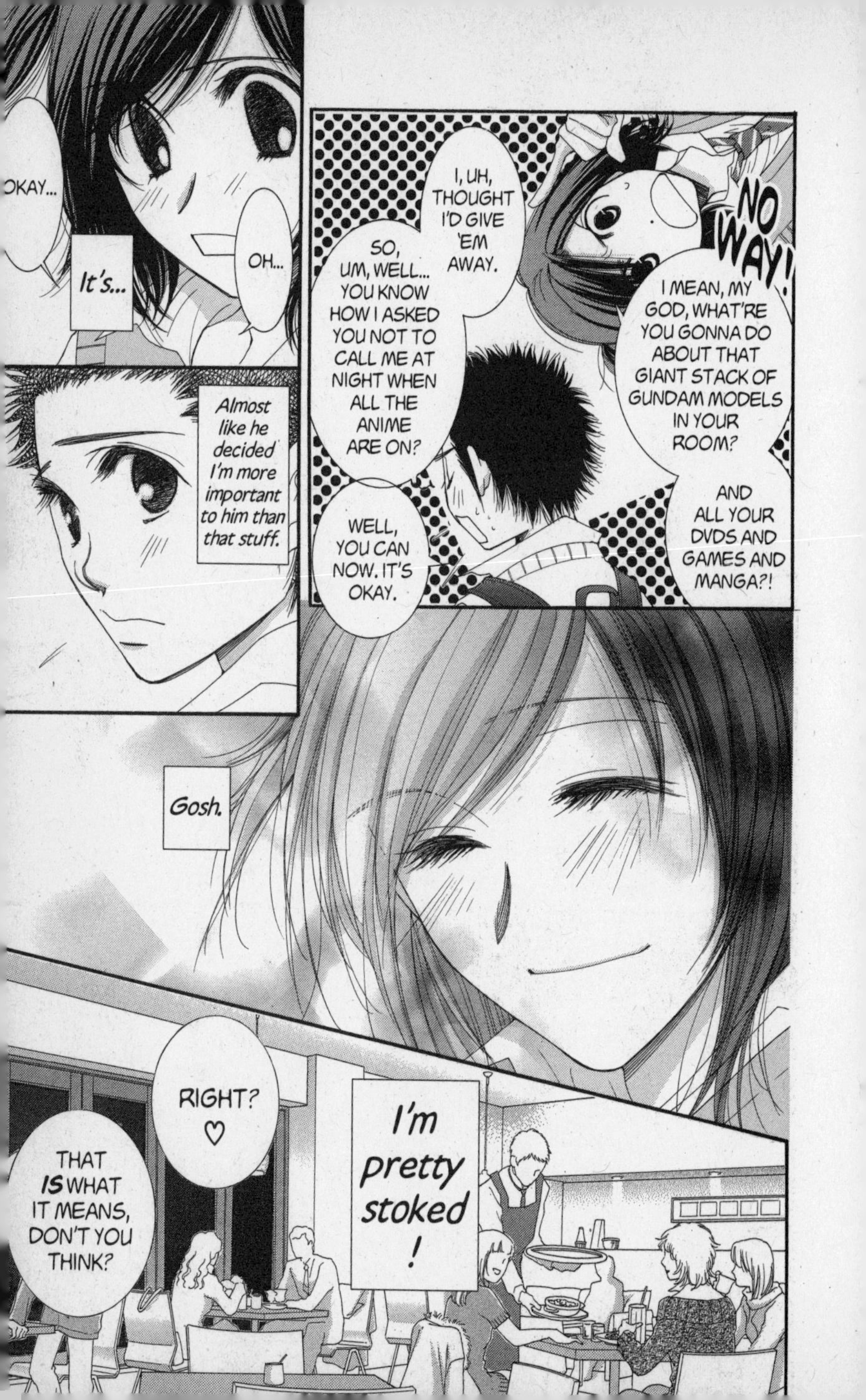

I, UH, THOUGHT I'D GIVE 'EM AWAY.
NO WAY!
I MEAN, MY GOD, WHAT'RE YOU GONNA DO ABOUT THAT GIANT STACK OF GUNDAM MODELS IN YOUR ROOM?
AND ALL YOUR DVDS AND GAMES AND MANGA?!
SO, UM, WELL... YOU KNOW HOW I ASKED YOU NOT TO CALL ME AT NIGHT WHEN ALL THE ANIME ARE ON?
WELL, YOU CAN NOW. IT'S OKAY.
OH...
It's...
OKAY...
Almost like he decided I'm more important to him than that stuff.
Gosh.
I'm pretty stoked!
RIGHT? ♡
THAT **IS** WHAT IT MEANS, DON'T YOU THINK?

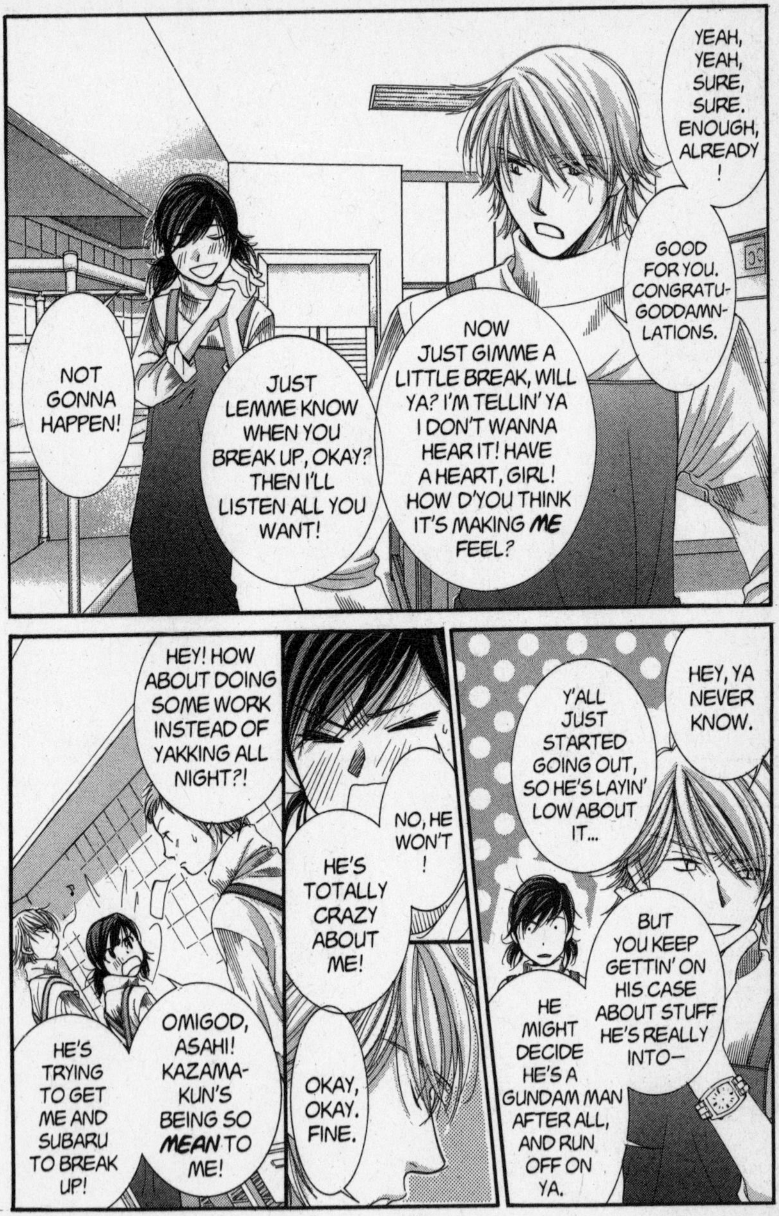
YEAH, YEAH, SURE, SURE. ENOUGH, ALREADY!
GOOD FOR YOU. CONGRATU-GODDAMN-LATIONS.
NOW JUST GIMME A LITTLE BREAK, WILL YA? I'M TELLIN' YA I DON'T WANNA HEAR IT! HAVE A HEART, GIRL! HOW D'YOU THINK IT'S MAKING ***ME*** FEEL?
JUST LEMME KNOW WHEN YOU BREAK UP, OKAY? THEN I'LL LISTEN ALL YOU WANT!
NOT GONNA HAPPEN!
HEY, YA NEVER KNOW.
Y'ALL JUST STARTED GOING OUT, SO HE'S LAYIN' LOW ABOUT IT...
BUT YOU KEEP GETTIN' ON HIS CASE ABOUT STUFF HE'S REALLY INTO—
HE MIGHT DECIDE HE'S A GUNDAM MAN AFTER ALL, AND RUN OFF ON YA.
NO, HE WON'T!
HE'S TOTALLY CRAZY ABOUT ME!
OKAY, OKAY. FINE.
HEY! HOW ABOUT DOING SOME WORK INSTEAD OF YAKKING ALL NIGHT?!
OMIGOD, ASAHI! KAZAMA-KUN'S BEING SO ***MEAN*** TO ME!
HE'S TRYING TO GET ME AND SUBARU TO BREAK UP!

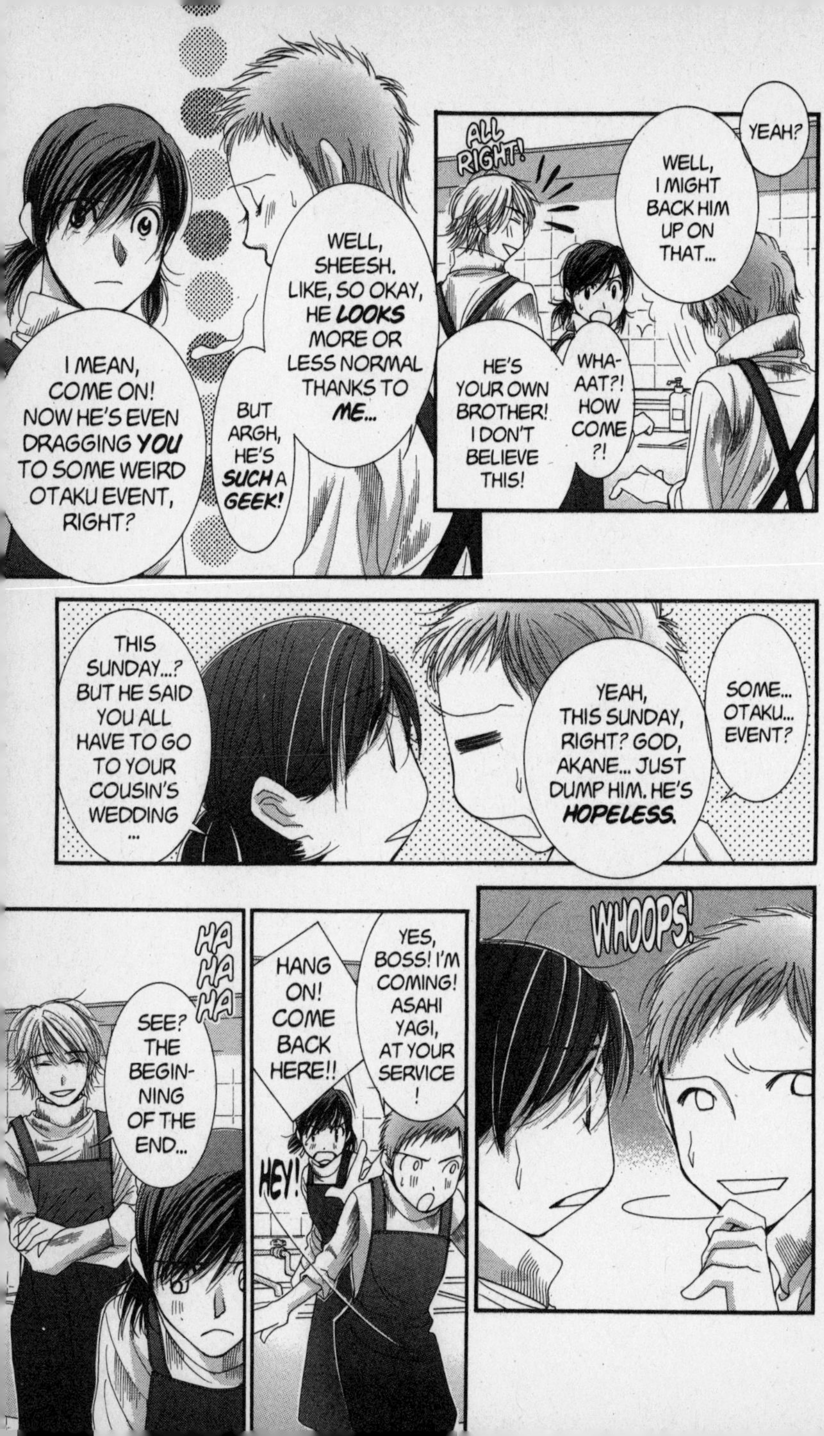
YEAH?
WELL, I MIGHT BACK HIM UP ON THAT...
ALL RIGHT!
WHA-AAT?! HOW COME?!
HE'S YOUR OWN BROTHER! I DON'T BELIEVE THIS!
WELL, SHEESH. LIKE, SO OKAY, HE **LOOKS** MORE OR LESS NORMAL THANKS TO **ME...**
BUT ARGH, HE'S **SUCH** A **GEEK!**
I MEAN, COME ON! NOW HE'S EVEN DRAGGING **YOU** TO SOME WEIRD OTAKU EVENT, RIGHT?
SOME... OTAKU... EVENT?
YEAH, THIS SUNDAY, RIGHT? GOD, AKANE... JUST DUMP HIM. HE'S **HOPELESS.**
THIS SUNDAY...? BUT HE SAID YOU ALL HAVE TO GO TO YOUR COUSIN'S WEDDING...
WHOOPS!
YES, BOSS! I'M COMING! ASAHI YAGI, AT YOUR SERVICE!
HANG ON! COME BACK HERE!!
HEY!
HA HA HA
SEE? THE BEGIN-NING OF THE END...

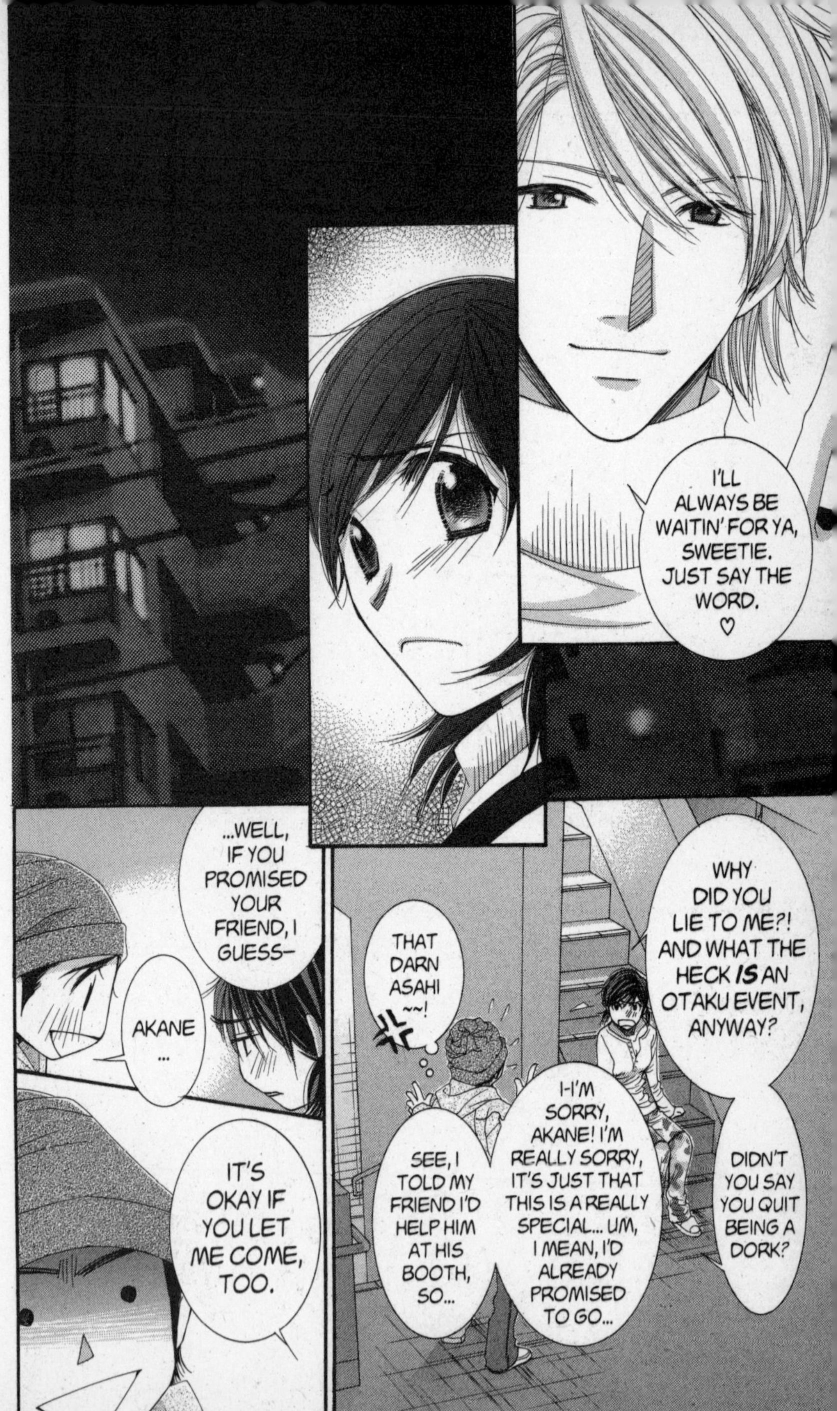
I'LL ALWAYS BE WAITIN' FOR YA, SWEETIE. JUST SAY THE WORD. ♡
WHY DID YOU LIE TO ME?! AND WHAT THE HECK ***IS*** AN OTAKU EVENT, ANYWAY?
DIDN'T YOU SAY YOU QUIT BEING A DORK?
THAT DARN ASAHI ~~!
I-I'M SORRY, AKANE! I'M REALLY SORRY, IT'S JUST THAT THIS IS A REALLY SPECIAL... UM, I MEAN, I'D ALREADY PROMISED TO GO...
SEE, I TOLD MY FRIEND I'D HELP HIM AT HIS BOOTH, SO...
...WELL, IF YOU PROMISED YOUR FRIEND, I GUESS–
AKANE ...
IT'S OKAY IF YOU LET ME COME, TOO.

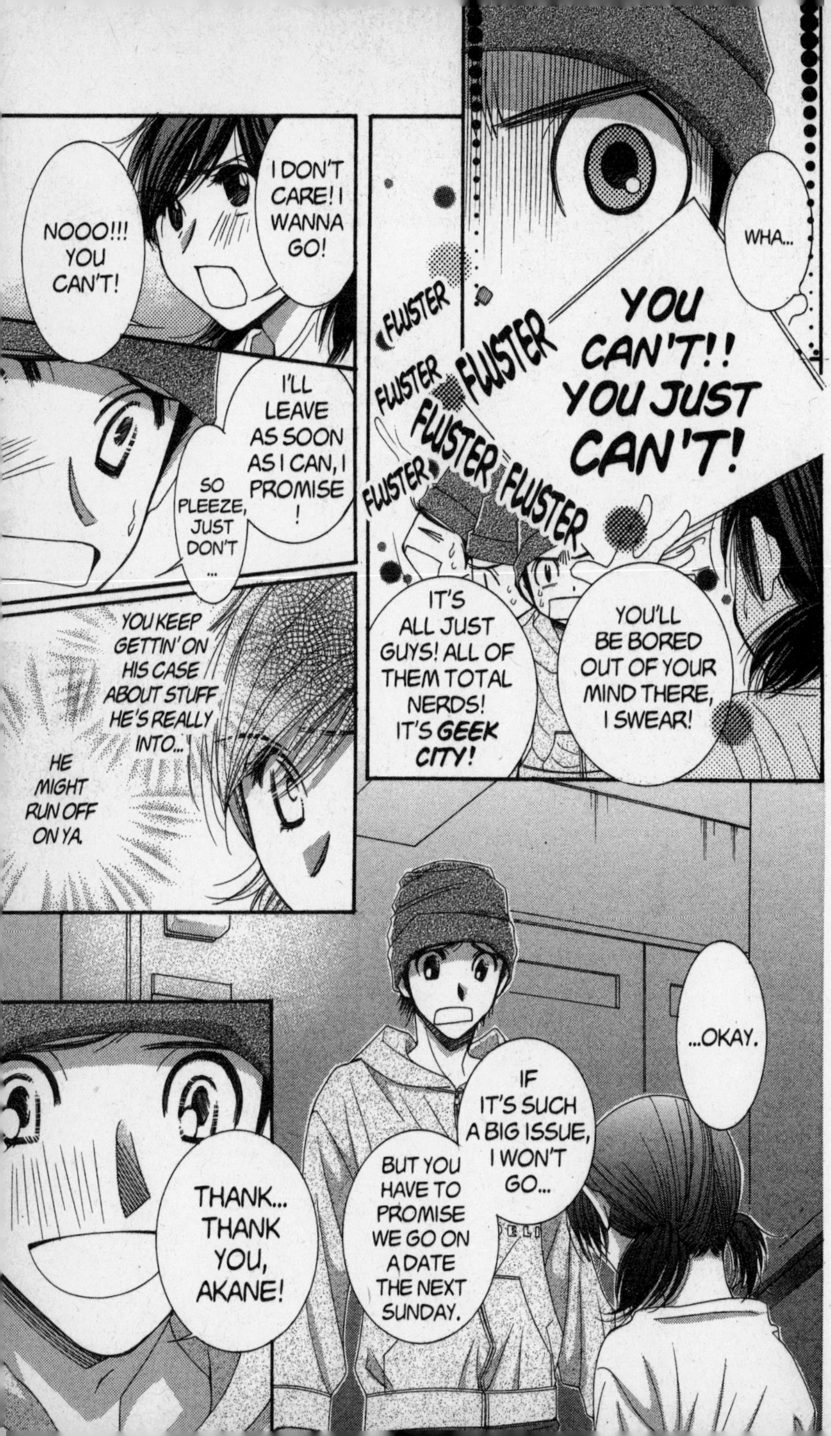

WHA...
YOU CAN'T!! YOU JUST CAN'T!
FLUSTER FLUSTER FLUSTER FLUSTER FLUSTER FLUSTER
YOU'LL BE BORED OUT OF YOUR MIND THERE, I SWEAR!
IT'S ALL JUST GUYS! ALL OF THEM TOTAL NERDS! IT'S **GEEK CITY!**
I DON'T CARE! I WANNA GO!
NOOO!!! YOU CAN'T!
I'LL LEAVE AS SOON AS I CAN, I PROMISE!
SO PLEEZE, JUST DON'T...
YOU KEEP GETTIN' ON HIS CASE ABOUT STUFF HE'S REALLY INTO...
HE MIGHT RUN OFF ON YA.
...OKAY.
IF IT'S SUCH A BIG ISSUE, I WON'T GO...
BUT YOU HAVE TO PROMISE WE GO ON A DATE THE NEXT SUNDAY.
THANK... THANK YOU, AKANE!

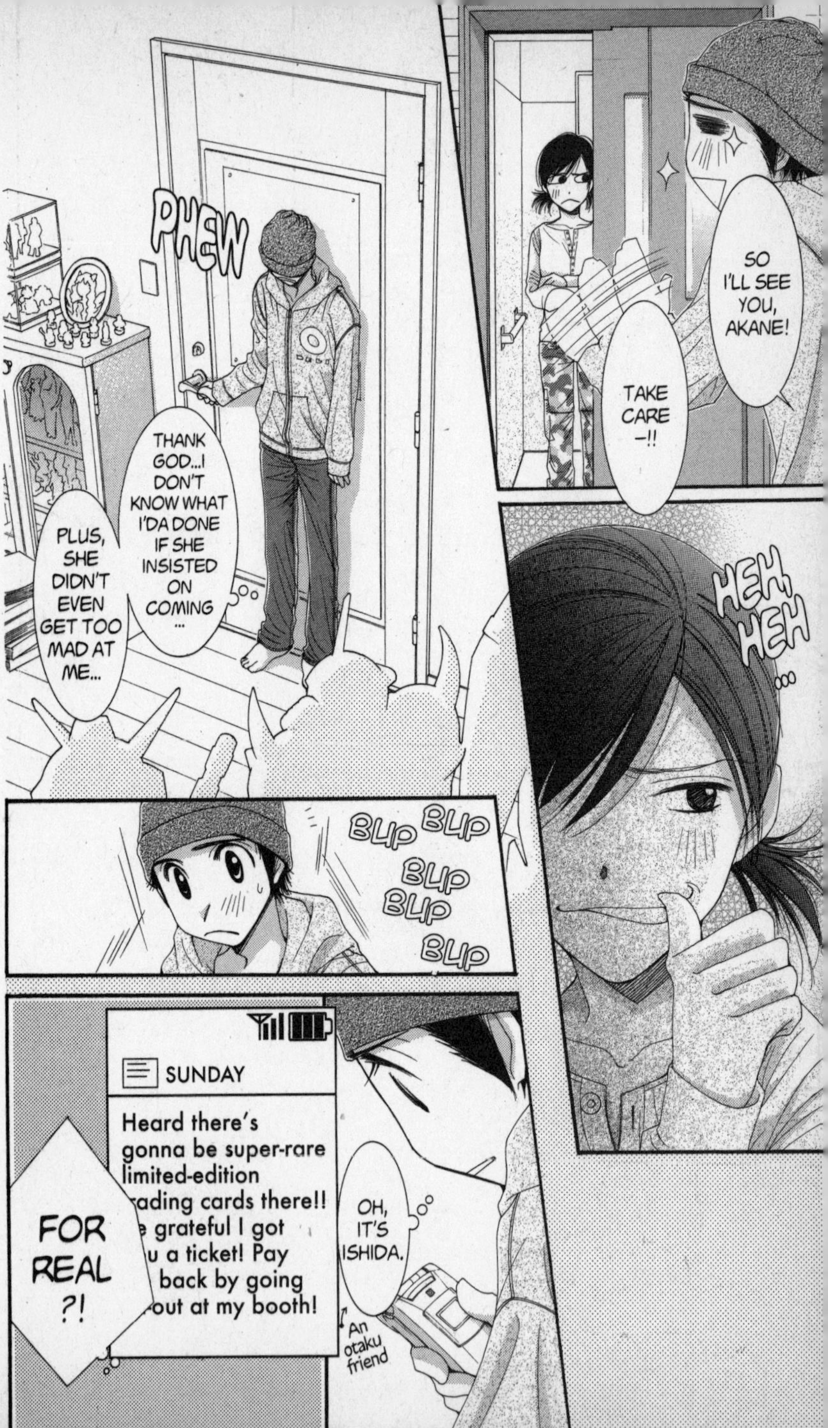
SO I'LL SEE YOU, AKANE!
TAKE CARE—!!
PHEW
THANK GOD...I DON'T KNOW WHAT I'DA DONE IF SHE INSISTED ON COMING...
PLUS, SHE DIDN'T EVEN GET TOO MAD AT ME...
HEH HEH...
BLIP BLIP BLIP BLIP BLIP
SUNDAY
Heard there's gonna be super-rare limited-edition
rading cards there!!
e grateful I got
u a ticket! Pay
back by going
-out at my booth!
OH, IT'S ISHIDA.
An otaku friend
FOR REAL?!

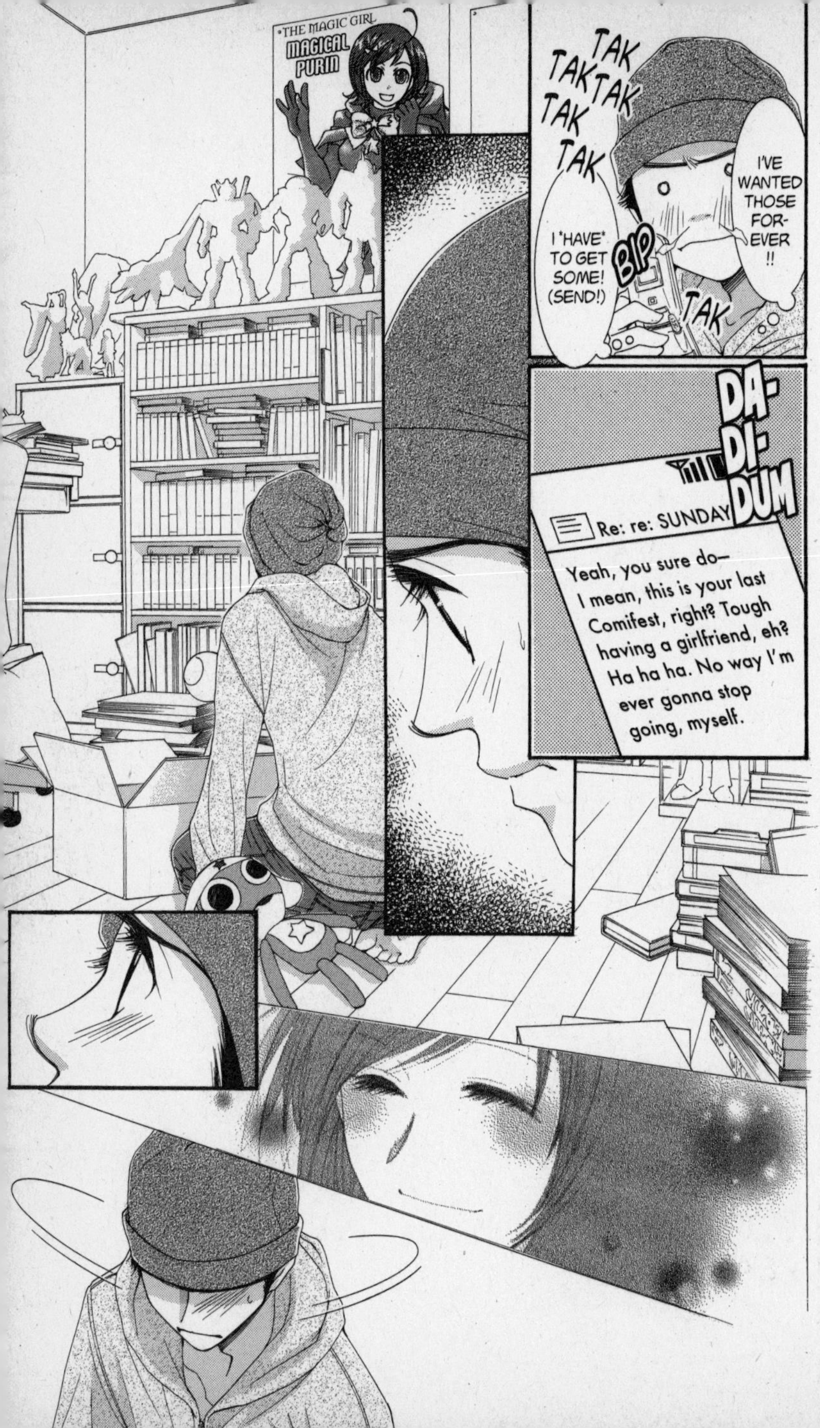
TAK TAK TAK TAK TAK TAK
I'VE WANTED THOSE FOR-EVER !!
I *HAVE* TO GET SOME! (SEND!)
BIP
TAK
DA-DI-DUM
Re: re: SUNDAY
Yeah, you sure do— I mean, this is your last Comifest, right? Tough having a girlfriend, eh? Ha ha ha. No way I'm ever gonna stop going, myself.
THE MAGIC GIRL
MAGICAL PURIN

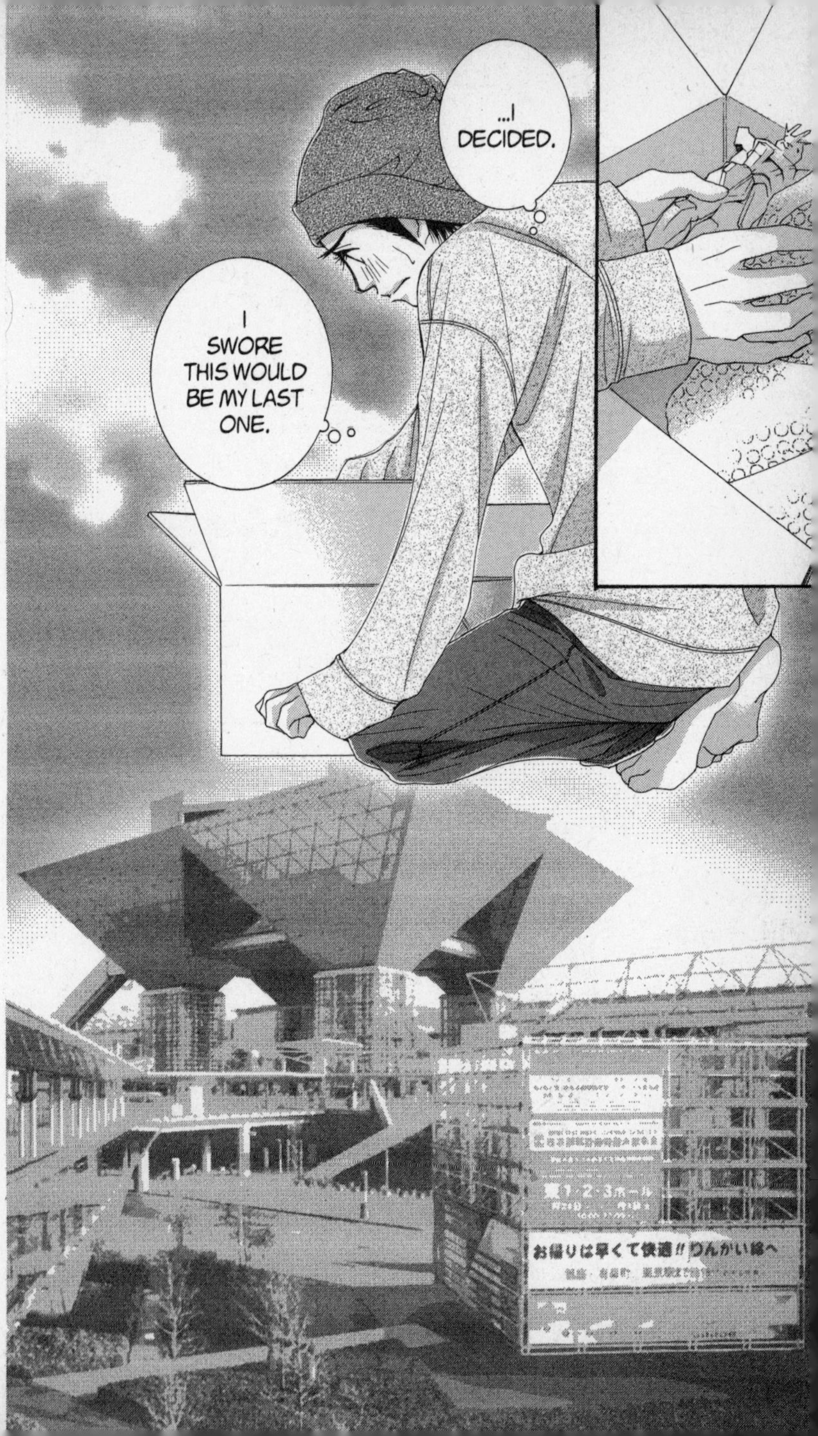
...I DECIDED.
I SWORE THIS WOULD BE MY LAST ONE.
東1·2·3ホール
お帰りは早くて快適!! りんかい線へ

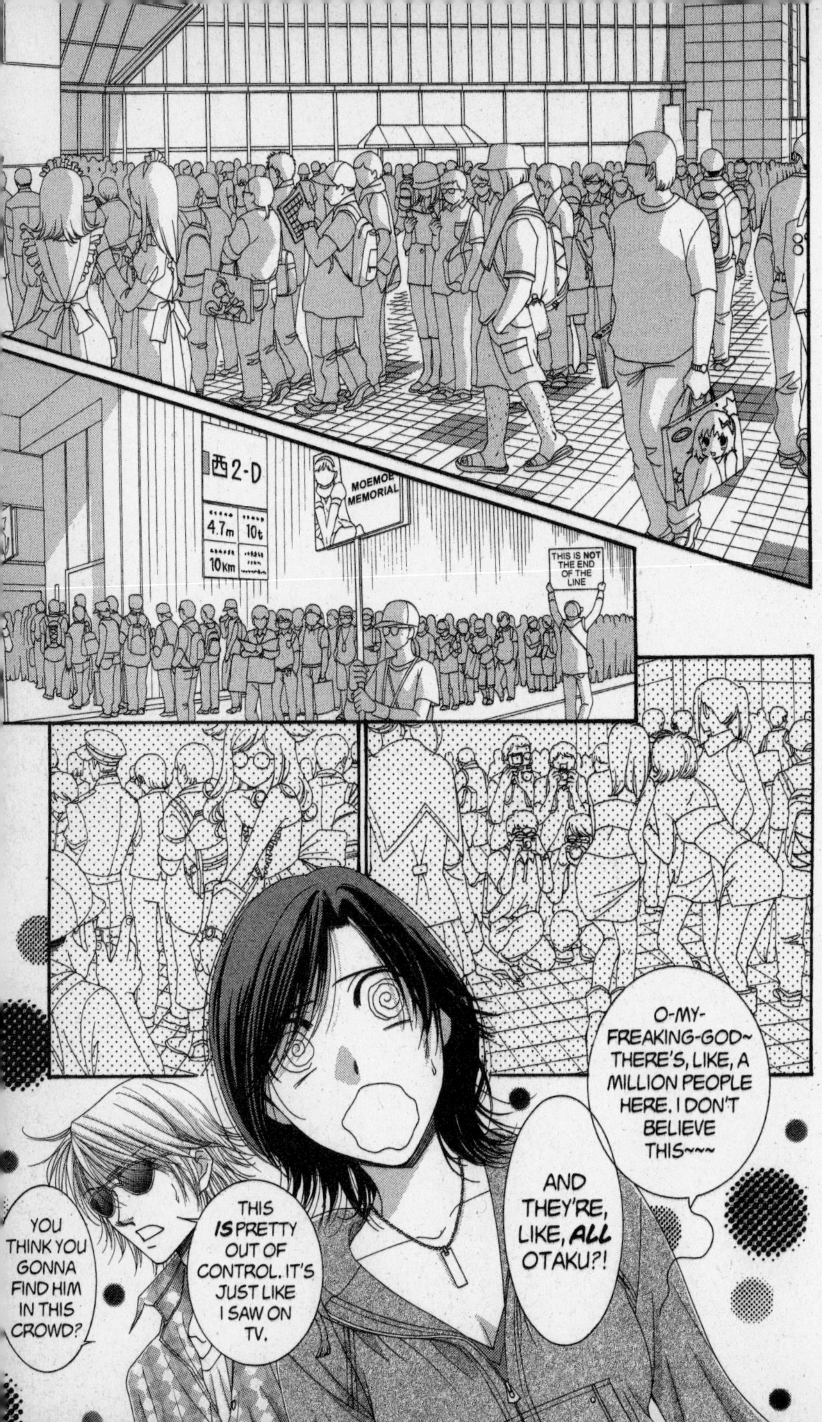
THIS IS NOT THE END OF THE LINE
MOEMOE MEMORIAL
西2-D
4.7m
10t
10km
O-MY-FREAKING-GOD~ THERE'S, LIKE, A MILLION PEOPLE HERE. I DON'T BELIEVE THIS~~~
AND THEY'RE, LIKE, ALL OTAKU?!
THIS IS PRETTY OUT OF CONTROL. IT'S JUST LIKE I SAW ON TV.
YOU THINK YOU GONNA FIND HIM IN THIS CROWD?

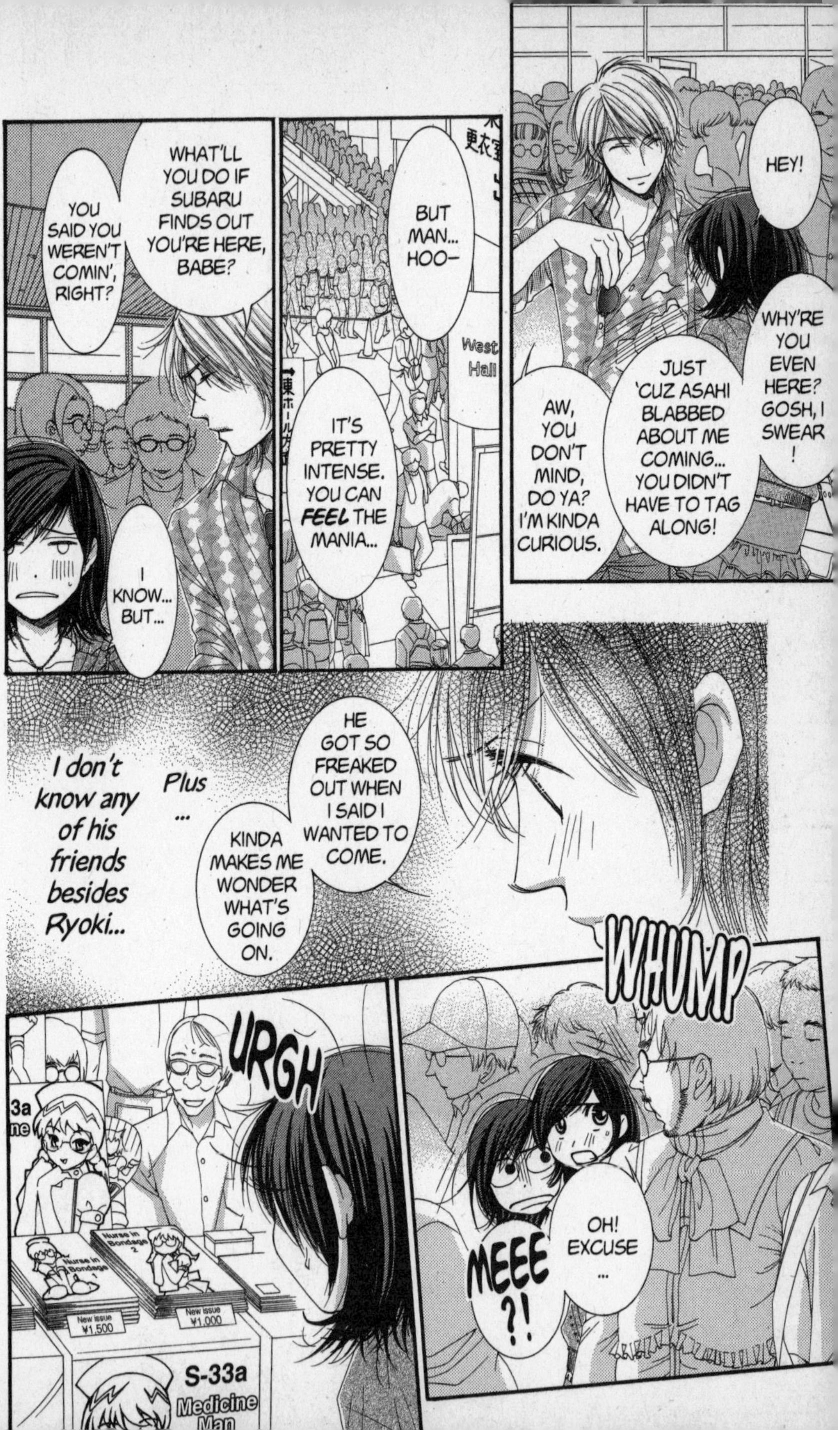
HEY!
WHY'RE YOU EVEN HERE? GOSH, I SWEAR!
JUST 'CUZ ASAHI BLABBED ABOUT ME COMING... YOU DIDN'T HAVE TO TAG ALONG!
AW, YOU DON'T MIND, DO YA? I'M KINDA CURIOUS.
更衣室
West Hall
BUT MAN... HOO-
IT'S PRETTY INTENSE. YOU CAN **FEEL** THE MANIA...
WHAT'LL YOU DO IF SUBARU FINDS OUT YOU'RE HERE, BABE?
YOU SAID YOU WEREN'T COMIN', RIGHT?
I KNOW... BUT...
HE GOT SO FREAKED OUT WHEN I SAID I WANTED TO COME.
KINDA MAKES ME WONDER WHAT'S GOING ON.
Plus ...
I don't know any of his friends besides Ryoki...
WHUMP
OH! EXCUSE ...
MEEE ?!
URGH
Nurse in Bondage 1
Nurse in Bondage 2
New issue ¥1,500
New issue ¥1,000
S-33a
Medicine Man

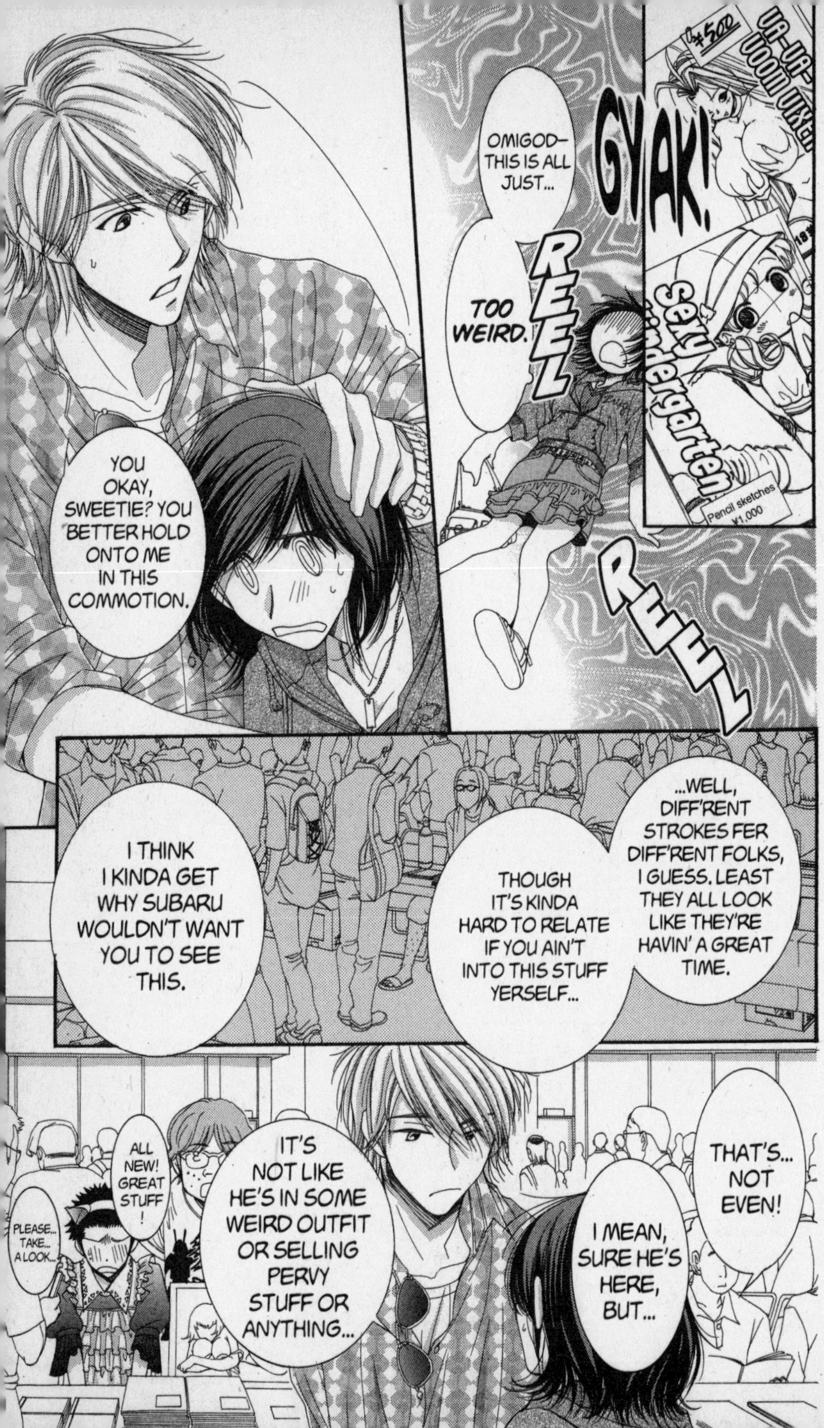
UA-UA-VOOM VIXEN
¥500
GYAK!
OMIGOD— THIS IS ALL JUST...
TOO WEIRD.
REEL
18
sexy indergarten
Pencil sketches ¥1,000
REEL
YOU OKAY, SWEETIE? YOU BETTER HOLD ONTO ME IN THIS COMMOTION.
...WELL, DIFF'RENT STROKES FER DIFF'RENT FOLKS, I GUESS. LEAST THEY ALL LOOK LIKE THEY'RE HAVIN' A GREAT TIME.
THOUGH IT'S KINDA HARD TO RELATE IF YOU AIN'T INTO THIS STUFF YERSELF...
I THINK I KINDA GET WHY SUBARU WOULDN'T WANT YOU TO SEE THIS.
THAT'S... NOT EVEN!
I MEAN, SURE HE'S HERE, BUT...
IT'S NOT LIKE HE'S IN SOME WEIRD OUTFIT OR SELLING PERVY STUFF OR ANYTHING...
ALL NEW! GREAT STUFF!
PLEASE... TAKE... A LOOK...

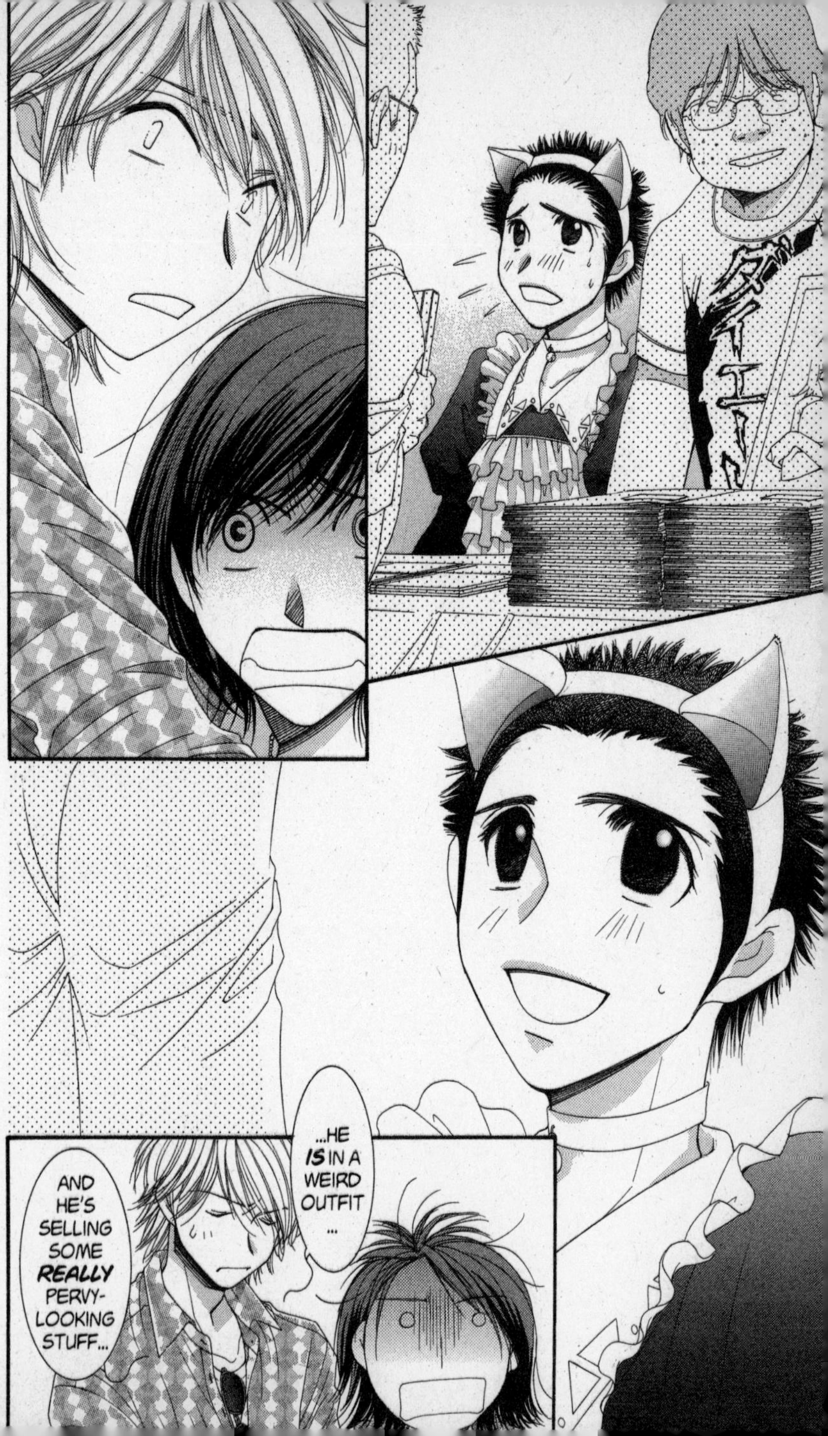
...HE *IS* IN A WEIRD OUTFIT ...
AND HE'S SELLING SOME ***REALLY*** PERVY-LOOKING STUFF...

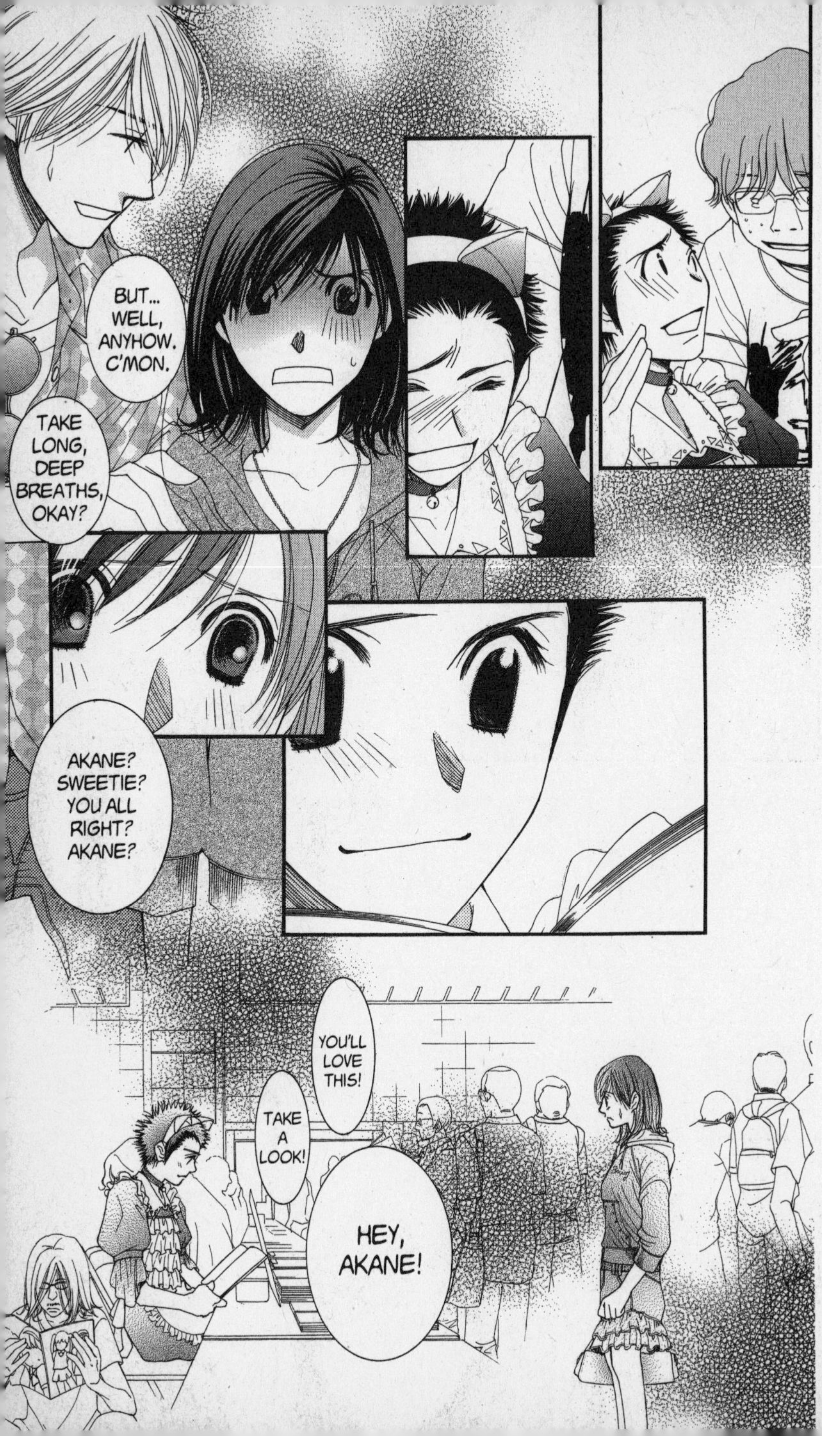
BUT... WELL, ANYHOW. C'MON.
TAKE LONG, DEEP BREATHS, OKAY?
AKANE? SWEETIE? YOU ALL RIGHT? AKANE?
YOU'LL LOVE THIS!
TAKE A LOOK!
HEY, AKANE!

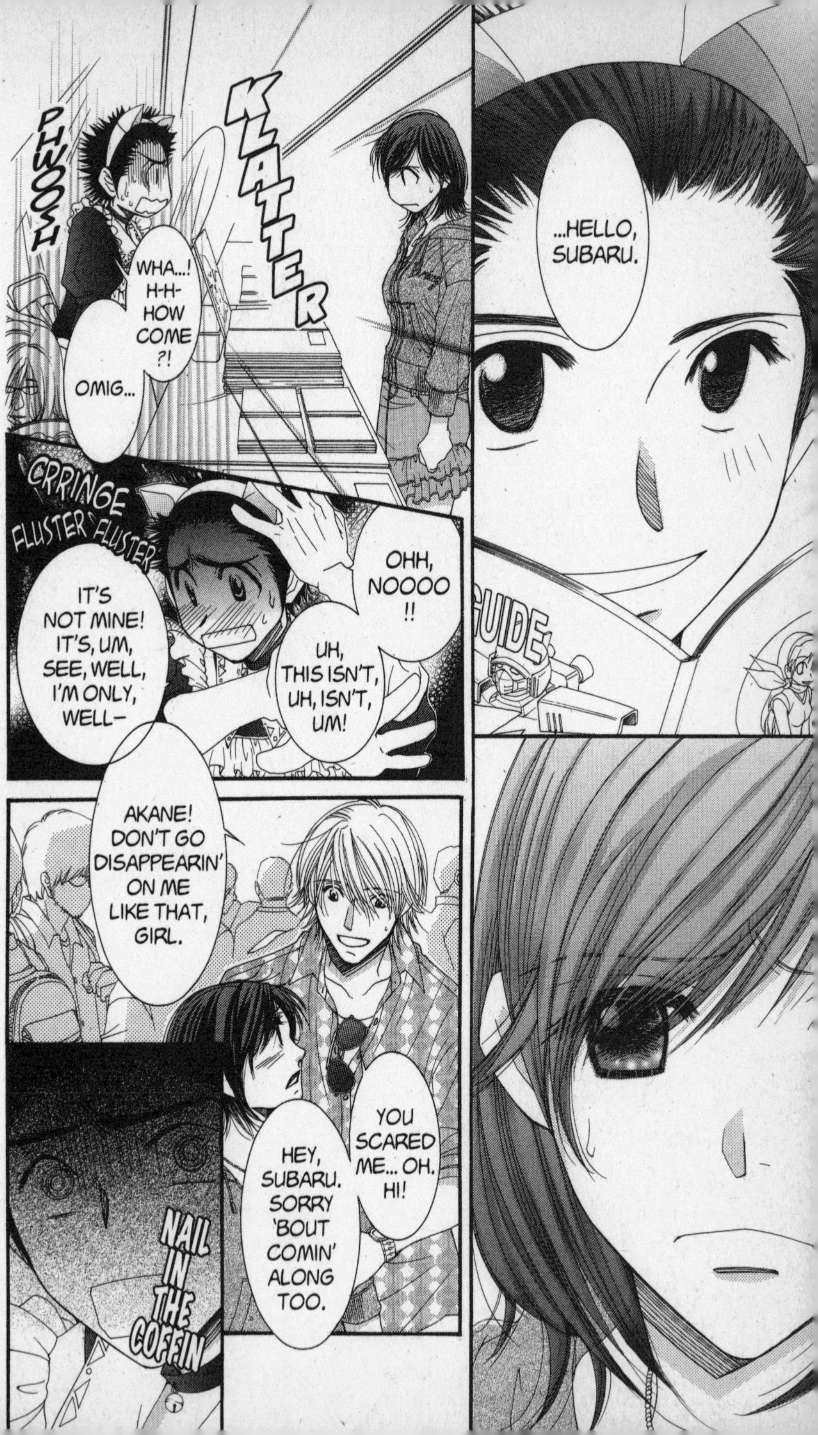

...HELLO, SUBARU.
KLATTER
PHWOOSH
WHA...! H-H-HOW COME?!
OMIG...
OHH, NOOOO!!
UH, THIS ISN'T, UH, ISN'T, UM!
CRRINGE
FLUSTER FLUSTER
IT'S NOT MINE! IT'S, UM, SEE, WELL, I'M ONLY, WELL—
GUIDE
AKANE! DON'T GO DISAPPEARIN' ON ME LIKE THAT, GIRL.
YOU SCARED ME... OH. HI!
HEY, SUBARU. SORRY 'BOUT COMIN' ALONG TOO.
NAIL IN THE COFFIN

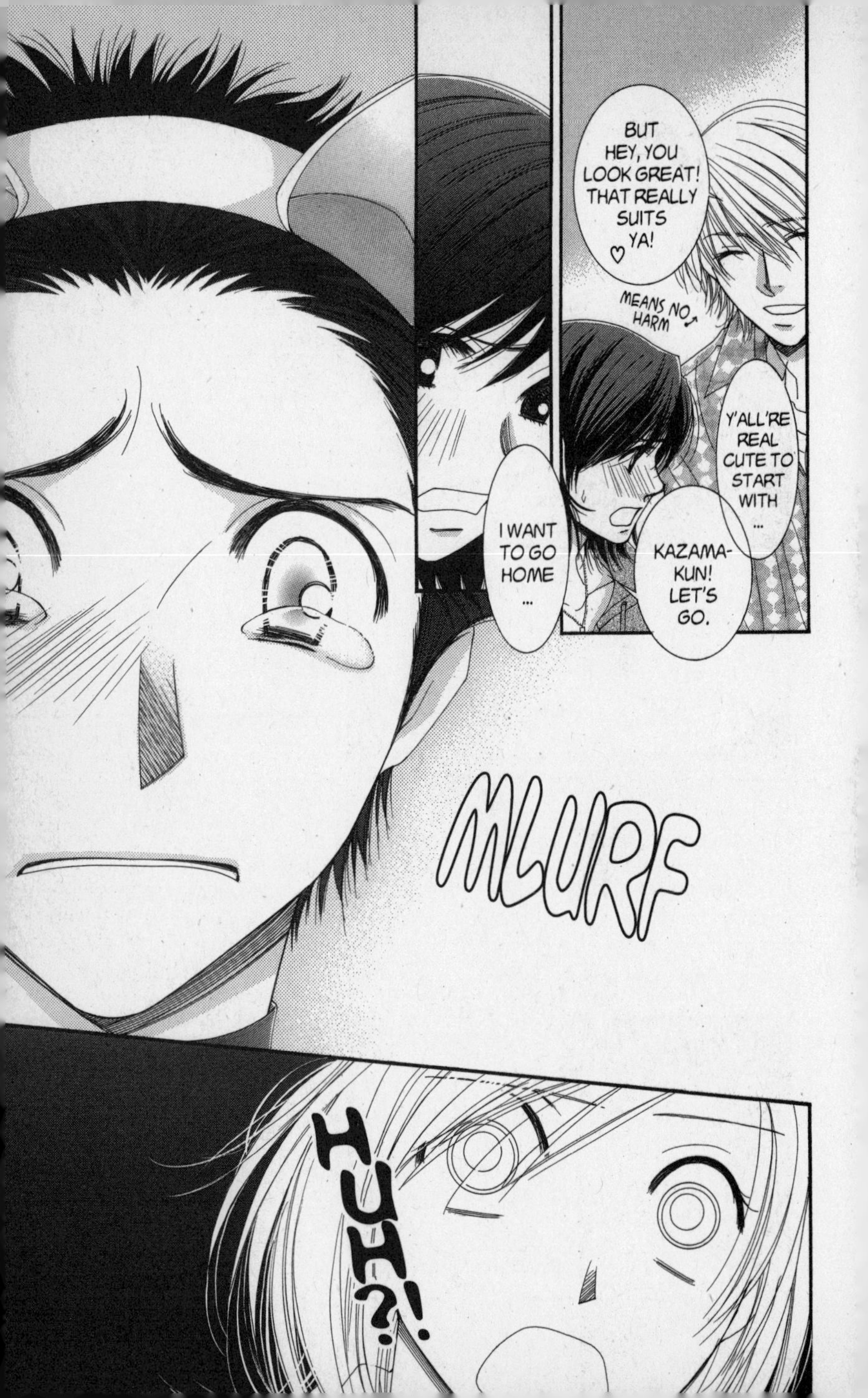
BUT HEY, YOU LOOK GREAT! THAT REALLY SUITS YA! ♡
MEANS NO HARM ♪
Y'ALL'RE REAL CUTE TO START WITH ...
KAZAMA-KUN! LET'S GO.
I WANT TO GO HOME ...
MLURF
HUH?!

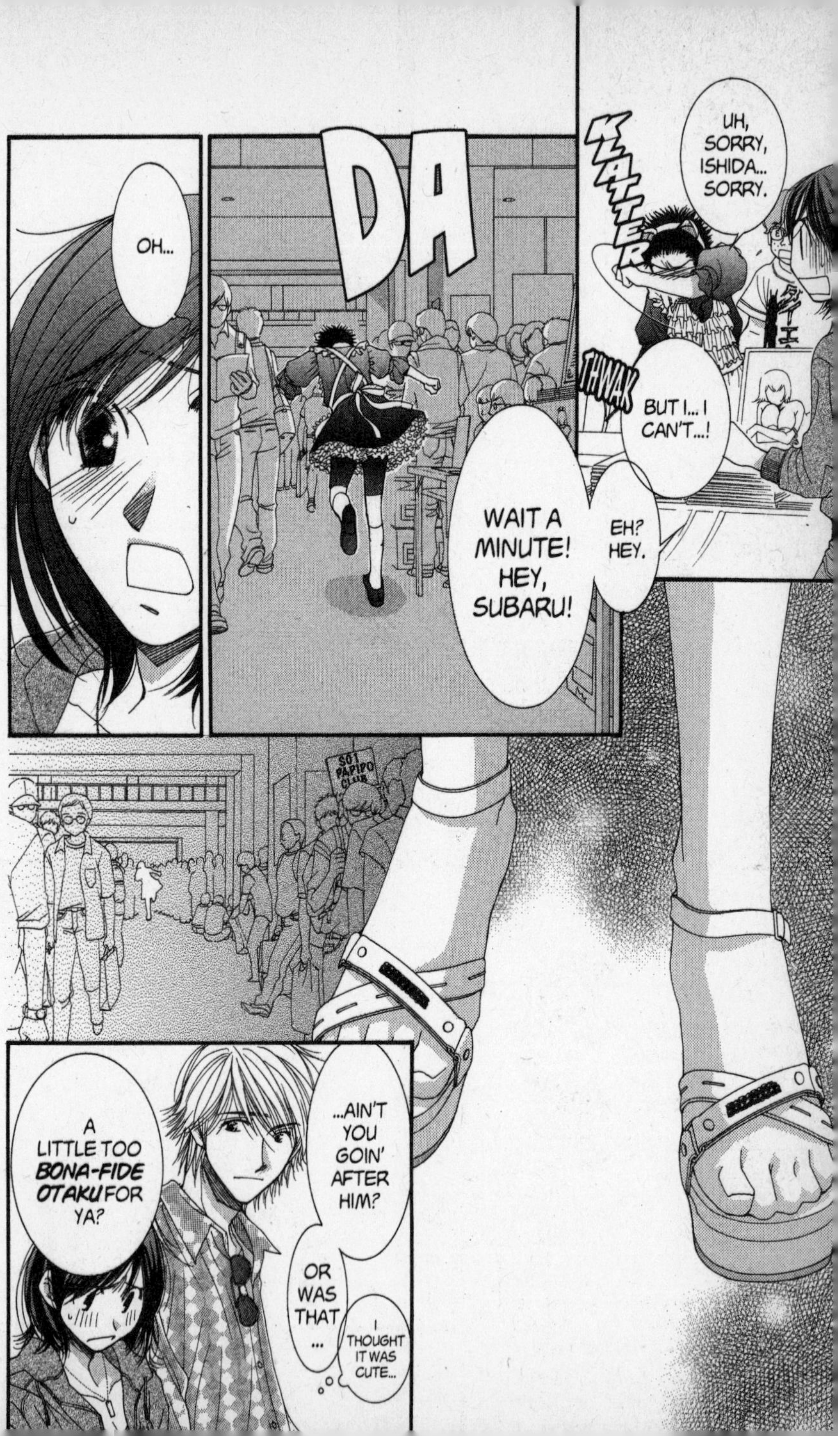
KLATTER
UH, SORRY, ISHIDA... SORRY.
THWAK
BUT I... I CAN'T...!
EH? HEY.
DA
WAIT A MINUTE! HEY, SUBARU!
OH...
...AIN'T YOU GOIN' AFTER HIM?
OR WAS THAT ...
A LITTLE TOO BONA-FIDE OTAKU FOR YA?
I THOUGHT IT WAS CUTE...

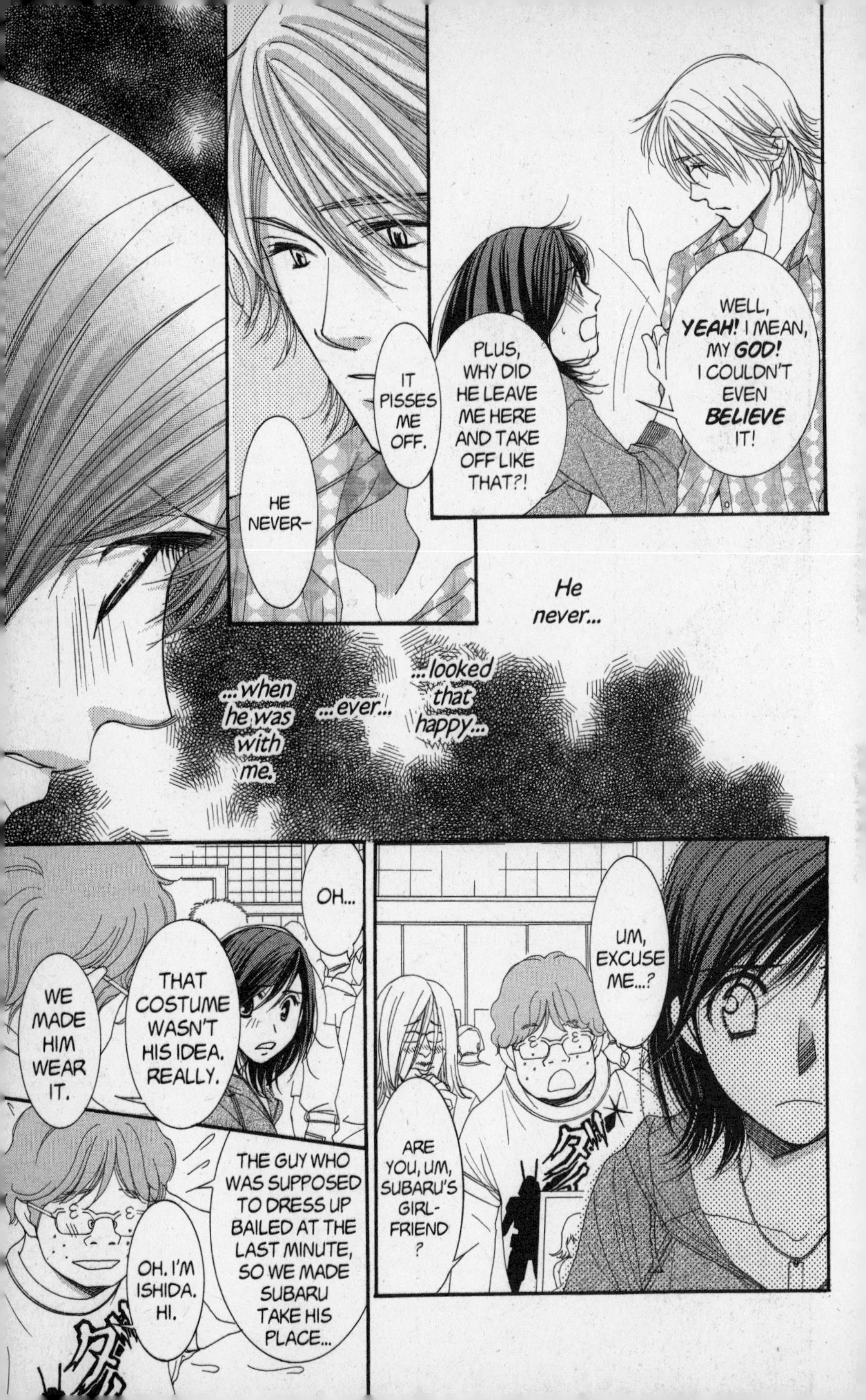
WELL, YEAH! I MEAN, MY GOD! I COULDN'T EVEN BELIEVE IT!
PLUS, WHY DID HE LEAVE ME HERE AND TAKE OFF LIKE THAT?!
IT PISSES ME OFF.
HE NEVER–
He never...
...looked that happy...
...ever...
...when he was with me.
UM, EXCUSE ME...?
ARE YOU, UM, SUBARU'S GIRL-FRIEND?
OH...
THAT COSTUME WASN'T HIS IDEA. REALLY.
WE MADE HIM WEAR IT.
THE GUY WHO WAS SUPPOSED TO DRESS UP BAILED AT THE LAST MINUTE, SO WE MADE SUBARU TAKE HIS PLACE...
OH. I'M ISHIDA. HI.

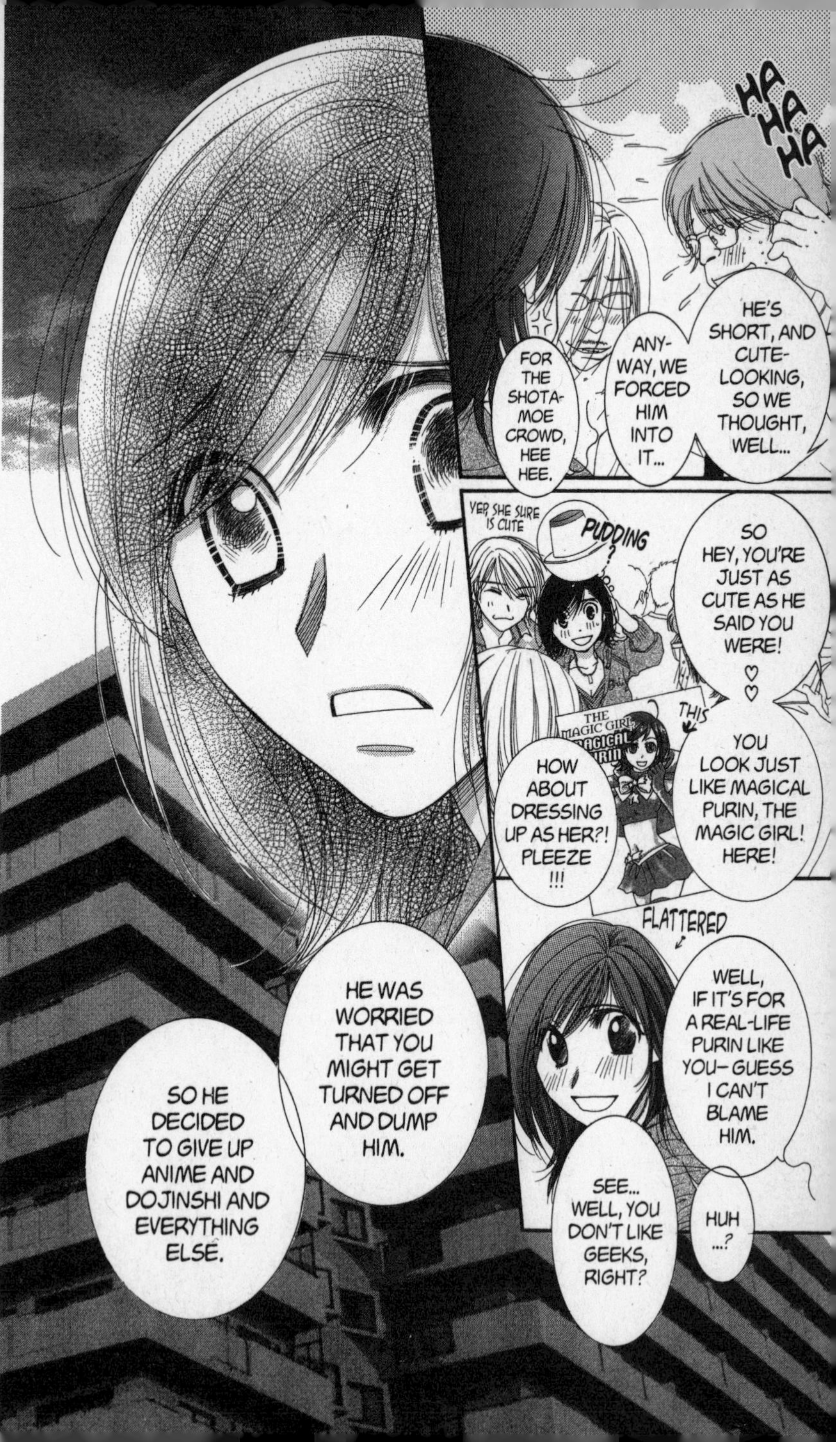
HA HA HA HA
HE'S SHORT, AND CUTE-LOOKING, SO WE THOUGHT, WELL...
ANYWAY, WE FORCED HIM INTO IT...
FOR THE SHOTA-MOE CROWD, HEE HEE.
SO HEY, YOU'RE JUST AS CUTE AS HE SAID YOU WERE! ♡ ♡
PUDDING?
YEP SHE SURE IS CUTE
YOU LOOK JUST LIKE MAGICAL PURIN, THE MAGIC GIRL! HERE!
THIS
THE MAGIC GIRL MAGICAL PURIN
HOW ABOUT DRESSING UP AS HER?! PLEEZE!!!
FLATTERED
WELL, IF IT'S FOR A REAL-LIFE PURIN LIKE YOU–GUESS I CAN'T BLAME HIM.
HUH ...?
SEE... WELL, YOU DON'T LIKE GEEKS, RIGHT?
HE WAS WORRIED THAT YOU MIGHT GET TURNED OFF AND DUMP HIM.
SO HE DECIDED TO GIVE UP ANIME AND DOJINSHI AND EVERYTHING ELSE.

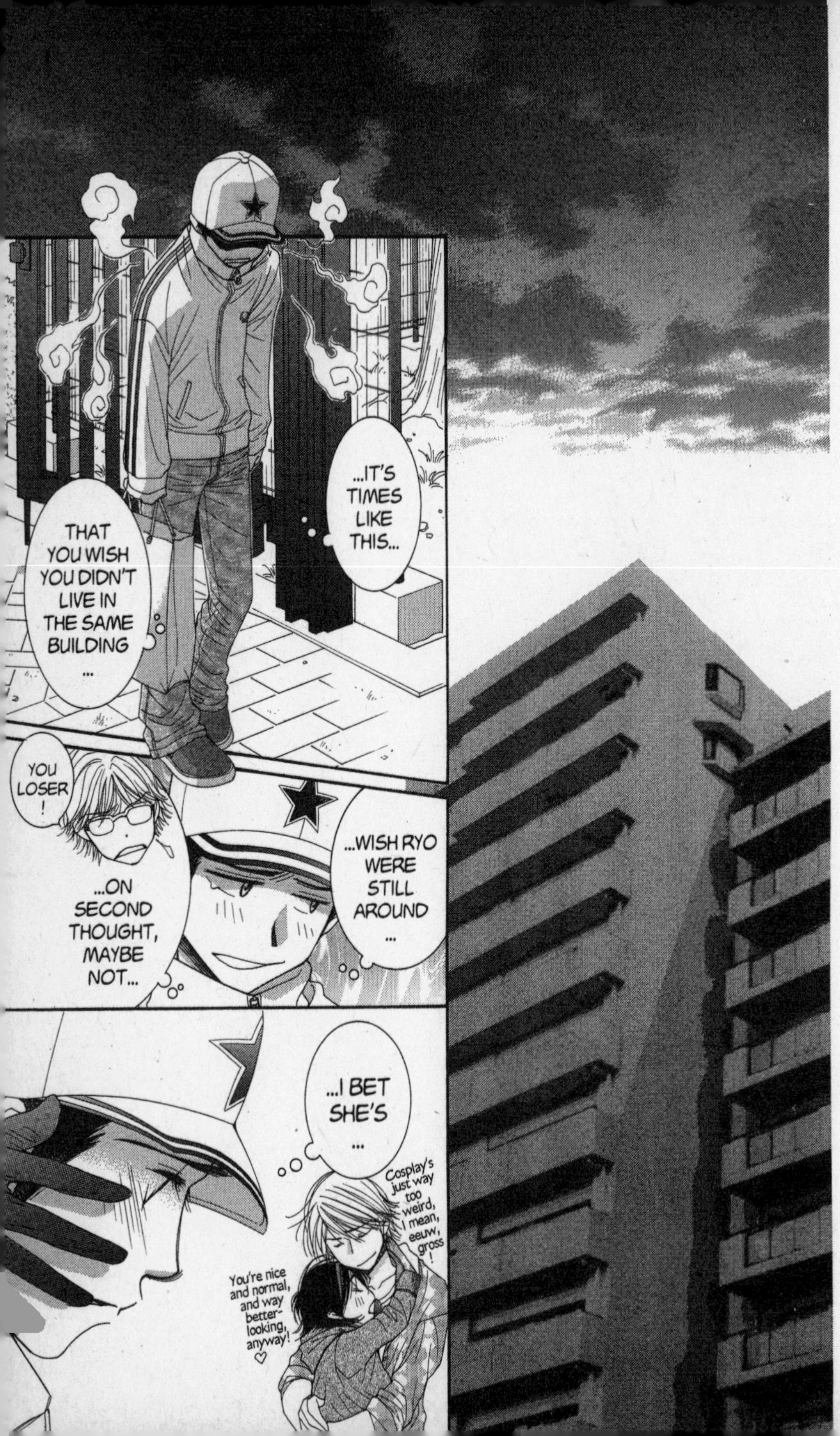
...IT'S TIMES LIKE THIS...
THAT YOU WISH YOU DIDN'T LIVE IN THE SAME BUILDING...
...WISH RYO WERE STILL AROUND...
YOU LOSER!
...ON SECOND THOUGHT, MAYBE NOT...
...I BET SHE'S...
Cosplay's just way too weird, I mean, eeuw, gross!
You're nice and normal, and way better-looking, anyway! ♡

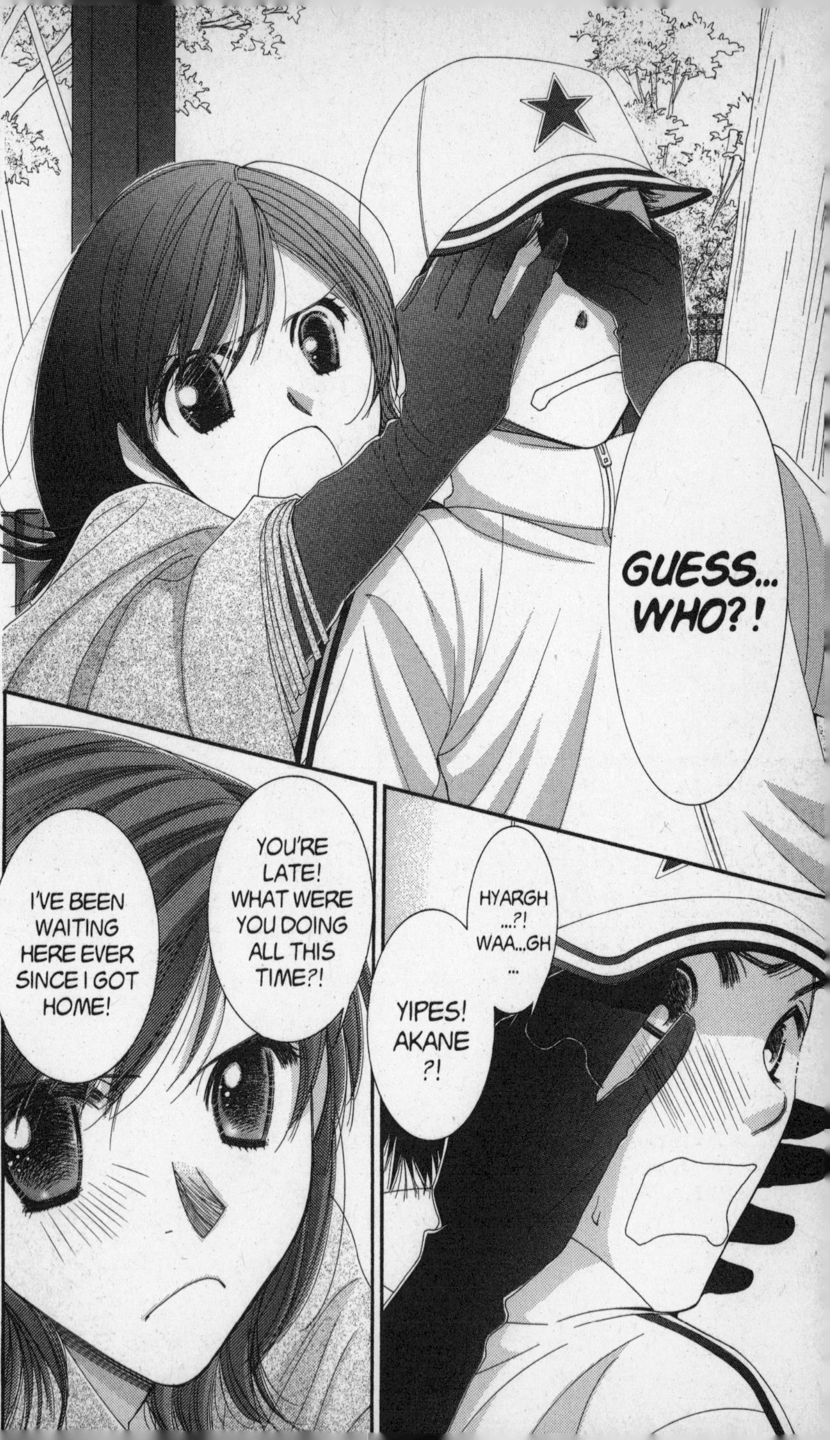
GUESS... WHO?!
HYARGH ...?! WAA...GH ...
YIPES! AKANE ?!
YOU'RE LATE! WHAT WERE YOU DOING ALL THIS TIME?!
I'VE BEEN WAITING HERE EVER SINCE I GOT HOME!

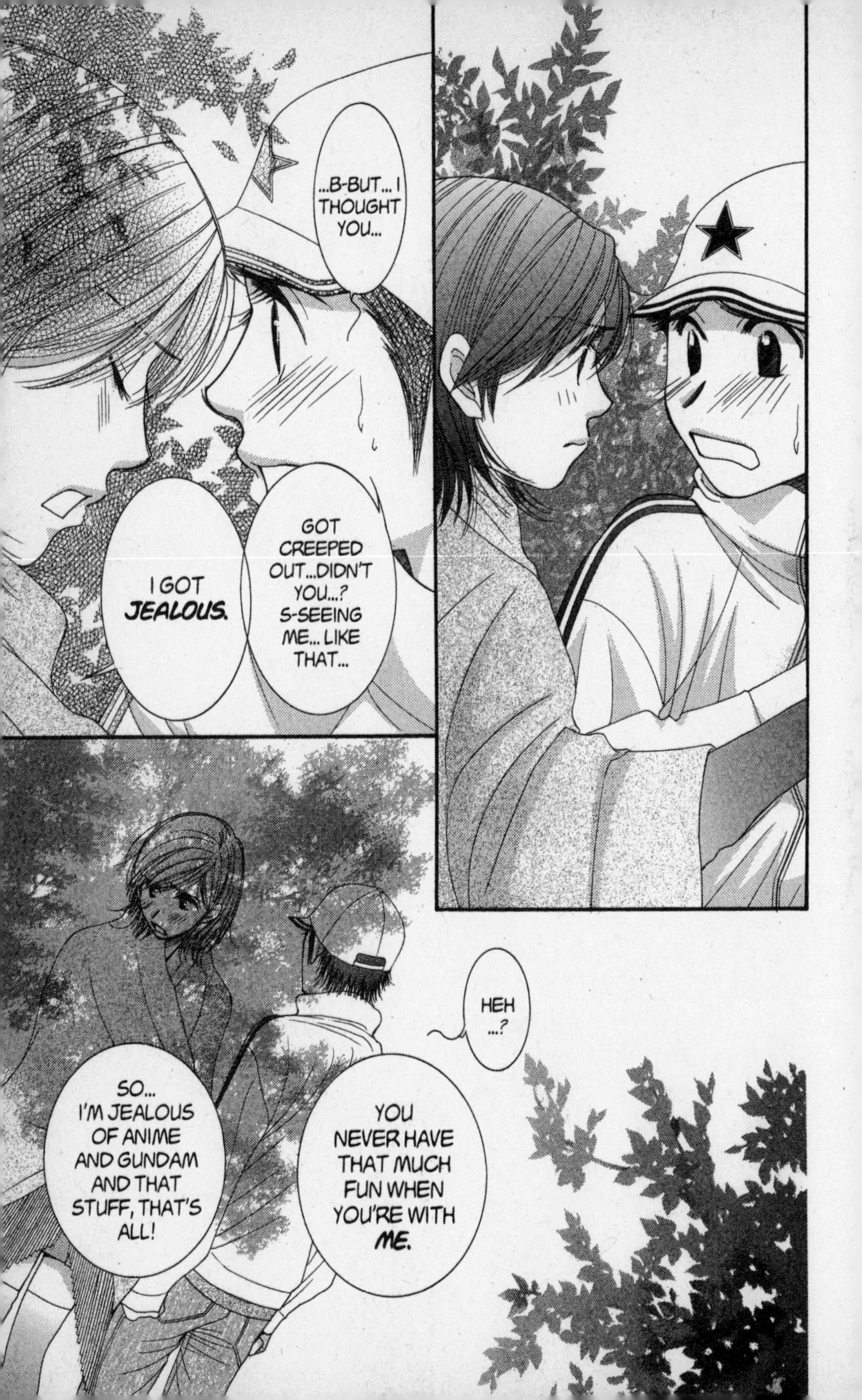
...B-BUT... I THOUGHT YOU...
GOT CREEPED OUT...DIDN'T YOU...? S-SEEING ME... LIKE THAT...
I GOT **JEALOUS.**
HEH ...?
YOU NEVER HAVE THAT MUCH FUN WHEN YOU'RE WITH **ME.**
SO... I'M JEALOUS OF ANIME AND GUNDAM AND THAT STUFF, THAT'S ALL!

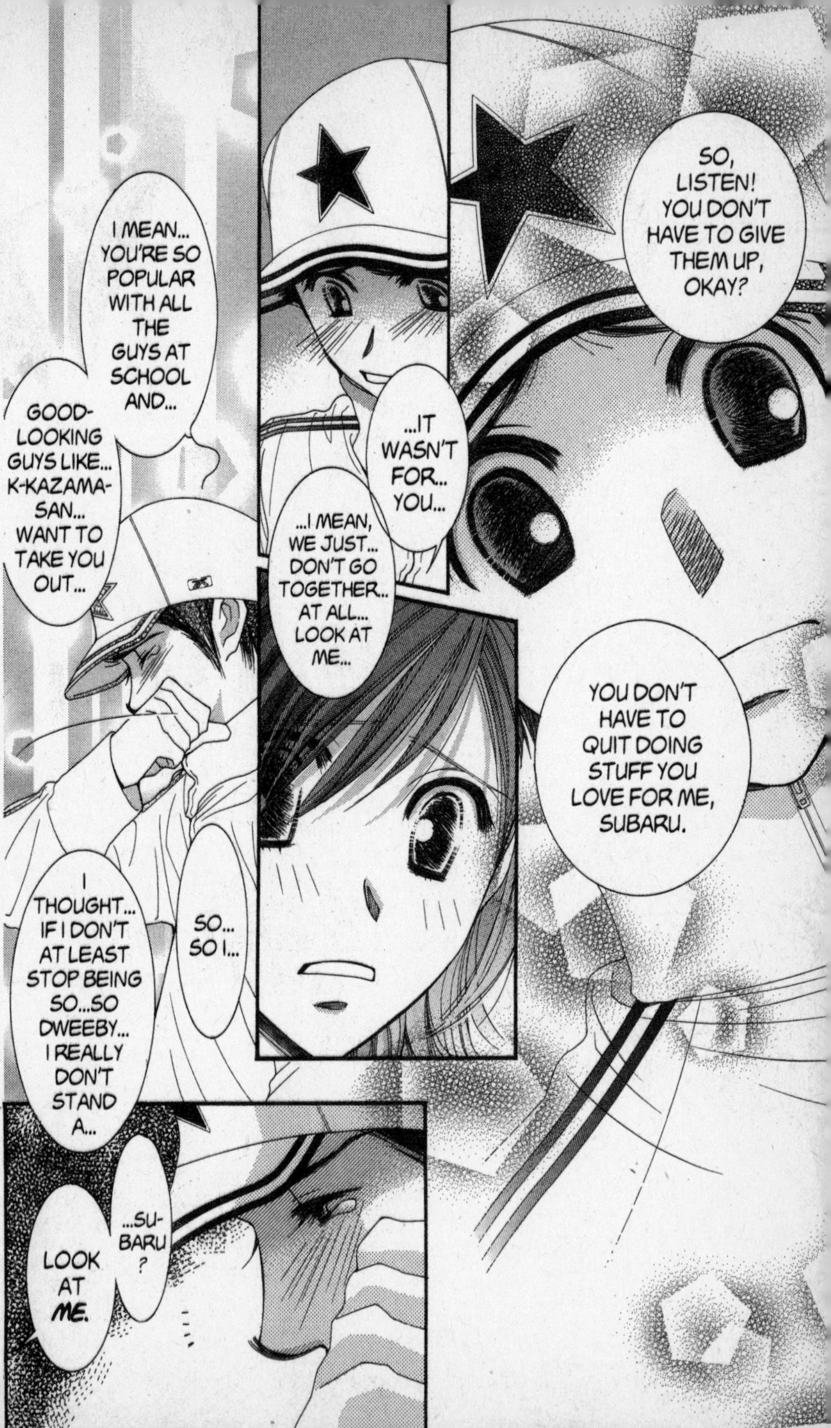
SO, LISTEN! YOU DON'T HAVE TO GIVE THEM UP, OKAY?
YOU DON'T HAVE TO QUIT DOING STUFF YOU LOVE FOR ME, SUBARU.
...IT WASN'T FOR... YOU...
...I MEAN, WE JUST... DON'T GO TOGETHER... AT ALL... LOOK AT ME...
I MEAN... YOU'RE SO POPULAR WITH ALL THE GUYS AT SCHOOL AND...
GOOD-LOOKING GUYS LIKE... K-KAZAMA-SAN... WANT TO TAKE YOU OUT...
SO... SO I...
I THOUGHT... IF I DON'T AT LEAST STOP BEING SO...SO DWEEBY... I REALLY DON'T STAND A...
...SU-BARU?
LOOK AT ME.

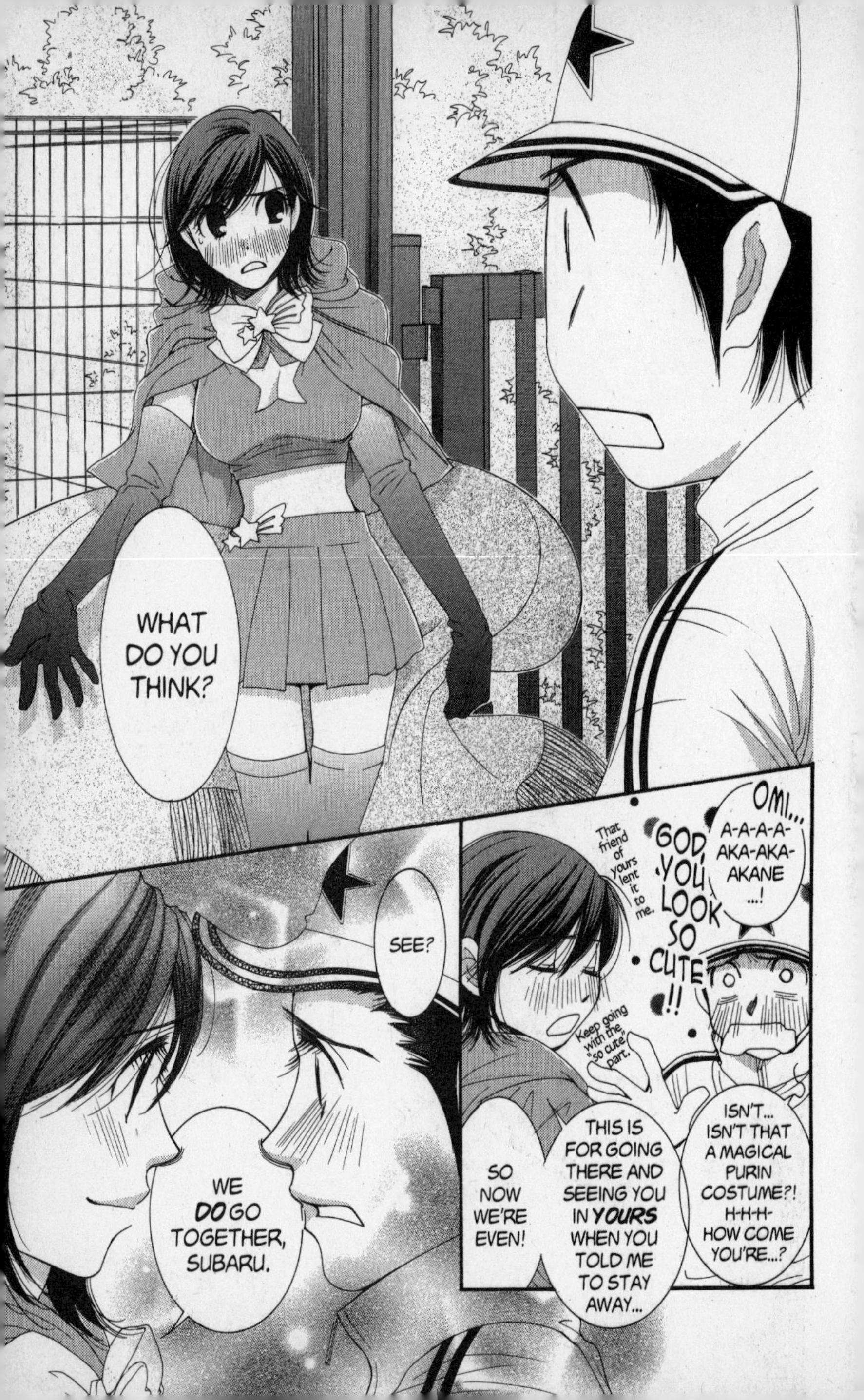
WHAT DO YOU THINK?
OMI... A-A-A-A-AKA-AKA-AKANE ...!
GOD, YOU LOOK SO CUTE!!
That friend of yours lent it to me.
Keep going with the "so cute" part.
ISN'T... ISN'T THAT A MAGICAL PURIN COSTUME?! H-H-H-HOW COME YOU'RE...?
THIS IS FOR GOING THERE AND SEEING YOU IN **YOURS** WHEN YOU TOLD ME TO STAY AWAY...
SO NOW WE'RE EVEN!
SEE?
WE **DO** GO TOGETHER, SUBARU.

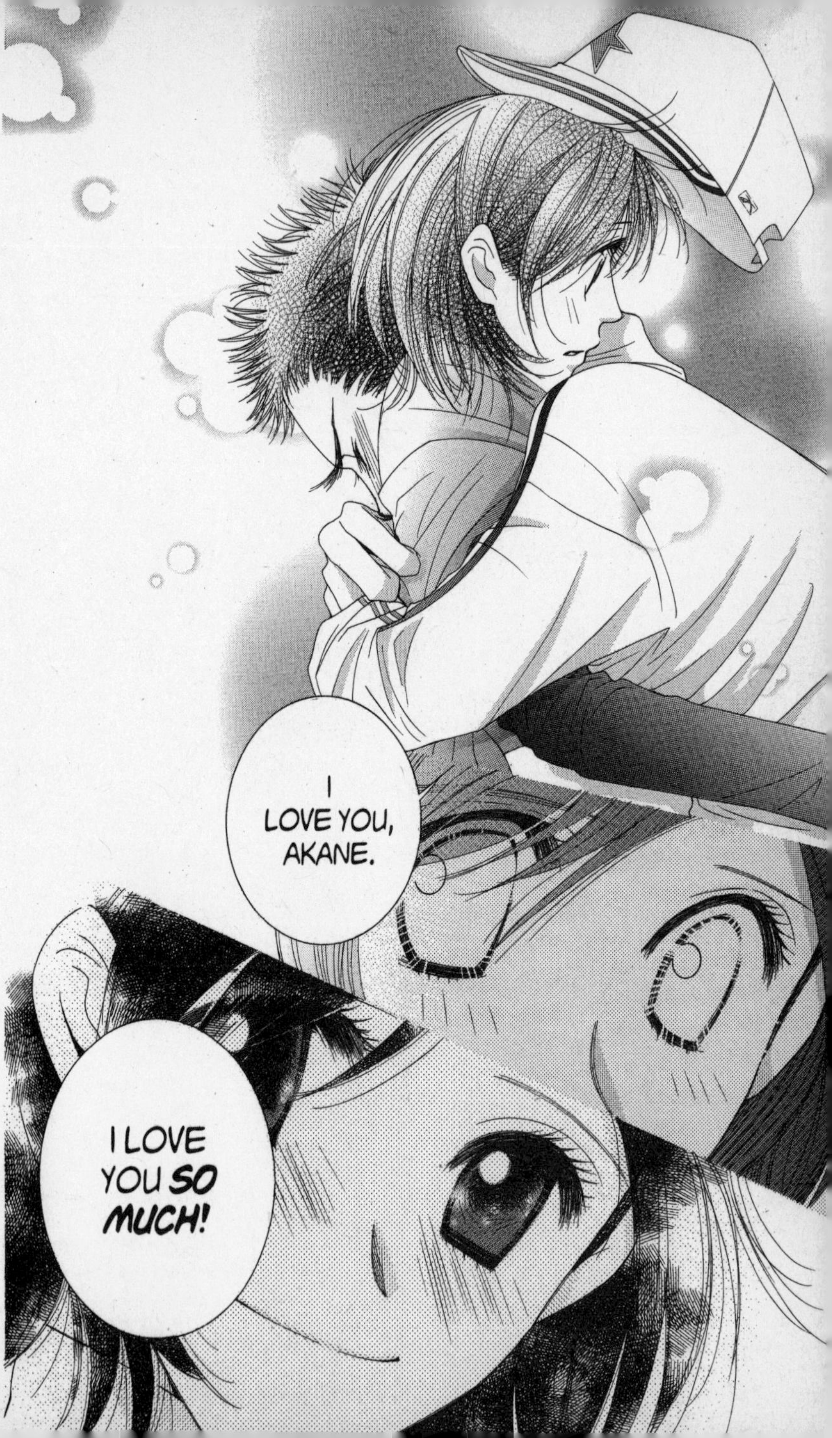
I LOVE YOU, AKANE.
I LOVE YOU SO MUCH!

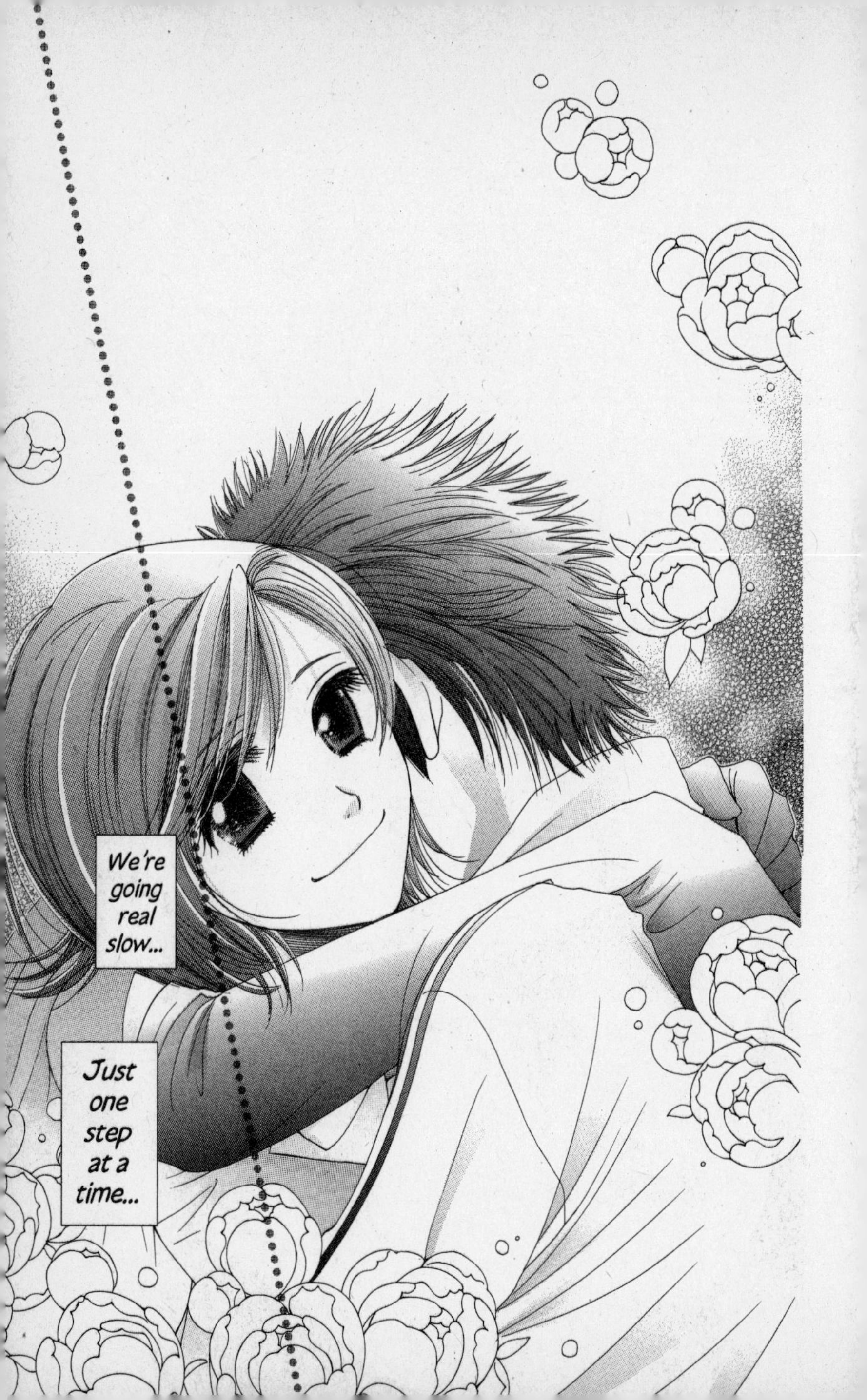
We're going real slow...
Just one step at a time...

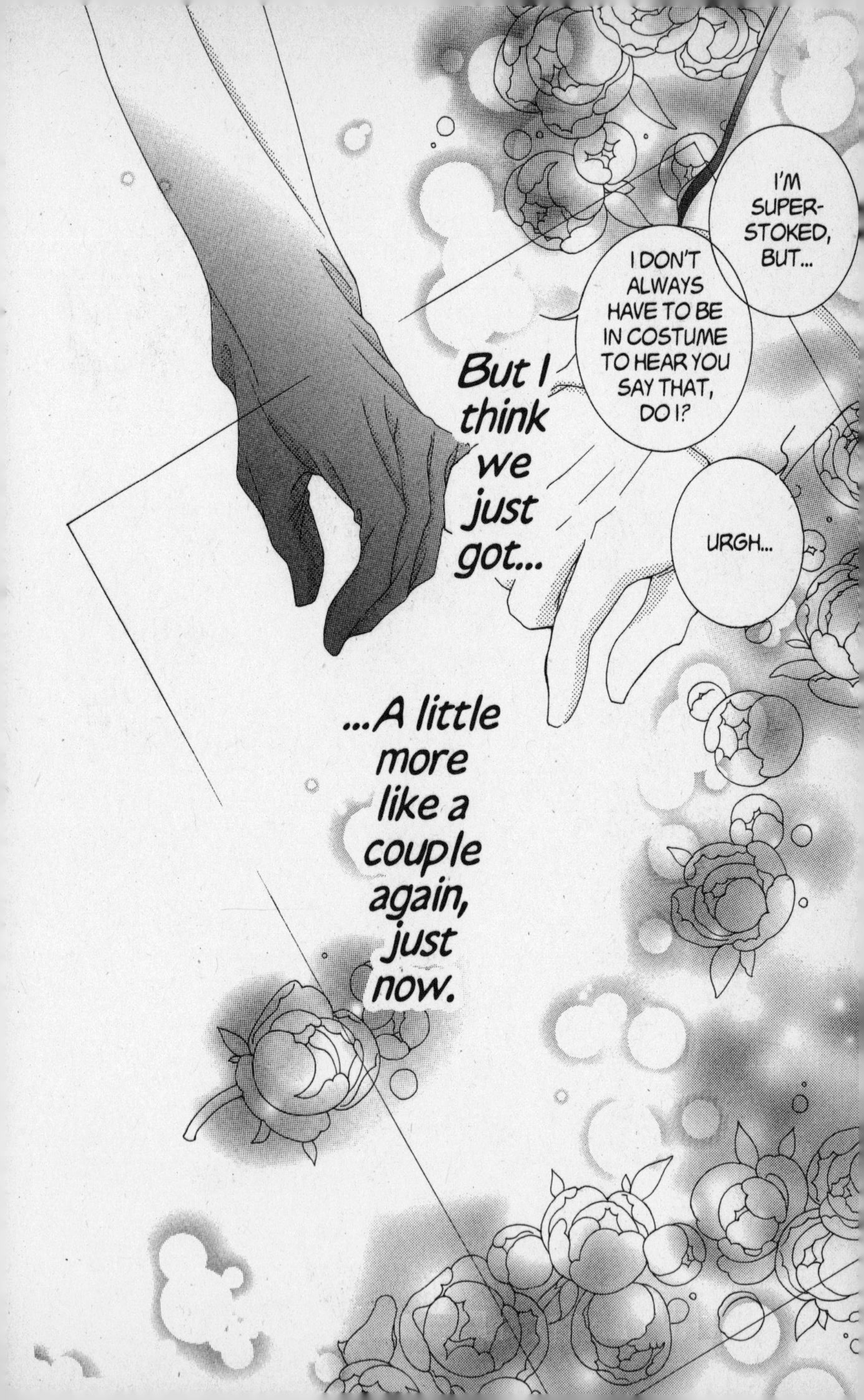
I'M SUPER-STOKED, BUT...
I DON'T ALWAYS HAVE TO BE IN COSTUME TO HEAR YOU SAY THAT, DO I?
URGH...
But I think we just got...
...A little more like a couple again, just now.

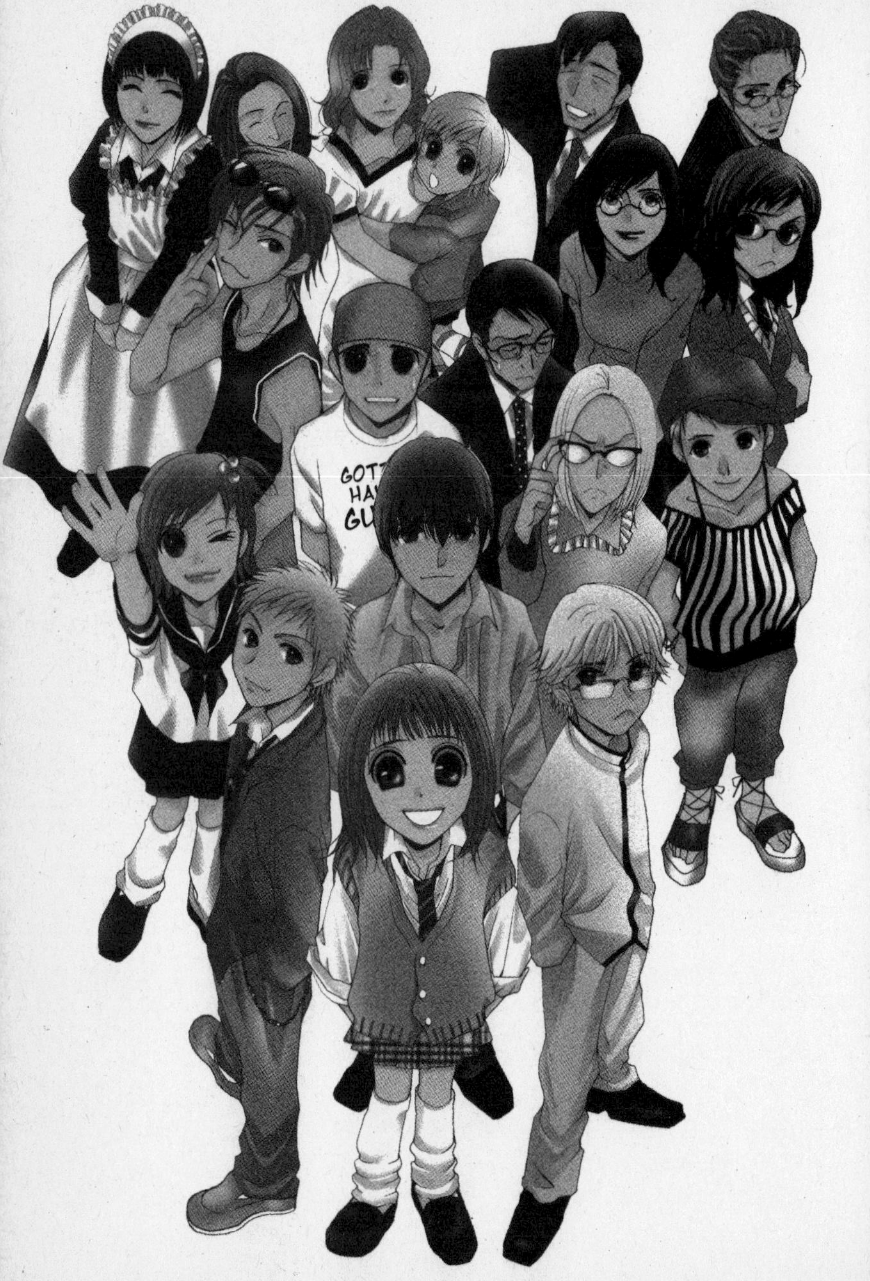

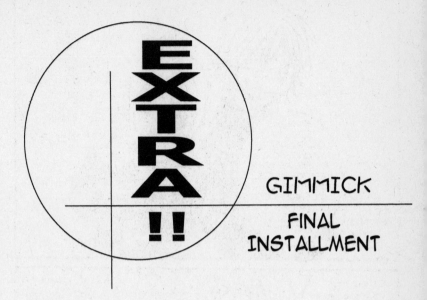

EXTRA !!

GIMMICK

FINAL
INSTALLMENT

Thank you for buying Hot Gimmick Vol. 12.
This is a bonus section, just for you
manga readers.
Read on!

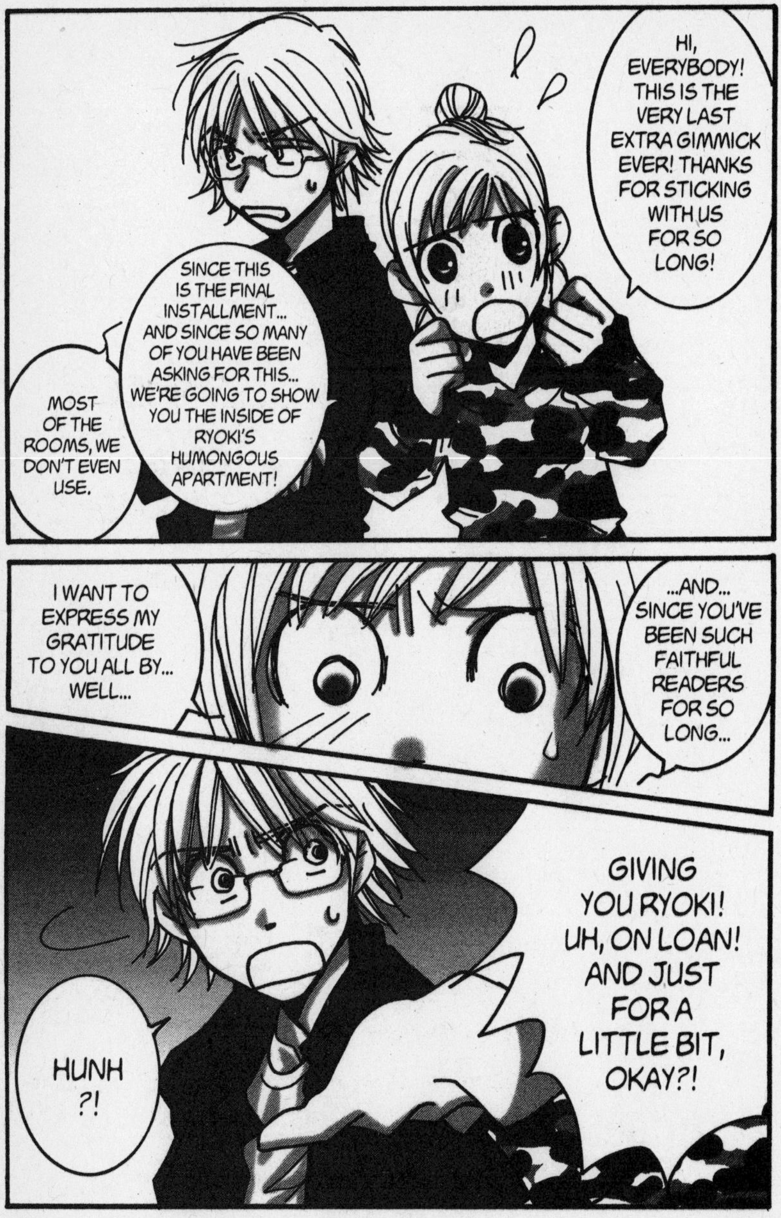
HI, EVERYBODY! THIS IS THE VERY LAST EXTRA GIMMICK EVER! THANKS FOR STICKING WITH US FOR SO LONG!
SINCE THIS IS THE FINAL INSTALLMENT... AND SINCE SO MANY OF YOU HAVE BEEN ASKING FOR THIS... WE'RE GOING TO SHOW YOU THE INSIDE OF RYOKI'S HUMONGOUS APARTMENT!
MOST OF THE ROOMS, WE DON'T EVEN USE.
...AND... SINCE YOU'VE BEEN SUCH FAITHFUL READERS FOR SO LONG...
I WANT TO EXPRESS MY GRATITUDE TO YOU ALL BY... WELL...
GIVING YOU RYOKI! UH, ON LOAN! AND JUST FOR A LITTLE BIT, OKAY?!
HUNH ?!

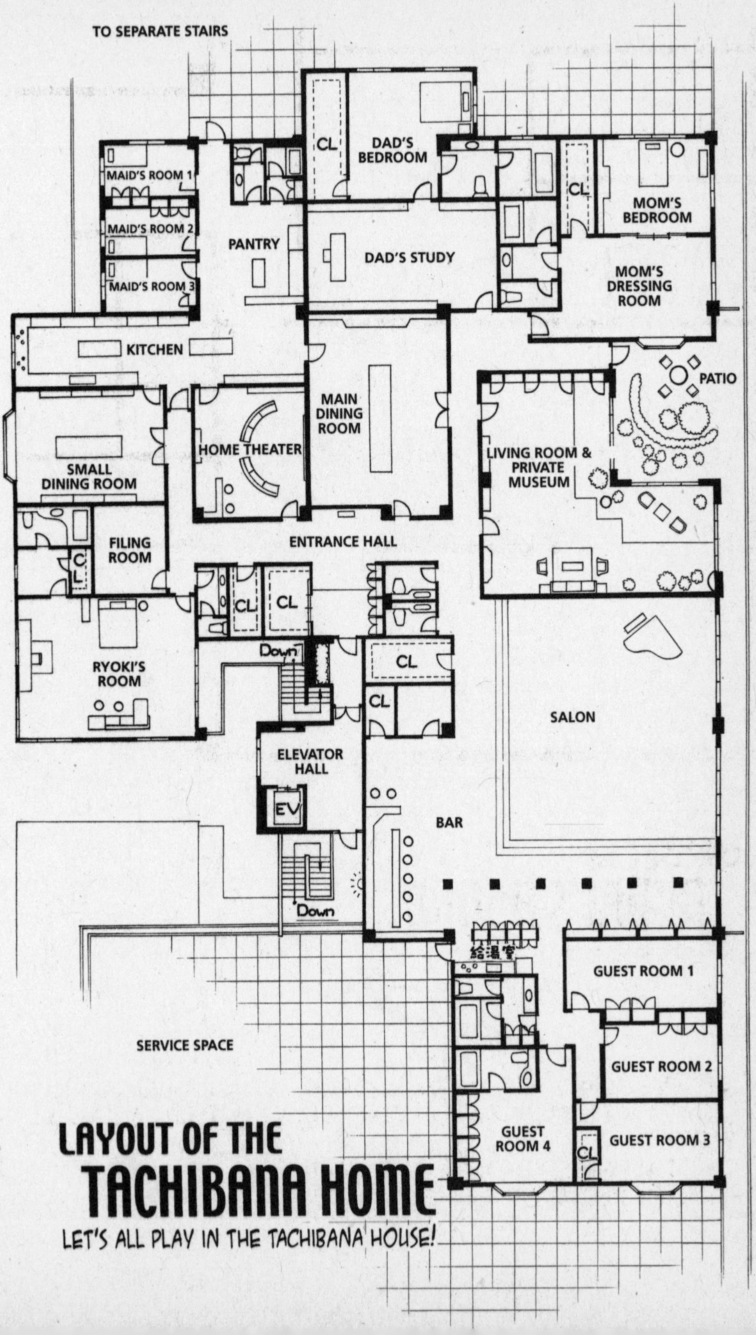
TO SEPARATE STAIRS
CL
DAD'S BEDROOM
MAID'S ROOM 1
MAID'S ROOM 2
MAID'S ROOM 3
PANTRY
DAD'S STUDY
CL
MOM'S BEDROOM
MOM'S DRESSING ROOM
KITCHEN
PATIO
MAIN DINING ROOM
HOME THEATER
SMALL DINING ROOM
LIVING ROOM & PRIVATE MUSEUM
ENTRANCE HALL
FILING ROOM
CL
CL
CL
RYOKI'S ROOM
Down
CL
CL
SALON
ELEVATOR HALL
EV
BAR
Down
給湯室
GUEST ROOM 1
SERVICE SPACE
GUEST ROOM 2
GUEST ROOM 4
GUEST ROOM 3
CL

LAYOUT OF THE TACHIBANA HOME

LET'S ALL PLAY IN THE TACHIBANA HOUSE!

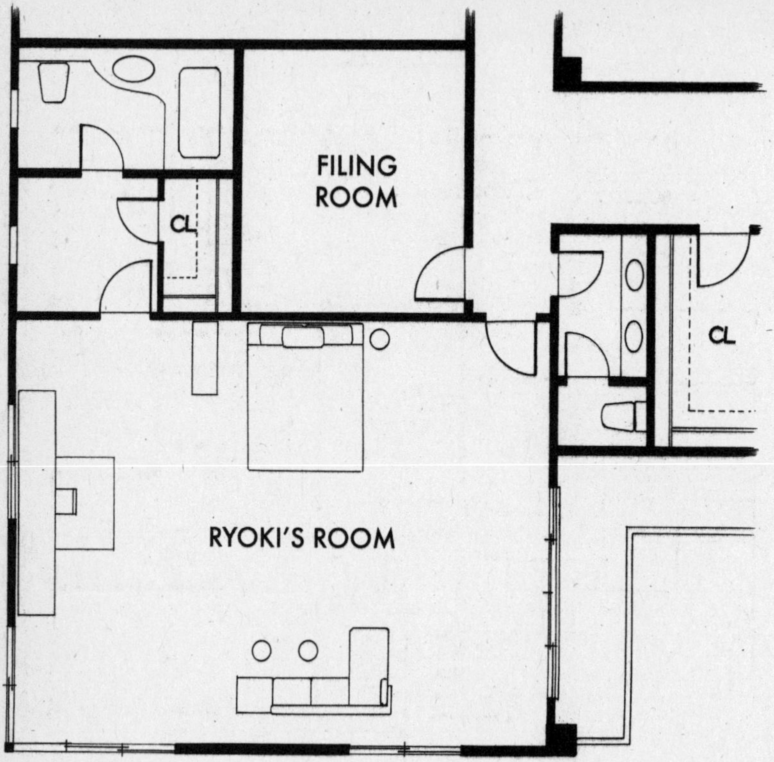
FILING ROOM
CL
CL
RYOKI'S ROOM

LAYOUT OF RYOKI'S ROOM

LET'S ALL PLAY IN RYOKI'S ROOM!

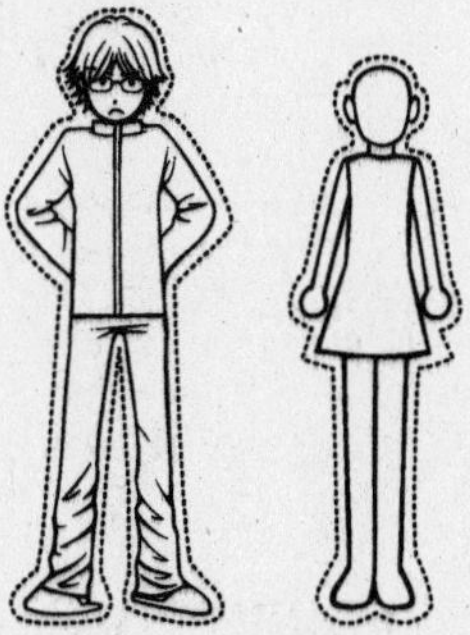

CUT OUT THE FIGURES OF RYOKI AND YOU, AT RIGHT. USE A COPY MACHINE TO ENLARGE OR REDUCE SIZE AS NECEESSARY.
YOU CAN SIT WITH HIM ON THE SOFA, OR LIE WITH HIM ON HIS BED, OR WHATEVER YOU WANT!

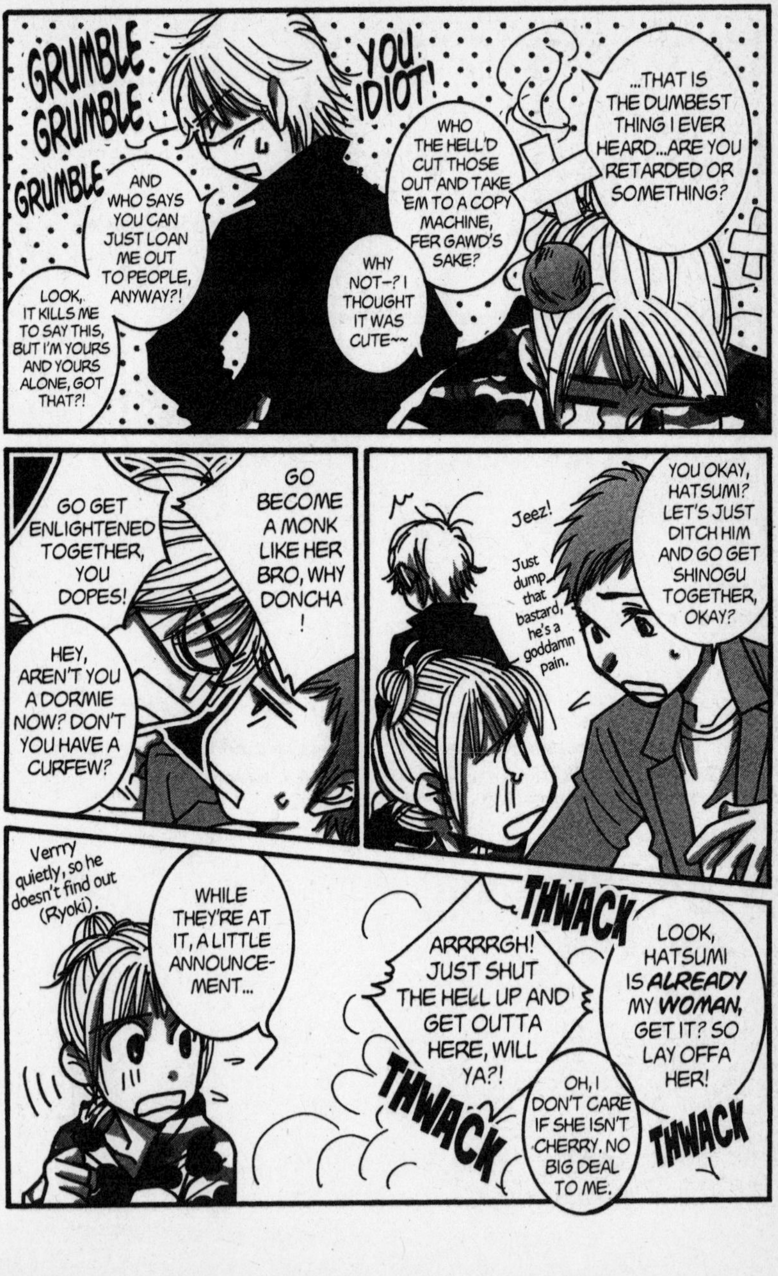
...THAT IS THE DUMBEST THING I EVER HEARD...ARE YOU RETARDED OR SOMETHING?
YOU IDIOT!
WHO THE HELL'D CUT THOSE OUT AND TAKE 'EM TO A COPY MACHINE, FER GAWD'S SAKE?
WHY NOT-? I THOUGHT IT WAS CUTE~~
GRUMBLE GRUMBLE
AND WHO SAYS YOU CAN JUST LOAN ME OUT TO PEOPLE, ANYWAY?!
GRUMBLE
LOOK, IT KILLS ME TO SAY THIS, BUT I'M YOURS AND YOURS ALONE, GOT THAT?!
YOU OKAY, HATSUMI? LET'S JUST DITCH HIM AND GO GET SHINOGU TOGETHER, OKAY?
Jeez!
Just dump that bastard, he's a goddamn pain.
GO BECOME A MONK LIKE HER BRO, WHY DONCHA!
GO GET ENLIGHTENED TOGETHER, YOU DOPES!
HEY, AREN'T YOU A DORMIE NOW? DON'T YOU HAVE A CURFEW?
LOOK, HATSUMI IS *ALREADY* MY *WOMAN*, GET IT? SO LAY OFFA HER!
THWACK
ARRRRGH! JUST SHUT THE HELL UP AND GET OUTTA HERE, WILL YA?!
OH, I DON'T CARE IF SHE ISN'T CHERRY. NO BIG DEAL TO ME.
THWACK
THWACK
WHILE THEY'RE AT IT, A LITTLE ANNOUNCEMENT...
Verrry quietly, so he doesn't find out (Ryoki).

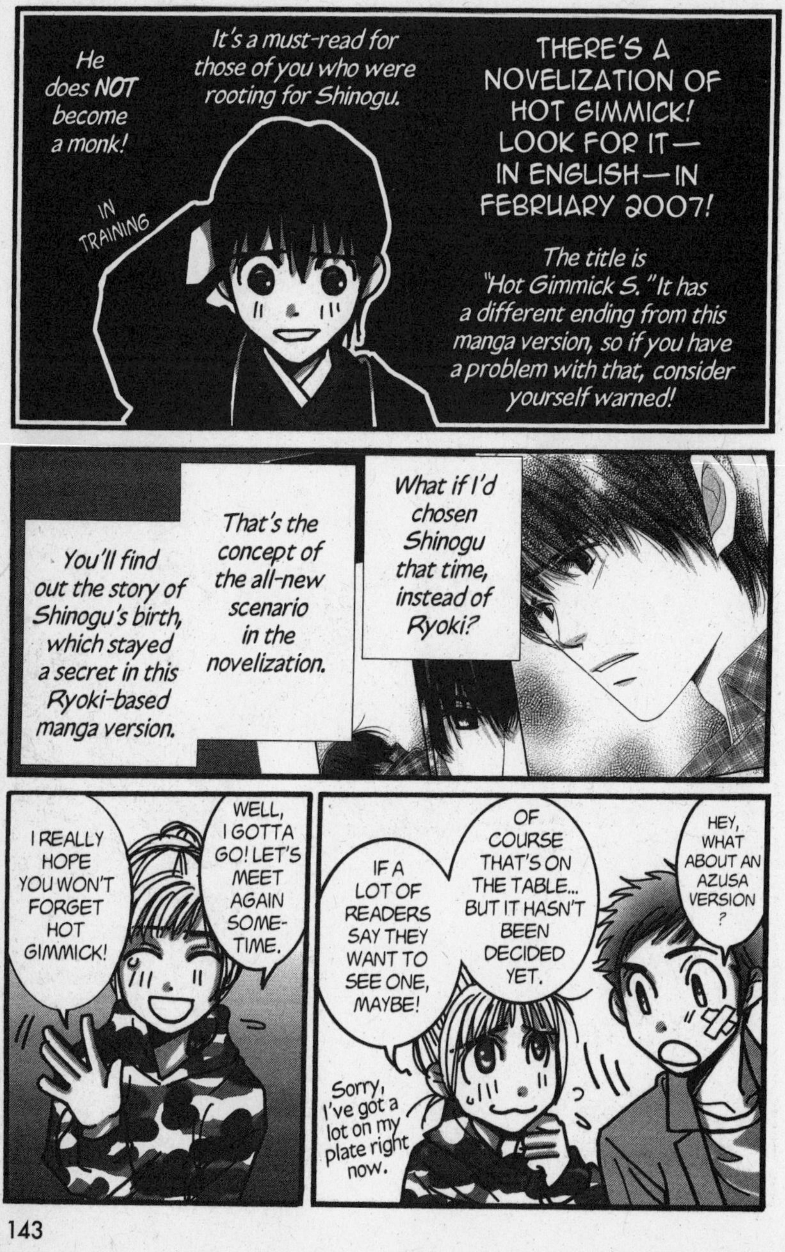
THERE'S A NOVELIZATION OF HOT GIMMICK! LOOK FOR IT—IN ENGLISH—IN FEBRUARY 2007!
The title is "Hot Gimmick S." It has a different ending from this manga version, so if you have a problem with that, consider yourself warned!
It's a must-read for those of you who were rooting for Shinogu.
He does NOT become a monk!
IN TRAINING
What if I'd chosen Shinogu that time, instead of Ryoki?
That's the concept of the all-new scenario in the novelization.
You'll find out the story of Shinogu's birth, which stayed a secret in this Ryoki-based manga version.
HEY, WHAT ABOUT AN AZUSA VERSION?
OF COURSE THAT'S ON THE TABLE... BUT IT HASN'T BEEN DECIDED YET.
IF A LOT OF READERS SAY THEY WANT TO SEE ONE, MAYBE!
Sorry, I've got a lot on my plate right now.
WELL, I GOTTA GO! LET'S MEET AGAIN SOME-TIME.
I REALLY HOPE YOU WON'T FORGET HOT GIMMICK!

hot gimmick

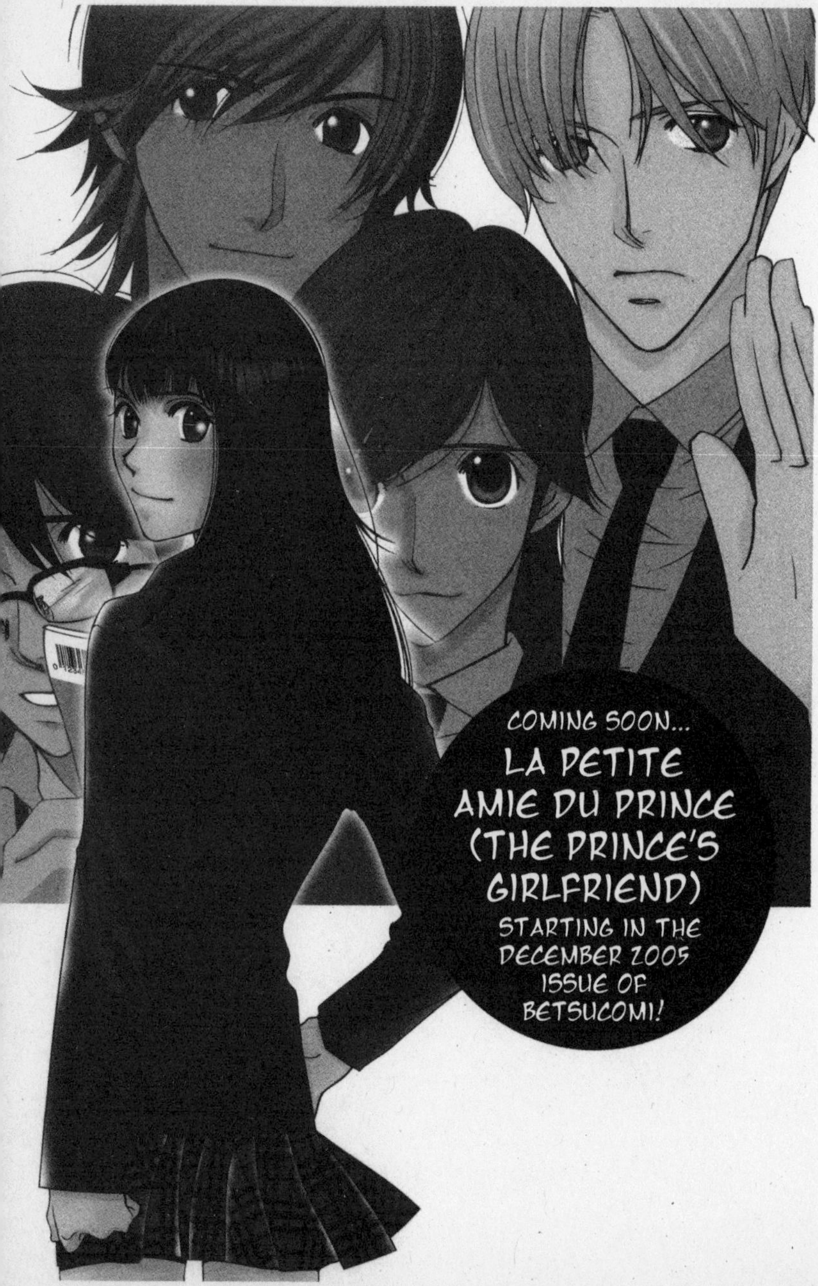
COMING SOON...
LA PETITE AMIE DU PRINCE (THE PRINCE'S GIRLFRIEND)
STARTING IN THE DECEMBER 2005 ISSUE OF BETSUCOMI!

THE NEXT PART IS A SHORT STORY CALLED "TEN DAYS."

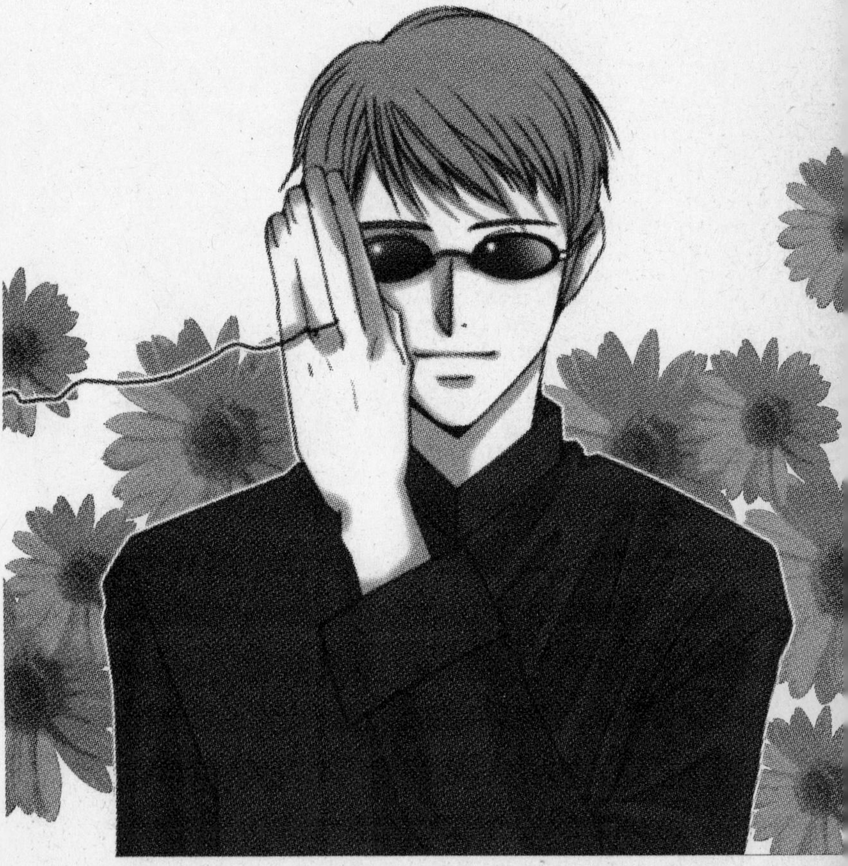

Ten Days

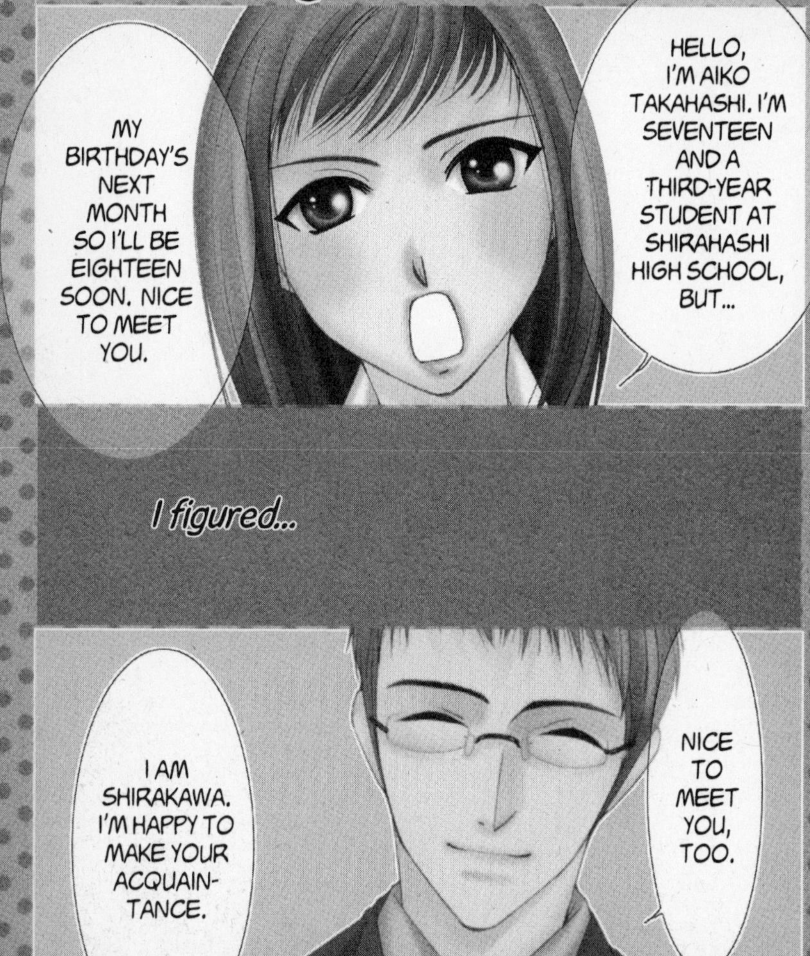

HELLO, I'M AIKO TAKAHASHI. I'M SEVENTEEN AND A THIRD-YEAR STUDENT AT SHIRAHASHI HIGH SCHOOL, BUT...
MY BIRTHDAY'S NEXT MONTH SO I'LL BE EIGHTEEN SOON. NICE TO MEET YOU.
I figured...
NICE TO MEET YOU, TOO.
I AM SHIRAKAWA. I'M HAPPY TO MAKE YOUR ACQUAIN-TANCE.
If I get married, life might be a lot easier.

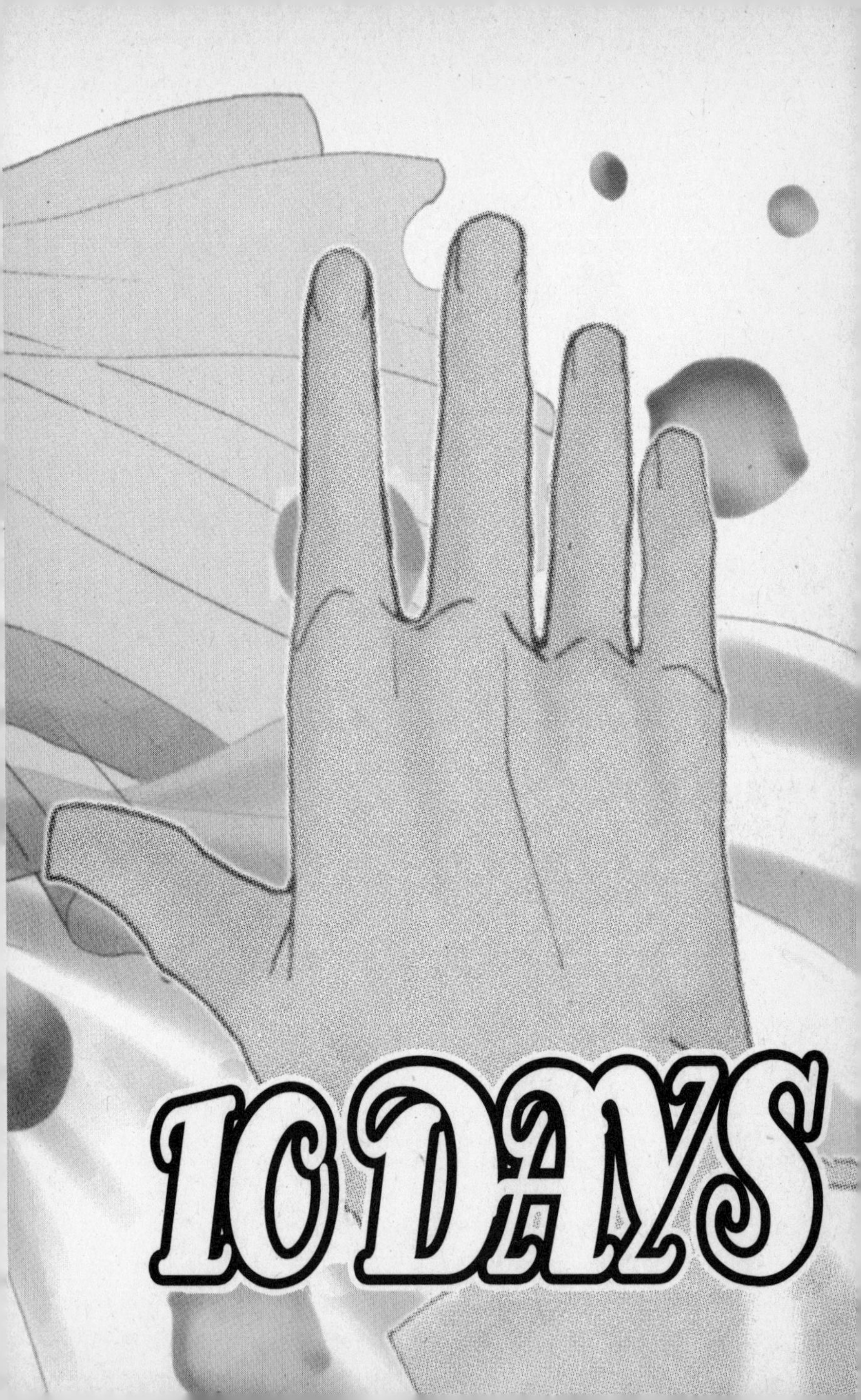
10 DAYS

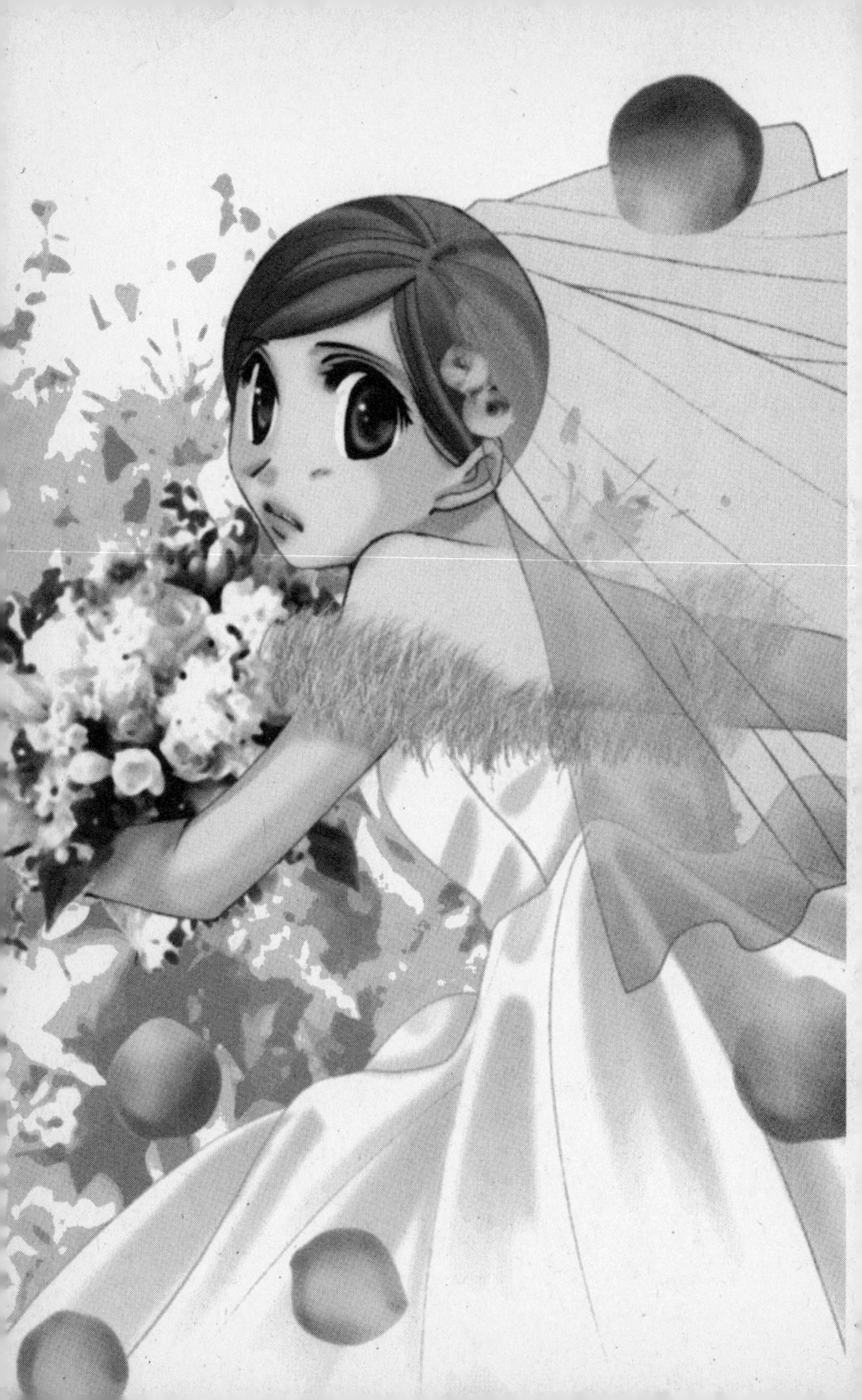

10 DAYS

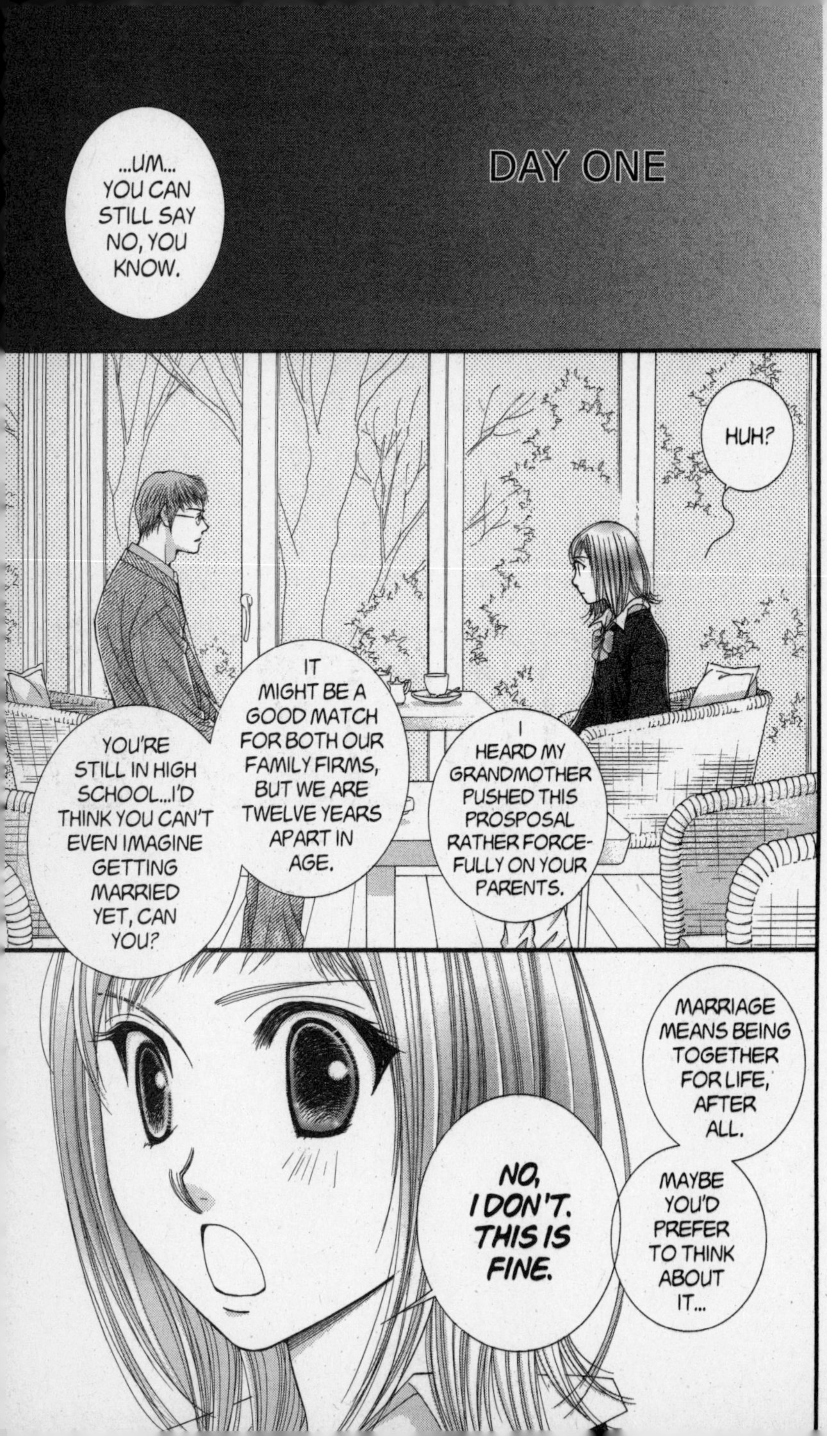
DAY ONE
...UM... YOU CAN STILL SAY NO, YOU KNOW.
HUH?
I HEARD MY GRANDMOTHER PUSHED THIS PROSPOSAL RATHER FORCE-FULLY ON YOUR PARENTS.
IT MIGHT BE A GOOD MATCH FOR BOTH OUR FAMILY FIRMS, BUT WE ARE TWELVE YEARS APART IN AGE.
YOU'RE STILL IN HIGH SCHOOL...I'D THINK YOU CAN'T EVEN IMAGINE GETTING MARRIED YET, CAN YOU?
MARRIAGE MEANS BEING TOGETHER FOR LIFE, AFTER ALL.
MAYBE YOU'D PREFER TO THINK ABOUT IT...
NO, I DON'T. THIS IS FINE.

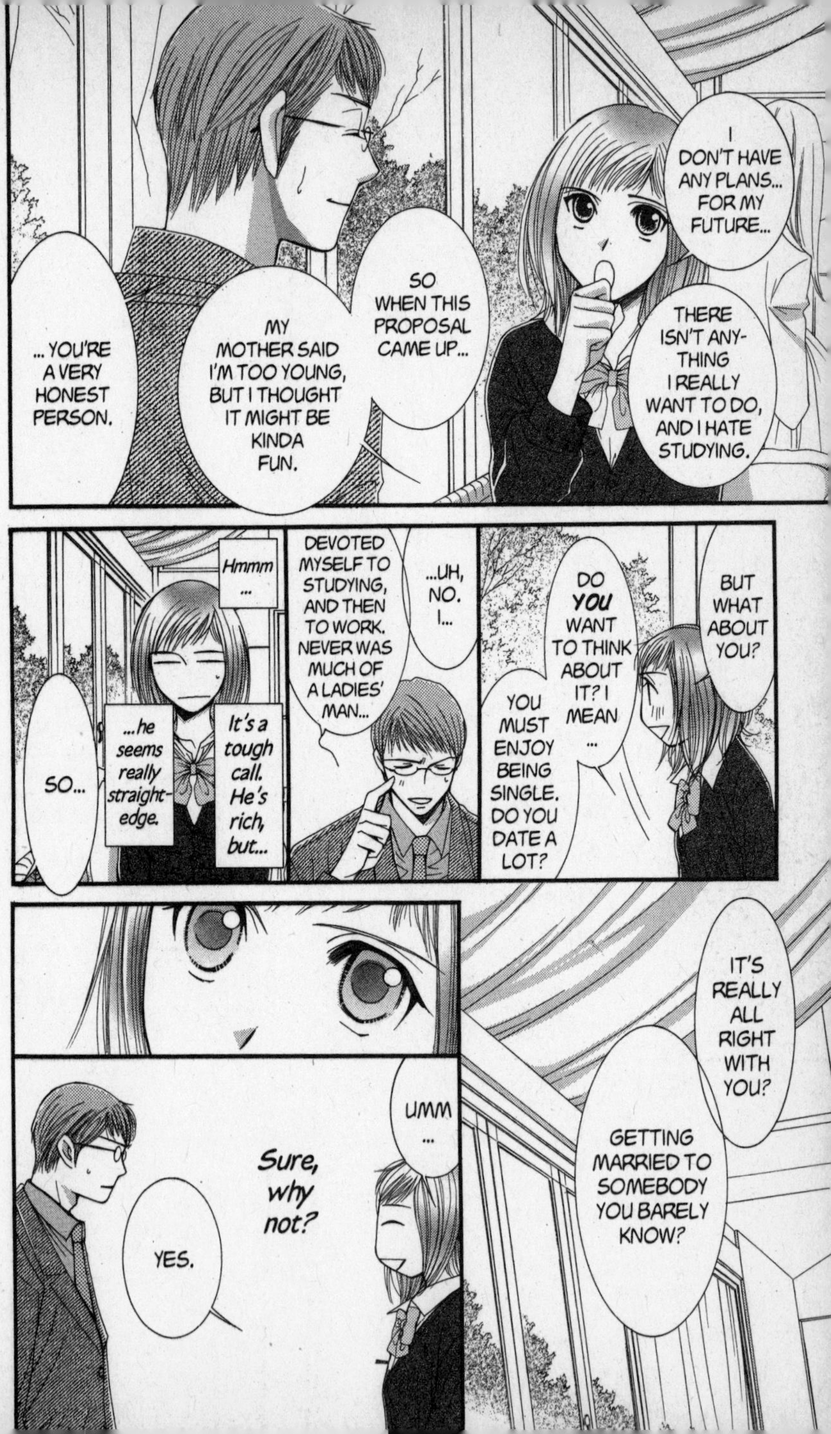
I DON'T HAVE ANY PLANS... FOR MY FUTURE...
THERE ISN'T ANY-THING I REALLY WANT TO DO, AND I HATE STUDYING.
SO WHEN THIS PROPOSAL CAME UP...
MY MOTHER SAID I'M TOO YOUNG, BUT I THOUGHT IT MIGHT BE KINDA FUN.
... YOU'RE A VERY HONEST PERSON.
BUT WHAT ABOUT YOU?
DO *YOU* WANT TO THINK ABOUT IT? I MEAN ...
YOU MUST ENJOY BEING SINGLE. DO YOU DATE A LOT?
...UH, NO. I...
DEVOTED MYSELF TO STUDYING, AND THEN TO WORK. NEVER WAS MUCH OF A LADIES' MAN...
Hmmm ...
It's a tough call. He's rich, but...
...he seems really straight-edge.
SO...
IT'S REALLY ALL RIGHT WITH YOU?
GETTING MARRIED TO SOMEBODY YOU BARELY KNOW?
UMM ...
Sure, why not?
YES.

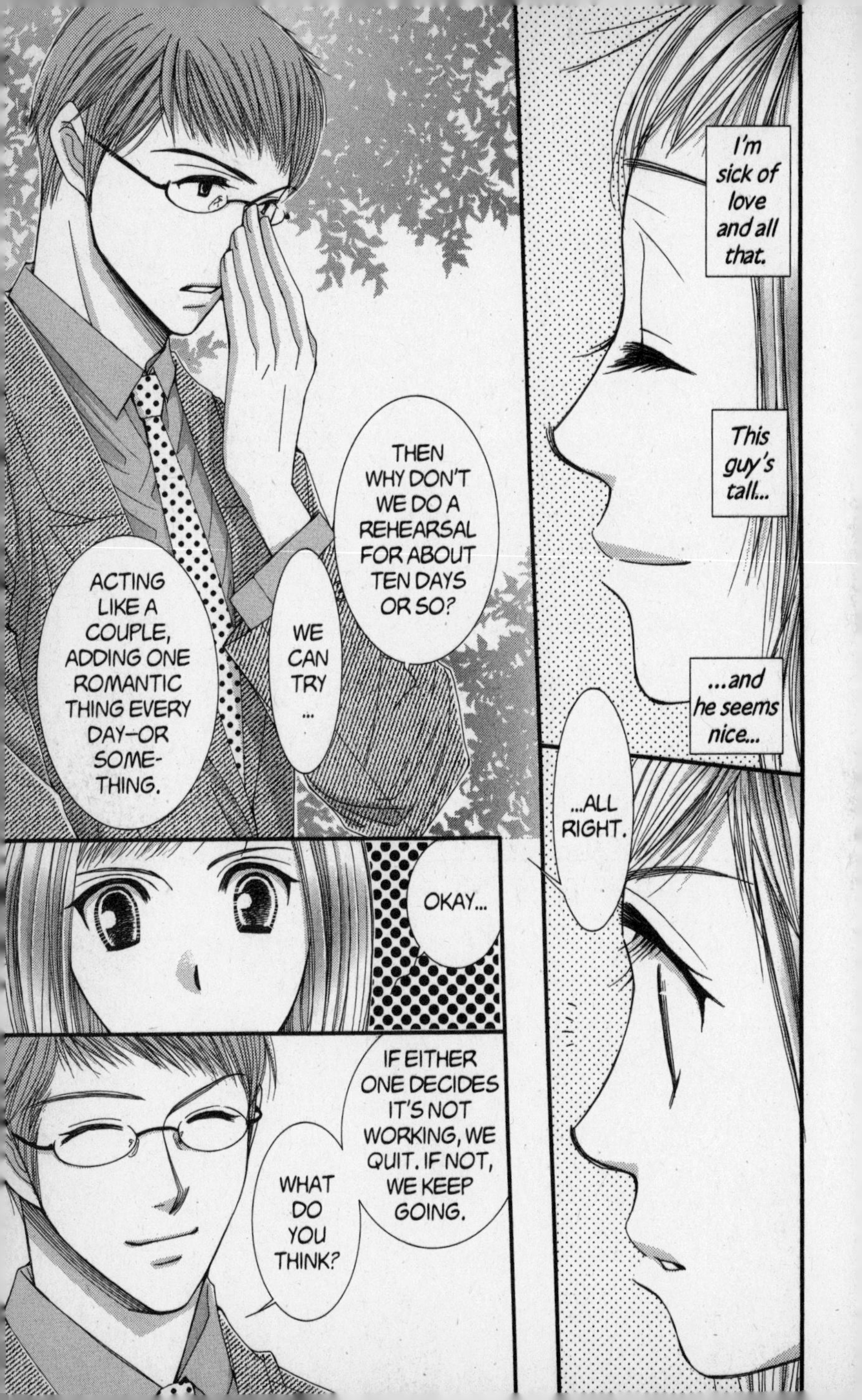
I'm sick of love and all that.
This guy's tall...
...and he seems nice...
...ALL RIGHT.
THEN WHY DON'T WE DO A REHEARSAL FOR ABOUT TEN DAYS OR SO?
WE CAN TRY ...
ACTING LIKE A COUPLE, ADDING ONE ROMANTIC THING EVERY DAY—OR SOME-THING.
OKAY...
IF EITHER ONE DECIDES IT'S NOT WORKING, WE QUIT. IF NOT, WE KEEP GOING.
WHAT DO YOU THINK?

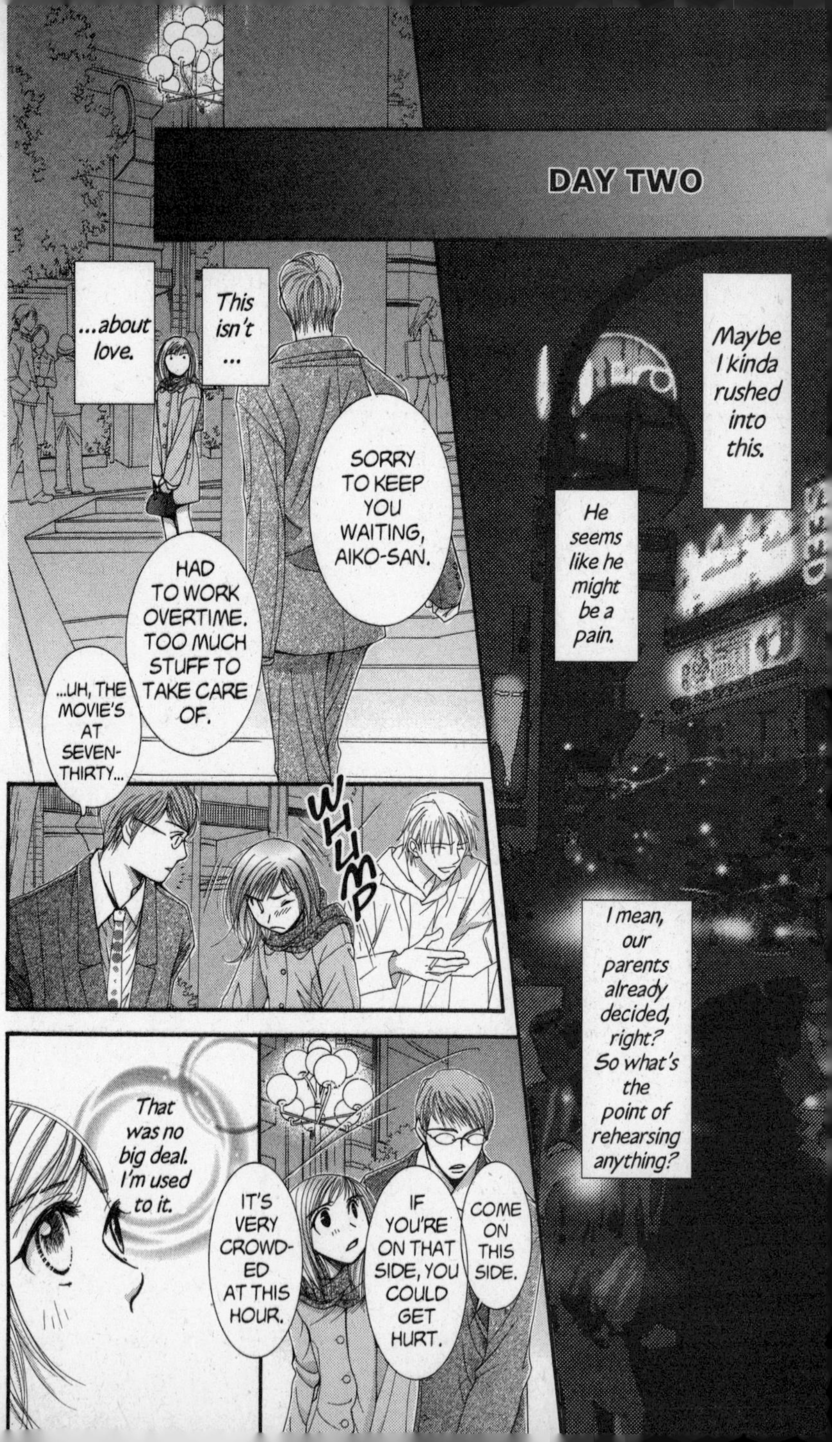
DAY TWO
Maybe I kinda rushed into this.
He seems like he might be a pain.
I mean, our parents already decided, right? So what's the point of rehearsing anything?
This isn't ...
...about love.
SORRY TO KEEP YOU WAITING, AIKO-SAN.
HAD TO WORK OVERTIME. TOO MUCH STUFF TO TAKE CARE OF.
...UH, THE MOVIE'S AT SEVEN-THIRTY...
WHUMP
COME ON THIS SIDE.
IF YOU'RE ON THAT SIDE, YOU COULD GET HURT.
IT'S VERY CROWDED AT THIS HOUR.
That was no big deal. I'm used to it.

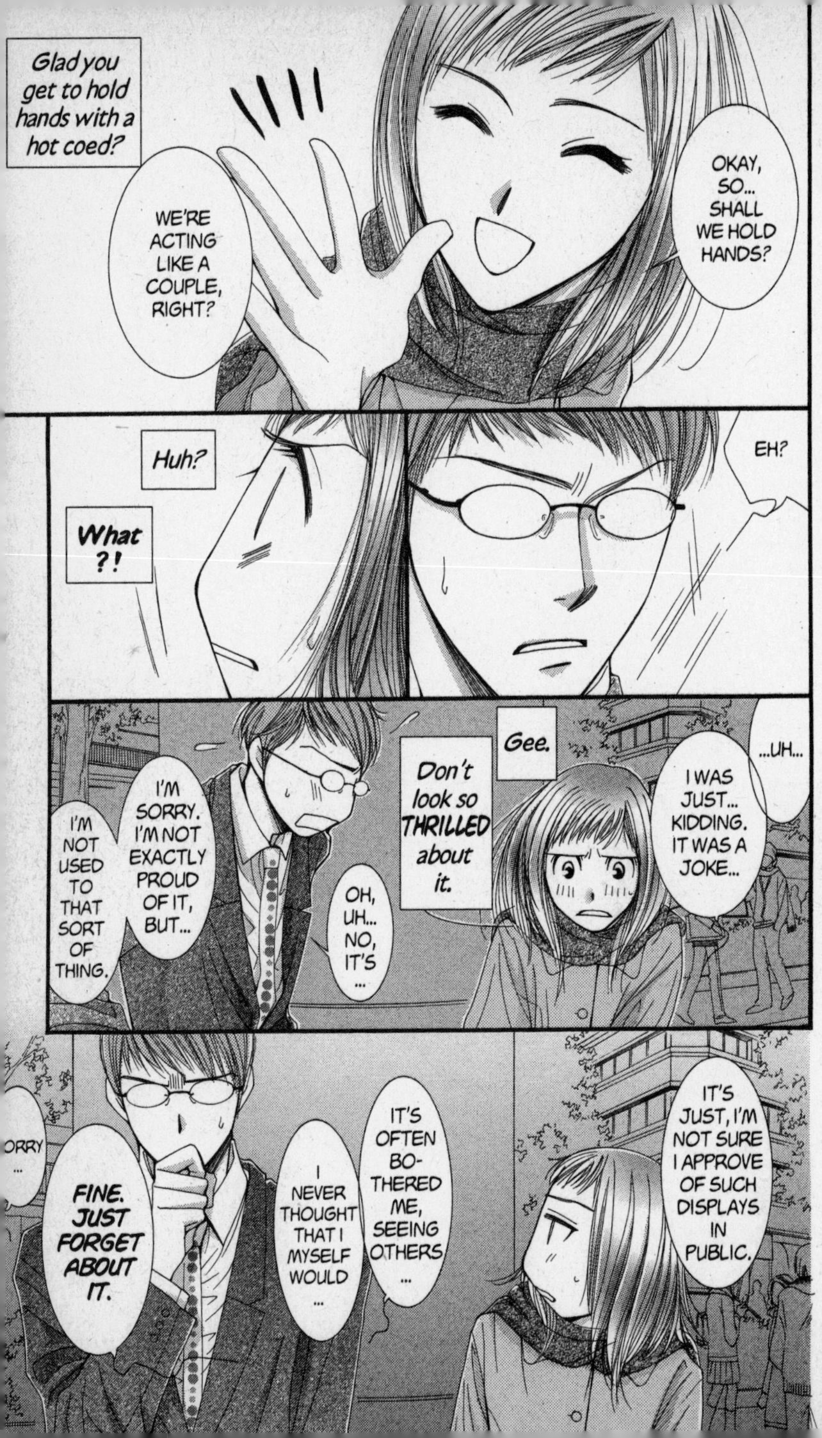
OKAY, SO... SHALL WE HOLD HANDS?
WE'RE ACTING LIKE A COUPLE, RIGHT?
Glad you get to hold hands with a hot coed?
EH?
Huh?
What ?!
...UH...
I WAS JUST... KIDDING. IT WAS A JOKE...
Gee.
Don't look so THRILLED about it.
OH, UH... NO, IT'S ...
I'M SORRY. I'M NOT EXACTLY PROUD OF IT, BUT...
I'M NOT USED TO THAT SORT OF THING.
IT'S JUST, I'M NOT SURE I APPROVE OF SUCH DISPLAYS IN PUBLIC.
IT'S OFTEN BO-THERED ME, SEEING OTHERS ...
I NEVER THOUGHT THAT I MYSELF WOULD ...
FINE. JUST FORGET ABOUT IT.
ORRY ...

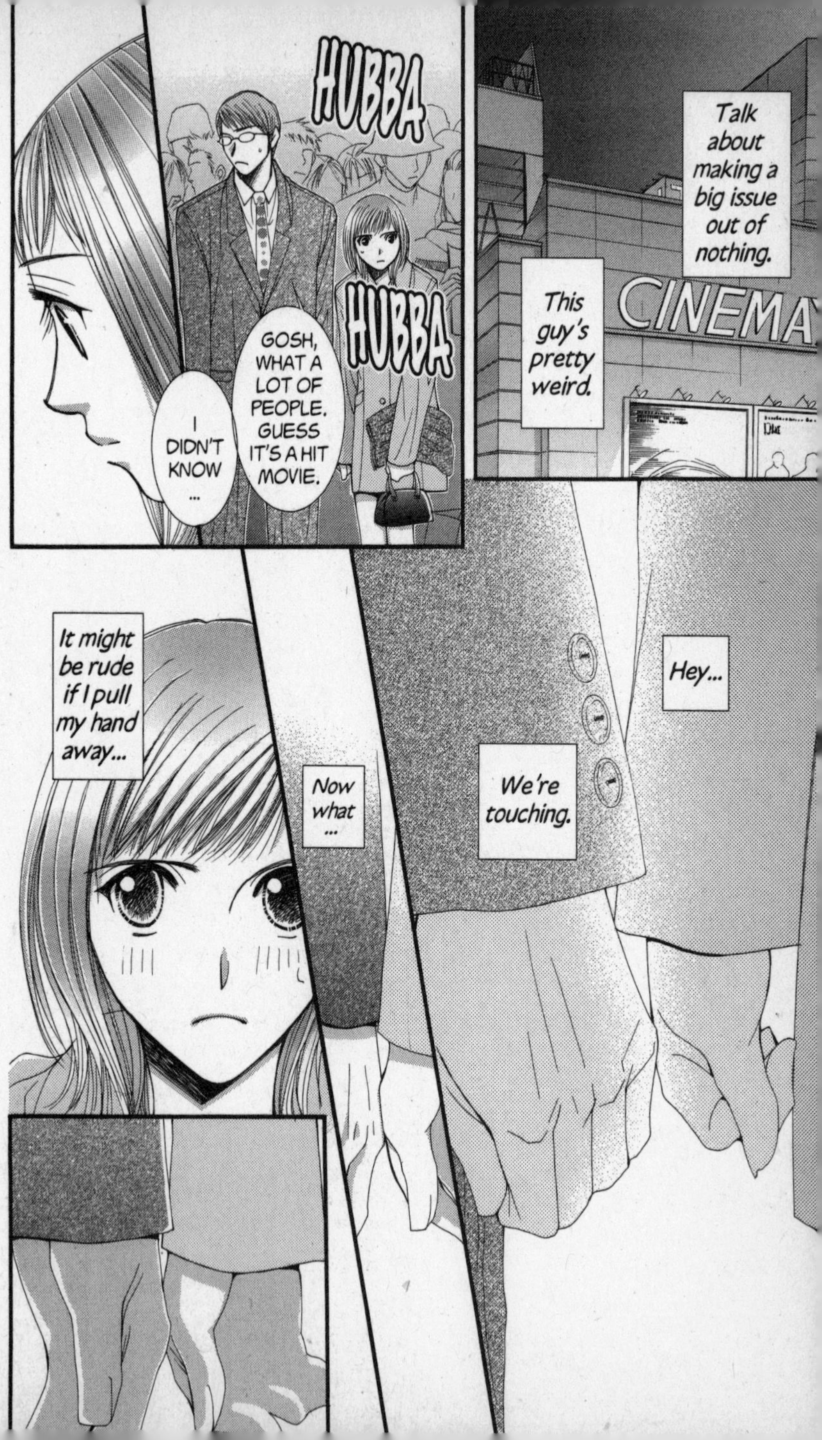
Talk about making a big issue out of nothing.
CINEMA
This guy's pretty weird.
HUBBA
HUBBA
GOSH, WHAT A LOT OF PEOPLE. GUESS IT'S A HIT MOVIE.
I DIDN'T KNOW ...
Hey...
We're touching.
Now what ...
It might be rude if I pull my hand away...

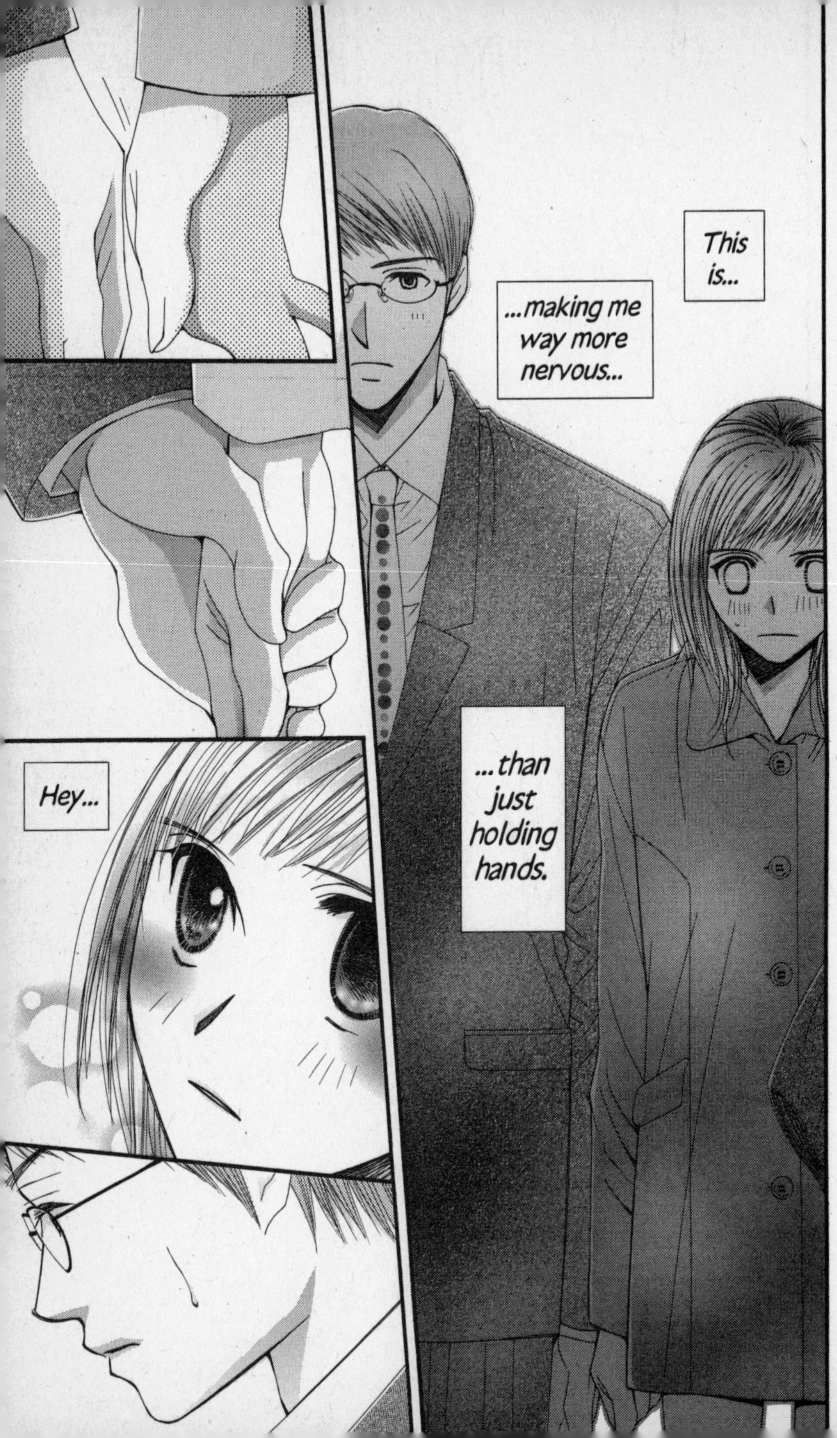
This is...
...making me way more nervous...
...than just holding hands.
Hey...

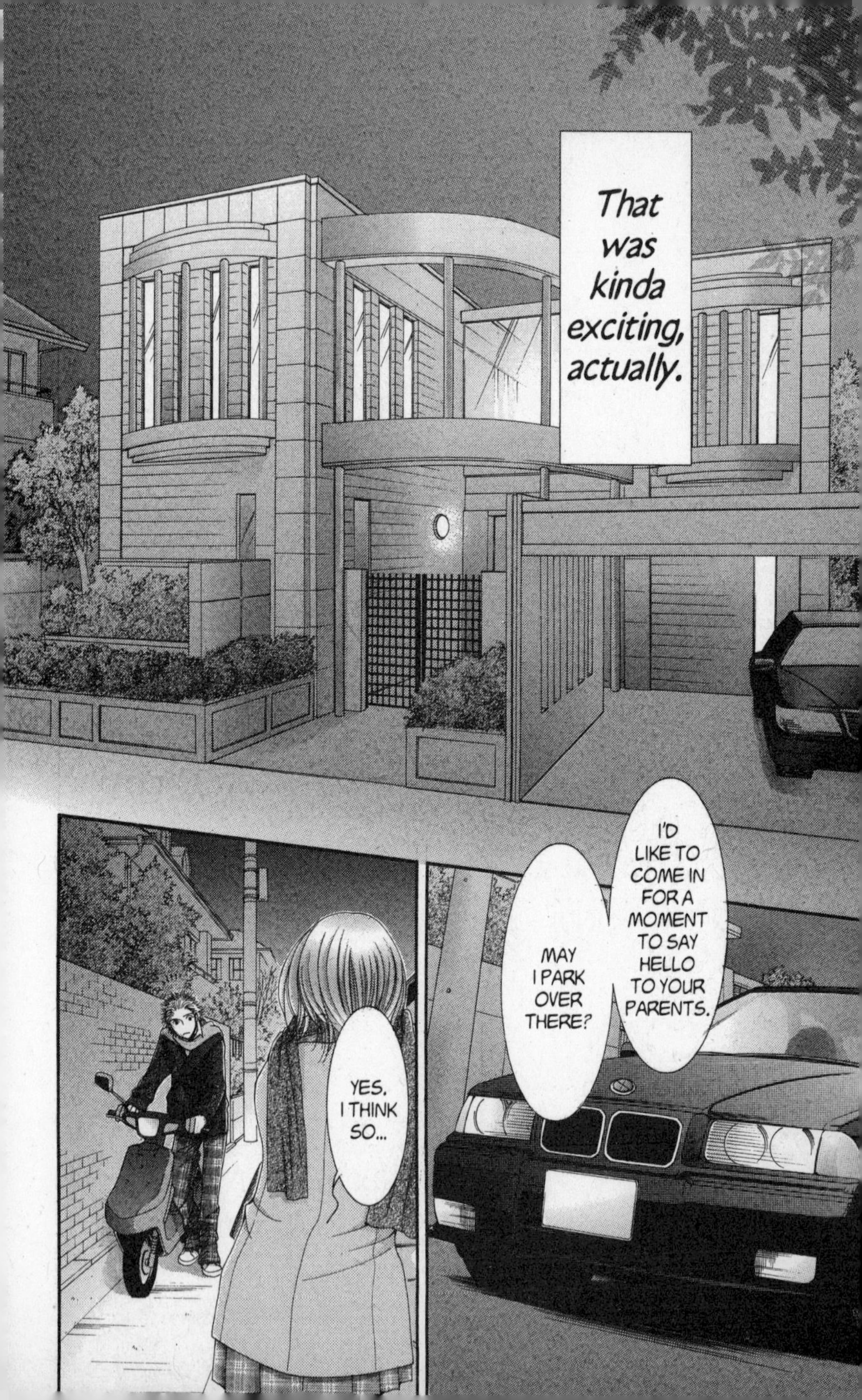
That was kinda exciting, actually.
I'D LIKE TO COME IN FOR A MOMENT TO SAY HELLO TO YOUR PARENTS.
MAY I PARK OVER THERE?
YES. I THINK SO...

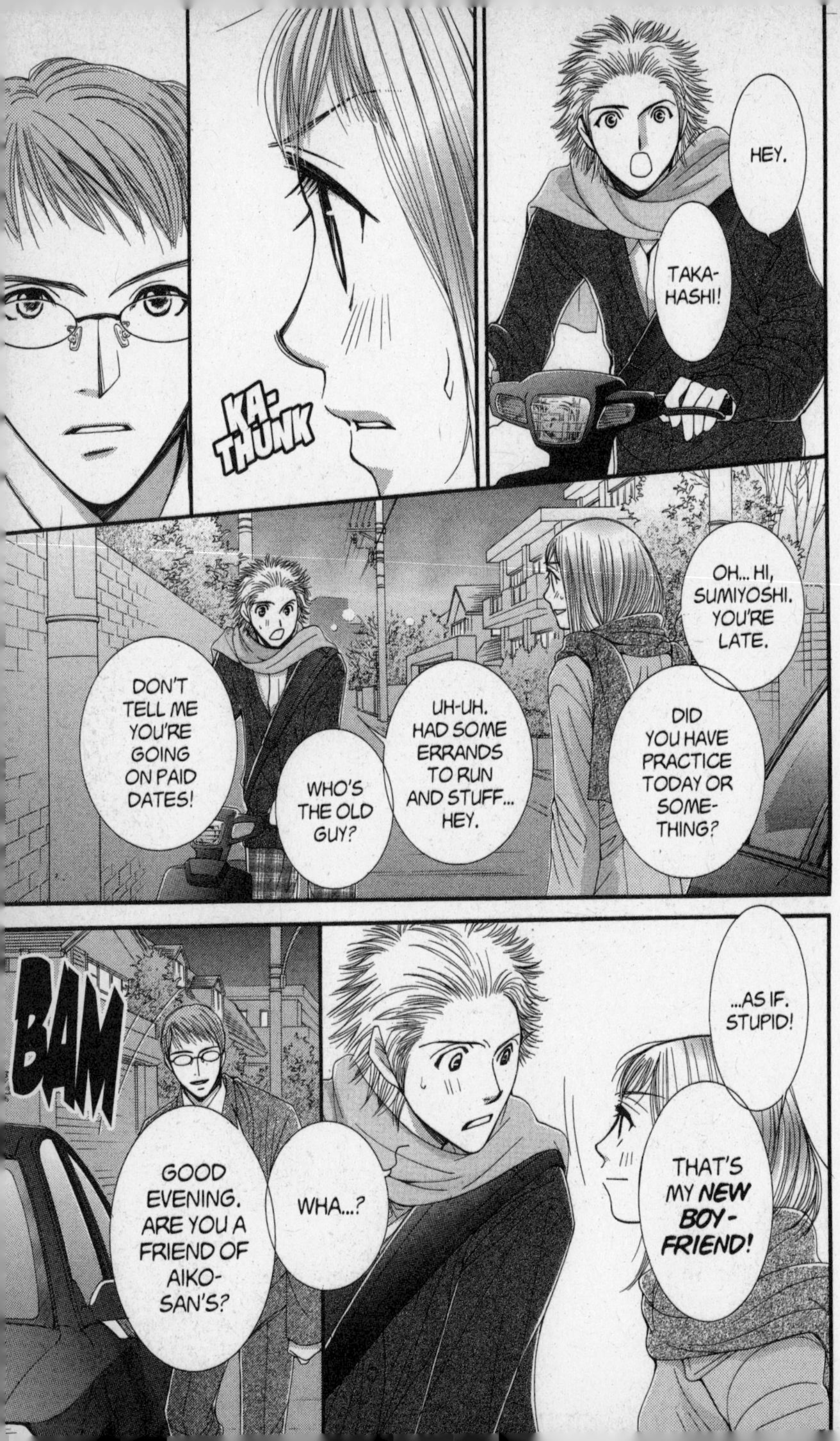
HEY.
TAKA-HASHI!
KA-THUNK
OH... HI, SUMIYOSHI. YOU'RE LATE.
DID YOU HAVE PRACTICE TODAY OR SOME-THING?
UH-UH. HAD SOME ERRANDS TO RUN AND STUFF... HEY.
WHO'S THE OLD GUY?
DON'T TELL ME YOU'RE GOING ON PAID DATES!
...AS IF. STUPID!
THAT'S MY ***NEW BOY-FRIEND!***
WHA...?
BAM
GOOD EVENING. ARE YOU A FRIEND OF AIKO-SAN'S?

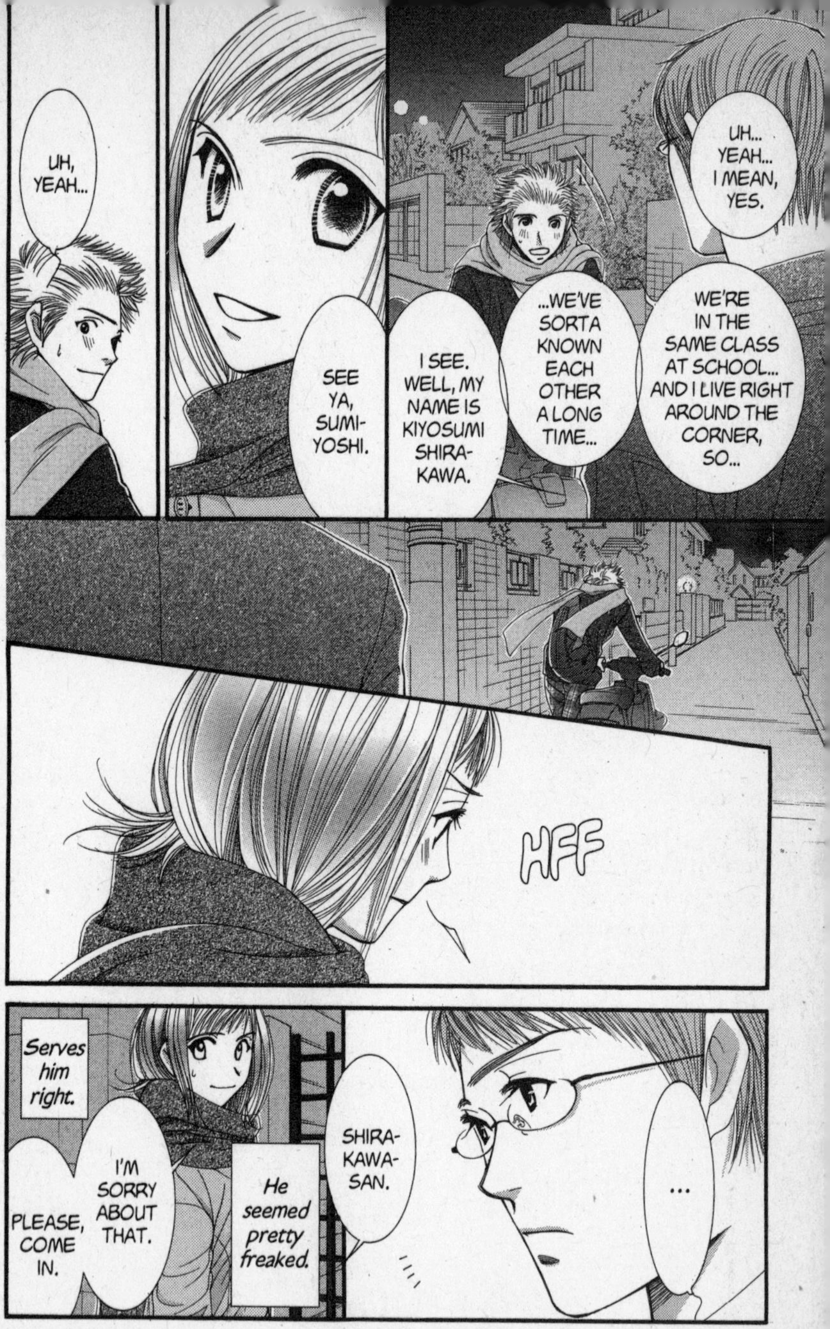
UH... YEAH... I MEAN, YES.
WE'RE IN THE SAME CLASS AT SCHOOL... AND I LIVE RIGHT AROUND THE CORNER, SO...
...WE'VE SORTA KNOWN EACH OTHER A LONG TIME...
I SEE. WELL, MY NAME IS KIYOSUMI SHIRA-KAWA.
SEE YA, SUMI-YOSHI.
UH, YEAH...
HFF
...
SHIRA-KAWA-SAN.
He seemed pretty freaked.
Serves him right.
I'M SORRY ABOUT THAT.
PLEASE, COME IN.

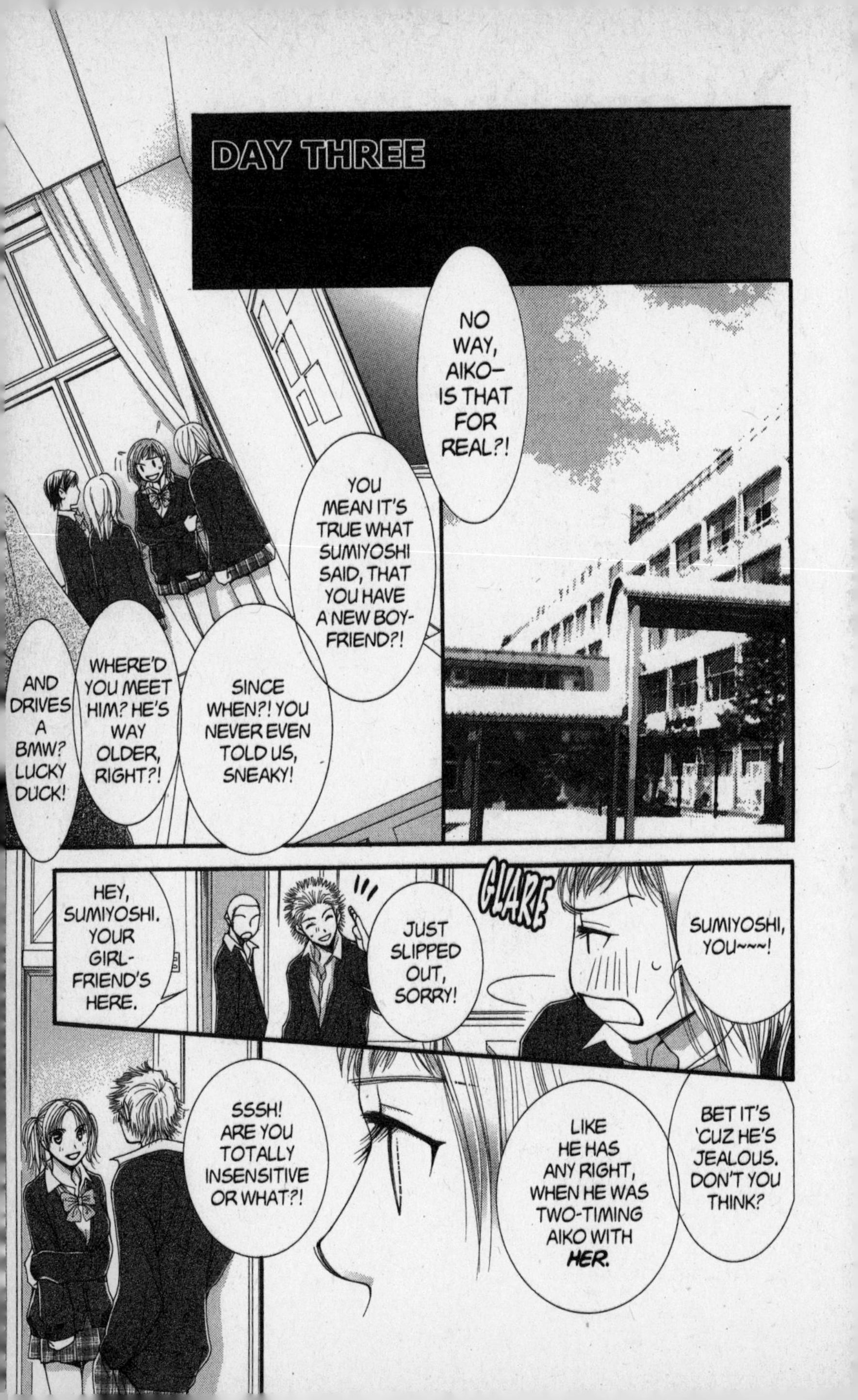
DAY THREE
NO WAY, AIKO— IS THAT FOR REAL?!
YOU MEAN IT'S TRUE WHAT SUMIYOSHI SAID, THAT YOU HAVE A NEW BOY-FRIEND?!
SINCE WHEN?! YOU NEVER EVEN TOLD US, SNEAKY!
WHERE'D YOU MEET HIM? HE'S WAY OLDER, RIGHT?!
AND DRIVES A BMW? LUCKY DUCK!
SUMIYOSHI, YOU~~~!
GLARE
JUST SLIPPED OUT, SORRY!
HEY, SUMIYOSHI. YOUR GIRL-FRIEND'S HERE.
BET IT'S 'CUZ HE'S JEALOUS. DON'T YOU THINK?
LIKE HE HAS ANY RIGHT, WHEN HE WAS TWO-TIMING AIKO WITH **HER**.
SSSH! ARE YOU TOTALLY INSENSITIVE OR WHAT?!

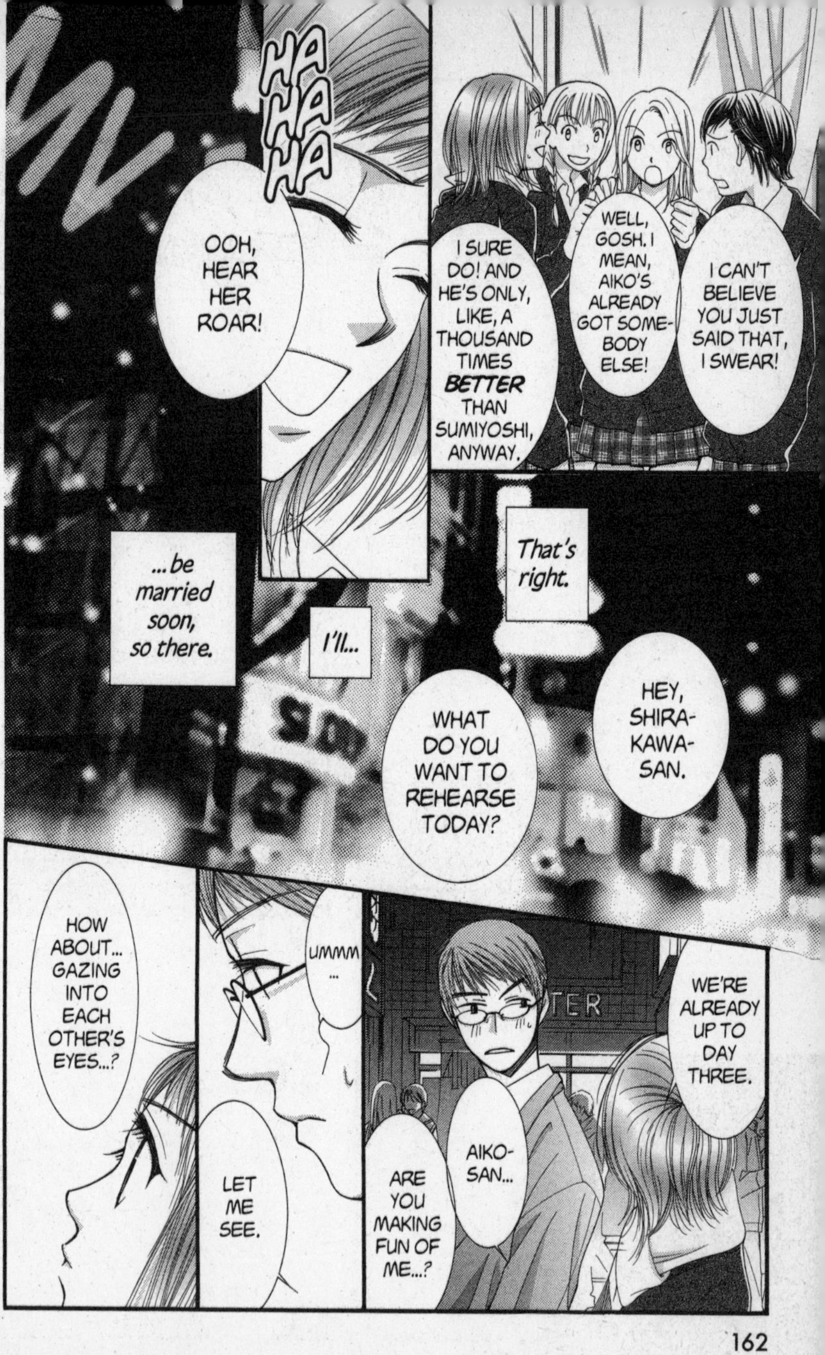
I CAN'T BELIEVE YOU JUST SAID THAT, I SWEAR!
WELL, GOSH. I MEAN, AIKO'S ALREADY GOT SOME-BODY ELSE!
I SURE DO! AND HE'S ONLY, LIKE, A THOUSAND TIMES **BETTER** THAN SUMIYOSHI, ANYWAY.
HAHAHA
OOH, HEAR HER ROAR!
That's right.
I'll...
...be married soon, so there.
HEY, SHIRA-KAWA-SAN.
WHAT DO YOU WANT TO REHEARSE TODAY?
WE'RE ALREADY UP TO DAY THREE.
AIKO-SAN...
ARE YOU MAKING FUN OF ME...?
UMMM...
LET ME SEE.
HOW ABOUT... GAZING INTO EACH OTHER'S EYES...?

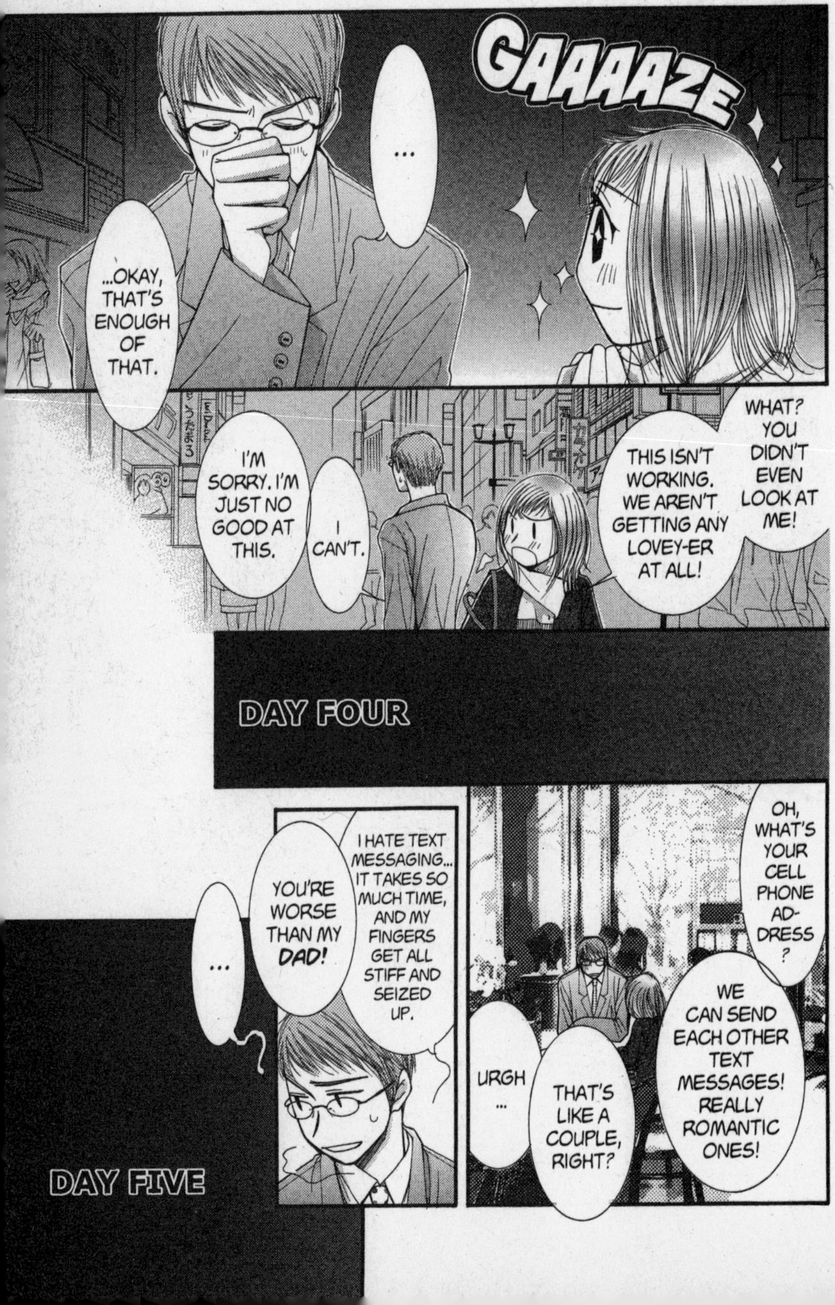
GAAAAZE
...
...OKAY, THAT'S ENOUGH OF THAT.
WHAT? YOU DIDN'T EVEN LOOK AT ME!
THIS ISN'T WORKING. WE AREN'T GETTING ANY LOVEY-ER AT ALL!
I CAN'T.
I'M SORRY. I'M JUST NO GOOD AT THIS.
DAY FOUR
OH, WHAT'S YOUR CELL PHONE AD-DRESS?
WE CAN SEND EACH OTHER TEXT MESSAGES! REALLY ROMANTIC ONES!
THAT'S LIKE A COUPLE, RIGHT?
URGH...
I HATE TEXT MESSAGING... IT TAKES SO MUCH TIME, AND MY FINGERS GET ALL STIFF AND SEIZED UP.
YOU'RE WORSE THAN MY DAD!
...
DAY FIVE

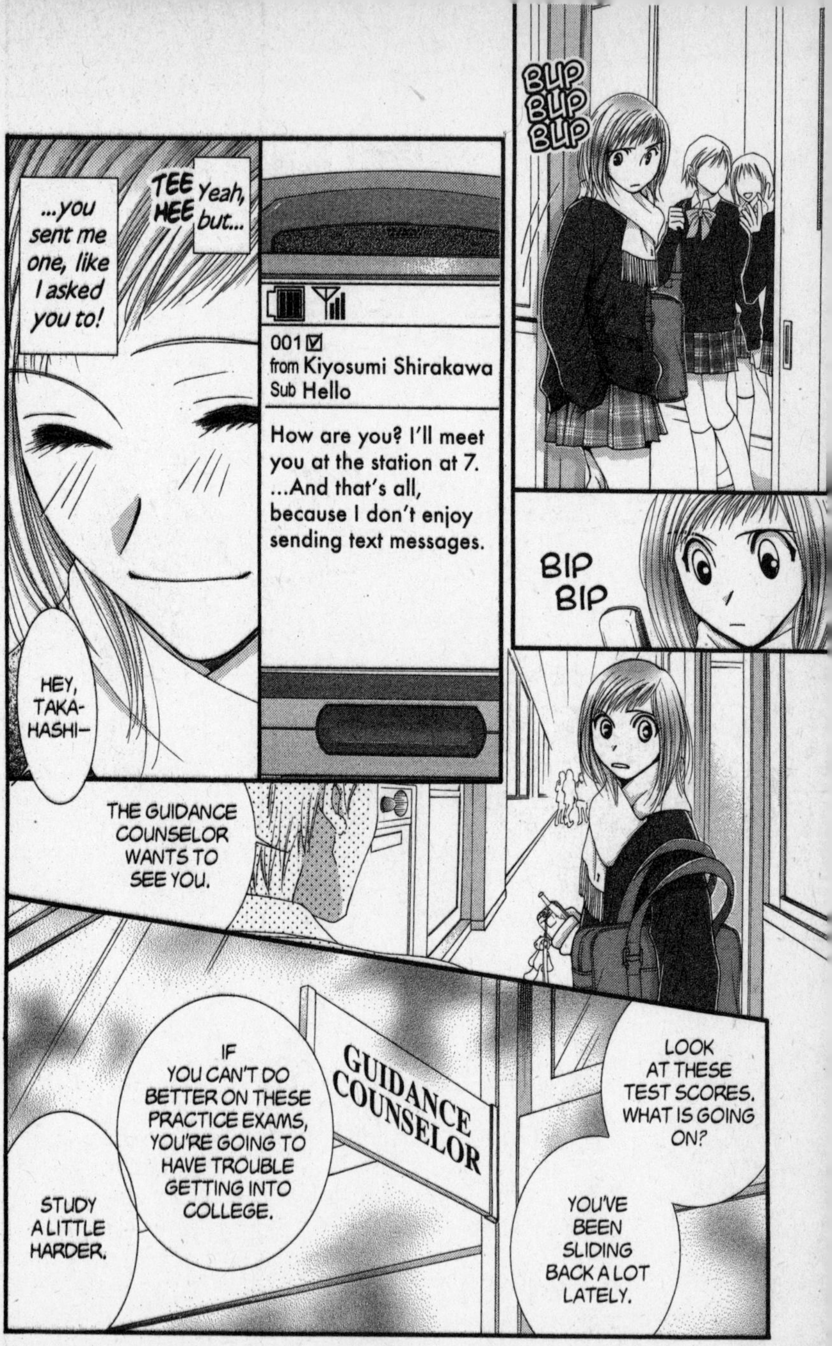

BLIP
BLIP
BLIP
BIP
BIP
001
from Kiyosumi Shirakawa
Sub Hello
How are you? I'll meet you at the station at 7. ...And that's all, because I don't enjoy sending text messages.
Yeah, but...
TEE HEE
...you sent me one, like I asked you to!
HEY, TAKA-HASHI—
THE GUIDANCE COUNSELOR WANTS TO SEE YOU.
GUIDANCE COUNSELOR
LOOK AT THESE TEST SCORES. WHAT IS GOING ON?
YOU'VE BEEN SLIDING BACK A LOT LATELY.
IF YOU CAN'T DO BETTER ON THESE PRACTICE EXAMS, YOU'RE GOING TO HAVE TROUBLE GETTING INTO COLLEGE.
STUDY A LITTLE HARDER.

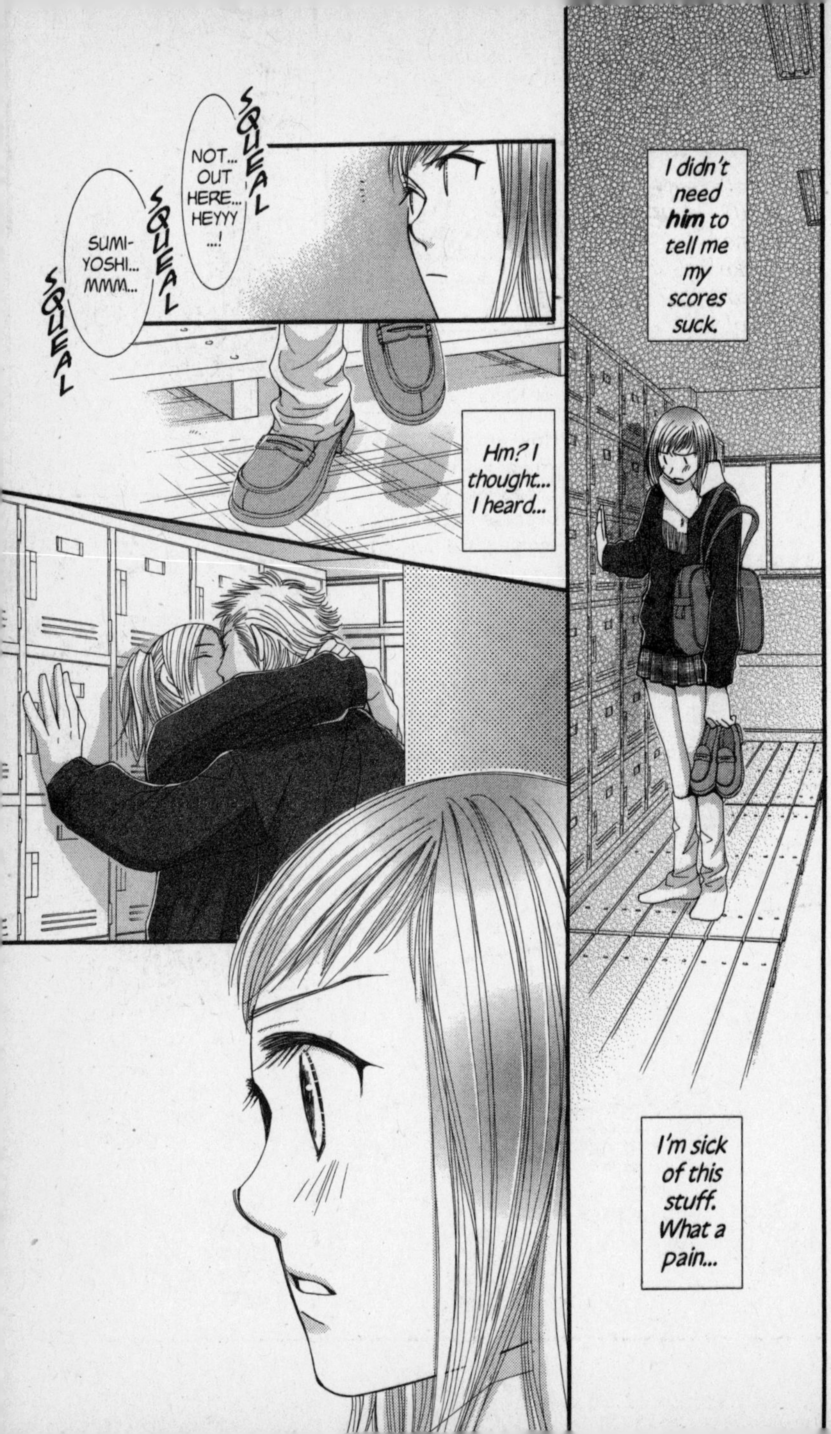
I didn't need **him** to tell me my scores suck.
I'm sick of this stuff. What a pain...
SQUEAL
NOT... OUT HERE... HEYYY ...!
SQUEAL
SUMI-YOSHI... MMM...
SQUEAL
Hm? I thought... I heard...

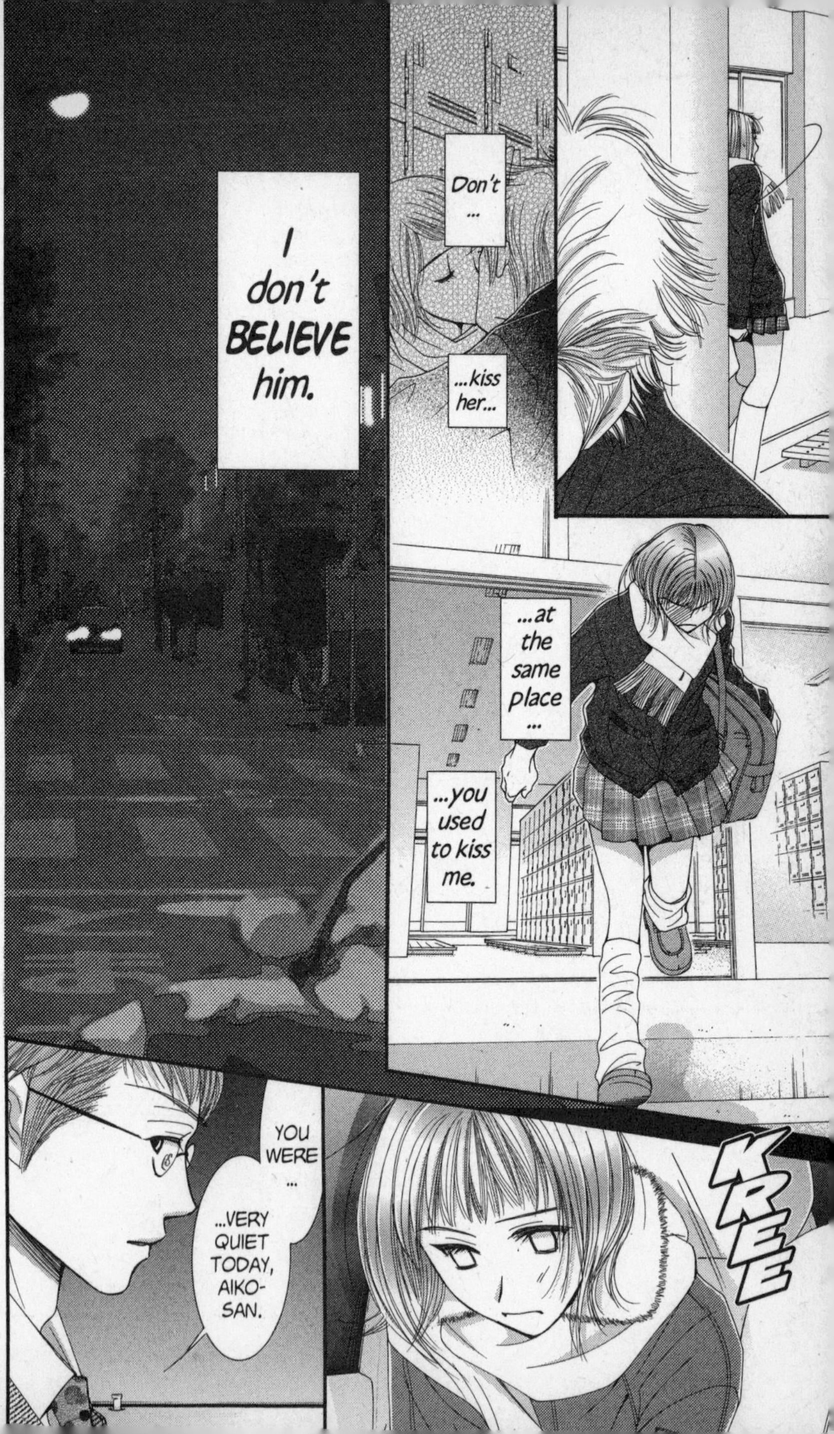
Don't ...
...kiss her...
...at the same place ...
...you used to kiss me.
I don't BELIEVE him.
KREE
YOU WERE ...
...VERY QUIET TODAY, AIKO-SAN.

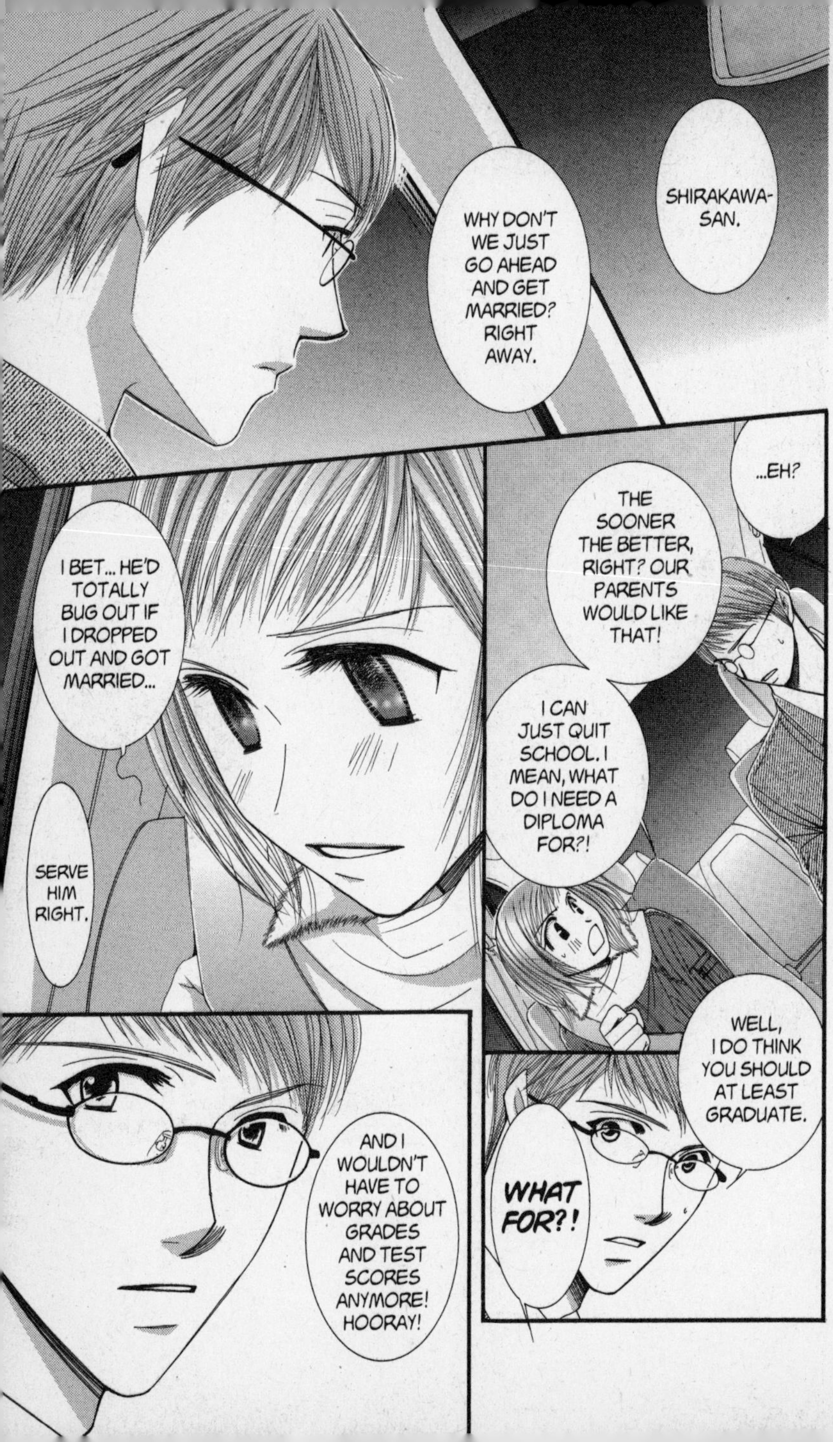
SHIRAKAWA-SAN.
WHY DON'T WE JUST GO AHEAD AND GET MARRIED? RIGHT AWAY.
...EH?
THE SOONER THE BETTER, RIGHT? OUR PARENTS WOULD LIKE THAT!
I CAN JUST QUIT SCHOOL. I MEAN, WHAT DO I NEED A DIPLOMA FOR?!
I BET... HE'D TOTALLY BUG OUT IF I DROPPED OUT AND GOT MARRIED...
SERVE HIM RIGHT.
WELL, I DO THINK YOU SHOULD AT LEAST GRADUATE.
WHAT FOR?!
AND I WOULDN'T HAVE TO WORRY ABOUT GRADES AND TEST SCORES ANYMORE! HOORAY!

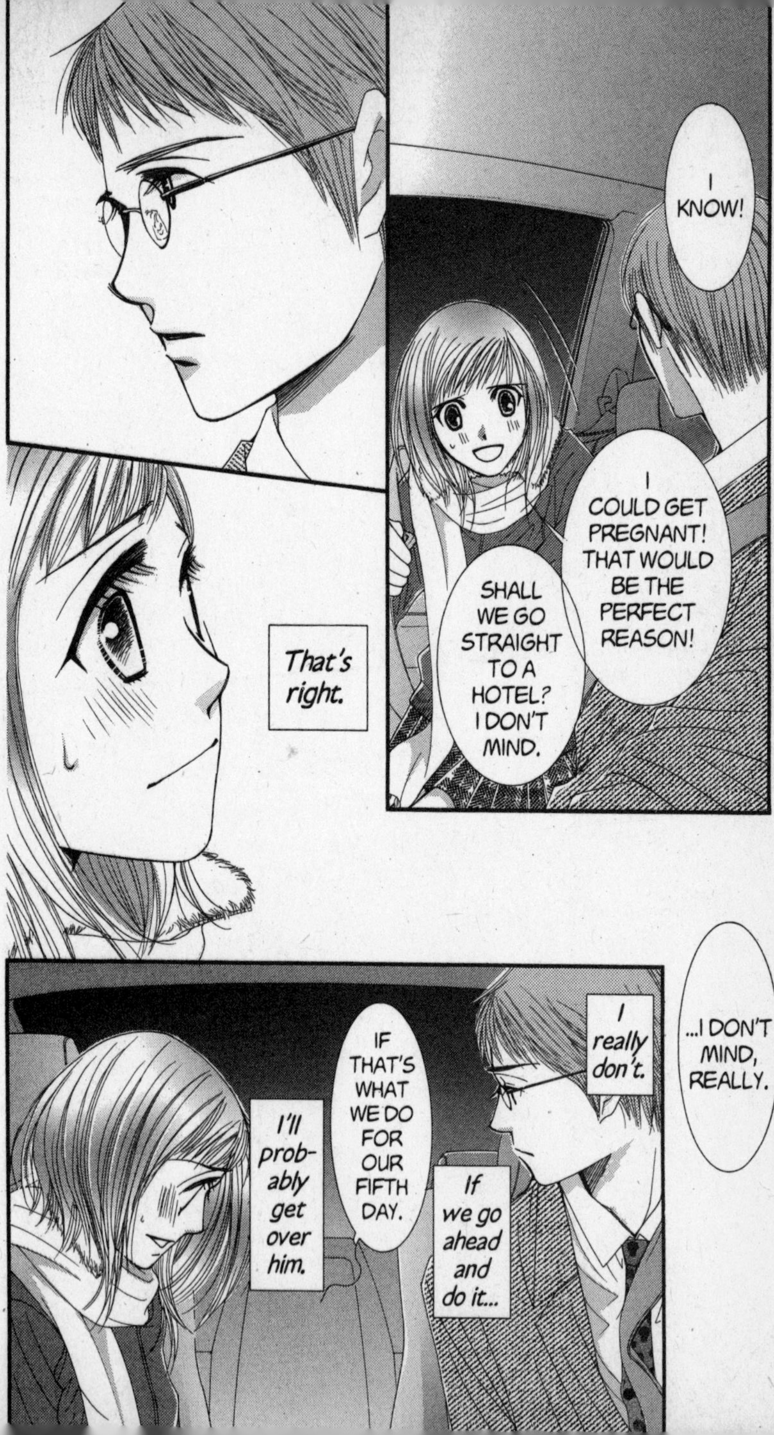
I KNOW!
I COULD GET PREGNANT! THAT WOULD BE THE PERFECT REASON!
SHALL WE GO STRAIGHT TO A HOTEL? I DON'T MIND.
That's right.
...I DON'T MIND, REALLY.
I really don't.
If we go ahead and do it...
IF THAT'S WHAT WE DO FOR OUR FIFTH DAY.
I'll probably get over him.

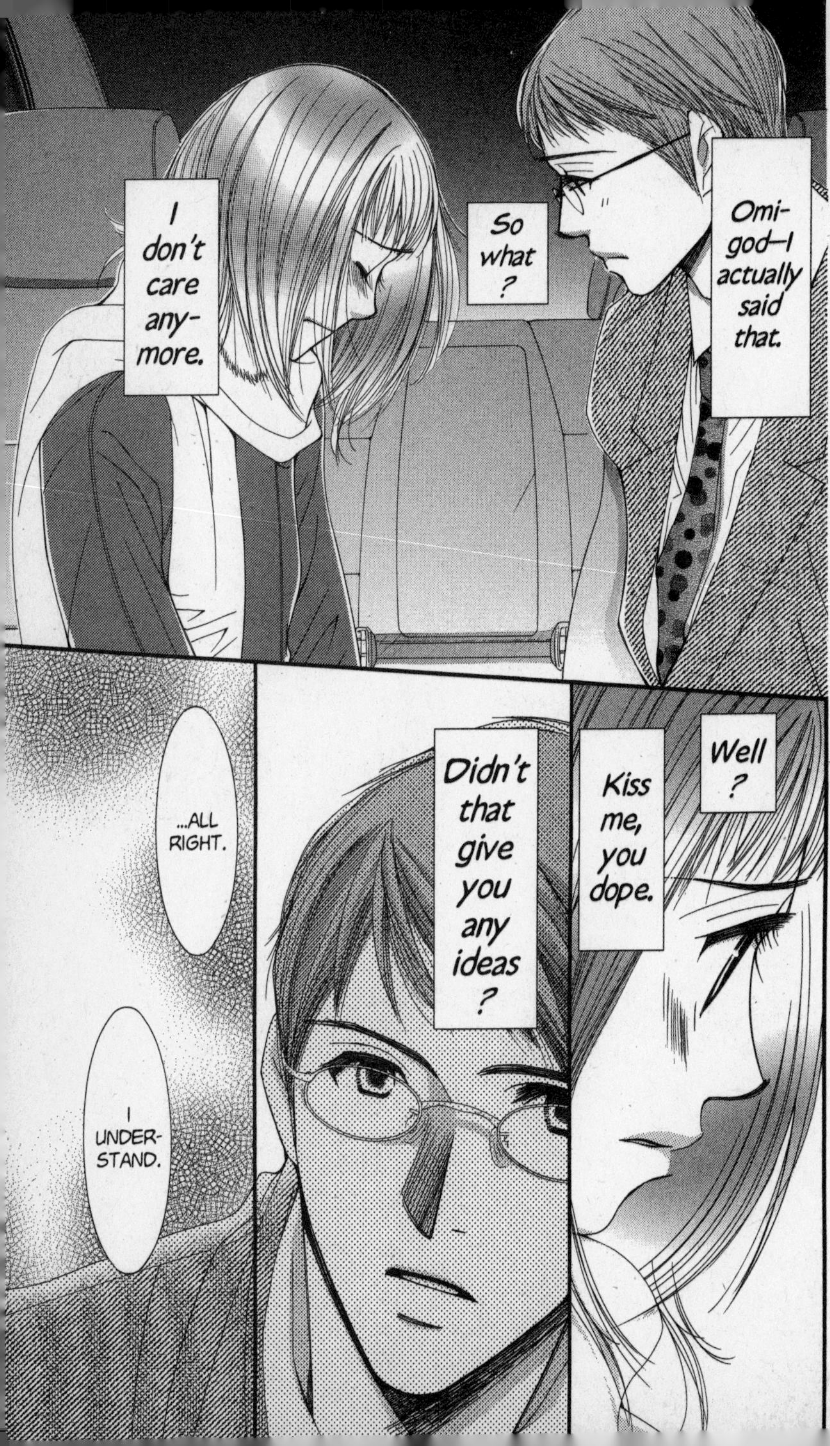
Omi-god—I actually said that.
So what?
I don't care anymore.
Well?
Kiss me, you dope.
Didn't that give you any ideas?
...ALL RIGHT.
I UNDERSTAND.

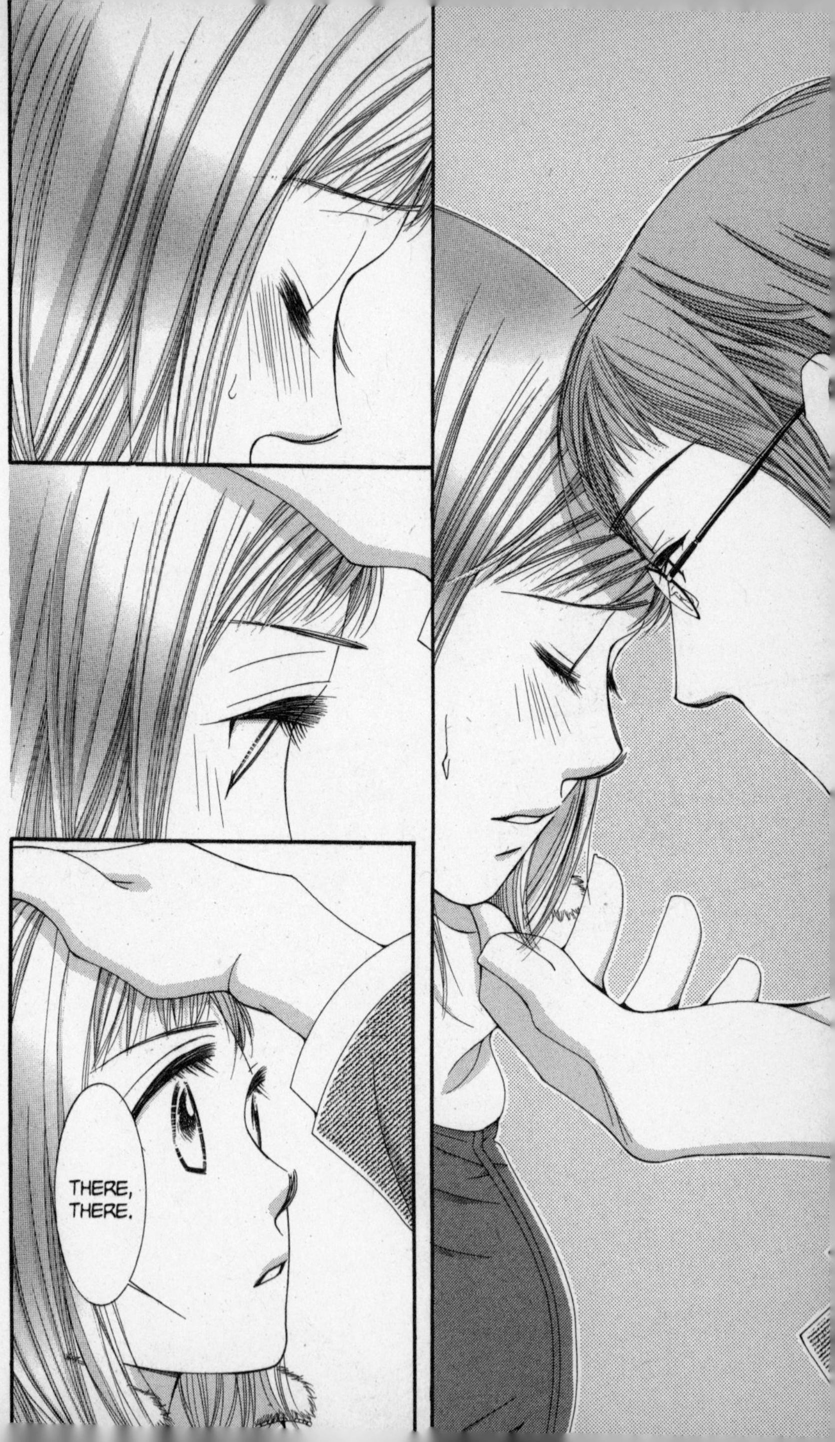
THERE, THERE.

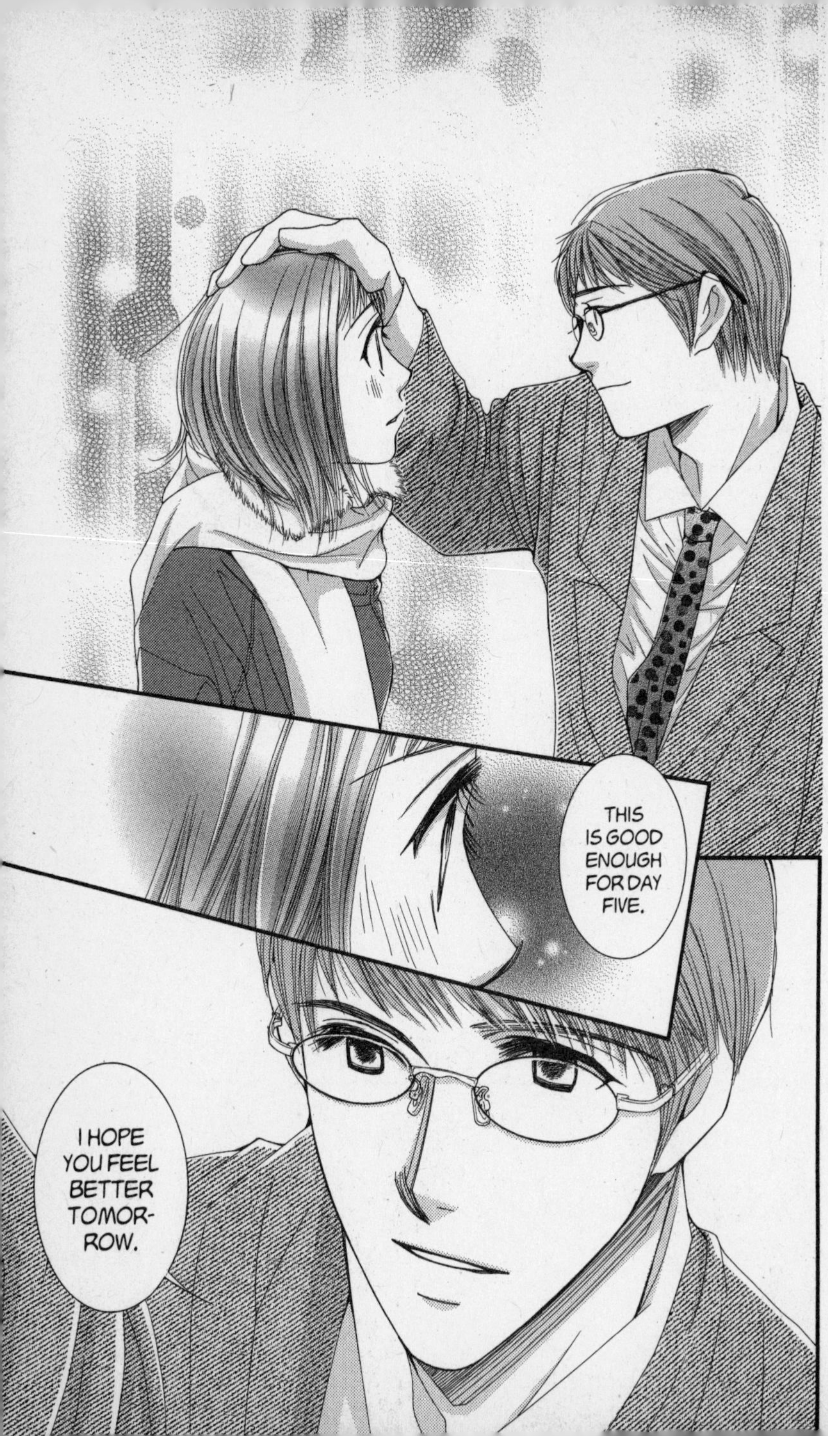
THIS IS GOOD ENOUGH FOR DAY FIVE.
I HOPE YOU FEEL BETTER TOMOR-ROW.

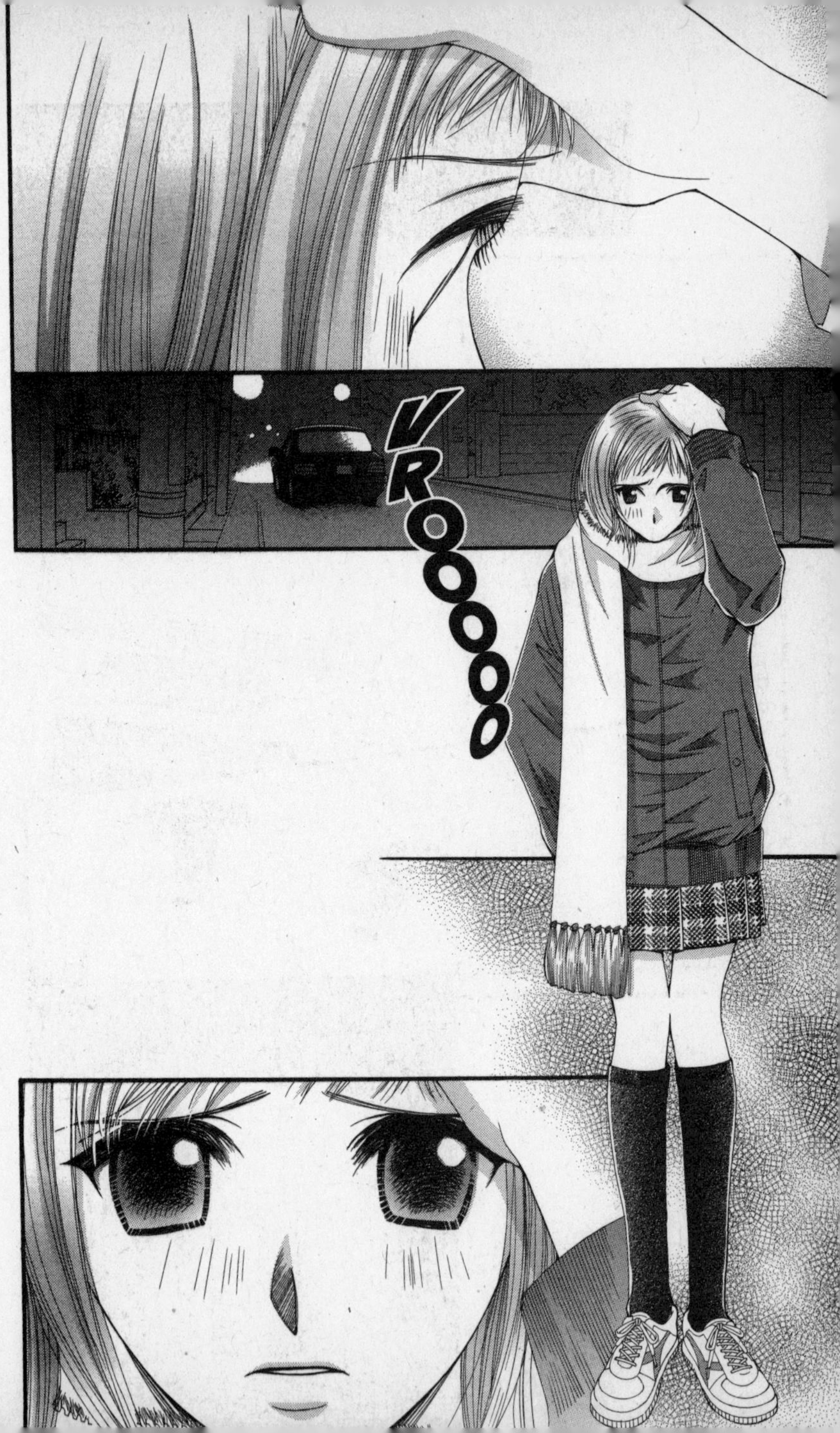
VROOOOOO

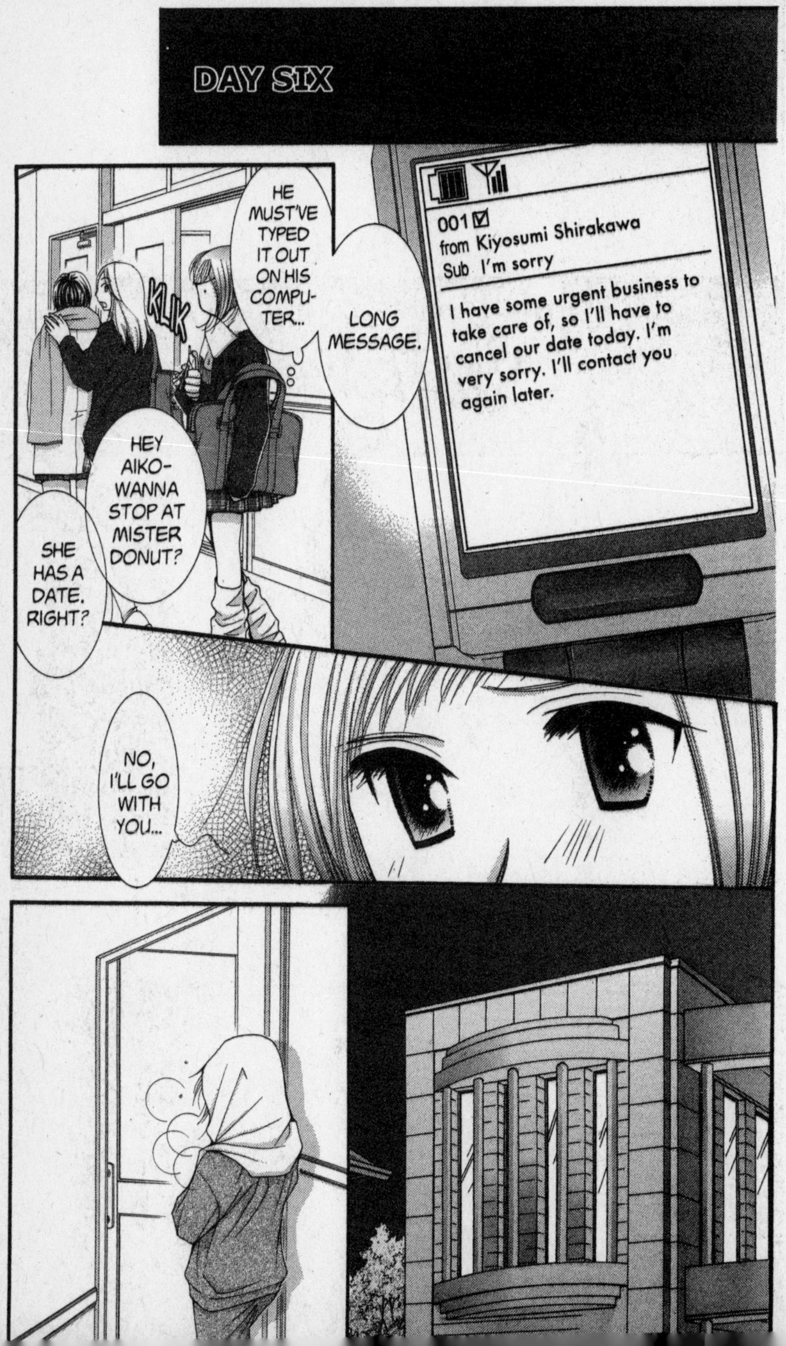
DAY SIX
001
from Kiyosumi Shirakawa
Sub I'm sorry
I have some urgent business to take care of, so I'll have to cancel our date today. I'm very sorry. I'll contact you again later.
LONG MESSAGE.
HE MUST'VE TYPED IT OUT ON HIS COMPUTER...
KLIK
HEY AIKO-WANNA STOP AT MISTER DONUT?
SHE HAS A DATE. RIGHT?
NO, I'LL GO WITH YOU...

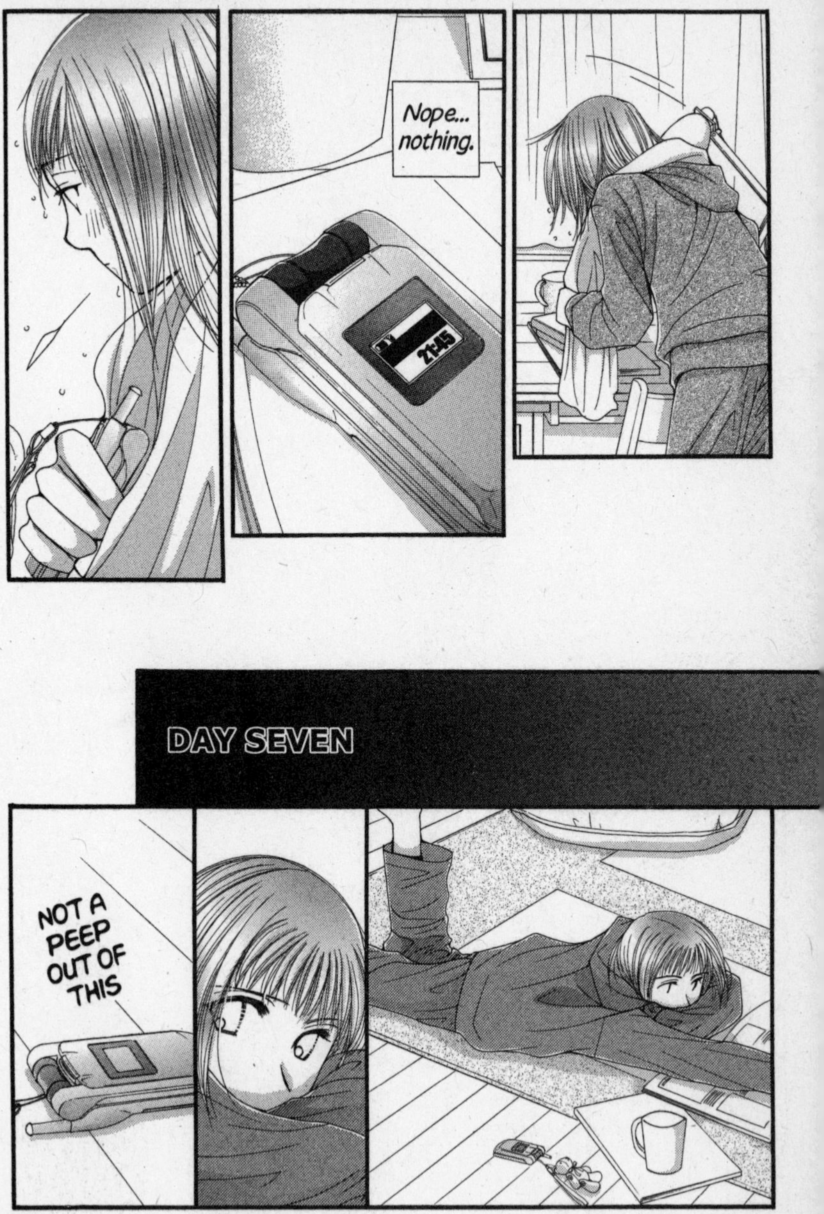
Nope... nothing.
21:45
DAY SEVEN
NOT A PEEP OUT OF THIS

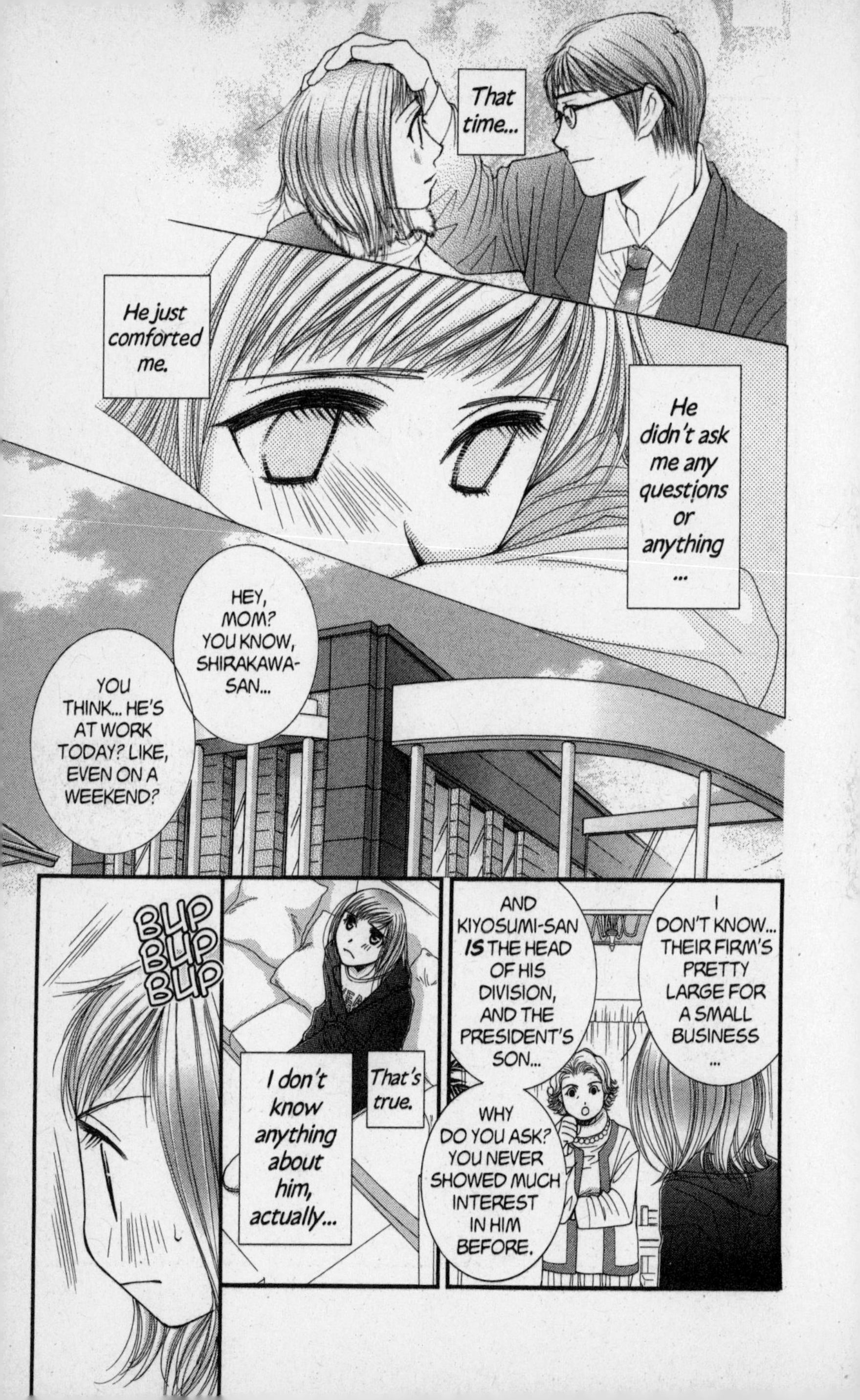
That time...
He didn't ask me any questions or anything ...
He just comforted me.
HEY, MOM? YOU KNOW, SHIRAKAWA-SAN...
YOU THINK... HE'S AT WORK TODAY? LIKE, EVEN ON A WEEKEND?
I DON'T KNOW... THEIR FIRM'S PRETTY LARGE FOR A SMALL BUSINESS ...
AND KIYOSUMI-SAN IS THE HEAD OF HIS DIVISION, AND THE PRESIDENT'S SON...
WHY DO YOU ASK? YOU NEVER SHOWED MUCH INTEREST IN HIM BEFORE.
That's true.
I don't know anything about him, actually...
BUP BUP BUP

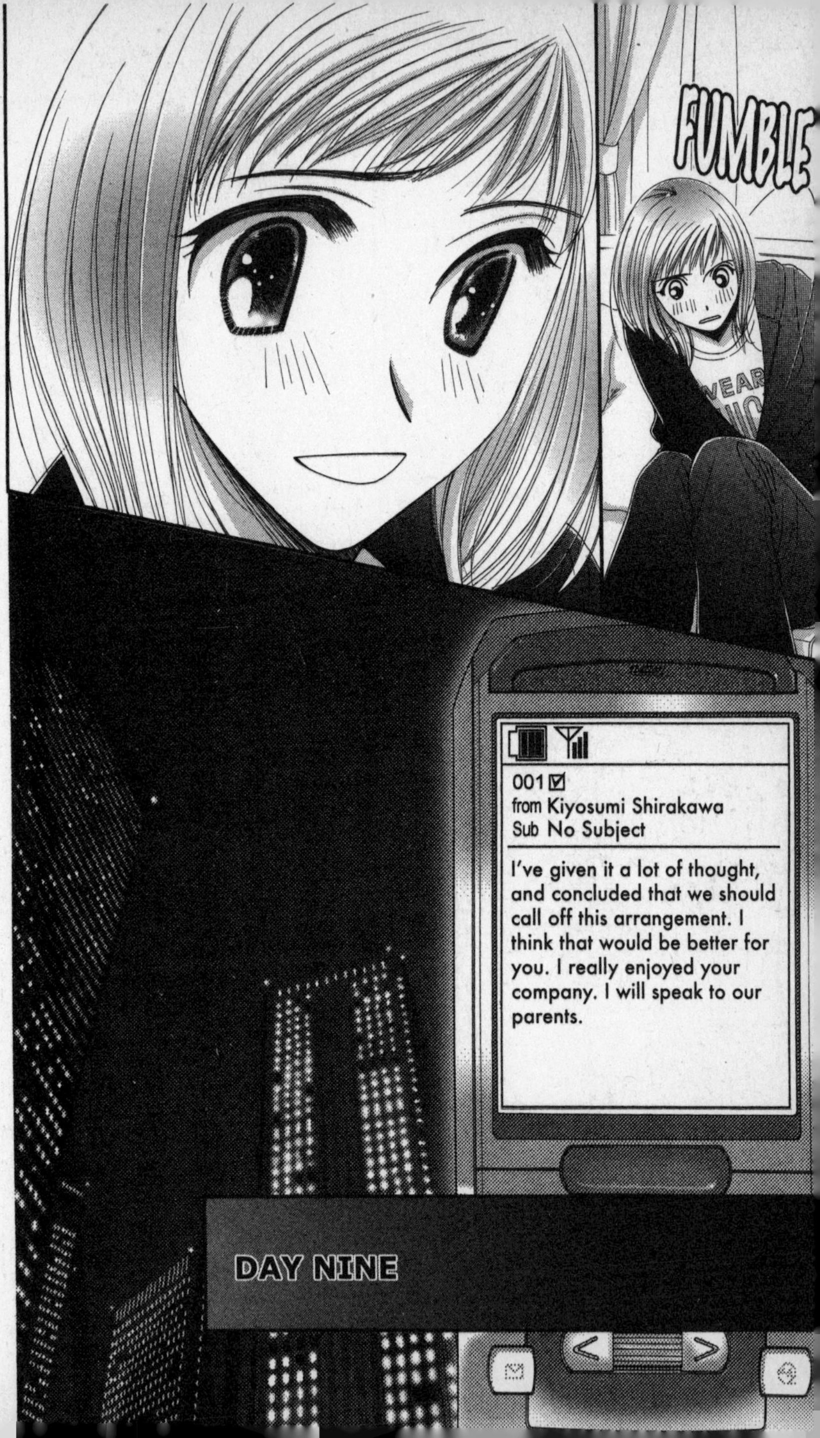
FUMBLE
001
from Kiyosumi Shirakawa
Sub No Subject
I've given it a lot of thought, and concluded that we should call off this arrangement. I think that would be better for you. I really enjoyed your company. I will speak to our parents.
DAY NINE

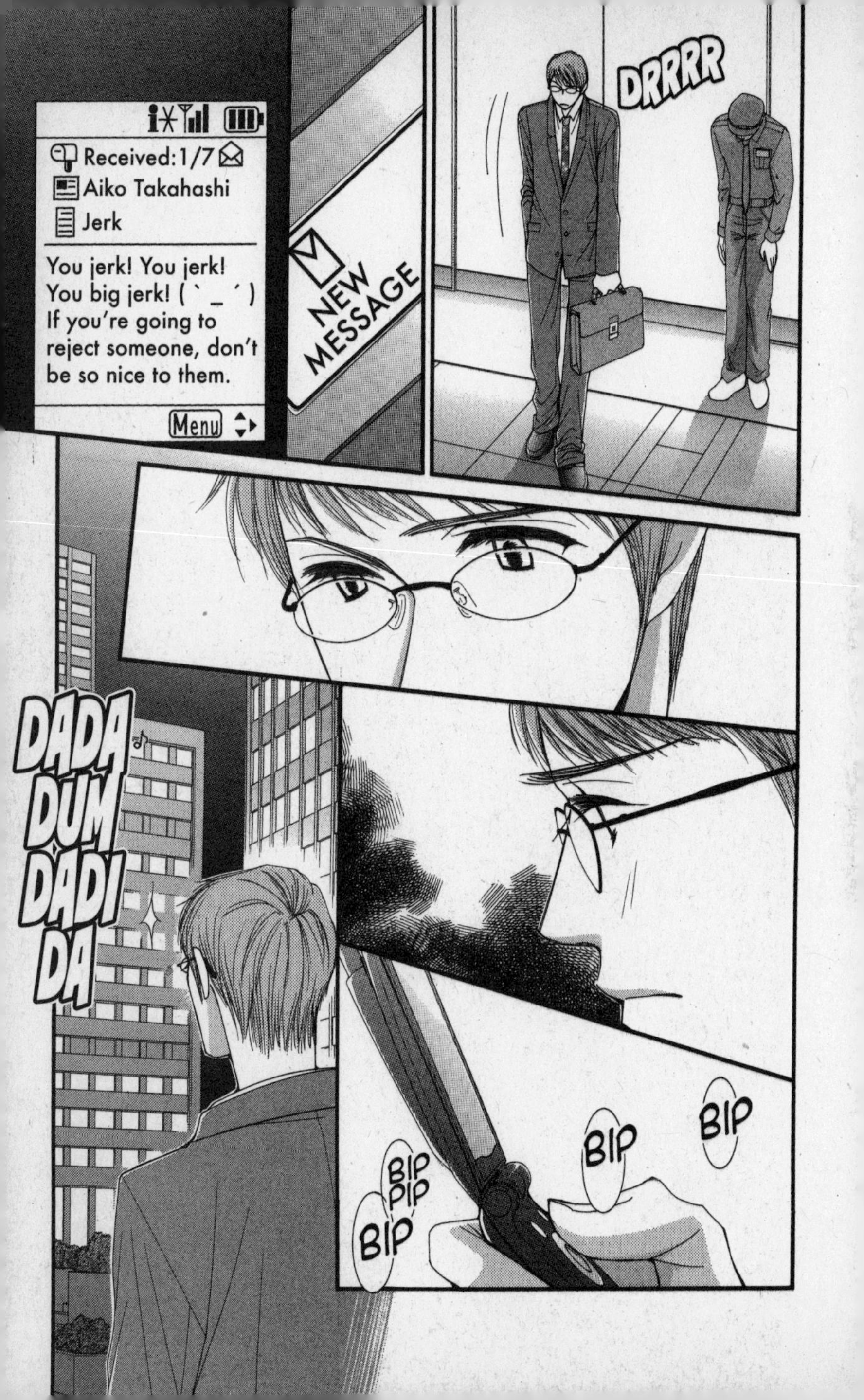
DRRRR
NEW MESSAGE
Received: 1/7
Aiko Takahashi
Jerk
You jerk! You jerk! You big jerk! (` _ ´) If you're going to reject someone, don't be so nice to them.
Menu
BIP
BIP
BIP PIP BIP
DADA DUM DADI DA

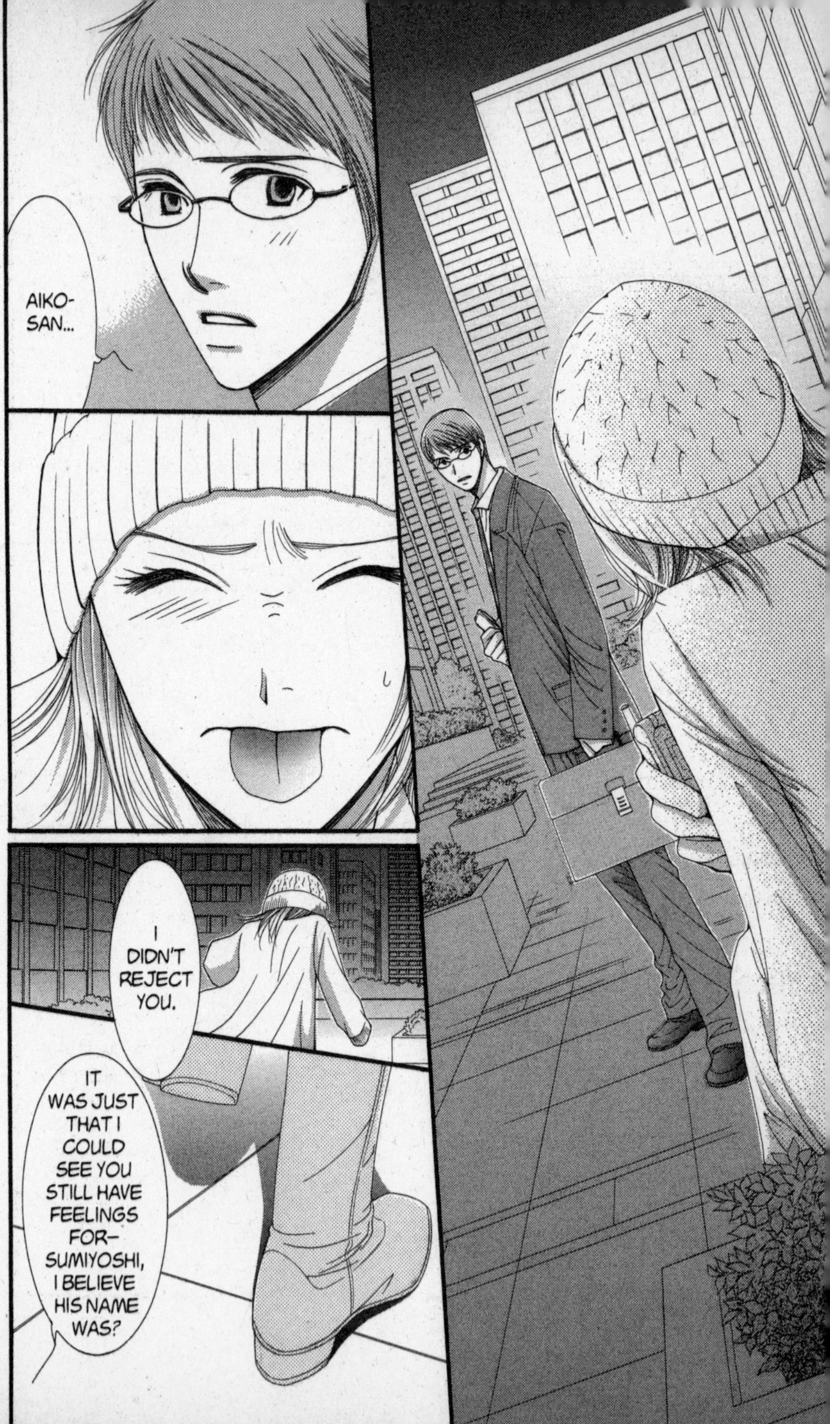
AIKO-SAN...
I DIDN'T REJECT YOU.
IT WAS JUST THAT I COULD SEE YOU STILL HAVE FEELINGS FOR– SUMIYOSHI, I BELIEVE HIS NAME WAS?

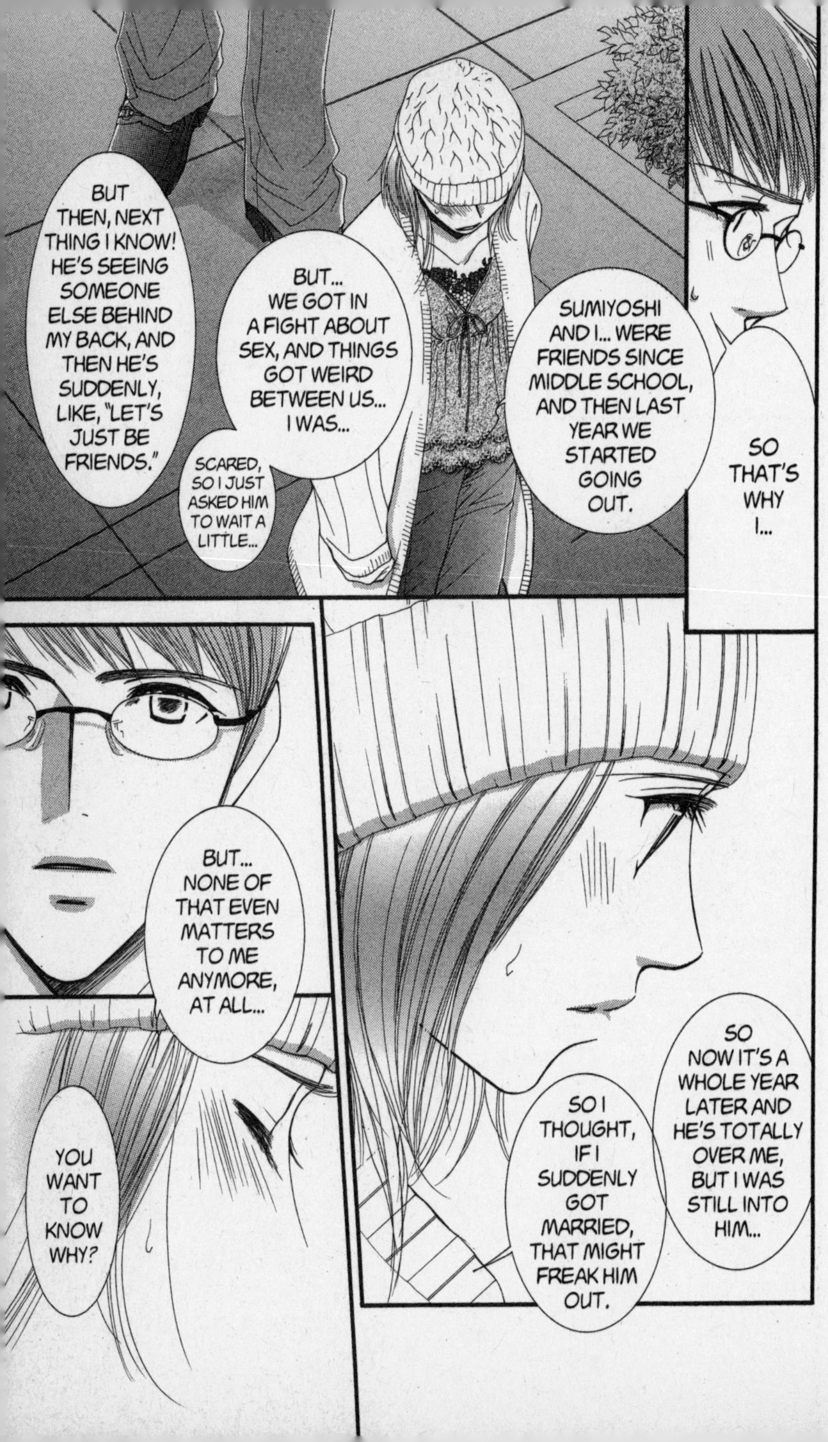
SO THAT'S WHY I...
SUMIYOSHI AND I... WERE FRIENDS SINCE MIDDLE SCHOOL, AND THEN LAST YEAR WE STARTED GOING OUT.
BUT... WE GOT IN A FIGHT ABOUT SEX, AND THINGS GOT WEIRD BETWEEN US... I WAS...
SCARED, SO I JUST ASKED HIM TO WAIT A LITTLE...
BUT THEN, NEXT THING I KNOW! HE'S SEEING SOMEONE ELSE BEHIND MY BACK, AND THEN HE'S SUDDENLY, LIKE, "LET'S JUST BE FRIENDS."
SO NOW IT'S A WHOLE YEAR LATER AND HE'S TOTALLY OVER ME, BUT I WAS STILL INTO HIM...
SO I THOUGHT, IF I SUDDENLY GOT MARRIED, THAT MIGHT FREAK HIM OUT.
BUT... NONE OF THAT EVEN MATTERS TO ME ANYMORE, AT ALL...
YOU WANT TO KNOW WHY?

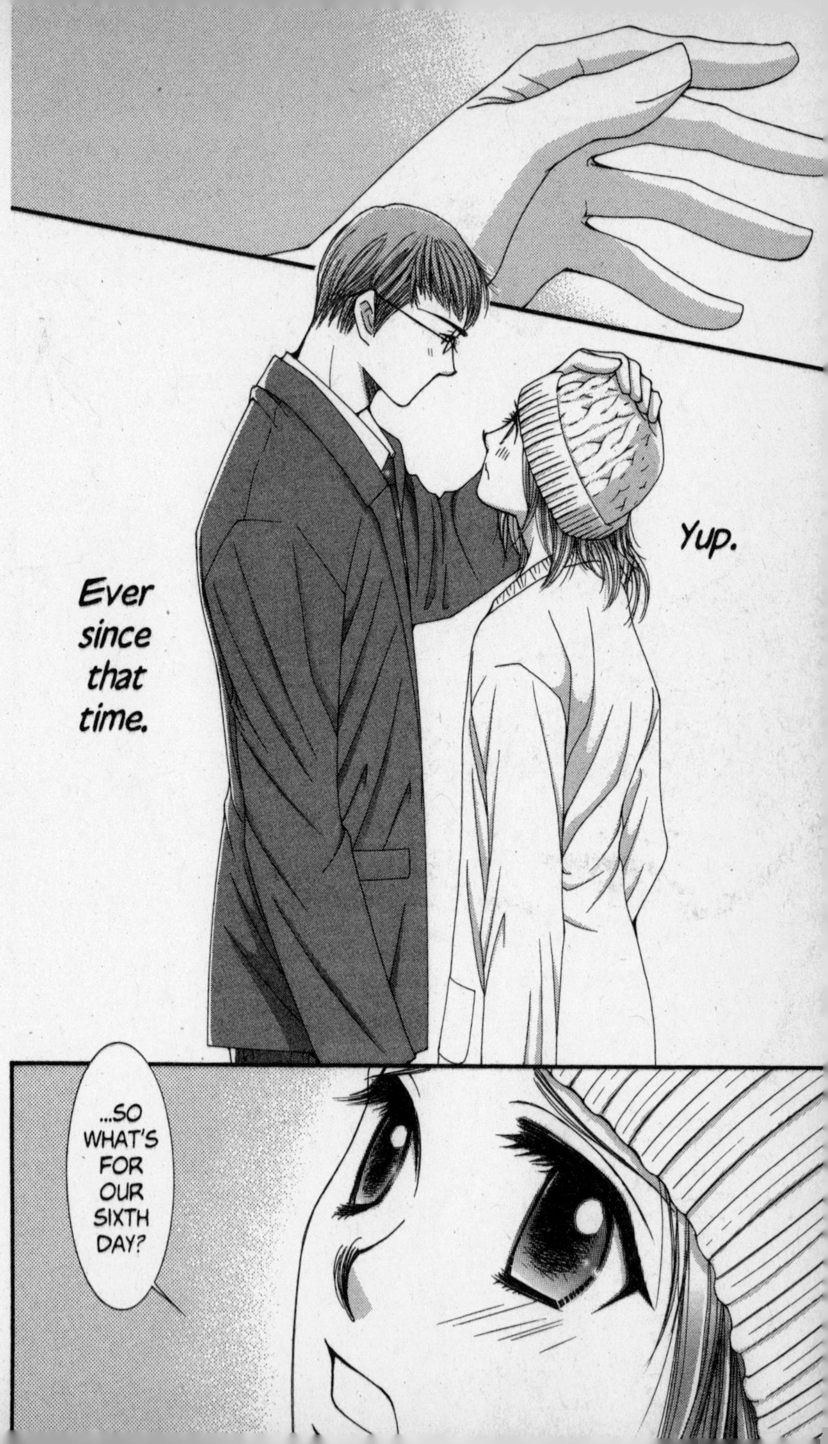
Yup.
Ever since that time.
...SO WHAT'S FOR OUR SIXTH DAY?

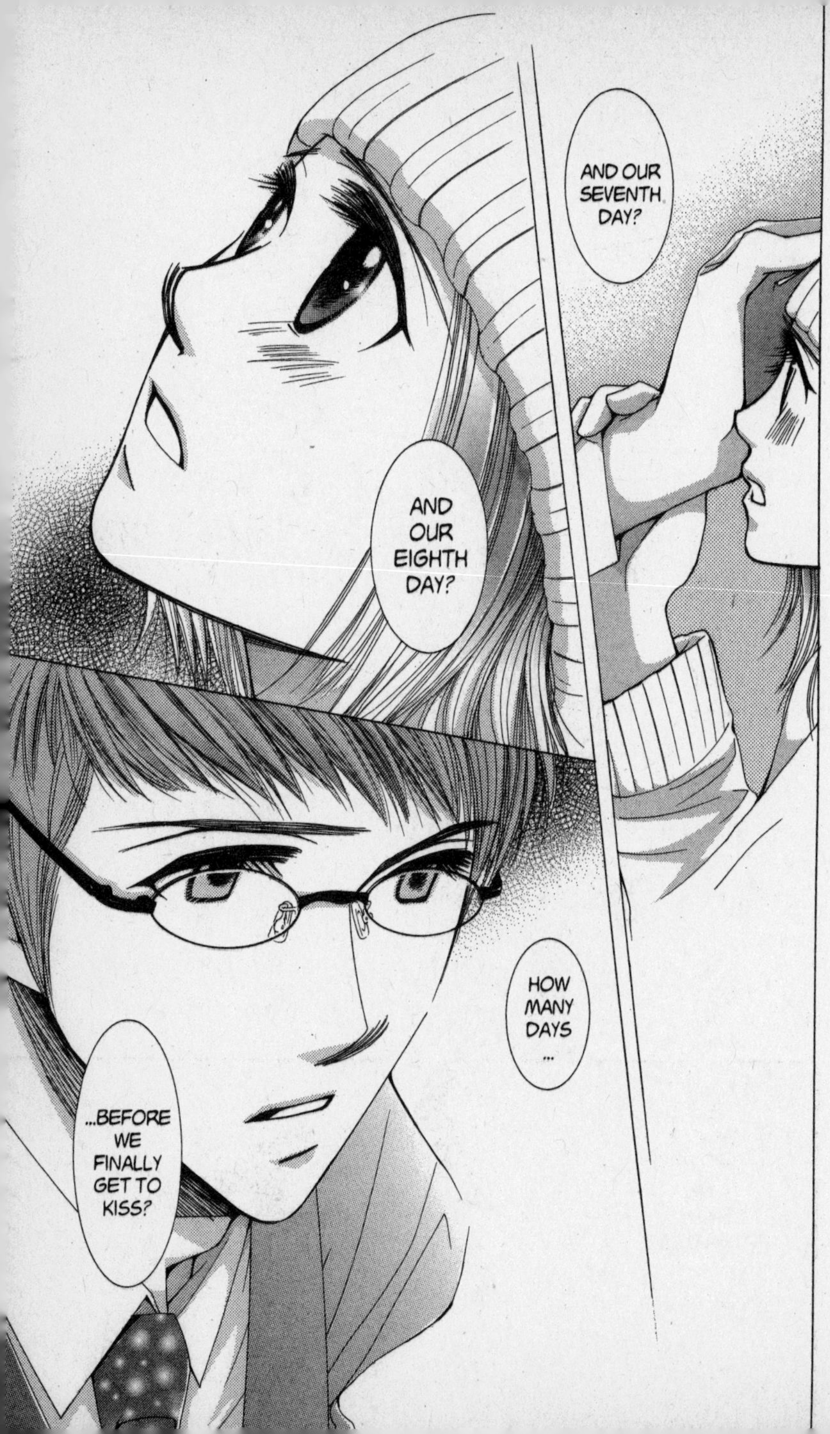
AND OUR SEVENTH DAY?
AND OUR EIGHTH DAY?
HOW MANY DAYS ...
...BEFORE WE FINALLY GET TO KISS?

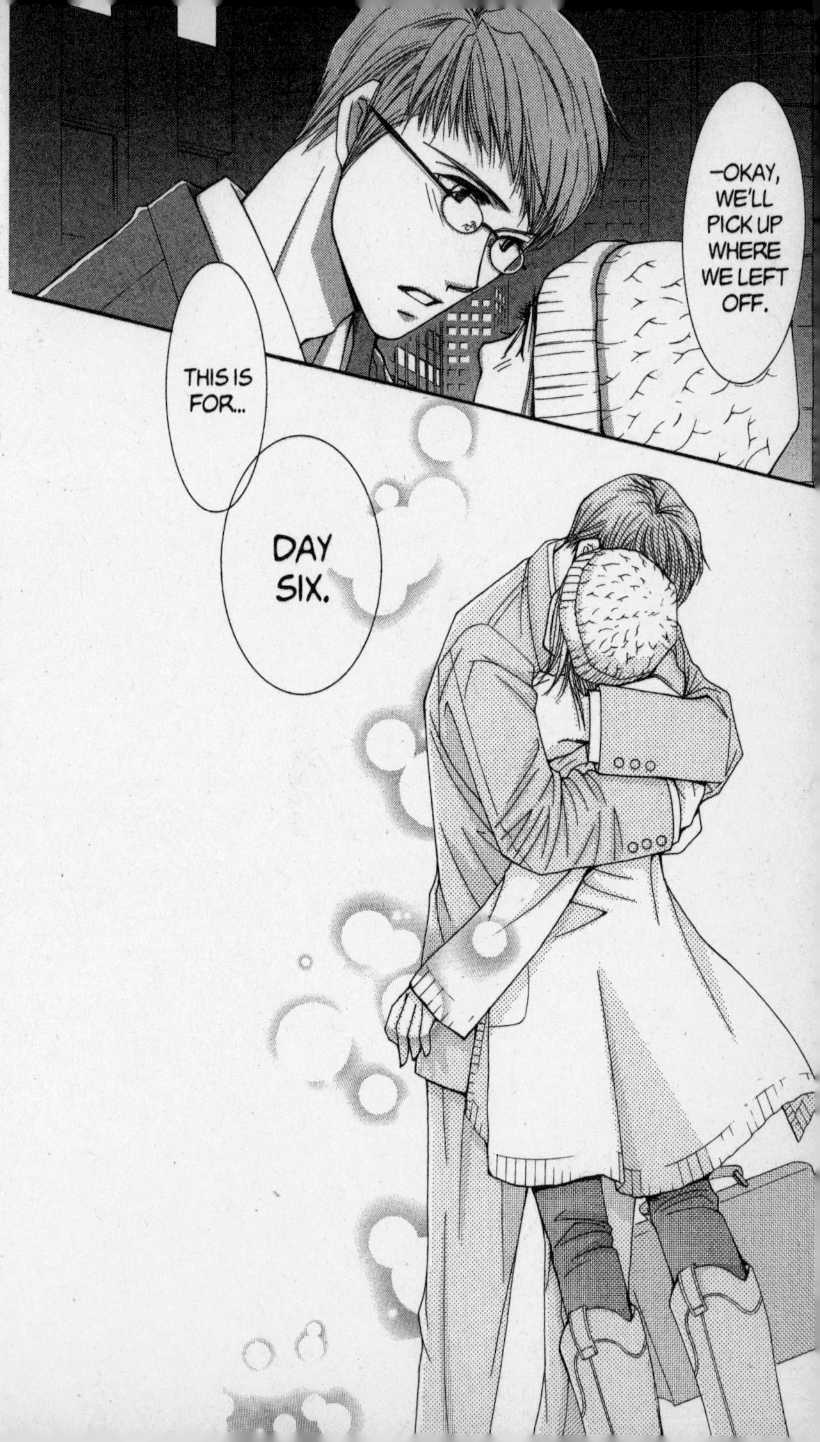
—OKAY, WE'LL PICK UP WHERE WE LEFT OFF.
THIS IS FOR...
DAY SIX.

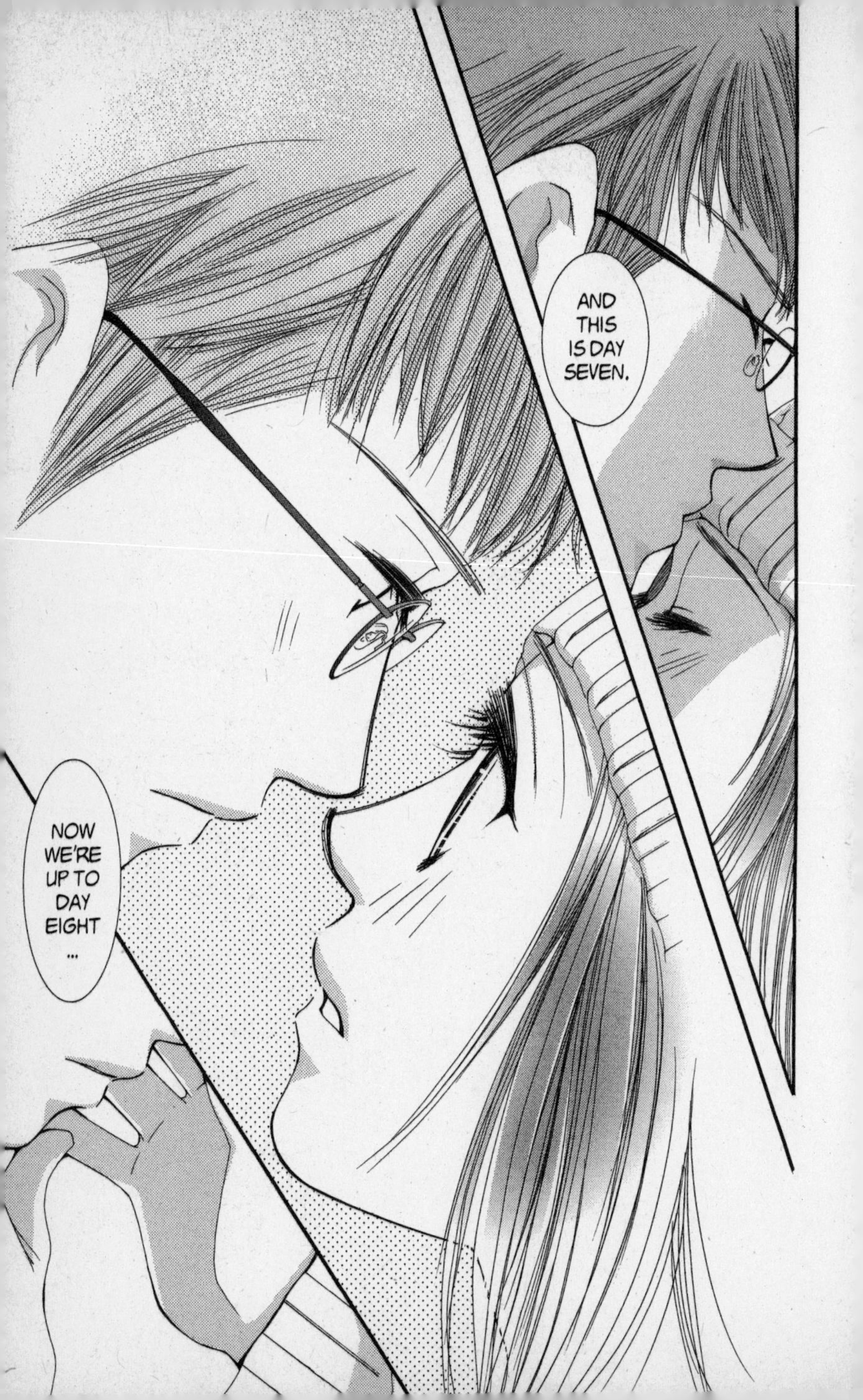
AND THIS IS DAY SEVEN.
NOW WE'RE UP TO DAY EIGHT ...

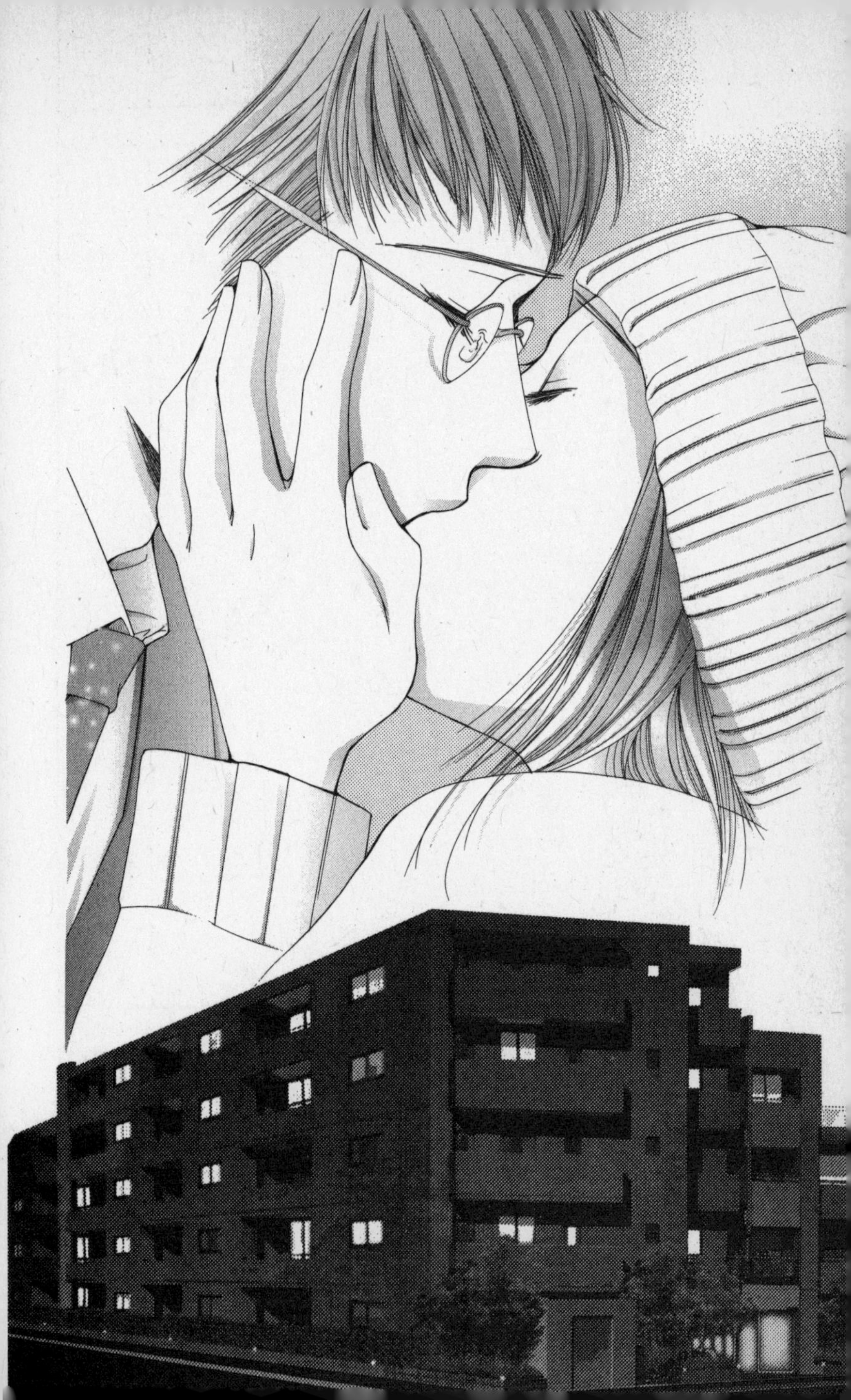

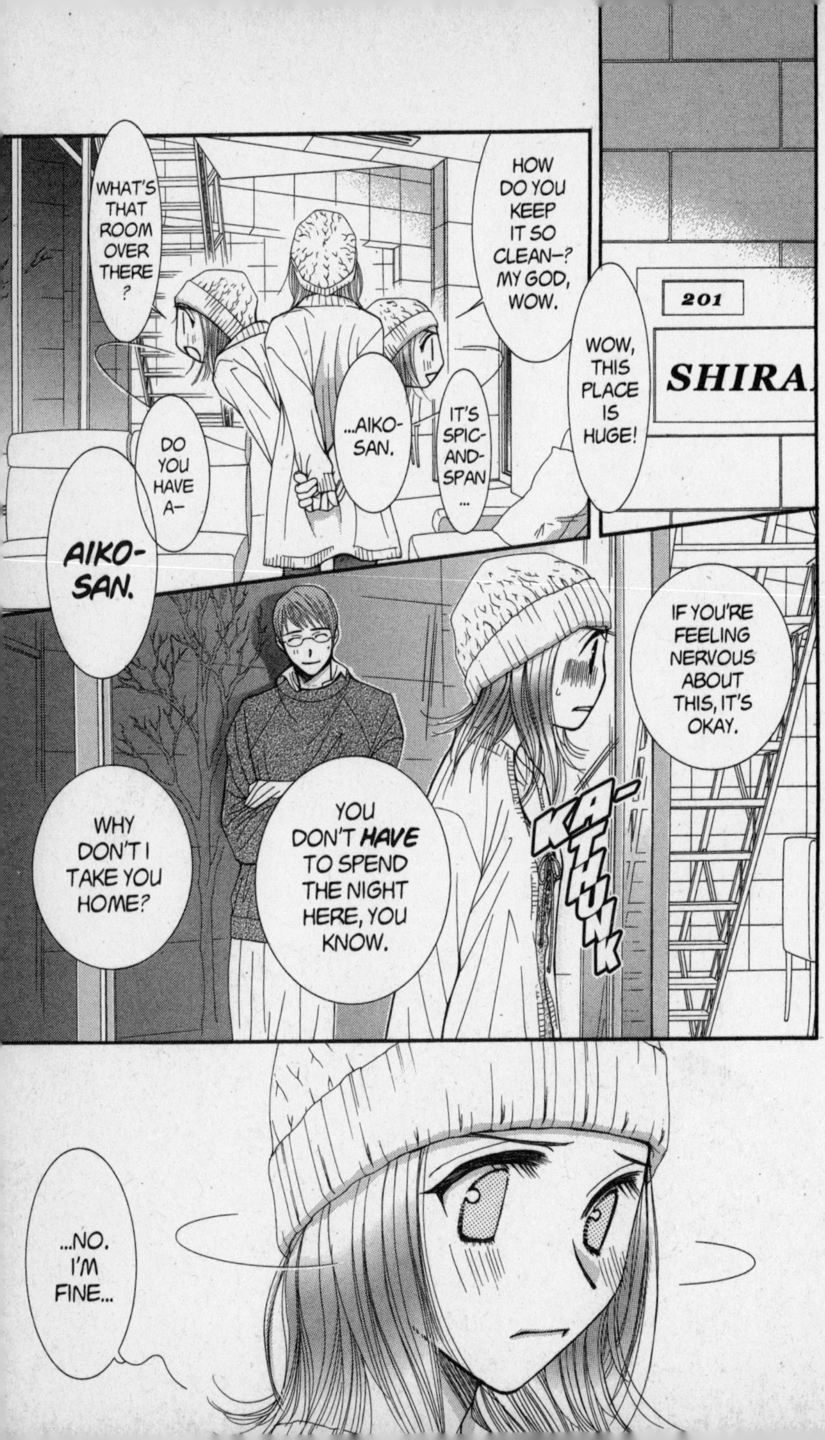
201
SHIRA
WOW, THIS PLACE IS HUGE!
HOW DO YOU KEEP IT SO CLEAN–? MY GOD, WOW.
IT'S SPIC-AND-SPAN...
...AIKO-SAN.
WHAT'S THAT ROOM OVER THERE?
DO YOU HAVE A–
AIKO-SAN.
IF YOU'RE FEELING NERVOUS ABOUT THIS, IT'S OKAY.
KA-THUNK
YOU DON'T **HAVE** TO SPEND THE NIGHT HERE, YOU KNOW.
WHY DON'T I TAKE YOU HOME?
...NO. I'M FINE...

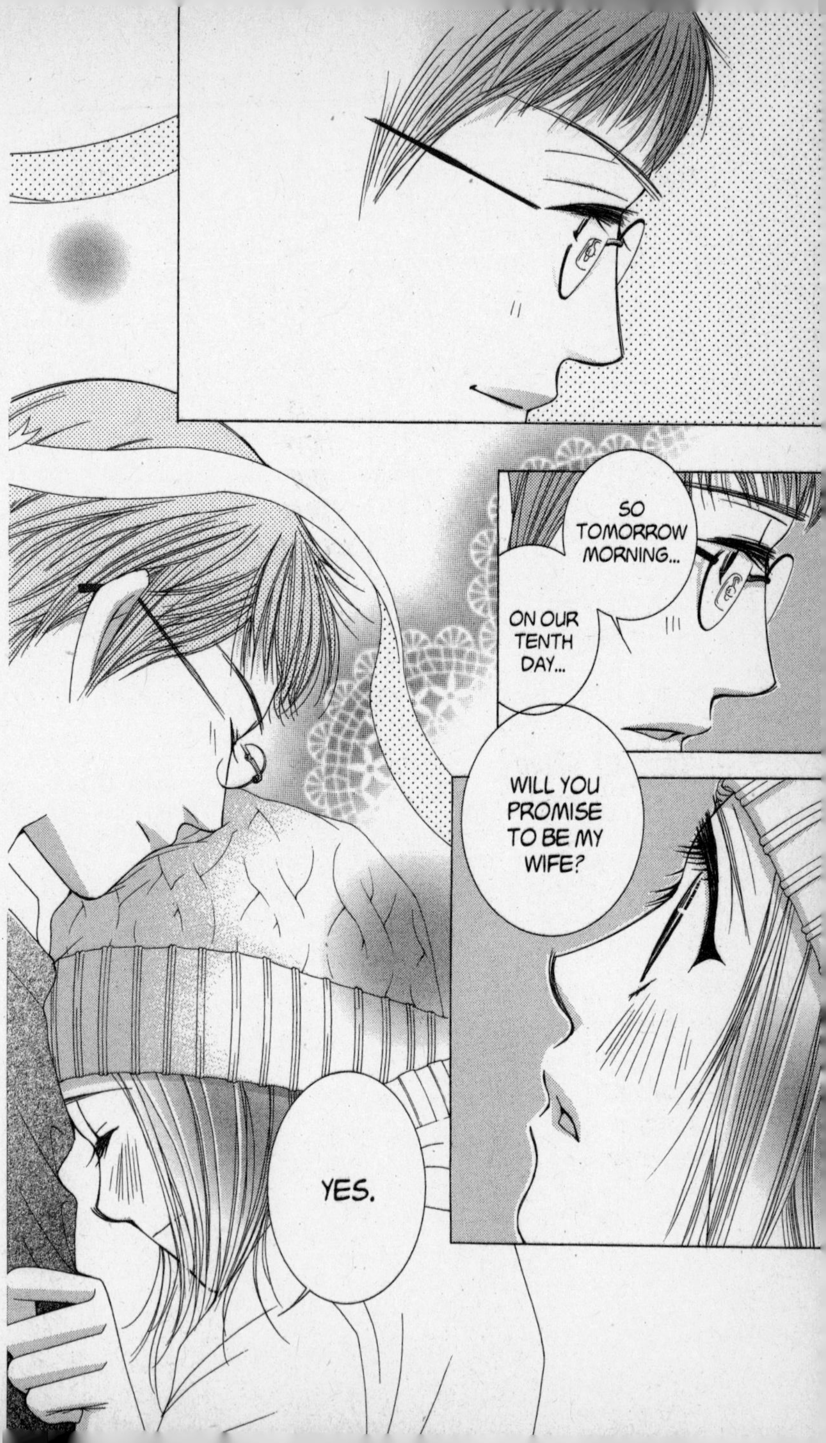
SO TOMORROW MORNING...
ON OUR TENTH DAY...
WILL YOU PROMISE TO BE MY WIFE?
YES.

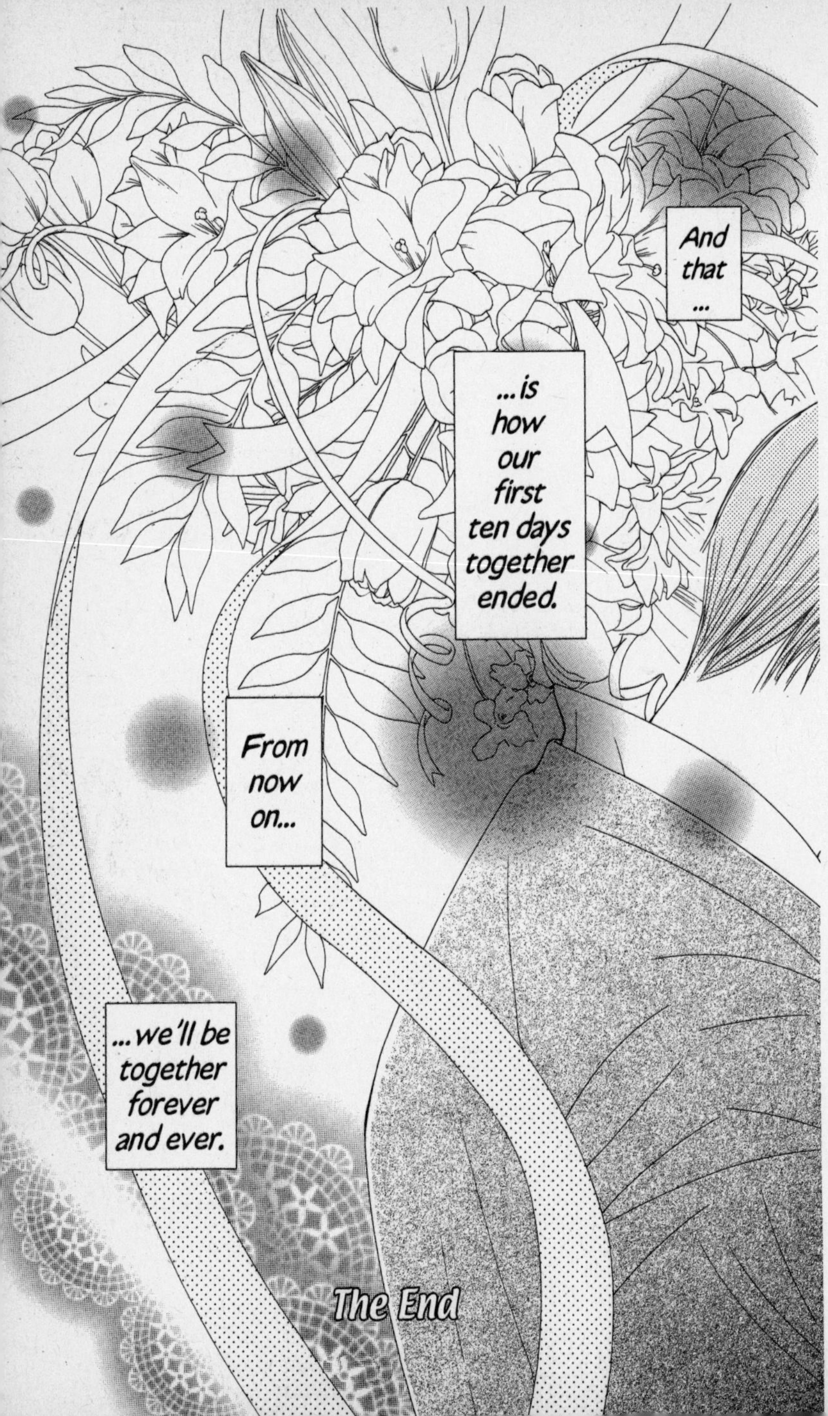
And that ...
...is how our first ten days together ended.
From now on...
...we'll be together forever and ever.
The End

HOT GIMMICK
Vol. 12

Shôjo Edition

STORY & ART BY MIKI AIHARA

ENGLISH ADAPTATION BY POOKIE ROLF

Touch-up Art & Lettering/Rina Mapa
Cover Design/Izumi Evers
Editor/Kit Fox

Managing Editor/Megan Bates
Editorial Director/Elizabeth Kawasaki
Editor in Chief/Alvin Lu
Sr. Director of Acquisitions/Rika Inouye
Sr. VP of Marketing/Liza Coppola
Exec. VP of Sales & Marketing/John Easum
Publisher/Hyoe Narita

Printed in the U.S.A.

Published by VIZ Media, LLC
P.O. Box 77010
San Francisco, CA 94107

10 9 8 7 6 5 4 3 2 1
First printing, September 2006

store.viz.com

PARENTAL ADVISORY
HOT GIMMICK is rated T+ for Older Teen and is recommended for ages 16 and up. This volume contains strong language and sexual situations.

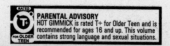

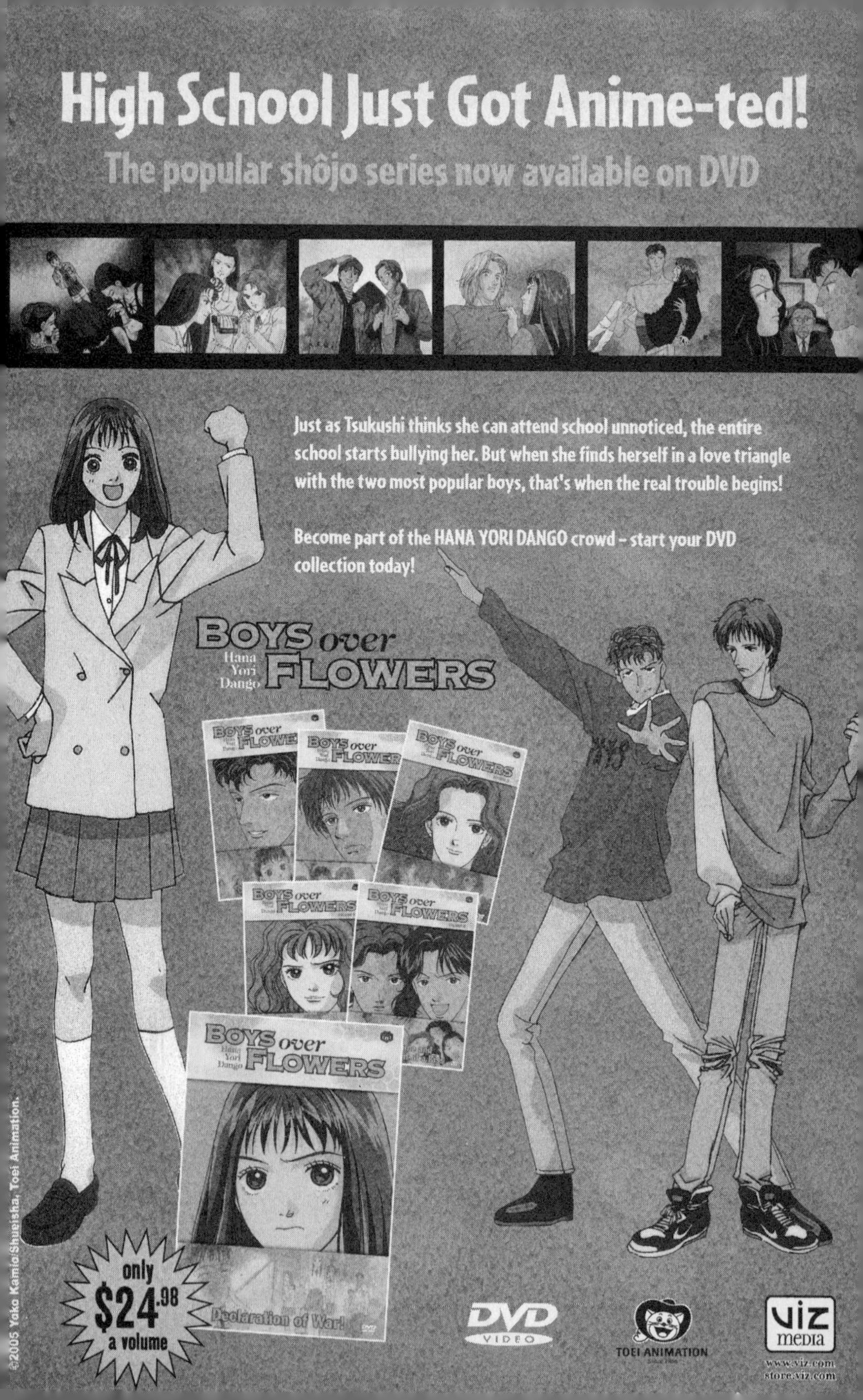
High School Just Got Anime-ted!
The popular shôjo series now available on DVD
Just as Tsukushi thinks she can attend school unnoticed, the entire school starts bullying her. But when she finds herself in a love triangle with the two most popular boys, that's when the real trouble begins!
Become part of the HANA YORI DANGO crowd – start your DVD collection today!
BOYS over FLOWERS
Hana Yori Dango
Declaration of War!
only $24.98 a volume
DVD VIDEO
TOEI ANIMATION
viz media
www.viz.com
store.viz.com
©2005 Yoko Kamio/Shueisha, Toei Animation.

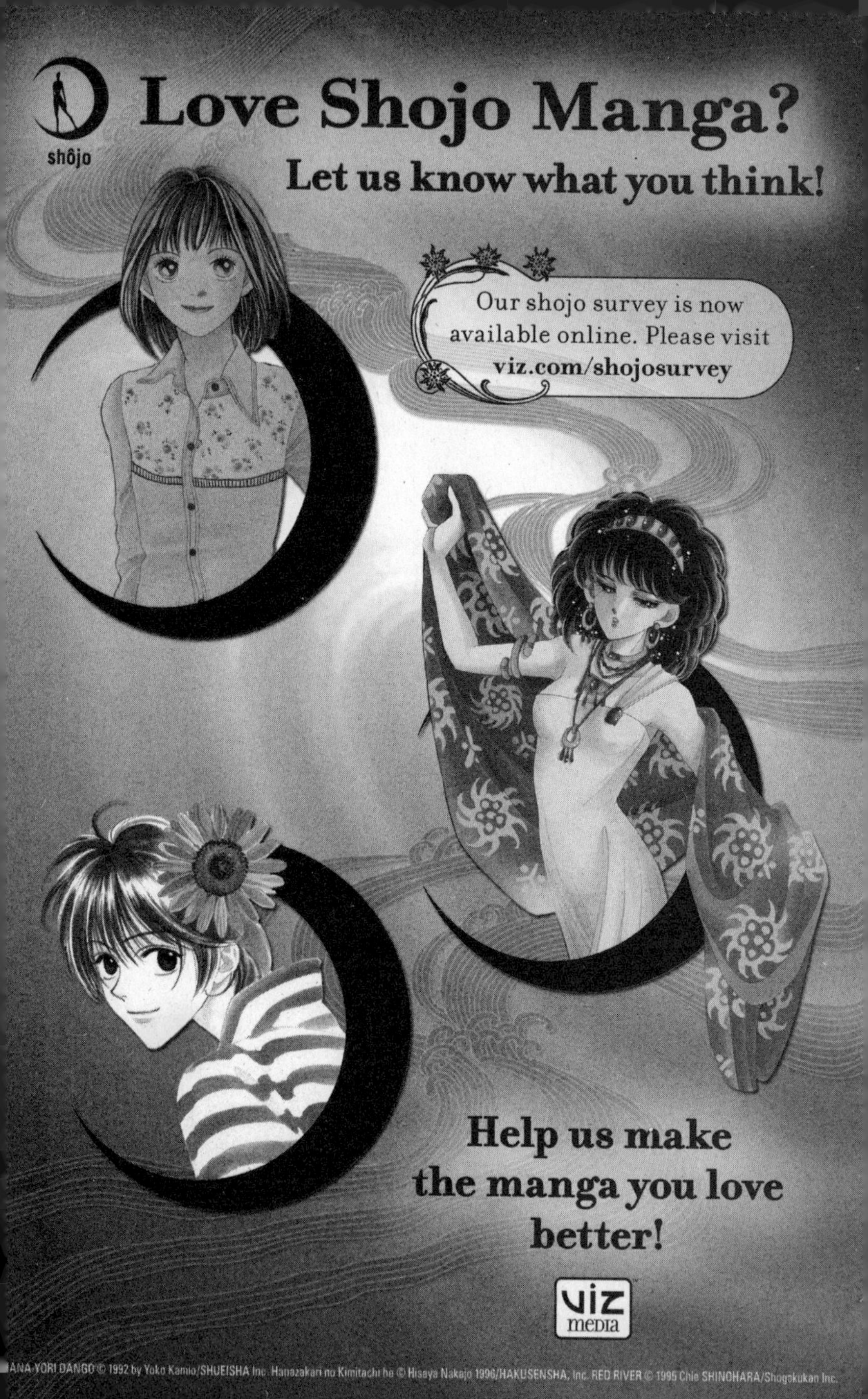